Also by Kirkpatrick Sale

Dwellers in the Land (1985)

Human Scale (1980)

Power Shift (1975)

SDS (1973)

The Land and People of Ghana (1963)

THE
CONQUEST OF
PARADISE

THE
CONQUEST OF
PARADISE

*Christopher Columbus
and the Columbian Legacy*

KIRKPATRICK SALE

Alfred A. Knopf
NEW YORK
1991

Copyright © 1990 by Kirkpatrick Sale

Library of Congress Cataloging-in-Publication Data

Sale, Kirkpatrick.
The conquest of paradise : Christopher Columbus and the Columbian
legacy / Kirkpatrick Sale. — 1st ed.
p.   cm.
Includes bibliographical references and index.
ISBN 0-394-57429-X
1. Columbus, Christopher Influences.   2. America—Discovery and
exploration—Spanish.   3. America—Discovery and exploration—
English.   I. Title.
E112.S16   1990
970.01'5—dc20   90-53069
                                          CIP

This book is printed on recycled paper.
Manufactured in the United States of America

Published October 12, 1990
Reprinted Twice
Fourth Printing, November 1991

For my wife
For those who were here first

Contents

THE
CONQUEST OF
PARADISE

Prologue

SURPRISING as it may seem from the present perspective, the
man we know as Christopher Columbus died in relative obscurity, his passing not even recorded at the time on the subcontinent
whose history he so decisively changed. But the true importance of
his Discovery became clearer with every passing decade as the New
World yielded up its considerable treasure to the Old, and as the
historical significance became appreciated in scholarly, and then in
popular, opinion. A half-century after his death it was certainly esteemed in the land that was its most obvious beneficiary—"the greatest event since the creation of the world," the Spanish historian
Francisco López de Gómara called it in 1552, "excluding the incarnation and death of Him who created it"—and by the end of the
sixteenth century even the French, notoriously stingy with praise for
non-Gallic achievements, were ready to admit, in the words of one
Louis Le Roy, that there was nothing "more honorable to our or the
preceding age than the invention of the printing press and the discovery of the new world; two things which I always thought could
be compared, not only to Antiquity, but to immortality." By the
time two more centuries had passed, and the full incredible panoramas
of the two new continents had become known (and in great measure
exploited) by the nations of Europe, there were few who would have
disagreed with the blunt assessment of the Scottish economist Adam
Smith: "The discovery of America, and that of a passage to the East
Indies by the Cape of Good Hope, are the two greatest and most
important events recorded in the history of mankind."

Replete as those judgments are, however, it really has not been
until the present century—indeed, until the retrospective provided
by the quincentennial of the First Voyage—that a fully comprehensive

measure of the Columbian achievement could be taken. Only now can we see how completely the Discovery and its legacy over the last five centuries have altered the cultures of the globe and the life-processes upon which they depend:

• It enabled the society of the European subcontinent to expand beyond its borders in a fashion unprecedented in the history of the world, and to come today to dominate virtually every other society it touches, Westernizing the great bulk of humanity, imposing its institutions and ideas, its languages and culture, its technologies and economy, around the earth.

• It enabled Europe to accumulate wealth and power previously unimaginable, the means by which it created and developed the most successful synergy of systems ever known, a mixture of humanism and secularism, rationalism and science, materialism and capitalism, nationalism and militarism—in short, the very structures of what we know as modern civilization.

• It enabled the vast redistribution of life-forms, purposely and accidentally, that has changed the biota of the earth more thoroughly than at any time since the end of the Permian Period, in effect re-joining the continents of the earth that were separated so many geological eons ago and thereby causing the extinction, alteration, and even creation of species at a speed and on a scale never before experienced.

• And most significant, it enabled humanity to achieve, and sanctify, the transformation of nature with unprecedented proficiency and thoroughness, to multiply, thrive, and dominate the earth as no single species ever has, altering the products and processes of the environment, modifying systems of soils and water and air, altering stable atmospheric and climatic balances, and now threatening, it is not too much to say, the existence of the earth as we have known it and the greater proportion of its species, including the human.

After five centuries, then, we have come to a unique position from which to judge the consequences of the Columbian discovery in their fullest dimensions. We can now appreciate especially what it means that it was the particular culture of one small promontory of the Asian landmass, with its particular historical attributes and at that historical moment, that was the cause of this event and its opulent beneficiary, and what has been the effect of the implantation of that culture throughout the world. We can now perhaps even bring ourselves to look with new eyes at the Discovery itself and the processes it unfolded, to reassess, with the wisdom of hindsight, the values and attitudes inherent in that culture and in the industrial civilization it has fostered.

In that spirit of reassessment this inquiry was undertaken. Columbus is above all the figure with whom the Modern Age—the age by which we may delineate these past five hundred years—properly begins, and in his character as in his exploits we are given an extraordinary insight into the patterns that shaped the age at its start and still for the most part shape it today. He is the figure as well who was primarily responsible for the ways in which the culture of Europe was implanted in the Americas, under not only Spanish flags but subsequent banners too, and his extraordinary career, very like his sailing routes, was the model for all those that came after. And he is the figure who, more than any other, provided the legacy by which European civilization came to dominate the American world for five centuries with consequences, we now realize, involving nothing less than issues of life and death.

This reassessment is particularly pertinent to the nation that not only is the foremost exemplar of the success of the transplanted culture but has lived out the Columbian legacy to its fullest, even taking as its greatest hero, as its very symbol, the Discoverer himself. For as Columbia, the personification invented for the newly formed United States at the end of the eighteenth century, he represents the soul and spirit of that nation and embodies what it takes to be its sense of courage and adventure, of perseverance and triumph, of brash indomitability. And thus it is in the United States that he is honored with more place names of all kinds—cities, counties, towns, rivers, colleges, parks, streets, and all the rest—than any other figure of American history save Washington, with more monuments and statues than have been erected to any other secular hero in the world. More than any other nation, the United States bears the honor, and the weight, of the Columbian achievement. More than any other nation, it is in a position to appreciate in the fullest its multiple, its quite consequential, meanings.

Interestingly, the Discoverer himself left us his assessment of the magnitude of his achievement, whose greatness he seemed not to doubt in the least. On his Fourth Voyage, his health none too good and his mind occasionally given to fantasy, he imagined that an apparition, presumably heavenly, came to him on shipboard one night and said:

> When He saw thee of an age at which He was content, marvellously did He cause thy name to resound throughout the land. The Indies, so rich a portion of the world, He gave thee for thine own, and thou hast divided them as it pleased thee, for He gave thee the power to do so. Of those barriers of the Ocean Sea which were closed with such mighty chains, He gave thee the keys, and thou wast obeyed through many lands, and thou hast gained an honorable fame throughout Christendom.

Whether the inspiration was the Lord's, as the Discoverer was pleased to think, the momentous achievement itself was certainly his, and its beneficiary was indeed the Christendom that eventually immortalized his name. Its legacy is now ours, now to comprehend and appreciate as never before.

Chapter One

1492

I

NO RELIABLE record comes down to us of the weather on that Friday morning in early August 1492 not long before dawn broke over the little port village of Palos, a few miles up the River Tinto at the southwestern corner of Castile, on the edge of the peninsula giving Europe its farthest thrust into the expanse of water then known as the Ocean Sea. Doubtless it promised to be another hot, Sahara-swept day, typical of Andalusia at that time of year, but doubtless too there were still in the air the last traces of the mountain *terral*, the gentle breeze that blows down from the Sierra Morenas toward the sea on summer nights. Low on the far western sky a pale, ghostly moon, a few days from full, would probably have still been visible.

What we do know is that, "at half an hour before sunrise," Cristóbal Colón, the designated captain general in charge of three small sailing ships that had been moored in the sheltered Palos inlet all summer, gave orders to weigh the anchors and begin the long voyage to the unknown reaches of the western seas. Long ash sweeps would have carried the vessels into the mid-channel of the Tinto to catch the ebb tide on its way out to the Gulf of Cádiz, and soon the deck crews would have unfurled and hoisted the canvas sheets to catch what they could of the morning's lingering breeze.

No excitement would have been aroused by the sight of those three vessels making their slow way to the sea: they were ordinary Mediterranean ships of the kind that had been used for more than a century along the Atlantic coasts, long ago proving themselves maneuverable and seaworthy. The first two were caravels, sleek and light all-purpose ships, three masts apiece, perhaps sixty to seventy feet long and probably just over twenty feet wide, each carrying two dozen men or so. Their names—or nicknames, rather, since nothing was painted on the transoms in those days and ships were known instead by the wharfside designations that local sailors gave them—could not have much pleased the Captain General, a man of many outward signs of piety: the name of the first, *Pinta*, although no doubt derived from that of some Pinto family in the region who owned the ship, actually meant "painted one," a *puta* to the sailors; and the name of the second, officially known as *Santa Clara* but called *Niña* after her owner, Juan Niño of nearby Moguer, meant "little girl," a title with many of the same implications.

The third ship was a nao, a somewhat larger, round-bellied vessel, perhaps a tenth again the size of the caravels, but bulkier, slower, and, as Colón was later to complain, "very heavy and not suitable for the business of discovery." Her original name was *La Gallega*, meaning she was built in Galicia, but her nickname then may have been *Marigalante*, which translates to "Dirty Mary" in sailing parlance, and if so the devout Colón would have had none of that; whatever the sailors may have called her on that voyage, she was known officially as *Santa María*, and thus she has come down to us today. This was the flagship of the fleet, holding the Captain General and the favored (that is, landlubberly) crew—two representatives of the royal court that was paying for the voyage, an *alguazil* (marshal) of the fleet, a secretary, an interpreter, and a surgeon—plus another three dozen men, all in a vessel whose deck dimensions could not have been much larger than those of a modern tennis court.[1]*

As the three ships made their slow way down the Tinto that morning, they would soon have passed close by a high, pine-covered hill off their port side, at the crest of which was the little Franciscan monastery of La Rábida, its bright whitewashed walls clearly visible even in the thin light of dawn. The Captain General may well have paused to give it a special farewell glance, for it was a place of some meaning for him. It was there that he and his son Diego had first stopped for hospitality and lodging during the dark days, seven years before, when they had arrived from Portugal, homeless and presumably poor. It was there that he had met (or perhaps gotten an introduction to) the noted Franciscan astronomer Fray Antonio de

---

*Superscript numbers refer to notes beginning on page 373.

Marchena, who gave the first sympathetic and supportive hearing to
his Grand Scheme of sailing westward into the Ocean Sea to find
wealth among distant lands and islands. It was there that he had left
Diego, under Minorite tutelage, for at least part of the time while he
spent hard, frustrating years traveling around the Castilian countryside after the peripatetic royal court in order to try to convince it of
the virtues of his treasured scheme. And it was there that he had met
Fray Juan Pérez, a former consort (possibly one of the confessors) of
Queen Isabella, who by all accounts was chiefly responsible for the
court's giving a last hearing to Colón when all seemed lost at the end
of 1491—a hearing that, after six long and fruitless years, finally led to
the ultimate royal assent, the acquisition and provisioning of the three
ships, and the embarkation of this little fleet on the river below.

But La Rábida signified something more than that, though Colón
might well not have known. It was located at the southwesternmost
point of the Spanish coast, Castile's face to the vastness of the Ocean
Sea, and it was for the Castilian mind a veritable symbol of that
kingdom's edge against the world and its eight-hundred-year-old history of struggle to advance that edge. In a very real sense Castilian
history can be defined as a series of encounters along a perpetual
frontier, as the kingdom devoted itself from the twelfth century on
to its holy Reconquista—the reconquest of Iberia from the infidel
Moors who had occupied the region since the ninth century. In that
long and bloody process—the successive waves of battles and sieges
and assaults and finally of conquest and settlement, in which Castile,
relentless and purposive, extended its territory century after century
southward from the Cantabrian mountains to the Mediterranean—
were shaped both the style of the Castilian monarchy and the character of Castilian society. Not for nothing that its heroes, like those
of certain other cultures, were men of those frontiers: unscrupulous
bandits like the famed El Cid, romantic knights and *caballeros* fighting
on horseback for land and ladies, grandees and *títulos* carving out
immense, prosperous estates of sheep and cattle—and of course, although he was not to be created for another hundred years yet, that
great quixotic *hidalgo* who so vividly lived in frontiers that he invented them where none existed.

*On January 6, 1492, four days after its formal surrender, Queen Isa-
bella of Castile and King Ferdinand of Aragon rode into the walled city*

of Granada, the last stronghold of the Islamic powers that had been in
Iberia for eight hundred years.* From the young caliph, Boabdil, they
took the keys of the Alhambra, the magnificent fourteenth-century
ocher citadel of the Moors, and ordered the crucifix and royal standard
to be raised at its highest parapets. Thus was the Reconquista complete.

Under the terms of the surrender agreement, all the conquered
Moors were to be allowed to remain in the territory and practice their
faith, unless they chose to convert to Christianity or emigrate across
the straits to Africa. Ten years later that agreement was abruptly
abrogated by the Spanish monarchs and all Moslems were ordered to
embrace Christianity or be expelled forthwith. Thereafter, in theory
at least, all of Spain was united as a Christian nation in service to the
pope of Rome.

As the three ships moved past the Minorite monastery and slowly
down the Tinto to the confluence with the River Saltés to starboard,
the *Pinta* under the command of Martín Alonso Pinzón would most
likely have been in the lead, as it was for much of the subsequent
journey.

Pinzón was not only an important shipowner in Palos but probably
one of the most experienced mariners in these waters—he was then
between forty-six and fifty, and apparently had been at sea most of
those years—and it was most likely his public support of Colón that
had persuaded the other sailors of the area to sign on for this voyage.
He may also have had enough experience at sea to have contrived the
same Grand Scheme that Colón himself had—at least his family and
friends said so, and so it was avowed some years later, during a
protracted lawsuit between the Spanish crown and the Captain General's heirs. In those proceedings, known collectively as the *Pleitos
de Colón*, it was claimed that Pinzón had been to Rome and seen
charts of new lands across the seas and even before Colón came along
"was about to seek them out at his own charge with two of his own
vessels." There is scant evidence to support such claims, but the
people of Palos at least took them seriously; there is today but one

---

*Properly the monarchs' names are Isabel and Hernando (or Fernando), and it seems a
shame that these have been rendered in English as Isabella and Ferdinand, losing the spice of
the Spanish original. That, however, is the convention, and I have chosen to follow it, as also
for the names of Spanish towns and cities.

statue in that town of the discoverer of the New World, and it is of Martín Alonso Pinzón.

The other crew members of the small flotilla seem to have been similarly seasoned sailors, all but four of them (a Portuguese and three Italians) Castilians, and they certainly were not hardened criminals, as myth would have it. (One, Bartolomé de Torres, had been in jail for killing a man in a fight, and three of his friends were caught trying to rescue him; they, and they alone, were the "criminals" who took advantage of the crown's offer to pardon those who would sail with Colón.) The captain of the *Niña* was Vicente Yañez Pinzón, Martín Alonso's younger brother and a man similarly born to the sea; Colón, of course, was captain of the flagship. And the owners of each ship were also on board, two as masters—those in charge of the administration of the crew—and one as an ordinary seaman. The pilots, who were primarily responsible for the navigation of the ships, were also veterans from Palos.

In addition to those in charge, each vessel probably shipped a carpenter, caulker, cooper, and marshal, as well as a variety of *marineros*, stewards, and gromets, or ship's boys. Each also had, oddly enough, a ship's surgeon, a personage who seems to have been largely superfluous for the whole journey, judging by the fact that the Captain General never once refers to the medical skills of any of them and that two of them were later left behind on Española, having been deemed unnecessary for the return trip.

Interesting, too, is what the three ships were *not* carrying.

Although the Captain General claimed to be advancing the cause of the Roman Church—he asserted to his sovereigns that the primary reason for the voyage was "to see the said princes and peoples and lands . . . and the manner in which may be undertaken their conversion to our Holy Faith"—there were no monks on board, no missionaries, no priests, no holy fathers, no men of the cloth of any kind. Although presumably he was also to deal with various princes and potentates (and was indeed carrying a Letter of Credence from Ferdinand and Isabella "to the Most Serene Prince _____," with the blank to be filled in on the occasion), there was no one on board with any diplomatic experience, no ambassador or minister, no one trained in any statecraft befitting a foreign court. And although there were likely to be some confrontations with "the said princes and peoples," there were no soldiers on any ship, nor any significant ordnance beyond some crossbows and arquebuses and a few small cannon. (The types of these last are not known, but Colón does later mention firing a lombard, a smallish, low-lying cannon mounted probably belowdecks on the flagship.) Nor, despite later illustrations by men who hadn't seen them to accompany accounts by those who hadn't been there, were there any "men at arms" with pikes, or cannoneers, or halberdiers, or archers, or soldiers of the line whatever. And there were not even any cooks (although each captain had a personal servant), inasmuch as the position of shipboard chef was not invented until well into the sixteenth century.

Most surprising, although the royal order to this little fleet was to "discover and acquire" all the new lands it was to come upon, not a single person on any of the ships is known to have had any training or skills as a naturalist, nor was anyone ever recorded during the voyage as having even the most rudimentary knowledge of flora and fauna, much less any ability to describe, record, analyze, or preserve any of the new specimens of life that might be found on those new lands. Colón himself came to regret this lack severely: when told by the islanders that one place had many spices growing, he wrote, "But that I don't know them gives me the greatest grief in the world, for I see a thousand sorts of trees . . . and of all them I recognize only this aloes." (And even then he was wrong: he loaded large quantities of what he took to be medicinal aloes on board, and it turned out to be a species of agave of no therapeutic value at all.) Nor, by the same token, was there anyone capable of, or interested in, making a sketch or drawing of any of the new sights—geological, biological, or anthropological—for the edification or even amusement of the audience back home; in fact, apparently not once in all of Spain's history of discovery did it send out an artist of any sort—not even during the century of El Greco and Velázquez—and the sole evidence of any Castilian visual sense is a few crude and inaccurate sketches, diagrams really, by Gonzalo Fernández de Oviedo in his *Historia general* of 1535–57.

Nor, finally, were there any jewelers or metallurgists. Although it was presumed that this voyage was to acquire, according to the crown agreements, "Pearls, Precious Stones, Gold, Silver, Spiceries, and other Things and Merchandise of whatever kind, name or description that may be," there wasn't anyone on board who knew gold from pyrite or pearl from chrysoberyl. One of the seamen was listed in the manifest as being a "silversmith" and charged with being an "assayer of minerals and washer of gold," but since this was one of the gromets, this was surely an overstatement at best. In any case, nothing is heard about his skills during the subsequent weeks, and at least once Colón loaded his ships with samples of gold "for your Sovereigns" that turned out to be nothing more than iron pyrite.

On August 2, 1492, the day before Colón sailed from Palos, the final deadline arrived for the expulsion from Spain of its entire Jewish population.

According to a royal decree suddenly issued only four months before, on March 30, and bearing the signature of the same royal official who subsequently authorized the orders for Colón's venture across the Ocean Sea, all Jews, of whatever age or station or position, were to be summarily expelled. The best estimates are that some 120,000 to 150,000 people were forced to flee from homes and lands their families had occupied for generations, in some cases centuries, and to take with them only their immediate personal possessions—not, however, their gold, silver, jewels, or currency, which were to be left behind for the crown and its agents.

It is hard to know how much credence to give it, but some sixty years afterward an old Spaniard in Guatemala asserted in a notarial deposition that he had been there, he really had, and seen the fleet of Colón's First Voyage as it sailed down the River Tinto that early morning. He was a gromet, he said, on a ship out of the nearby port of Huelva that was riding deep in the water with an overloaded cargo of Jews—Sephardim, so called from the Biblical term for westernmost lands—one of the many such boatloads leaving Spain packed to the gunwales with unfortunate emigrants that day.

Of this agonizing exodus, the turmoil of which must have affected every harbor in Spain, the Captain General has almost nothing to say, referring to it but once in all his writings. That single entry, in the introduction that he appended to his account of this initial voyage and addressed directly to the king and queen, notes casually that "thus, after having expelled all the Jews from your kingdoms and dominions, in the same month of January" they commissioned him to make his journey—and even then he got the date of expulsion wrong by seven months.[2]

Meeting with the River Saltés, the three ships turned hard to port to follow the larger river out through the channel to the gulf, between the piney hills and scrub brush of the mainland and the marshy islands and sandy *bancos* to seaward. In the terse account of the Captain General, the little fleet slipped past the river's mouth and "departed . . . from the bar of Saltés at 8 o'clock," their course set toward the south, and "afterward to the southwest and south by west." The ocean breezes now filled the sails, the gray-green swells slapped against the hulls, the first watch took its posts, and the momentous journey thus began.

Of the importance of that journey none of the ninety men aboard those ships could have had any doubt, though they could not of course have known or even dreamed just how fateful and consequential it was to be in world history, not even the man whose abiding passion it had apparently been for a decade or more. They knew, each of them, that this was a journey off into the uncharted western parts of the Ocean Sea, undertaken at the explicit and highly unusual orders of the king and queen, whose decree had been read in the Palos town church a few months before: "We have commanded Cristóbal Colón to set out with a fleet of three *carabelas armadas* as Our Captain of the same, toward certain regions of the Ocean Sea to perform certain things for Our service." (Not only that, but the monarchs, not noted for their regal generosity, had actually put up the bulk of the money for the voyage and were paying its sailors at the going rate, four months' salary in advance: something must have been up the royal sleeve.) The men aboard also knew, each of them, that for decades, perhaps centuries, mariners and geographers and travelers had told of places of fantastic wealth out there on the farther edge of the ocean, and there was every reason to suppose that those stories of golden cities and magical fountains and fist-sized jewels might well come true for them, and to hope that they might return to Palos with riches beyond a grandee's dreams.

There would be dangers, of course, even the most hardened *marinero* would have acknowledged that. Not a risk of falling off the edge of the earth or of going so far over the rim you couldn't get back: no serious sailor, no one who had seen ships disappear over the horizon and return without incident, could believe that sort of landlubberly twaddle. But the journey was scheduled to be a very long one—all three ships were provisioned for a full year in an age when two weeks without putting into port was a rarity—and it would take them well out of sight of land, unlike the voyages along the African coast. There was always the problem of the winds, for it was well known that the fair wind that takes you out can be the foul wind that prevents your coming back, and on a lengthy trip such as this the prospect of not finding that favorable homeward breeze, the western wind the Greeks called Zephyr, could send a certain chill through even the hardiest soul. And of course there was no way of knowing what kinds of people—or, if the stories be true, monsters —might be out there, on land or sea: the well-known wild men and dog-heads and cyclopes and hairy giants, the one-breasted amazons who enslaved men, the anthropophagi who roasted and ate human flesh, the sirens and mermaids who lured sailors to their deaths.

The Captain General too knew of all these risks, and indeed it is likely that he knew far more about the monstrous races from his extensive reading in the bizarre travel literature of the fifteenth century than any of his crew.* But he had had many years to prepare for just this opportunity, so he told us later many times over, and to consider just how serious were the risks ahead. He had spent a number of years at sea—just how many is uncertain, and his own claims ("I have been at sea for twenty-three years" in 1492, "I have passed 40 years in this employment" in 1501) are not only inconsistent but certainly exaggerated—and he may have sailed as far south as the African Gold Coast and possibly as far north as Iceland (or at least Bristol).[3] He knew of—indeed, it seems from his reading that he carefully studied—the current stories about the fabled rich islands in the western ocean (Antillia, Brasil, Ymana, St. Brendan's Isle, Ventura, Satanazes, and on and on), and he also would have known of the several decades of Portugal's attempts to find them and the stories told around the docks of Lisbon and Porto Santo by those who claimed they had. He may possibly have had a useful map of some kind, and later on at sea he does say he showed Martín Alonso Pinzón "a chart" which "had depicted certain islands on that sea," but there

---

*We actually have some idea of what Colón's reading was like, since seven of his personal volumes, most with extensive marginalia (called *postille*, or postils, by scholars in this field), have survived and are preserved today in the Biblioteca Colombina in Seville. Three of the books are full of travelers' fancies and descriptions of monstrous beings: Marco Polo's *Orientalium regionum* and an Italian résumé of 1485; Pierre d'Ailly's fanciful *Imago mundi* and other treatises (1480–83); and Pliny's classic *Historia naturalis* in Italian translation (1489). The others were Pope Pius II's *Historia rerum ubique gestarum* (1477); Plutarch's *Lives* in a 1491 Castilian translation; a *Summula confessionis* of St. Antonius of Florence (1476); and Seneca's *Tragedies*. Colón's son Fernando listed, in chapter 6 and 7 of his biography, a number of other sources he assumed his father read, including some of similarly dubious reportorial veracity.

is no way of knowing if it was something of real value or merely another fanciful depiction of imagined worlds like other surviving maps of the period. And there is some reason to suspect that he may have had, who knows how, some idea of the wind patterns across the Atlantic, for he did select routes both out and back that were so accurate in making use of prevailing air currents that sailing ships use them to this day.

He may well have been as able a captain, as both sailor and student, as any voyage of discovery in 1492 could have had. And yet it is pertinent to add that this man, here on the high seas with the fate of ninety men, and perhaps Spain as an empire, in his hands, had likely never before, as near as we can reconstruct his career, been the captain of any ship larger than a rowboat, much less a fleet.

On the night of August 10, 1492, with the power and money of Ferdinand of Aragon behind him, Rodrigo de Borja, a Spanish member of the noted Borgia family, bribed, threatened, argued, and black-mailed his way into becoming the supreme pontiff, Vicar of Christ and Pope of the Church of Rome, taking the papal name Alexander VI. A man of great wealth and unabashedly high living, he was, despite his holy vows, the father of an unknown number of children in both Castile and Rome, including Cesare and Lucrezia, later to become famous in their own right, so to speak, and even in his own time acknowledged as the ultimate symbol of a papacy then in the dregs of a century-long decadence.

His papacy was marked by policies that encouraged almost contin-uous and disastrous warfare through much of the Italian peninsula, by the open auction of lucrative ecclesiastical offices to the richest and most corrupt of his holy curia, and by his own personal chicaneries in office, including bribery, sexual assignations, live-in mistresses, and oral readings of pornography from the papal library. All in all, he was a fitting continuation of the venal and incompetent pontifical line that was, in just a few years' time, to precipitate the reaction we know as the Reformation.

The quarters of the Captain General on his flagship were not spacious. He would indeed have had his own cabin, below the poop deck at the far aft of the ship (and so was the only person on board, court representatives included, with sleeping quarters), but it was a space of perhaps ten feet by twenty, with two small side windows and a doorway in front, room enough for a bunk bed and writing table and little more. So except for the hours when he was sleeping or eating or filling in his daily journal, Colón would likely have spent his time—especially on that shakedown morning as they moved into the open sea—surveying the ship from the poop deck and calling down to the helmsman or pilot in the binnacle, below the quarterdeck, from which the ship was steered.

The Captain General at this point in his life was—well, let us say *about* forty years old and by no means young, and not enter here into the great debate about his date of birth.[4] He was, according to his second (and "illegitimate") son, Fernando, whose biography of his father is the first we have, "a well-built man of more than average stature"; according to the contemporary historian Oviedo, he was "of good stature and appearance, taller than the average and strongly limbed." His hair, which had been "very red" in his youth, had gone quite white (not a few historians surmise it was because of his difficulty in winning support for his Grand Scheme), and his ruddy face, "tending to bright red," was lined and, according to one who knew him, bearded. The life expectancy of adults in late-fifteenth-century Europe is not known, or knowable, but it is sure that recurrent famines and epidemics took a heavy toll, even among the better-off —"thousands of details demonstrate the precariousness and brevity of life in those far-off times," the French historian Fernand Braudel has said—and the age of forty was indeed well advanced; Charles V of France died at forty-three with the reputation of being "a wise old man."

A man of forty thus might not have all that much time left to fulfill himself, or his dreams, and it would not be surprising if Colón knew that well, particularly since his dreams were so outsized, beyond the contemplation of most other men. They all hung in the balance with the voyage that started that morning: if this venture came to nothing, there would be no more for Cristóbal Colón.

It is hard to know from his later writings exactly what impelled those dreams, but the standard historians' line that the European conquest of America was driven by "God, gold, and glory" would seem to be pretty much on the mark in his case. Of his dedication

to God and his belief that he was God's chosen instrument of re-
demption, smarmy though it was at times, there is little doubt; it
was, indeed, obsessive and not entirely salutary, as we may judge
from his later frenzied preoccupation with the kind of bizarre millenarianism, complete with Second Coming and Final Judgment, that
seems to have infected the entire age. His dedication to gold was
equally evident, and would even determine the course of every one
of his explorations in the Caribbean: "Gold is most excellent," he
wrote after his last voyage, and "whoever has it may do what he
wishes in the world." And his compulsion for glory, for personal
glory, to shower not only upon himself but upon his entire lineage,
had occupied him so much during the past half-dozen years that he
nearly jeopardized his entire scheme by insisting on grandiose benefits, titles, honors, and privileges far beyond those usual for a man
of his station; and they continued to occupy him until, in the last
years of his life, he thought of little else.

God, gold, and glory, then, were the stuff of this man's dreams,
as they were the motivations for the millions who would follow him.
What does that say, ultimately, about a man, about the culture whose
product he was?

*Sometime in 1492, less than twenty years after the introduction of
printing to Spain, Elio Antonio de Nebrija, historiographer royal to
Queen Isabella, published in Salamanca a grammar of the Castilian
language, the first such work ever compiled for a European vernacular.
A grammar is a typical work of what one might call the encyclopedic
mentality to which Renaissance Europe aspired and that was to sustain
its vaunted scientific method: it is intended to be all-inclusive and
exhaustive, neutral and nonjudgmental, ostensibly without political
point of view or social purpose, and meant only to be a list, a catalogue,
an inventory.*

*"What is it for?" Isabella is said to have asked, in a burst of prac-
ticality, when Nebrija's book was presented to her by a royal courtier.*

*"Your Majesty," the courtier is reported to have answered, "lan-
guage has always been the companion of empire."*

*Friday, 3 August. We departed Friday the 3d day of
August 1492 from the bar of Saltes at the eighth hour.*

We proceeded with strong sea winds until the setting of the sun toward the south sixty miles, which are 15 leagues; afterwards to the southwest and south by west, which was the course to the Canaries.

The first entry in the record of this voyage by the Captain General does not seem like much, to be sure. But the very fact that he kept such a journal at all is extraordinary and, for history, extraordinarily fortunate. This event, indeed, has its place in history as much because of Colón's foresight in deciding to keep a daily record of his voyage as because of any of the rather inconsequential islands he happened to find in the course of it: it is this that gives us not just the fact but the texture and substance of the event, permits it truly to *become* an event, something that takes on color and life and historical heft.

The *Journal* (the *diario de a bordo* as it was then, known usually in Spanish as the *Diario de Colón*, in English as the *Journal of the First Voyage*) is, as far as we know, the first log designed for a wider audience than other mariners or royal marine archives—it is in fact addressed to Ferdinand and Isabella but was undoubtedly crafted with an eye to Clio—and thus concerned with matters other than tides and winds and currents and the like. It is remarkably detailed and wide-ranging, especially when compared to the accounts of many other voyages even in the centuries to follow, and in contrast to some other important voyages—Cabot's, for example, the Corte Reals', Balboa's—for which we have no substantial record at all.*

Despite all that, from the point of view of the modern historian, the *Journal* is still slight and superficial, not to mention at times confusing as to places seen and distances traveled. Take that fateful August Friday, for instance, about which we would like to know so much—the dimensions of the ships and their rigging, say, the provisions and other cargo, the activities in Palos and along the shore, and especially what was going on in the mind of the Captain General. All we have are those two bare sentences, some fifty meager words, about winds and distances. Plus this one line, in an introduction added some time later: "I departed from the said harbor well supplied with very many provisions and many seamen, on the third day of the month of August of the said year, on a Friday, at half an hour before

---

*For the important voyages of John Cabot, the nominal European discoverer of North America, there survives no log, no journal, no diary, no firsthand letters, no shipmates' versions—not even a lading bill, not so much as a solitary signature of the captain's.

sunrise, and I took the route for the Canary Islands of Your High-nesses."

That is all Colón ever said about that day; that is *all* that is positively known about the departure of the First Voyage.

Do not be deceived. Other versions of the departure add a good deal more color and many more details, some complete with extensive descriptions of the cargo and illuminating psychological profiles of the captain and crew, not to mention conversations held on shipboard and descriptions of the clouds overhead. But those are, we must understand, fabrications, inventions, novelists' figments masquer-ading as historians' truths. Indeed, there is probably no other area of modern history with more elaborate fantasies pretending to be sober fact than in Columbian studies, even in works by the most celebrated and reputable.

It might be fun to believe that Colón embraced his friend García Fernández on the Palos dock just before departure and said, "If it please God, we shall be here again within the year"—the version of a popular nineteenth-century writer, Charles Paul Mac Kie. Or that Colón and the deckhands crossed themselves and knelt as they passed by La Rábida, listening to the last chords of the friars' morning hymn—the fantasy put forward as fact in Samuel Eliot Morison's 1942 Pulitzer Prize–winning biography. Or that Isabella and Fer-dinand were right down there at the Palos dockside when Colón reluctantly said farewell and turned to join his piked and armored crewmen in the longboats—the charming scene engraved by Theo-dore de Bry in 1594. It might be fun to believe such stuff, but it is the stuff of imagination not history.

No, all that we can truly depend upon here is the word of the Captain General's *Journal*. And even that, I am constrained to say, is not wholly reliable. For one thing, we cannot always trust the version of events put forth by Colón, who was not above lying and exaggerating for effect. Beyond that, the original manuscript of the *Journal* has not survived, and what we have is an abstract, or close paraphrasing, of it, with some direct quotations, made by the ad-mirable friar Bartolomé de Las Casas perhaps in the 1530s, four decades after the fact, and he was working from a version copied from Colón's original by a scribe who was apparently not all that sophisticated or literate. Thus there is room for error, and a need for caution.

The few other sources for information about the First Voyage also merit caution. The biography of Colón by his son Fernando (who was only four at the time) comes to us only in an Italian version, not the original Spanish, and it is known to be full of inaccuracies; the works by court humanist Peter Martyr ("First Decade," 1511), Oviedo (*Historia general*, 1535), and Las Casas (*Historia de las Indias*, 1550s) appeared well after the fact and, because none of the authors was in Palos or on shipboard, all had to rely on later stories spun by Colón or on dockside gossip of the crew. One additional source is that collection of depositions called the *Pleitos*, in which surviving members of the first crew were asked a series of questions by royal notaries; but the answers, taken down over the years between 1513 and 1536, well after the event, cover only a limited range of material that happened to interest the crown, and the witnesses were generally partisan, sometimes contradictory, and often inaccurate.

So we are thrust, perforce, on the pages of the *Journal*, and from there we will learn such as we can. It is about all we have of reliable, incontrovertible evidence—for the scenes of departure, for the eventual landfall, for the entire momentous voyage—and where it fails us we must be frank to acknowledge conjecture, and sail, as historians must, with the companions of "probably" and "likely" and "perhaps" through the shoals of the past.

On April 9, 1492, Lorenzo de' Medici, pleased to be known as "il Magnifico" and for more than twenty-two years the generous and crafty omnipotent ruler of Florence, died. Of his two sons, the elder, Piero, succeeded him as ruler and managed to destroy the family oligarchy within two years, finally being expelled by the apocalyptic sermonizer Girolamo Savonarola and his band of republican opportunists; the second, Giovanni, pope from 1513 to 1521, fared hardly better, for under his reign the Protestant Reformation began, with the posting of the Lutheran theses in 1517.

It is the examples of Lorenzo in his rule of Florence and later of Cesare Borgia in his domination of northern Italy that were the inspirations for the document of political amorality, chicanery, duplicity, violence, and self-interest called The Prince, *written by the Florentine Niccolò Machiavelli in 1513 and said to be the foundation of modern political science.*

Saturday, 4 August. They proceeded to the southwest by south.

Sunday, 5 August. They proceeded on their course, and between day and night made more than forty leagues.*

The journey from Palos southwest by south to the Canary Islands, where Castile even now was in the process of establishing a colony that might do for her what the Azores had done for Portugal, was about 700 miles.

The fleet had favorable winds, for they made somewhere between 80 and 120 miles a day, but they were hampered by a faulty rudder on the *Pinta* and did not catch sight of Grand Canary until daybreak on Thursday, August 9. (They were actually aiming for the Canary island of Lanzarote and missed it by more than a hundred miles, such were the state of fifteenth-century navigation and the skills of the Captain General.) For three days they lay to, "owing now to contrary winds, now to calms," and not until Sunday were they finally able to put into port, the *Pinta* limping into Grand Canary, the *Santa María* and *Niña* sailing on to the island of Gomera eighty miles to the west.

Just why Colón chose to sail to the Canaries is not quite clear. It is true that they were the westernmost possessions of Castile—but they were 700 miles to the south and represented a considerable deviation for a fleet that would presumably have been aiming due west. It may have been, as some have suggested, that he had picked up somewhere (perhaps during his time in the Madeiras) an idea that he would find easterly winds at that latitude, and if so, that was no doubt the most important single decision in his entire navigational career, for that is exactly what happened; all the Portuguese voyages of discovery over the previous decades, by contrast, had headed due west from the Azores, 800 miles north, and all had run into the contrary westerly winds common at that latitude. Or it may have been pure dumb luck, as others have suggested, inspired by an idea that his ultimate destination was on the same latitude as the Canaries, so that the only navigation he would have to do on the ocean would

---

*Controversy surrounds the proper length of Colón's "league," with various authorities suggesting 3.18, 2.89, 2.82, and 2.67 nautical miles, but for general purposes it may be taken as roughly 3 nautical miles (c. 3.5 land miles); for Colón it was equivalent to 4 miles, but the trouble is we do not know what length of mile he used.

be to steer into the setting sun and hold the rudder. We do not know; the Captain General says not a word about it.

In truth, we do not even know where he was going.

And that brings up the nagging, nettling questions that we cannot evade if we are concerned with what is in the mind of the Discoverer: what *did* he seek? where *was* he planning to go, anyway?

The usual answer, which the storybooks and conventional historians prefer, is that he was heading for China (or Cathay, as he might have called it) and its outlying islands, including the fabled isle of Cipango, which we know as Japan—or, to use the usual fifteenth-century term for the eastern regions of Asia, "India" or "the Indies."

This is certainly what Colón himself wanted the world to believe, and he never tired of pointing out in later letters and accounts how for years he had been putting forth the idea of an "enterprise of the Indies" only to have it received with nothing more than "laughter and mockery." This was also what he himself declared in the prologue to his *Journal*: "Your Highnesses . . . thought to send me, Cristóbal Colón, to the said regions of India," and later, "to take my course and sail so far that I would reach the Indies."[5] This also seems to be the import of two documents Colón took along with him on the First Voyage: one, an official passport (in Latin) saying that he was authorized to sail "toward the regions of India [*ad partes Indie*]," the other an all-purpose letter of introduction to foreign potentates from the sovereign king and queen, who "have learned with joy of Your esteem and high regard for Us and Our nation"—possibly a reference to the story in Marco Polo that the rulers of the East were eagerly waiting to welcome Europeans and receive their doctrine of Christ. And finally, this is suggested also by a document in the archives of Simancas that confirms a payment to King Ferdinand's treasurer "for the three caravels that their Highnesses sent to the Indies" and "to pay Xristoual Colón who sails with the aforesaid fleet."

It is notable too that this theory was accepted without question by all of the initial historians of the Indies, from Fernando to Las Casas and beyond. But it is also notable that all of them are simply relying on the word of Colón and the documents that he left behind, in which the idea of an "enterprise of the Indies" was painstakingly crafted.

There are reasons to give it credence. It is *not* true, as convention has it, that the trade route by land across the Middle East had been closed by the Turkish conquest of Constantinople—the Venetians, for example, continued regular trade with the East for spices, drugs, and luxuries until the 1520s—but it is true that both Portugal and Spain had some interest in opening their own sea routes to Asia. Long-distance trade even then was seen as a more profitable venture than domestic commerce, because one could always find something plentiful here that was scarce there, on distant shores, and vice versa; and for a Europe then stirring with the beginnings of its capitalist revolution this meant a place for increasing amounts of loose money. And it would seem probable that a budding nation such as Spain that was seeking outward expansion would think more in terms of establishing an Oriental trade with known empires of wealth and known sources of desirable goods than, say, searching for new lands of uncertain value.

And yet against all that there have to be put certain serious queries and doubts.

There is almost no reliable record for anything in Colón's life before his dealings with the Castilian court in the late 1480s, and nothing anywhere to show that he ever had a Grand Scheme of any kind, much less one to the Indies. The common notion of there being some kind of *Empresa de las Indias* festering in his soul since the days in Portugal is entirely unsubstantiated, the only evidence for it being Fernando's account, supplied presumably by his father, and well after the fact. It is possible that such a plan existed, but as Columbus scholar Henry Vignaud points out, "A scheme for reaching the Indies by way of the West rests, in the last resort, solely on the unsupported testimony of the man whose interest lay in maintaining the assertion—on the word of Christopher Columbus, who was not a truthful man." It might well have been that Colón had nothing so specific in mind when he petitioned the Sovereigns—it is reasonable to think he may have intended only to search for the fabled islands, as many Portuguese and English sailors before him,* or perhaps for some entirely new lands at the east end of Asia, neither Cathay nor Cipango but "some island or land of great importance" before them, as Fernando himself at one juncture suggested.

Certainly the prologue is not much help on this point, since it

---

*As Colón might have known, there is no mention of the Indies or Asia as a destination in any of the (admittedly limited) records of the Portuguese voyages to the west in the years between 1431 and 1486; one in 1484 speaks of searching for an island, one in 1486 of an unspecified mainland.

seems clearly to have been added to the *Journal* at some later time and might have been written only *after* Colón convinced himself (or after he wanted to pretend to Ferdinand and Isabella) that the sparse islands he had reached were really among those that Marco Polo had promised were off the China coast, and that he should be sent back for a *second* voyage regardless of how meager the treasures were on this one. There is some support for the idea of this late conjuration of a near–Asian discovery in the fact that Colón does not ever mention the Indies (in his own words) at any time or in any document before the *Journal* entry of October 17, or China before the entry of October 21.

There are other problems, too. In the formal documents drawn up between Colón and the Spanish monarchs to authorize this voyage —papers known collectively as the Capitulations, and unquestionably genuine (although copies)—there is no reference to "the Indies," or Cathay, or any specific land of the Orient. All that is said, and it is said no fewer than nine times, is that Colón was authorized to "discover and acquire" certain "Islands and Mainlands" in the Ocean Sea. That reference to "discover and acquire" is also troubling, since it would be hard to imagine the Sovereigns sending Colón to discover what was already occupied and acquire what was already owned by the sovereign power of the Grand Khan or some other Eastern potentate. Moreover, since they then granted him the right to call himself "Viceroy and Governor-General" of any lands he finds, they could hardly have been thinking of those already claimed and settled and governed; they, at least, must have had new territories in mind. That, too, is the conclusion from the evidence in the *Pleitos* depositions of the original crew, because no sailor—and who else would have been more likely to know the true destination?—mentions that Colón said anything about a voyage to the Indies or the Orient, only to "new lands."

Moreover, it has always seemed something of a mystery why Colón, if he really planned to go to Cathay and the realm of the Grand Khan, whose magnificence Marco Polo had celebrated, would take with him little trinkets and beads and bells to trade with: that was the sort of truck the Portuguese had used for barter with the tribes who lived along the African coast, not the kind of treasure one would put before an imperial majesty of the likes of the exalted Khan. In fact, Vasco da Gama got into trouble a few years later when he finally arrived in India and went before a local rajah with nothing more than the trading trinkets of Africa; Portugal's next voyage, in 1500, went out with thirteen vessels and a rich cargo of gifts and European trading goods. One might have thought that Colón would more likely have taken the approach of Jean Nicolet, who in exploring the Great Lakes more than 140 years later took along a mandarin robe of damask embroidered with flowers and multicolored birds, just in case he should come upon a retinue of the Khan and need to dress accordingly.

And was his subsequent behavior any more like that of a peaceful ambassador intruding into the realm of a powerful sovereign kingdom? At every island Colón came to, as he boldly claims in his *Journal*, he went through an elaborate ceremony of taking "possession" of the land and planting the flag of Castile and León, in full view of the inhabitants, as if this was territory entirely unowned and up for grabs. And he did this without even the semblance of an army, not even trained soldiers, carrying only the most limited sorts of armaments, as if he knew full well that there was no Oriental empire or likelihood of resistance here.

Those who have cast doubt on the idea that Colón was aiming for the Indies—what we may call the Vignaud school, after the man who spent several long and painstaking books arguing this case—have never been able to prove their thesis, in spite of these substantial doubts. However, those who take the India-all-along position—what we may call the Morison school, after the scholar who has been the Discoverer's greatest champion in this century—have not been able to allay those doubts satisfactorily, either.[6] Perhaps it is best to conclude that this issue, like so many of those in the Columbian corpus, can never be resolved and that we will likely never know for sure the vision in the Captain General's mind as he began his expedition. Not very satisfactory for those who demand certainty in their historical tales, but it is an area, being both deep and murky, in which the historian and the sailor might each be able to feel at home.

On December 7, 1492, as he descended the marble stairs of the Palace of Justice in Barcelona, King Ferdinand was attacked by an assailant who rushed at him from behind and slashed at his neck and shoulder with a sword. Only the heavy chains of office that the king wore around his neck prevented his decapitation; as it was, he was severely wounded, falling to the steps in a pool of blood and crying, according to the chroniclers, "Help, holy Mary! Treason! Treason!"

The assailant, Juan de Cañamás, was captured, tortured, hanged, and thereafter burned at the stake.

Thursday, 6 September. He departed this day in the morning from the harbor of Gomera, and shaped a course to make his voyage. . . . And he went all that day and night in very light winds and at morning found himself between Gomera and Tenerife.

Friday, 7 September. All Friday, and Saturday up to three hours of the night, he lay in very light winds.

Saturday, 8 September. At the third hour of night, Saturday, the northeast wind began to blow and he shaped his way and course to the west . . . and made nine leagues that day and night.

We are now an entire month later. The little fleet has had a somewhat exasperating time in various Canary ports and waters, first searching for a vessel to substitute for the rudder-wounded *Pinta*, then waiting in vain for the local governess of Gomera to return home with another vessel to swap, and finally going ahead and having the *Pinta* repaired, "very well with much work and care." At last, on the morning of September 6, the Captain General was able to set sail again, only to succumb to the greatest frustration a sailor knows (and how much greater for these sailors): to be becalmed on a flat, unmoving ocean.

Not until the early hours of September 9 did the wind finally begin to come in from the northeast, the sails puff and begin to fill, and the three ships, their helmsmen with eyes attentive to the compass box before them, head on their fateful course: west, due west. Thus to achieve what may fairly be called the most important journey in the history of the human species: the journey that began the long process by which a single culture came to dominate as never before all the other cultures in the world, to impose its languages in their mouths, its clothes on their backs, its values in their hearts, and to accumulate to itself the power that now enables it to determine nothing less than the destiny of the world.

Chapter Two

Europe

I

"The End of the World Is Near"

IT WAS late in the year 1492 that the renowned Nuremberg printer Anton Koberger commissioned several leading German artists to create a series of some two thousand woodcuts for a massive *Book of Chronicles* being written by Hartmann Schedel, a physician, scholar, and man of letters, which he planned to publish the following year. One of the studios he selected employed a young Nuremberg artist, Albrecht Dürer, then just twenty-one years old but already recognized (not least by himself) as a man of genius.

Among the assignments apparently given to young Dürer was to produce a *Dance of Death*. This theme, a recurrent one ever since the terrible plagues that ravaged Europe in the fourteenth century and still unexpectedly, mysteriously, and devastatingly visited European cities throughout the fifteenth century, grew in popularity as the decades passed. It exemplified perfectly the preoccupation with morbidity at all levels of society—princes as well as peasants, for none was exempt—a preoccupation that came to be called at the time "the culture of death." Popular treatises offered lessons on *ars moriendi*, the art of dying; mystery plays and pageants in town squares and cathedrals featured endless deathbed scenes replete with hovering, fearsome black angels; high and popular art, spread in part by the new printing press, presented scenes of rotten corpses, writhing skeletons, decaying bodies eaten by wriggling worms, and everywhere the grinning, lascivious, triumphant smile of Death himself. The

Dance of Death, in which bodies in various stages of putrefaction cavorted in their last exercise on earth, was by now a ubiquitous sight, found in frescoes and engravings, stained-glass panels and funerary statues, from London to Naples; it was the perfect drone for the threnody that resounded through an age of which historian Johan Huizinga has written, "No other epoch has laid so much stress as the expiring Middle Ages on the thought of death."

But Dürer's version, as one might expect, rose far above the usual depiction of this grisly scene. Here is not only terror and melancholy but also a kind of sickly joy and morbid delight as three dancing skeletons, one with flesh still drooping and entrails hanging, prance wildly above a grave from which a fourth corpse emerges, hand upraised, to join the dance being played for them by the ghastly piper, cloaked in shrouds, who leads their final tune. With the skill for infinite detail for which he later became famous, Dürer made all too clear the obsession, the psychotic fascination, of that age, that culture, with incomprehensible and ever-present Death. "By far the most gruesome example of these works of art," the German scholar Paul Herrmann writes, "it is terrible to behold, and it is meant to be so."

It is, in truth, a fitting illustration for the volume for which it was planned, a history of the world that would announce, as many of the time already believed, that the present age, "in which iniquity and evil have increased to the highest pitch," is the penultimate age of humankind, to be followed, and in not too many years, by the Day of Judgment and the end of the world.

The end of the world: the idea was taken quite seriously by Europe of the late fifteenth century—not as a mere conceit, not as a metaphor or theological trope, but as a somber, terrifying prediction based solidly on the divine wisdom of biblical prophecy and the felt experience of daily life. The protean German historian Egon Friedell, who calls this period the "incubation" of the Modern Age, argues that "there was a general feeling of the world's end, which, expressed or unexpressed, conscious or unconscious, permeated and dominated the whole era." Or in the words of Joseph Grünpeck, the official historian to the Hapsburg emperor Frederick III, "When you perceive the miserable corruption of the whole of Christendom, of all praiseworthy customs, rules and laws, the wretchedness of all classes, the many pestilences, the changes in this epoch and all the strange happenings, you know that the End of the World is near. And the waters of affliction will flow over the whole of Christendom."

In such an atmosphere it is not surprising that so much of Christendom reacted with an explosion of messianic millenarianism—Armageddon at hand, the terrible words of St. John come true ("Woe, woe, woe, to the inhabiters of the earth"), the reign of the Antichrist, the triumph of the serpent "which is the Devil," a thousand years of misery. The British historian Norman Cohn has filled a long book with the evidence of this strange but obviously very prevalent strain of Christianity in the late Middle Ages, and the only conclusion one can reach after his elaborate recitation is that for countless hundreds of thousands of Europeans manifestly millenarian—Ranter or Thuringian, Amaurian or Taborite, Free Spirit or Franciscan—there must have been hundreds of thousands of others resonating with the same sensibilities.

Among whom—and "resonating" is the right word—was one Cristóbal Colón, lately of Palos and now embarked on his mad, brave adventure across the Ocean Sea. The end of the world was apparently an abiding, perhaps even obsessive, preoccupation of his, and he was concerned to determine exactly how many years remained until the Final Judgment. For this he pored over Revelations and Isaiah at length, but most important to him was Pierre d'Ailly's *Imago mundi* (complete with opuscula), in his copy of which he made no fewer than 848 marginal notes and calculations. His conclusion: "St. Augustine says that the end of the world will come in the seventh millennium from its creation; the holy theologians follow him, especially the Cardinal Pierre D'Ailly. . . . According to this calculation, there are lacking about one hundred and fifty-five years for the completion of the seven thousand, at which time the world will come to an end." In other words, Armageddon around 1650. And this he believed.

Whether the end of the world was understood to be as imminent as tomorrow or as distant as several generations off, the effect on the soul of Europe was pretty much the same. "A general feeling of impending calamity hangs over Europe," in the words of Huizinga, "a sombre melancholy weighs on people's souls." The evidence is everywhere: in the replicas of the Dance of Death, of course, in the immediately popular first edition of *Danse Macabré* in 1485, in the melancholy love songs of northern Europe, in the diaries of the young grandees of Spain, in the diatribes from Italian pulpits, in Georges Chastellain's chronicles of unlucky princes, in this typical stanza of the French poet Eustache Deschamps, one of his dozens of "monotonous and gloomy variations" on this theme:

> *Time of melancholy, and of temptation,*
> *Age of tears, where envy and torment blend,*
> *Time of lassitude and of condemnation,*
> *Age of decadence before the end.*
> *Time full of horror, deceiving all around,*
> *Age of lies, with pride and envy rife,*
> *Time without honor, nor sense nor judgment sound,*
> *Age of sadness and the fore-doomed life.*

And Huizinga, who devotes a substantial part of his classic *Waning of the Middle Ages* to this phenomenon, concludes, "Always and everywhere in the literature of the age, we find a confessed pessimism. As soon as the soul of these men has passed from childlike mirth and unreasoning enjoyment to reflection, deep dejection about all earthly misery takes their place and they see only the woe of life."

The woe of life. It is five centuries in the past for us, and a world without much that we now take for granted—without flat plates and table forks, and liquor and rubber and nightclothes and easy chairs and, important to remember, without the idea of progress or the optimism of the affluent—and so it is difficult even to imagine that sense of woe, much less feel it now. It thus deserves a closer look, a brief examination of at least a few of the darker landscapes of that age.

Violence What Huizinga calls "the violent tenor of life" in the fifteenth century was so pervasive—death was so daily, brutality so commonplace, destruction of the animate and inanimate so customary—that it is shocking even in our own age of mass destruction.

At the simplest level there was the violence of everyday life, suggested by this picture of fifteenth-century Spain by the contemporary historian Lucio Marineo Siculo:

Many cities and towns of Spain cruelly worn out by many and most cruel thieves, murderers, adulterers, by infinite insults and sacrilege and all kind of delinquents . . . Some of them, scorning laws both human and divine, took all justice into their own hands. Others, given to gluttony and laziness, shamelessly violated wives, virgins and nuns. . . . Others cruelly assaulted and robbed tradesmen, travelers and people on their way to fairs. Others, who had greater power and greater folly, seized lands and castles of the Crown, and sallying thence with violence robbed the fields of their neighbors.

At another level there was the sanctioned violence of local authorities whose punishments were meted out on a daily basis on the scaffolds of the public squares in almost every town and city. "Judicial cruelty," Huizinga calls it:

> Torture and executions are enjoyed by the spectators like an entertainment at a fair. The citizens of Mons [in Flanders] bought a brigand, at far too high a price, for the pleasure of seeing him quartered, "at which the people rejoiced more than if a new holy body had risen from the dead." The people of Bruges, in 1488 . . . cannot get their fill of seeing the tortures inflicted, on a high platform in the middle of the marketplace, on the magistrates suspected of treason. The unfortunates are refused the deathblow which they implore, that the people may feast again upon their torments.

On a higher level still, there was the Church-sponsored violence known as the Inquisition, which went, methodically and heartlessly, after any variety of heretic or dissenter, reformer or mystic, attempting to do by the sword—or by the torturer's rack and the auto-da-fé—what it could not do by word or prayer, under whose jurisdiction countless millions were imprisoned, by whose decree countless hundreds of thousands were killed. The Inquisition in Spain was the most brutal of all in the fifteenth century, in part because it was, uniquely, under the control of the crowns of Castile and Aragon. It was in fact the only truly national institution within their territory and as such their single most potent (and indeed most popular) instrument for creating the nation-state that was to be Spain. The Inquisition, under royal direction from 1483, was the one whose strictures Cristóbal Colón would have been careful to heed, and whose ministrations, evidenced in clouds of smoke billowing from town squares throughout the land, he would have witnessed daily.

Then, finally, there is the violence of nation-states such as Spain, just then forming in Europe, and the principalities, duchies, margravates, republics, seigneuries, dominions, earldoms, and noble factions and royal families of all sorts, each one struggling to determine which should dominate in that formation and how wide its scope should be. To them, deadly violence was nothing less than the daily stuff of politics. Internally the savagery of brother against brother and cousin against cousin—complete with kidnapping, torture, mutilation, fratricide, patricide, assassination, and fomented rebellion—went on year after bloody year, as in the faction fights in the royal house of Scotland throughout the fifteenth century, the decades-long wars of White Rose and Red in England, and the crude battles between disputatious families in Castile, of which the contemporary historian Father Juan de Mariana wrote: "It was the custom of men to carry the title of kingship in the point of their lances and in their weapons," and "The strongest is the one who captures the jewel, and who wins it from his opponent without regard for the laws which are silent in the face of the clamor of arms, of trumpets and drums." When tired of that internecine pastime, the possessors of power would wield it just as brutally upon disobedient or disliked fellow citizens, as in the slaughters by the various tyrants struggling to rule the collapsing Italian city-states, the ruthless repression of sectarian and peasant revolts in the German provinces, the revival by Ferdinand and Isabella of the Santa Hermandad (Holy Brotherhood) as their private and lawless police force, and the vigilante-turned-terrorist VEHM in the Holy Roman Empire under Frederick III. And among each other the rising states would practice the same sort of relentless violence—officially called war—providing the fifteenth century with a steady spate of battle and siege and slaughter, whose reverberations touched every corner of the subcontinent and whose severity reached levels not merely double and triple but *ten and fifteen* times what they were just three centuries before.

Disease The devastation that was the Black Death had somewhat abated by the middle of the fifteenth century, but its resilient virus could and did surface for another three centuries in regions and localities all over Europe, and it is accurate to say that no family was untouched by its deadly grip. Perugia, for example, was struck by plague at least eight times in the fifteenth century, with the loss of thousands; Hamburg, Nuremberg, and Cologne each had more than ten epidemics, with casualties sometimes of more than 50 percent, it is said; and Catalonia, which had been stricken by the plague four times in the fourteenth century, was hit another six times in the fifteenth, and its population of some 430,000 in 1365 had shrunk to less than 278,000 by 1497.

But the plague was only part of the daily—and always mysterious—fate of Europe. As one history of medicine puts it:

> During the Middle Ages, European humanity was plagued with epidemic diseases as never before or since, and these were variously attributed to comets and other astral influences, to storms, the failure of crops, famines, the sinking of mountains, the effects of drought or inundation, swarms of insects, poisoning of wells by Jews and other absurd causes. The real predisposing factors were the crowded condition and bad sanitation of the walled medieval towns, the squalor, misrule, and gross immorality occasioned by the many wars, by the fact that Europe was overrun with wandering soldiers, students and other vagabond characters, and by the general superstition, ignorance and uncleanliness of the masses.

And then it goes on to suggest the consequences: besides plagues, both bubonic and pulmonary (the latter, new to Europe in the fourteenth century, was especially devastating), leprosy, ergotism, scurvy, chorea, smallpox, measles, diphtheria, typhus, tuberculosis, and influenza, every one of which was not just debilitating but potentially deadly.

Deadly, and deadly on a scale, a daily scale even, that is difficult now to imagine. Listen to the rabble-rousing Savonarola, in 1496, intoning this image from his pulpit in Florence:

> There will not be enough men left to bury the dead; nor means to dig enough graves. So many will lie dead in the houses, that men will go through the streets crying, "Send forth your dead!" And the dead will be heaped in carts and on horses; they will be piled up and burnt. Men will pass through the streets crying aloud, "Are there any dead? Are there any dead?"

And that is not prophecy, really, nor rhetoric; it is clinical observation. Or more simply, Thomas à Kempis: "How can it even be called a life, which begets so many deaths and plagues?"

Famine   It is not that food for the general populace was abundant or particularly nutritious at *any* time in the fifteenth century—wheat and barley were the staple, in most places the only, crops, and they provided little besides bread and soup—but that yields at all times were chancy and often meager. One year's bad harvest meant hunger; two, disaster. "Famine constantly visited the continent," Fernand Braudel notes soberly at the start of his masterly history of European society, "laying it waste and destroying lives." Nor, remember, were there the palliatives of potatoes and corn that saved the poor so often in later years: they were yet to be discovered in their native land, the New World.

Soils throughout Europe varied widely in quality, as did agricultural techniques, but even such a relatively privileged area as France experienced at least seven general, country-wide famines in the fifteenth century and innumerable local ones. As to the Mediterranean basin, marked by thin and none too fertile lands, it "was always on the verge of famine," Braudel notes, and Spain compounded its agricultural crisis by choosing sheep over tillage and allowing its *hidalgos* vast uncultivated holdings. Castile endured at least four serious general famines of which we have record in the fifteenth century, and a poor region such as Andalusia suffered from grain crises and famine with heartbreaking frequency: 1400–02, 1412–14, 1421, 1423–26, 1434–38, 1442–43, 1447–49, 1454, 1458–59, 1461–62, and 1465–73, for a total of thirty-five years. No wonder that an old Spanish proverb had it, "If the lark flies over Castile, she must take her grain of barley with her." No wonder that the word *carestía* recurs in the diaries and chronicles of the era: dearth, scarcity, want.

The tolls of such famines are largely unrecorded, folded into the count of death rates that were always high, and they most often accompanied epidemics of disasters anyway. One does get a sense, however, that many hundreds of thousands were victims of famine, one way or another, every year—even two centuries later, we know, as much as a third of the Finnish population died in the 1696 famine, and the electors of Burgundy in 1662 recorded that "famine this year has put an end to over ten thousand families in your province and forced a third of the inhabitants, even in the good towns, to eat wild plants." From such details we may glimpse the situation at the close of the fifteenth century.

The social costs of recurrent famines were in any case high. Most often it was the countryside that felt the ravages first, and there that those who still had the strength took to open rebellion, of which we have some record if only because the official troops would be called out to put them down with force. But the severest famines touched the towns and cities, too, and the range of disruption there went from open robbing and looting and uncontrolled pillaging in suffering towns, to outright riots and rebellions, often again suppressed with nothing short of massacres. In Seville in 1462, one Garci Sánchez wrote: "At seven o'clock another hunger riot started in Seville. The mass of the people armed themselves and searched for bread. The gangs went from house to house searching for bread and saying that it had been stored away as a remedy for hard times. Everyone hid their valuables, thinking that they wished to loot their coffers. This lasted till mid-day." From the tone of it one is tempted to assume that such disturbances were hardly uncommon.

A somber age, then, and little wonder its preoccupation with death, little wonder its sense of impending doom. Famine, disease, violence, these the companions of the day, the season, the year, the lifetime however short. A French poet at the end of the fifteenth century left this anguished prayer:

> *War we suffer, famine, too, and death;*
> *Cold, heat, day, night, sap our breath;*
> *Fleas, scabmites, and vermin show their wrath*
> *Upon us daily. In short, have mercy, Lord,*
> *Upon us wicked persons, whose life is short.*

In the face of all of this, the institutions of the time knew no answers, no palliatives. The once stable customs and values of the medieval world no longer held; everywhere, as Friedell puts it, there was

the definite, though generally unconscious rejection of all earlier dominants of existence. There is a sudden collapse of all the standards and "truths"—religious, ethical, philosophical, economical, erotic, and artistic—which, till then firmly established and believed, had guaranteed, seemingly forever, the orientation of man in past, present, and future. [It was] a catastrophic collapse of all values . . . a radical loosening of all bonds.

In place of the old universals there were now dualities, schisms, multiplicities, infinitudes: not for nothing is this the age that invents polyphony and counterpoint in music and double-entry bookkeeping in commerce, that knew such a babel of vernacular languages that Leonardo da Vinci at the time feared "the generation of man will come to pass as not to understand each other's speech."

"This was a civilization that had lost its bearings," say Bruce and William Catton in their survey of the era, and the evidence of that is everywhere: what authority, after all, could make sense of these times, these long decades of upheaval and despair? What was there to trust in an era of uncertainty, how find peace when there was violence all around, where look for harbor when the winds brought only tempests?

The Church? Corrupt and decadent, without authority or comfort, and quite unable to predict or explain or even to assuage the catastrophes that befell on every side; the Inquisition, we should remember, was a sign not of strength but of weakness, not of fervor but of rot. "No man in these days builds churches or founds monasteries," reported Abbot Trithemius of Sponheim, accurately, in 1493.

The prince, the seigneur? Generally, without concern; if concerned, without compassion; if compassioned, without power to aid and heal. "A prince," after all, as Machiavelli wrote just a few years hence, "cannot do all the things for which men are esteemed good, for, in order to maintain the state, he is often obliged to act contrary to humanity, contrary to charity, contrary to religion."

The state, then? It was there, and growing, but so far little more than the fledgling construct of this or that temporarily more powerful lord, concerned more with higher taxes and usurpations of power than with anything like the solace and security that, at least in theory, nations would come to provide their citizens. The lot of most people, as Nicholas of Cusa put it, was "to live . . . subject to servility and umbrage to those who rule them," with few defenses against that arbitrary authority, and of rights and comforts almost none at all.

To what, then, could a bewildered and despondent Europe turn? As it happened—but of course it was not so happenstantial as all that—there were three responses open to a battered Europe at that time, responses that were shaped by powerful social and intellectual forces still early in their development but with such inherent strength that they would come to mark, and would go on to sustain, the Modern Age right to the present.

There was, first, that response of the Renaissance, primarily on the Italian peninsula but soon throughout the entire (at least the educated) subcontinent, that goes by the name of *humanism*. In an age of lost certainties and ebbing faith, it proffered what might be seen as the most tangible, the most fundamental, object of all, and endowed it with both corporeal virtue and a kind of divine uniqueness. Humanism swept through fifteenth-century Europe not merely because it created an effective substructure for the classes of wealth and power, but because it provided a flood of answers, and with the authority of antiquity, to fill the gaping holes of doubt and disbelief for all.

De dignitate et excellentia hominis was the title of Giannozzo Manetti's influential book, published in the 1440s, and therein was the simple message of the humanistic vision. In the face of that dignity and excellence, given its full range, all of the era's obstacles—political, intellectual, practical—would surely crumble, as the Florentine humanist Marsilio Ficino made clear in his *Theologica platonica*, published in the early 1480s: "The immense magnificence of our soul may manifestly be seen from this: man will not be satisfied with the empire of this world, if, having conquered this one, he learns that there remains another world which he has not yet subjugated. . . . Thus man wishes no superior and no equal and will not permit anything to be left out and excluded from his rule." This is not merely the classical "man the measure." This is a new, unrestrained "man the imperialist," and how fitting a description it is of the age on which Europe was to embark—and how apt, we may conjecture, it must have seemed to at least one former Genoese.

But humanism does not, in its philosophical excesses, stop there: next is nothing less than "man the divine." Ficino put it simply: "And so he strives to be as God everywhere." No blasphemy there, no sacrilege, for it is merely the recognition of what was truly in God's plan, the elevation of the human above all species. Leon Battista Alberti, a Renaissance man par excellence, expresses it in this paean to man: "To you is given a body more graceful than other animals, to you power of apt and various movements, to you most sharp and delicate senses, to you wit, reason, memory, like an immortal god." And for another Florentine, Giovanni Pico della Mirandola, the possibility for every human was nothing less than "to regenerate thyself a godlike being." A Renaissance it was indeed: a rebirth of the human in the image of God.

Not that humanism sought to put forth a new *morality* in place of a Christian creed shredded by a century and more of cynicism and scurrility; not at all. It promoted rather a new secular pragmatism that overrode the old questions of morality, and Machiavelli, although he shocked even some of his compatriots with his blunt assertions of it, was merely its most open acolyte. What works, in the here and now, for this society of humans, at this time, is what matters: after all, we are building not the Heavenly City but the earthly one. The modern historian Lauro Martines, in his study of Renaissance Italy, points out that all along humanism was meant "to provide upper-class citizens with a sense of unity and direction in their lives. And this was a consciousness oriented more frankly toward worldly ends. Sin would have to be de-emphasized and morality redefined [toward] a psychological consciousness that was more in keeping with worldly goals." Hence, by the fifteenth century, "the demands of worldliness were taken in, absorbed, and became the psychological consciousness not only of literati but also of the social groups at the top." Hence also—and the linkage is neat—both "money and authority had no more able and wheedling defense than that found in humanist encomia."

When humanism spoke of the "dignity of man," one should note, it meant primarily "man" in the broader sense of "human." But it *also* meant the male human, and especially the wealthy, urban, positioned, accomplished male; most assuredly it did not include, except in the most casual way, woman. For this was a Europe in which patriarchy was deeply ingrained: the patriarchy of the Church, with an infallible father at its top, of the principality and the state, with their hierarchical forms of dominance, of the very family itself, with the male in both legal and ecclesiastical eyes the reigning power in the home. In the chain of being, it was understood that the biological entity that came just below man was woman.

A second, closely related response of that era was *rationalism*, particularly that form of it which now goes by the name of science.

It was a decidedly anomalous way of looking at the world, but European rationalism—that promulgation of logical, straight-line, objective comprehension which finds its apex in the scientific method—proved to be the ideal instrument for the time and place. With it philosophers and scholars, and very soon all educated people, could provide a picture of the world in its smallest detail that quite did away with any need to suppose a God, or gods, or miracles or magic or mysticism or metaphysics. Let the old religions falter and fail; science would be the new faith.

The task of achieving this triumph of European rationalism was immense, and it took a whole range of disparate talents—humanists, artisans, painters, surgeons, alchemists—and decades before it was ascendant, centuries before it was commonplace. For there were age-old habits of thought to dispel, fundamentally different modes of perception to supplant. "What they had to do was not criticize and combat faulty theories," a modern scholar of the early scientists has written, "they had to do something different. They had to replace the framework of the intellect itself, to restate and reform its concepts, to evolve a new approach to Being, a new concept of knowledge, a new concept of science, and even to replace a pretty natural approach, that of common sense, by another which is not natural at all." It was like trying to say that cannonballs and feathers fall at the same speed.

What they had to achieve, in short, was—in Schiller's later masterful phrase—the "de-godding of nature." At the time, even with the best efforts of the Church, there still lingered in many places in Europe the common wisdom that gods and spirits inhabited the elements of nature—trees, certainly, streams and rivers, forests, rocks—or in some parts of the Church itself, that nature was sacred because God was immanent in all that He created. The task of rationalism, through science, was to show—no, better, to *prove*—that there was no sanctity about these aspects of nature, that they were not animate or purposeful or sensate, but rather nothing more than measurable combinations of chemical and mechanical properties, subject to scientific analysis, prediction, and manipulation. Being de-godded, they could thereby be capable of human use and control according to human whim and desire, and Europeans—uniquely, as near as we can tell, among all cultures—could assume, in Descartes's words, that humans were the "masters and possessors of nature."

One reason that the new rationalism gained such credence in Europe at this time was that, in a manner of speaking, it came up with the goods. The technologies it spawned, and the ones accepted and implemented by the political and commercial powers of the era, were there to be seen and marveled at, very soon a part of everyday life: the public clock, for example (which now at the end of the fifteenth century first began to strike at the quarter hour), and eyeglasses (which came into general use only at the middle of the century), and pane-glass windows (increasingly common, especially in houses of the rich), and the double-rigged three-masted sailing ship (common in both northern and southern Europe by the last part of the century). But none was more significant, in immediate impact as well as in subsequent durability, than—there is dark irony in their conjunction, so typical of objective rationalism—the printing press and the gun.

The perfection of movable type in the 1440s and the availability of good, cheap paper to replace expensive parchment created a printing industry in Europe that was widespread and well-established by the 1470s; by 1500, it is said, there were 110 places on the subcontinent, from Toledo to Stockholm, with at least one printing press and some with three or four. Within the comparatively short period of half a century—from 1454 to 1501, known to scholars as the Age of Incunabula (which marvelous word actually means "swaddling clothes")—there were, by one estimate, 20 million books printed, in at least 40,000 separate editions. And while one could hardly gainsay the positive effects of such an explosion, it is fair nonetheless to point out that something may have started to be lost in the substitution of the machine for the human, the impersonal for the individualistic, quantity for quality, uniformity for spontaneity: it was the beginning, it is not too much to say, of the industrialization of philosophy and the mechanization of thought.

The century's other triumphant technology (in many respects, from metallurgy to specialization, a related one) was that of armaments, made possible by the development of "corned" gunpowder from the 1420s and more sophisticated gun bores and firing mechanisms from the 1460s. With the invention of the arquebus sometime in the later part of the century, allowing individual soldiers to have powder-fired weapons, and then with the perfection of mobile and large-bore cannon in the 1480s (proven by the French in the field in 1494), allowing a fairly small army to have devastating and mobile firepower, the basics of modern mechanized warfare were established. "By the end of the fifteenth century," two economic historians write, "when both cannon and small arms were in common use, gunpowder had profoundly altered the military, governmental, and industrial aspects of medieval civilization." Profoundly altered, indeed: one might more accurately say that it very quickly destroyed it entirely.

But one further consequence of the rise of a rationalistic science goes beyond the technological achievements, as great as those are. It is what we may call the culture of science, the bed from which it grows and which it in turn fertilizes: a milieu of restlessness, curiosity, movement, impatience, and zeal, of the need to explain and explore and overturn and unveil as no other society seems to have felt before. Peter Mathias, a British historian of science who deals with this phenomenon, notes that it is the spread not of scientific *knowledge*, which is truly possessed by only a few, but of scientific *attitudes*, which are absorbed by many, that characterizes Europe from the fifteenth century on. Science and technology in this context, he notes, "give evidence of a society increasingly curious, increasingly questing, increasingly on the move, on the make, having a go, increasingly seeking to experiment, wanting to improve." It is heroic and Promethean, perhaps, but it is also dangerous and Faustian, and Friedell may not be off the mark in calling it a "daemonic emotion."

A final response of the fifteenth century to its bewildering circumstances was, naturally, of a piece with the first two: *materialism* and, in its everyday economic guise, capitalism. The impulse to treasure the material here-and-now, the tangible, in a world of both corporeal uncertainty and spiritual vacuity would seem to be perfectly normal, as we see it today, and yet it appears to have been something quite new for Europe, at least in the frank and far-reaching way it was now expressed. The touched and seen, the rationalistically "real" and the scientifically quantifiable, slowly take on an importance that they had had at no other time and place.

We see it best probably in the art of the age: in the love of objects in precise detail that obsesses Dürer, for example, or especially Leonardo, as his notebooks endlessly attest; in the almost palpable look of material things in a van Eyck portrait; in the elaborate complexities that fill those Bosch paintings to the bursting point. The artists of the time, in the words of Kenneth Clark, "had, to a supreme degree, the power of making their thoughts visible," giving to their works what he calls an "atmosphere of liberal materialism." That materialism celebrated the objects of the outward world, made "realistic" now through perspective, anatomy, foreshortening, all the skills of the Renaissance trade, in a style that stands in stark contrast to virtually all of the art of the preceding centuries since the fall of Rome. The realism of the age was materialism in paint and marble.

Not that this was the first era in which the human soul coveted and strove for wealth—but perhaps the first in which the possession of material goods began so markedly to replace other values at the center of ethical and religious pantheons. All of the trappings and rigamarole that other societies in other eras had used to deflect, disguise, deflate, or deny their love of material wealth were here, in a forthright and practical Europe, gradually dispensed with. Where else would we likely find a man like the great printer Aldus Manutius placing above the door of his shop, the soon-to-be-famous Aldine Press in Venice (and at about the time of the First Voyage), a sign reading: "Talk of nothing but business, and despatch that business quickly"? Where else would we find the hero of a hortatory dialogue saying, as does a character in an Alberti piece, "A man cannot set his hand to more liberal [beneficial] work than making money"? Where else would we find eulogies, such as those for Matteo Palmieri, who died in Florence in 1475, praising a man for knowing "how much riches contribute to a civic life led with dignity"? This is a frankness of material lust one encounters rarely in the historical record.

This straightforward materialism, developed over long decades with sophisticated humanism and rationalism as its companions, created the essential conditions for the success of that economic system we have come to call capitalism. (The word itself was unknown in the fifteenth century, of course—it doesn't exist until the eighteenth, doesn't take on its present meaning until the late nineteenth.) Other contributory elements, to be sure, had also come into being by the late fifteenth century—credit lines, currency transfers, bills of exchange, maritime insurance, international banking, and the accumulation of metals and moneys themselves—but it was materialism's pattern of mind, its order of values, its reinterpretation of the world, that really permitted all these other instruments to develop in Europe, and mesh, and flourish.

The process was naturally a long one, starting well before the fifteenth century and continuing after, but in that century one clearly sees the beginnings of its triumph, and even contemporaries started to sense the undermining of the old values and the emplacement of the new. The idea of a "just price," which so dominated medieval economics that guilds would ostracize those who tried to charge more than the set figure for their goods, now gave way to the concept of "what the traffic will bear"; earlier notions of "good goods at a fair price" were displaced by a revival of the old Roman motto "Let the buyer beware"; the practice of usury, once regarded as a sin ("Thou shalt not lend upon usury to thy brother"), was first allowed to be the province of Jews ("Jews are as necessary as bakers," a Venetian reported in 1519) and then became the territory of any element of society. God, in short, and the restraints which He was presumed to have placed on the medieval economy, lost out to Mammon in this new unbridled form; and the Church had not the power (or, in truth, given its quite extensive worldly interests, the desire) to do anything about it. Lewis Mumford, in *The Condition of Man*, encapsulates it thus: "The whole moral change that took place under capitalism can be summed up in the fact that human purposes, human needs, and human limits no longer exercised a directive and restraining influence upon industry: people worked, not to maintain life, but to increase money and power and to minister to the ego that found satisfaction in vast accumulations of money and power." We should be careful to watch such a process.

Whatever one can say about these new forces to which the mind, the very culture, of Europe was turning—or to which it was succumbing, it might be better said—they were unquestionably powerful, proficient, and persuasive, and they would prove to be the essential skeletonic structure of the Modern Age. Indeed, as they developed not only independently but, even more, synergistically, they may be said to have created the very body and substance of that age.

And they were all nurtured by, and in turn nurtured, one last element of the age rather slower to develop, although its beginnings were visible now: the accretion of civic power we call the nation-state. The idea of the nation, much less the concept of nationalism, was so far insufficiently developed to provide an alternative allegiance for this age of bewilderment and despair. But the essentials were there, and it was only a matter of time before they were melded into a significant new political instrument, one that found itself in harmony with the pragmatic, accumulative, mechanistic, and essentially amoral strains I have mentioned. The new humanists and scientists and capitalists proved to be natural allies of the princes of this incipient state—and those princes who understood this soonest, and learned to use these alliances, won the day in the decades to come, and took unto themselves and their houses the elements not just of royalty, which is something ancient, but far more important, of nationhood, which is something new.

Nationalism was a potent instrument, indeed. It would have been so if it depended on nothing more than the moneylending of bankers and the large-bore artillery of armies, as in large part the government of the Spanish nation-state did for its century-long ascendancy. How much more potent when it could add the ancient wisdom and imaginative self-glorification of the humanists, the practical technics and manipulations of the scientists, the treasures and leverage of the capitalists; and more potent still when it found in this mesh of values all that justified and enshrined its growth and ultimate consolidation.

There is much that can be said about this extraordinary process of European state-building, but it suffices for now to know that it was a new phenomenon on the political horizon—just as a new continent appeared on the geographic one—and that it represented a configuration of power never before known, whose consequences would be spread as far as its representatives explored and settled. To Arnold Toynbee—and this in the fullness of age, not in his youthful *Study of History*—the rise of the nation-state was the crucial phenomenon of this era: "The major political change in Western Christendom in the course of the quarter of a millennium 1303–1563 was the transfer of power and revenue from the Papacy, and from other organs of the Western Church (e.g. monasteries), to local secular governments."

Thus we may begin to see the broader dimensions of the culture of Europe as it existed on that morning when Cristóbal Colón set sail and began the process that was to implant that culture not only in the two continents of the New World he was to find but in the islands and shores beyond them, around the globe. For the next five centuries, through a long process of aggrandizement and absorption, this culture came to prevail throughout virtually all the earth—and in those countries where it secured itself more or less intact, particularly in North America, as in those countries where it imposed itself by imperialism and industrialism, its priorities and visions, its preconceptions and powers, pretty much determined the fate of the earth.

It may be too much to see this, as for example Friedell does, as five hundred years of "that long unbroken Crisis of the European soul" expressing "one of the most rudimentary, childish, and primitive periods in the history of the human spirit"; or as the scholar Frederick Turner has put it, the method by which "a world millions of years in the making vanished into the voracious, insatiable maw of an alien civilization." Perhaps it is best to see it simply, in the words of the contemporary Spanish humanist Hernán Pérez de Oliva, as the means by which Spain would "unite the world and give to those strange lands the form of our own." But it was in any case a process by which Europe was able, eventually, to overcome its own desperate frailties and terrors, and find not only gold and silver and precious ores beyond imagining, not only foods that would sustain its population for centuries (potatoes, manioc, corn, tomatoes, among others), not only drugs it would take into its pharmacopoeia (some two hundred at various times), not only vast resources of timber and furs and hides and water power, but the huge continent on which the people of Europe would spread themselves and their culture.

In the dark twilight of fifteenth-century Europe, the overriding question, for those still able to ask questions at all, was how to survive the misery and suffering and violence that seemed to be rushing the world to its end. The answer that came, that was on its way to being born as the little fleet headed due west from the Canaries, was the conquest of Paradise.

Chapter Three

1492

II

*Sunday, 9 September. He made that day 15 leagues. . . .
In the night they made a hundred and twenty miles at ten
miles per hour, which is 30 leagues. . . .
Monday, 10 September. On that day and night they
made sixty leagues. . . .
Tuesday, 11 September. That day they sailed on their
course, which was west, and they made 20 leagues and
more. . . . That night they made nearly twenty leagues. . . .*

For the first ten days at sea after their departure from the Canaries,
the three small vessels under the command of Cristóbal Colón scud-
ded before brisk trade winds into the waters of the Ocean Sea where
no ship had ever gone before. All was uneventful, at least in the sense
that delights the seaman: the ships were under full sail, making remarkably good distances of 150 miles or more a day, and though the
sea was up, it was on the stern and the skies were clear and the
weather balmy without hint of storms. In another sense, of course,
each day brought the excitement of new waters and new experiences,
a world of new birds and fish and vegetation and trade-wind clouds,
and with each day the distance from home, and the anxiety, stretched
farther.

The winds full, the miles swift: they may not have known where
they were headed, but they were getting there awfully fast. (Unusu-
ally fast, in fact: the Captain General was lucky to have the trade
winds following him still, since in normal years they slacken off in
the latitudes he pursued.) But here is a strange thing. The Captain

General chose not to tell the crew—or "the people," as he phrased it in the *Journal*, using the customary expression that conveyed some of the egalitarianism common to Iberian ships of the time—the correct distances that the fleet was making. He began the ruse, according to Las Casas, on Sunday, September 9: "He made that day 15 leagues, and decided to reckon less than he made, so that if the voyage were long the people would not be frightened and dismayed"; and the next day, similarly: "He made 60 leagues . . . but he reckoned only 48 leagues in order not to frighten the people if the voyage should be lengthy."

Here is the source of the story of Colón's famous "false log," although it seems very doubtful that it was a written log at all, in spite of one entry on September 25 claiming "he wrote up two routes on this voyage." More likely this was rather a series of offhand estimates the Captain General would toss out at the end of the day when he made his reckonings, and he would note this occasionally alongside his "true" figure in the *Journal*. After all, it is highly unlikely that any of the crew would have had access to any logs, real or fake, or that any of them would be literate, in any case.

But longitudinal reckoning in those days was an extremely tricky business—there were no instruments to give an accurate measurement, and the best any seaman could do would be to try to judge the speed of the ship against some passing flotsam or the froth stirred up by the bow. Hence any seaman could make as accurate a guess as the Captain General; and indeed the pilots of the ships, experienced sailors all, kept their own estimates, which Colón at several points on the passage asked for to compare with his. Hence, also, there would be no way to "fool" the sailors on all three ships with false reckonings, since if they couldn't calculate (or estimate) an accurate distance themselves they could certainly get it from the captains and pilots.

Stranger than that, though, is the Captain General's reasoning. The idea seems to be, as his son Fernando put it, "that they might not think themselves so great a distance from Spain as they really were," but then that meant simply that they must have known they were farther away from their destination—a cause, one would have thought, for much greater consternation. There was no doubt that they *did* know how far it was to their destination, for Fernando assures us that his father "had often told them they must not expect to strike land until they had sailed seven hundred and fifty leagues west of the Canaries." So after these first ten all-out days, with Colón having told them they were only 350 leagues from the Canaries (while he himself reckoned 400), each one of them could figure that they were then 400 leagues from their goal—not what would normally seem conditions to comfort a crew on a voyage of discovery. "When will we get there?" is surely a more common cry than "How far are we from home?"

And the irony is that Colón's *announced* "false" figures to the crew were considerably more accurate than his own "true" figures in the log; ironic, too, that the figures kept by the pilot of the *Santa María* turned out to be more reliable than the Captain General's, for on October 1, when Colón in private decided he was 707 leagues from the Canaries (although his separate entries add up to 675 leagues), the pilot figured 578 leagues, the crew were told 584—and the correct distance was probably 575 leagues.

Now what does all this strange flimflam say about the character of its creator? Was he merely being cautious, in his own peculiar way, using a harmless ruse in order to assure a peaceful voyage? Is this "entirely proper and ethical," as Samuel Eliot Morison says, since "mariners are an odd tribe, little understood by landsmen," and "ignorant seamen" are easily frightened by anything outside their experience? Or is this deception part of a darker side of the Discoverer, rooted in an obsession with keeping the sailing route and distance a secret from the sailors who might be future competitors—as he himself says later, "in order to confuse the pilots and seamen who charted the course [*carteava*] so that he would remain master of that route to the Indies, as in fact he remained, since none of them showed on their charts his true route, because of which no one could be sure of his route to the Indies" (February 18)?[1]

The deception here—even more, the *self-deception*—is too symbolic of all we encounter in the inner workings of Cristóbal Colón, time and again, not to be counted a significant element in his basic temperament. It is almost as if he had an imperfect understanding of the line between truth and falsity—or perhaps more accurate, he did not consider that distinction morally or technically important, so long as higher ends were involved. Only in a world where logic is supreme are such distinctions necessary and important; to many a mind of the late Middle Ages the idea of "fact" or "truth" might be murky indeed, and faith, or a belief, or a received opinion, might be equally weighty. For Colón, at any rate, these distinctions were regularly blurred, and the resultant deception and deceit, conscious and unconscious, have created a good deal of confusion about the man and his motives, even among his contemporaries and companions and certainly among his subsequent chroniclers. They created, too, as we shall see, that failure to distinguish the real world from the illusory, the experienced from the imagined, which we call madness.

In the summer of 1492, Castile had sent an armed expedition to conquer the island of Palma, in the Canaries, one of the last two islands there still not under the control of the Iberian monarchy. Like other expeditions before, this was to use the full force of European power to suppress and eliminate the Guanches, a people who had been on the islands for centuries, and to implant outposts for European agriculture and trade.

The Canaries, islands known to the ancients, had been rediscovered in 1336 and settled by Europeans, in bloody battles with the natives, from the early fifteenth century on. Many European princes and trading houses established colonies there, but over the decades Castile proved the dominant power and, despite the Guanche resistance, eventually occupied and secured most of the territory. In 1479 Portugal relinquished its claims in favor of Castile; after another four years the island of Grand Canary was under firm Castilian control; and the island of Palma, after the siege beginning this summer, fell in 1493, with Tenerife to follow three years later. By 1496 the Canaries became the first overseas possession of what was to become a worldwide Spanish empire.

In the twenty years of its conquest Castile learned several lessons. European armaments, supplemented by armor, horses, dogs, and a good deal of treachery, were superior to any resistance by peoples without guns, however brave and fierce they might be. The lure of land and riches would attract any number of Iberian soldiers and hidalgos, *no matter how risky the invasion might be, so long as they were guaranteed the spoils of conquest and a few titles. Populations far from Europe seemed to be peculiarly subject to diseases and sharp population die-offs, a fortunate effect for the intruders—who, though they did not know it, introduced the deadly pathogens. And after the disruption of a conquered ecosystem, when native species were extinguished or displaced, new species from Europe, aggressive and more opportunistic, grew in their stead.*

The Guanches, who once numbered between 80,000 and 100,000, after less than two centuries of conquest and settlement were extinct.

We might well begin to look at this pattern of deception and confusion with the question of Colón's birthplace. He is curiously unforthcoming on so elemental a matter: the only direct reference we have is in a will of 1498, in which he says, "I being born in Genoa" and "Genoa . . . in it I was born," and there is not one other substantiation in all of his writings. (Even that will is not completely reliable, since we do not have the original and must rely on a royal "confirmation" dated three years later, whose text, the most recent experts agree, is not entirely trustworthy.) The presumption of his Genoese birth is based also on four notary documents of undoubted authenticity—one of them, from 1479, says "Cristoforus Colombus, a citizen of Genoa"—and we have every reason to believe that the man to whom they refer is indeed the later Spanish admiral. But the fact that Colón does not mention his birthplace in any other private or public document is rather strange, and it has led to all kinds of speculation, most of it quite wild, about where he must have been born. In the last century, according to one count, there have been no fewer than 253 scholarly articles and books on the specific question of Colón's origin, with rival claims from Corsica, Greece, Chios, Majorca, Aragon, Galicia, and Portugal, not to mention France and Poland; but since none of them has yet stood up to scrutiny, it seems reasonable for now to accept the Genoese site, which is in fact favored by a quarter, the more reasonable quarter, of these works.*

The confusion as to Colón's birthdate is perhaps a more understandable sort of muddle, if one considers the general disregard paid to such matters in that age, but the fact that Colón offers such disparate versions throughout his life does imply a strange sort of in-

---

*An attendant question as to whether Colón was Jewish has been put forth most explicitly by Salvador de Madariaga and Simon Wiesenthal. But inasmuch as this idea is supported by no direct evidence whatsoever, and the circumstantial evidence is both thin and often unsavory (Madariaga even argues that Colón's great love of gold proves his Jewish blood), there is no reason to give it credence.

difference here, if not outright deception. Not so understandable is the complete mystery we confront when we try to discover his life before he began his petition to the Spanish majesties in about 1486. True, first-rate documentation on many historical figures of five centuries ago tends to be slim, particularly on those who are not of noble birth and are comparatively trackless before they accomplish the deed for which they become known; but it is also true that this Colón attracted a great deal of attention, at least in Spain, in the years after 1493, and it might be thought that he would be asked to supply some complete and coherent picture of his early years. Apparently not, for no such depiction survives, and all we have of contemporary accounts are sketchy, romantic, sometimes contradictory stories, presumably originating with a Colón for whom exaggeration about his valor and steadfastness would come naturally.* Of reliable information there is precious little indeed, and of solid independent documentation there is, I regret to say, nothing.

The stories are colorful enough, many of the kind a man would be happy to have told about his early years, and traditional historians retail them unabashedly. There is, for example, the story of Colón's being shipwrecked off the Portuguese coast in 1476 and making his way to shore only by clinging to a ship's oar, a story of Fernando's for which there is no supportive evidence; there is the one about his being a pirate captain for King René of Anjou and deceiving his shipmates by a trick of the compass into sailing across the Mediterranean at night, a tale Fernando recounts from a purported 1495 letter of his father's for which there is no supportive evidence and so many unlikely circumstances as to make it almost laughable; and there is the one about his going into the mapmaking business with his brother Bartolomé and earning a living in Lisbon with his fine hand and talent for bookselling, a story rendered by several Italian historians who didn't even know Colón and to which not even Fernando gives enough credence to include in his account. These are the sorts of tidbits that historians even now, even the most serious, choose to put into their biographical stews to enhance the flavor—but they are merely conjectural and unverifiable, however tasty.

The fault is not that of the historians alone, obviously, for the trail

---

*His son Fernando, for example, admits that his father died "before I made so bold as to ask him about such things; or, to speak more truly, at the time such ideas were farthest from my boyish mind." As a result, his version of the early Colón, thin as it is, is full of errors and speculations.

that Colón left behind is so confused and incomplete, from his birth-date and birthplace on, as to suggest more than mere carelessness about fact-and-fiction on his part, and even more than the paucity of authoritative documents in an age before printing was common-place. The darkness there suggests rather that he was a man truly without a past that he could define, without a home, or roots, or family, without ever a sense, or love, of place. His early years are dark because, in a sense, they are empty.

Let us look.

If Genoa was indeed the place of his birth, it hardly registers on his soul: nowhere does he refer to the home in which he was born or the way he spent a single moment of his early years, nowhere does he draw comparisons with the seasons or the climate or the vegetation of the region he presumably was raised in, nowhere does he talk about growing up with his father or mother or whatever other family he had.* Nor did he ever find a home elsewhere, as near as we can tell: most of his first twenty years or so were probably spent at sea, when not in Genoa; he was off and on in Lisbon (and at sea) for four years in the 1470s, then on Porto Santo and Madeira (and at sea) for the next four or five years; after 1485 he was in Castile and moving around without anything like a permanent abode (Palos, Cordova, Salamanca, Puerto de Santa Maria, then following the Sovereigns to Seville, Madrid, Guadalupe, Malaga, Jaen, Seville . . .) during the next seven years. He was, peculiarly, a man who never knew a settled life or an identity with any one stretch of earth, whose only real home from childhood on seems to have been the sea, an inconstant and limitless sea whose interminable gray waves offer no habitation for the human animal; a man whose strongest wish, it seems, was always to go somewhere else, who by his own account was consumed for at least a decade by the compulsion to sail to the uncharted West,

---

*Nowhere, also, does he use a word or phrase of substance in any Italian dialect, including Genoese. Indeed, it is hard to see how, even assuming a Genoese birth, one could really construe Colón as an "Italian" (if one can even talk about such a thing as an "Italy" at this date), although Italians since the Risorgimento, and Italo-Americans most vigorously, have certainly tried to make him one. There is no record of his being able to either read or write any Italian language, certainly not the Tuscan that became standard Italian (although one postil in his copy of Pliny is in garbled Italian, it may well be his brother Bartolomé's); his Genoese was in any case quite distinct from the other dialects of the peninsula, hardly "Italian" at all; nor did he show any acquaintance with the great Italian authors, scholars, or artists. The languages he wrote were Castilian, with a little Portuguese mixed in, and Latin, and he chose first the former and then the latter as the languages of his own name; all the surviving letters and documents with his authentic signatures, *including* the letters he wrote to Genoese friends or the Banco di San Giorgio in Genoa, are in Castilian.

and who once he had made the journey was not content until he had gone out again and yet again, until he had gone to the next island, and the next, and the one beyond that . . . a restless, rootless man.

Family ties, similarly, were negligible, at least from the record he left. Of his Genoese family, none but the sparsest mention in his wills of 1498 and 1506, with grants for his brothers and a bare phrase about praying to "the souls of my father and mother." Of his presumed marriage in Portugal, to one Felipa Moniz Perestrello, no mention at all, not even the date of their wedding (perhaps 1479), the date of birth of Diego, their only child (perhaps 1480), or the date of his wife's death (perhaps 1484)—nor, from a man we know to be quite capable of passion on other matters, are there any love letters, poems, or other memorabilia, no descriptions at all, not even a fond remembrance in old age. And of his mistress from his days in Cordova, Beatriz Enríquez de Arana, again only the barest intimation that he wished Diego (*not* Fernando, whose mother she was) to be sure she could "live honestly" after his death—as he put it in his 1506 will, with a certain mysteriousness, "for the satisfaction of my conscience, because this matter weighs heavily upon my soul, the reason for which, it is not fitting to write here."*

Perhaps most revealing of all, this is a man without a settled *name*, and it is hard not to believe that a confusion, or at least inconstancy, of that kind reflects some sort of true psychological instability. Presumably born with the name *Cristoforo Colombo* (or *Christofferus de Columbo*, as one Genoese deposition has it), he became *Christobal* (or *Christovam*) *Colom* (or *Colombo*) in Portugal, and then usually *Cristóbal Colón* in Spain, the form used for the decade of his greatest fame (though on occasion he would be called *Christoual*, or *Colomo*), and in the Capitulations before the First Voyage he is *Xρõual de Colón* and *Xρõual Colón*, with the Greek abbreviation for "Christ," and that is the form he used the *only* time he himself rendered his own full name, in the prologue of the *Journal*. As if that were not confusing enough, starting in 1493 he often chose to sign himself simply *Xρ̃o* FERENS, a deliberate reference to the saint whose name he bore and hence to his own great accomplishment in carrying Christianity across the ocean as St. Christopher had borne the Christ child across the river; we should not ignore also the deliberate imitation

_____

*Oddly, Fernando in his biography gives her even shorter shrift: he mentions her not at all.

of royalty and high aristocracy in the use of a first name only. Perhaps it is fortunate that he probably never saw the particular Latinized version of his name that has become standard in the English-speaking world, for that would have only confused him further.*

The Spanish have a word, perhaps known to Colón, *querencia*, which implies not merely a "love of home," as the dictionaries say, but a deep, quiet sense of inner well-being that comes from knowing a particular place of the earth, its diurnal and seasonal patterns, its fruits and scents, its history and its part in your history and your family's. It is that place where, whenever you return to it, your soul releases an inner sigh of recognition and relaxation. Colón, alas, was a man never to know *querencia*, never truly to inhabit any one environment, always to go through his life without that most basic of touchstones, a home.

Perhaps the stuff of which discoverers are made, it might be said. "The world owes all its outward impulse to men ill at ease," as Hawthorne puts it in his *House of the Seven Gables*. "The happy man inevitably confines himself within ancient limits." Whatever else, not once did Colón give signs of being a happy man.

On December 19, 1492, Vincenzo Colombo was hanged from the tower on the main dock of the city of Genoa.

Vincenzo Colombo was not, as near as exhaustive research can tell, any relation to Cristoforo, though they were both Ligurians and both at times sailed out of Genoa. Vincenzo was an out-and-out pirate who as captain of a twenty-eight-oar brigantine plied a very successful career in the western Mediterranean, it seems, as did hundreds of other brave sailors, many of them Genoese. Successful, that is, until in December 1491 he had the misfortune to pick on a ship that had the favor of King Charles VIII of France. The ship was coming back from the Middle East with a heavy cargo of silks, pearls, and spices, some of which it decided to offload to a small boat in the waters off Genoa. Vincenzo happened to be lurking there, captured the boat, and sailed happily off to Corsica.

Charles VIII was not pleased, and he demanded of the duke of

Columbus is only one of several Latin possibilities, and by no means the most popular in his day. Several Latin versions of his letter to the Sovereigns after the First Voyage use the form *Christoforus Colom* (also *Cristoferi Colom*); some use the form *Colonus* from the Spanish, and this is the Latin form advocated by his son Fernando: *Christophorus Colonus*.

Milan, who demanded of the governor of Genoa, that this corsair who had violated the safety of Genoese waters be hounded down and punished. Hearing of this, Vincenzo wrote a letter protesting to the governor that he was doing only what any loyal son of Genoa would do in looting foreign ships, but the hunt for him continued nonetheless and in late 1492 he was finally captured, jailed, tried, and sentenced to death. On the afternoon of his hanging he signed a notarized testament as to the kinds and numbers of goods he had stolen; the document suggested no guilt or remorse.

Attempts have been made over the years to connect Vincenzo with Cristoforo, perhaps as pirates-in-arms, sometimes to identify them as the same man. However little we know about Colón's early career— and he may well have spent part of it as a corsair, as he suggests— there is scant reason to suppose he ever served with Vincenzo, no reason at all to suppose they were identical.

Monday, 17 September. The pilots took the north, marking it, and found that the compass needles varied to the northwest a full point; and the sailors were fearful and depressed and did not say why. The Admiral was aware of this and he ordered that the north again be marked at dawn, and they found that the compasses were correct.

It was just eight days into the voyage from the Canaries that the compasses of the fleet—those essential instruments upon which all oceangoing navigation and the life of each oceangoing seaman depends—went haywire, at least in nautical terms. The compasses did not point north, and that was fearful, indeed, something simply not in the experience of any European sailor or the manuscript of any ancient geographer. This perplexity struck to the very core of Europe's understanding of the seas.

It is hard to overestimate the role of the magnetic compass in Europe's technological conquest of the ocean.* There were other important navigational instruments—the astrolabe, the cross-staff,

---

*Some of the power of the instrument is suggested by its etymology: the Spanish *brújula* derives from a suggestive mixture of the Italian *bùssola* (compass) and the Murcian *brujería* (witchcraft).

the quadrant—but none had the ease and accuracy of the compass, none was so useful on lengthy voyages out of sight of land. It was a borrowed invention, not native—the Chinese had the compass already in the twelfth century, and it probably made its way to Europe across the Indian Ocean, reaching Italy in the late fourteenth—but like many other borrowings it was put to particularly good use by a culture just then beginning its restless searches for salvation beyond its shores. In fact, along with other improvements in navigation and ship design in the fifteenth century, it became the centerpiece of a technological superiority that finally enabled the subcontinent of Europe to develop a seafaring power far beyond what its size or population would suggest. Combined with the concerted development of armaments and their installation on shipboard from the middle of the fifteenth century, the compass gave Europe the ability to dominate all the oceans of the world for the next four centuries. In this one instance, Fernand Braudel argues, Europe's technological acumen did give it an important edge over the other developed civilizations of the earth: "This time, technology—ocean navigation—did create 'asymmetry,' an advantage on a world scale." And although other maritime cultures might have tried to compete on the seas, only Europe was so interested in global dominance, only Europe—mark the verb—" 'needed' the rest of the world, needed to venture outside its own front door."

And now, with the three ships west of the Canaries, the chief instrument on which that superiority depended seemed to be failing them. Little wonder that "the mariners took fright."

What in fact had happened is that the ships had sailed to a point on the earth where one can see the normal diurnal *rotation* of the North Star, a phenomenon not visible from Mediterranean latitudes. So when they took their sights the sailors found the North Star first to one side and later to the other of "true" north determined by the compass—and they assumed that since the star, being fixed and eternal and unvarying, could not be at fault, it had to be the machinery. And if the compasses were wrong, all of them on each ship, then there were no certainties left and the fleet would have no way of knowing where on the vast seas it was—or how to get back home.

At this point the deceptive ingenuity of the Captain General proved itself equal to the occasion. He did *not* assume that he had discovered a "westerly variation" of the compass, as some writers suggest, comparable to the easterly variation known in the Mediterranean (not until his third voyage out did he suggest this alternative, and there is no hint of such an idea in the *Journal*); rather he proposed to the sailors—on the spur of the moment, it would seem—that "the reason was that the star appeared to move and not the needles," and a few days later, "it appears that the Star moves like other stars, and the compasses always point true." There is no possible way for Colón to have come to this by experience, nor had he any way to be certain there was any truth to it; but as it turns out, it was quite correct and apparently accepted by the crew, for no further signs of their "fright" are reported. How remarkable that the Captain General came to such a deception, and so readily—and so accurately.

In the fall of 1492, from his new eminence in Rome, Pope Alexander VI officially absolved the Florentine humanist Giovanni Pico della Mirandola from the sin of heresy, thus clearing the way for the popular young scholar to regain position and stature in his native city.

Pico had come into difficulties with a treatise he wrote around 1486 called De hominis dignitate oratio—*Oration on the Dignity of Man —whose unabashed humanism and celebration of the near divinity of the human species, especially in its mid-Renaissance, Florentine form, was understandably regarded as heretical by the previous, somewhat more demanding pope, Innocent VIII. It was Pico's position, as that of a good many humanists of the period, that man had a right to rule over the rest of creation, and that indeed God specifically told man to be "constrained by no limits, in accordance with thine own free will." It was a message that many, particularly those engaged in such as discovery and conquest, would choose to heed.*

Two years after his pardon, Pico, still suffering from the punishments inflicted during his years as a "heretic," died, at the age of thirty-one.

Thursday, 20 September. *This day he steered west by north and westnorthwest because the winds were very variable in the calm weather. They probably made no more than seven or eight leagues.*

After the brisk breezes of the first ten days, on September 19 the winds fell and during the next week or so were variable, sometimes up, sometimes dying to gentle gusts when the sea would be "very smooth like a river." The fleet made sometimes eight or ten, sometimes twenty leagues or more, but with considerable tacking and frequent calms. It was the sort of weather that allows seamen plenty of time to think.

Both Captain General and crew kept finding signs of the land that they were eager to encounter. At first there was a "tern" and a bosun bird, which the Captain General said "never depart from land more than 25 leagues," and two days later "many bunches of very green weed, which had recently (as it seemed) been torn away from land," and this too he interpreted as a sign "that they were near some island." He was, as he would continue to be, quite wrong about the species of the sea: the birds were almost certainly oceanic animals that typically fly thousands of miles from land; the green weed was the gulfweed of the Sargasso Sea, which is similarly pelagic and has nothing to do with islands. They were then more than 750 miles from the nearest spot of dry earth.

Daily the "signs" continued: on September 17 some crabs, "sure signs of land"; on the eighteenth a cloudbank, "which is a sign of being near land"; on the nineteenth a windless drizzle, "which is a sure sign of land"; on the twenty-first a whale, "which is a sign that they were near land, for they [whales] always stay near." It is surprising ignorance, this, for a man who claimed to have spent twenty-three years plying the ocean, even if we allow that he was sailing where no one had been before and could not be expected to know every bird on the wing, and that he was trying to keep up the morale of a crew concerned to get to a landfall. None of his climatic or biotic observations was correct, and it is something of a wonder that he kept on recording them even when it turned out time after time that they were erroneous and no land appeared. It was the sort of pretense to natural history that he curbed but did not abandon in the face of the astounding variety of the biota he was about to encounter in the New World.*

Tensions must have been rising on all three ships. The "signs of land" never turned out to bring it any closer, and the Captain General's repeated assurances that they probably indicated unimportant

---

*As to his powers of natural observation, it took Colón sixteen days of looking at that strange Sargasso weed, day after endless day, before he noticed, and recorded, that it "bore something like fruit," in fact the globules that keep the weed masses afloat. "Strange," Morison says, "that he did not observe them earlier."

nearby islands instead of the magnificent land he said he was making for must have worn thin. On several occasions the captains and pilots of the three ships conferred, and once on September 22 Colón sent a chart to Martín Alonso Pinzón on the *Pinta*, who studied it for three days before sending it back; there may have been some who wondered whether the Captain General knew as much about where he was going as he had been saying. By the end of September the fleet had gone three weeks without sight of land, very probably farther than any European seamen had ever gone before without putting into port, and even by Colón's "false" reckoning they were close to 1,800 miles out into an apparently endless ocean with still no guarantees of lands ahead or sure enough winds to take them back.

But it was not until October 10, a full month after leaving the Canaries and still nothing but endless water, that the *Journal* mentions any open dissension in the crew: "Here the people could stand it no longer, and complained [*quexavase*] of the long voyage." Out of this entry, plus some fanciful embellishment by Fernando and Oviedo, and some unreliable testimony in the *Pleitos* decades later, was concocted the famous story of the Columbian "mutiny." The *Journal* has no mention of mutiny on the voyage out, or anything close to it—there is only one earlier reference to the crew's being "all worked up" on September 22 about not finding winds strong enough for the return trip—and this particular incident about "the long voyage" was handled, according to the Captain General, with what appears to be seemly dispatch. In Las Casas's paraphrase: "The Admiral cheered them as best he could, holding out good hope of the benefits they would have," meaning the anticipated gold and treasure. "And he added that it was useless to complain since he had come to find the Indies, and so had to continue until he found them, with the help of Our Lord."

Why the chroniclers treated such a complaint, which under the circumstances seems only reasonable and was apparently neatly contained, as an outright rebellion—"open mutiny," in Morison's language—is something of a puzzlement. That may be the story Colón gave to his son and other writers back in Spain, for on the homeward journey, four months later, when he was feeling particularly bitter toward Martín Alonso Pinzón, Colón referred to that time when "the people who all with one voice were determined to return and to rise against him in protest" (February 14)—a typical, moody exaggeration that could not be true since he obviously could not have gone on if the entire crew had opposed him. That may also be the story that subsequent historiofabulists, contriving the brave lone hero against the world, liked to believe. But the closest thing to substantiation comes from the *Pleitos*, evidence taken from crew members anywhere from sixteen to forty-five years after the event, and the best they do is support the idea that there *was* a fuss in the fleet in early October, there *may* have been grumblings and complaints against the Captain General, and there *was* a meeting of the ships' captains at which it was agreed that the voyage should go on a few days more—three days, maybe four—and if nothing was encountered by then they'd best consider returning home. That's the "mutiny." The single suggestion out of all those documents that the seamen themselves had any evil intent is from the deposition of a man who was in his eighties in 1536 when he testified and who, as it turned out, was not even in the crew.

All of this mutiny story has once more the smell of deception, perhaps even self-deception—of Colón trying, through self-serving stories to his son and gullible chroniclers, to create the image of the valiant lone visionary against the disbelieving multitude. It is more reasonable to suppose, however, that indeed perturbation was expressed after a month at sea with nothing more to show for it than the sighting of a few "terns" and a whale, and that as a result a meeting of the senior crew was called and opinions expressed, exactly the sort of thing that was regularly done on all Iberian voyages of the time. Just a few years earlier, for example, in 1488, Bartholomew Diaz had been forced to turn back after rounding the Cape of Good Hope because his crew had voted against his sailing on and decided that seven months of finding their way around the tip of Africa was enough for this time out. There is no way to know whether it was one of the Pinzóns at that meeting who said, *"Adelante, adelante,"* as some *Pleitos* statements aver, or whether it was Colón who urged them, "On! Sail on!" as the lovely romantic poem by Joaquin Miller put it in the nineteenth century; all we know is that they did indeed keep sailing westward, and many of them must have thought that night of the ancient motto of the city of Palos: "Trust in God and hammer on!"

On they went, and at a fair clip, too: 59 leagues on October 10, Colón recorded, another 27 during the day on the eleventh, another 18 or so before midnight, and more than 4 in the two hours after midnight into October 12. On the eleventh they found a green reed, some cane, and a little stick apparently carved by hand—and here at last there were some real indications that land was nearby, and "with these signs," the Captain General wrote, "everyone breathed more easily and grew cheerful."

The moon on the evening of October 11, off to port, was just a few days past full, and the skies were clear. Around ten o'clock Colón, standing on the sterncastle, thought he saw a light on the horizon, but "it was so uncertain a thing that he did not wish to declare that it was land," so he called the royal steward, who said he too saw the light, and the royal inspector, who said he could see nothing. The Captain General still thought he could see something out there, "like a little wax candle lifting and rising," but no one on either the *Pinta* or the *Niña*, sailing ahead of the flagship, raised the call, so he merely told his crew to keep "a sharp lookout on the forecastle, and to watch carefully for land." He added that "to him who first sang out that he saw land he would later give a silk doublet," and this "besides the other rewards that the Sovereigns had promised, which were a 10,000-maravedi annuity [about $70 a year in gold, when an able seaman would make about 12,000 maravedis in a good year] to whoever should first sight it."*

Sometime around "two hours after midnight" the lookout on the *Pinta*, Juan Rodríguez Bermejo, gave out the cry of *"Tierra!"* and the ship fired its cannon as a signal to the others that land was ahead. And there, "at a distance of 2 leagues," was their long-awaited goal in sight. Sails were lowered, and the three ships prudently lay to until daylight to make their landing.†

*The translation of currencies from centuries past so that they make some sense to present readers is difficult indeed. In general I have tried to suggest the buying power of the various units at the time, and also put the amount in terms of gold where pertinent; for the most part I have translated that gold into dollar amounts calculated in U.S. dollars *before* 1933, when the United States joined the rest of the world in abandoning the gold standard. This can also be translated into the fixed price of $35 an ounce that the United States established subsequently, a rate that was itself abandoned in the 1970s, or into the market price of $400 or thereabouts for which gold was selling in 1990. The maravedi in these terms was a copper coin worth about .0103 gram of gold in 1492, so 10,000 maravedis would equal 103 grams or around $70 in pre-Depression dollars, $129 in fixed-rate dollars, and about $1,400 in 1990 dollars.

†And so we honor October 12 as Columbus Day—at least nowadays we do, although it was not until 1934 that the U.S. government made it an official holiday. But according to our present Gregorian calendar, the day of discovery is really October 23. Colón operated by the Julian calendar, which was found to be way off the celestial mark in the sixteenth century, and the new calendar, first adopted in 1582, cut ten days off the old one. So anytime we celebrate the Columbian landfall on October 12 we are actually honoring October 1, when Colón merely "steered on his route west."

It was his moment of triumph, and it may seem wrong to take anything away from the Captain General as he savored his success. (Nothing of the emotions that must have overwhelmed him at that moment, though, is recorded in the *Journal*, nor does he ever refer in later writings to this singular hour.) But it is fitting to note that Colón appropriated the 10,000-maravedi reward (and presumably the silk doublet) to himself, on the grounds that *he* had really seen the lights of the island earlier in the evening and deserved the stipend. Upon his petition, Ferdinand and Isabella in 1493 dutifully assigned him the legacy, raising the money either from a special tax on butcher shops in Seville, according to one source, or from an explicit confiscation of Jewish goods in the hands of suspect *conversos,** according to another, although it was not actually so very much money, one would have thought, for the normal coffers to supply. And this even though when Colón seems to have sat down on October 13, to enter the previous days' excitement in his *Journal*, he made the calculations that told him that when he "saw" those lights he was at least forty nautical miles from the island they eventually came upon, and at that distance there was no way he could have seen anything at all.

On November 9, 1492, Charles VIII of France and Henry VII of England signed the Peace of Etaples, which officially put an end to the Hundred Years' War, some thirty-nine years after the formal hostilities had ended. It also, in theory, ended France's claims to Brittany and forced Charles to disclaim support for Perkin Warbeck, the Yorkist pretender to the throne of England. With its signing, both sides affirmed a lasting peace between the two dynasties—which lasted exactly thirty years, until Henry VIII, born just the year before the treaty, invaded France in 1522.

Charles, to be sure, had no intention of disavowing war—only, temporarily, war with Henry VII. This same month he gave orders for the development of France's new mobile artillery, whose power he intended to test as soon as possible against the feuding city-states of the Italian peninsula. Less than two years later he launched the

---

Conversos was the polite term for those Jews who had chosen to convert to Christianity instead of fleeing Spain, although their loyalty always remained suspect and they were a prime target of the Inquisition; *marranos*, which means "hogs" or "filthy ones," was the derogatory term.

invasion of northern Italy, in which that artillery proved successful beyond his reckoning, thus beginning a long process of warfare between France and Aragon, both with Italian interests, and a long process of Italian disintegration and decline.

The citizens of Florence, however, might not have been taken by surprise. For in the same year of 1492 the demagogic preacher Savonarola had predicted that outside forces would invade Italy—the thought was absurd! impossible!—and that when they came they would be heartily welcomed by the battered and weary populations of Florence—ridiculous! Like many of his predictions, this one proved to be correct, one of the reasons the pope banned him from further preaching in 1495.

[*Friday*, 12 *October. At*] *daylight Friday . . . they reached an islet of the Lucayas, which was called Guanahani in the language of the Indians. Soon they saw naked people, and the Admiral went ashore in his armed longboat.*

Very well: landfall. The much-sought prize. The question is—the first question, anyway, directly related to the nagging one about their intended destination—*where did they suppose they were?*

Did the Captain General (or as we may fairly style him now, the Admiral, for he had fulfilled his pledge) believe that he had come upon one of those 7,448 islands that Marco Polo had said were to be found in the Sea of China, one of them the opulent island of Cipango, where the roofs were of gold and the streets of marble? This may have been Colón's first thought, since the very next day he became impatient with this first coral outpost and declared that "in order not to lose time I intend to go and see if I can find the Island of Cipango."

Did he believe that he had reached a desolate outisland at the gateway to the kingdom of the Grand Khan, and that just beyond would be the magnificent cities and untold riches of Cathay? If so, he gave no sign of it at this point, and not until a week later, on October 21, did he first declare that he was "determined to go to the mainland and to the city of Quisay [Quinsay] and to present Your Highnesses' letters to the Grand Khan."

Did he imagine that he had come to one of the fabled islands— well, perhaps not *this* one, for it seemed somewhat deficient in riches and cities, but nearby . . .—that he had heard and read so much about, Antillia or St. Brendan's Isle or its equivalent? After all, it could be that "island or land of great importance" that Fernando says he "had hope of finding . . . between the end of Spain and the known end of India."

Did he perhaps think he had reached what Fernando called "the unknown eastern part of India" that "had [not] been seen or discovered by others," lands not part of the Khan's realm, or any other potentate's, but that would be his alone? That would explain his subsequent action the next morning in marching right in and claiming it for his Sovereigns, with the full pomp of blithe possession.

Or did he possibly suppose that he had come to an outlying part of an entirely new and unexplored mainland, not Cathay, not the Indies, not the Golden Chersonese, but that land across the seas whose existence, the contemporary Oviedo says, was "notorious"? He would certainly have heard talk about such a place, either from his time in Portugal (from which a dozen voyages had gone out in the fifteenth century, several of them returning with reports of land) or his presumed trip to Bristol (from which expeditions were undertaken at least from 1480); maybe this unprepossessing little island foretold that new mainland.

Alas, we have no real way of knowing what was in the Admiral's mind that portentous dawn. He never said what he then thought he had come upon or where, in the world, it was. Later, in the report of this voyage to the Sovereigns, he maintained that he was somewhere, somehow, in the Indies, or off the coast of China, although precisely where he did not divulge.

Until, at the end, he realized he had come upon a New World, and it was Paradise. That would be closest to the mark.

And the second question is: *where in fact were they?*

Not that it matters so much, perhaps, in the long run. *Any* landfall would undoubtedly have led to the same long process of European expansion, and the fact that it occurred on one of the most modest extrusions of limestone and coral in the world—a spot so inhospitable that apparently not even the local Tainos made permanent habitation there—was quite unimportant. The same fate would have befallen history no matter which island of the Caribbean, or perhaps whichever part of the mainland, this first brave European fleet had come upon. It certainly would not have mattered much to those who made the landfall—nor does it, in the broader picture of the conquest of America, to us.

And yet it is surely the most uncertain and controversial point in all Columbiana, and that is a matter of wider significance. Colón could easily have described the features of the island with such precision that we would know today, even assuming the effects of time, just which of the Bahamian reef islands he encountered. Or he could have gone ashore with his astrolabes and quadrants and compasses and charts and determined its geographical position with enough precision that we would be able to locate it with certainty today. Or he could have tried to erect there a sufficiently enduring monument, a cross carved upon stone, for example, complete with triumphant inscriptions, that might have marked the spot for centuries. But he did none of that.

The Admiral had led his fleet across 3,000 miles of ocean to at least a small body of land, and who knows how many riches beyond, and yet he did not determine, with precision enough for later generations ever to know, where it was that he had achieved his dream.

We may safely leave the incredible thickets, perhaps I should say whirlpools, of the "Landfall Question" to scholars and mariners and tourist officers and obsessed amateurs from now until the decacentennial; and we may safely rest assured that no answers of certain authority will be forthcoming. The number of islands that have been seriously put forth for the landfall honor—discarding those that are offered only by small outisland hoteliers and local history buffs—stands today at *twelve*: San Salvador (formerly Watlings), Grand Turk, Caicos, Cat, Mayaguana, Crooked, Conception, Eleuthera, Egg, Plana Cay, Rum Cay, and Samana Cay. (There are actually not many other islands in the general area left for nomination, for which we should perhaps be grateful.) A case for each of them can be made—*has* been made—with some persuasiveness, or at least I am usually persuaded by each one as I read it, and each new author will declare with some assurance that the issue has now at last been put beyond dispute; a recent claimant has in fact come forth after the expenditure of more than a million dollars and with the imprimatur of the National Geographic Society.

Yet of course they cannot all be right, and the only sensible conclusion to reach is clearly that the answer to the Landfall Question can never be decided. It is, again, something that falls into that inevitable—and for the modern temperament unsatisfactory—area of the unknowable.[2]

But I do think it is fair to ask why it is that Colón left the world this conundrum. Two answers suggest themselves, both in keeping with the Admiral's character. First, it seems likely that he did not care. He was not in search of small, wooded, coral islands—he had made it plain several times on the journey out that he was not interested in stopping at the various islands he and the crew supposed were nearby, because "it was better to go at once to the mainland, and later to the islands." The goal was not *land*, at least not in the Admiral's heart, but rather *gold*, the wealth of the fabled lands beyond the seas, of which he had the right to "take and keep for himself the tenth part of the whole," according to the official agreements with the crown. Time and time again, and beginning in fact the very next day, Colón openly declared his single-minded interest in finding gold, and his every movement from now on was bent to that purpose. So what matter this inhospitable outisland?

A second motive, not contradictory, might have been that Colón wanted to keep the location to himself, for his own purposes of wealth and glory, and so decided to prevent his own crewmen and subsequent mariners (especially Portuguese) from following his trail to treasure. He was even willing, and this seems significant, to deceive his Sovereigns: he was careful not to put anything definite in the log he prepared for them, nor did he provide a "chart of navigation" or map of "the lands of the Ocean Sea in their proper positions under their bearings" as he had promised to do in the prologue. Indeed, the Sovereigns were put out by all this, and in a letter of September 15, 1493, six months after Colón's return, they wrote with unusual bluntness, as if they had said it before, "We have need to know the degrees within which the islands and land you discovered fall and the degrees of the path you traveled." Such evasiveness does seem extraordinary, if not downright treasonous, and yet there is no indication in any extant record that Colón ever acceded to their majesties' demands.

Eventually, to be sure, both Colón and the Sovereigns, as well as the other Spanish captains making their way to the Caribbean, forgot entirely about this small and unprofitable piece of Bahamian coral while they set their sights on larger islands of greater promise. There were no further known requests for its location, indeed no further known interest in it at all until the nineteenth century. Only in 1825, with the first publication of Las Casas's version of the *Journal*, did people begin seriously wondering where the landfall of that voyage was—and by then it was too late to find out. The Admiral kept the secret to himself, and will forever.

Sometime in 1492, Martin Behaim, a cosmographer then at work in Nuremberg, presented to the public a round ball on which he had placed a parchment map of the world, an Erdapfel *as he somewhat quaintly put it, today the oldest existing globe of the earth. That globe, now in the German National Museum in Nuremberg, is remarkable as much for its gold and cerulean beauty as for the ingeniousness of its shape. But it is perhaps most remarkable because it reflects the mainstream cartographical thinking of 1492: there is nothing between Europe and Asia but Cipango and assorted scattered islands. There is room there for a small Bahamian island, perhaps even something the size of Cuba or Española, but no room for two new continents: the distance from the Canaries to Cipango is less than 3,000 miles, about 7,000 miles shy of the actual extent.*

Behaim, though born in Nuremberg, is known to have been in Lisbon in the 1480s, where he married a woman of the minor nobility, possibly joined King João's considerable cosmographical staff, and possibly was knighted. He went back to Nuremberg in 1487 or 1490, and on the basis of what he claimed to have learned in Portugal the city authorized him to produce a globe with the most up-to-date geographical information available. In this task he had the help of Hartman Schedel, the man who was even now putting the finishing touches on his Nuremberg Chronicle, and one Hieronymus Müntzer (known by the interesting Latin name of Monetarius), a learned physician.

Late in 1493 Behaim returned to Lisbon and presented to King João an impassioned letter from the learned Müntzer urging him to consider sending a fleet of discovery westward across the ocean: "O what glory you will gain if you make the habitable Orient known to your Occident [and] make those Isles of the Orient tributaries, and their kinds, amazed, will quietly submit to your sovereignty." It also urged that the king put such a fleet at the command of Behaim, "deputed by our King Maximilian especially for this purpose," and suggested that he and other learned mariners should "set out from the Azores and sail the breadth of sea" forthwith.

King João might or might not have trusted Behaim as a navigator—he was in general something of a liar and a boaster—and he might or might not have realized by then that sailing westward from the Azores would put any fleet directly into contrary winds. But what he did know—for Admiral Colón had put in at Lisbon and told him in March, five months before the Müntzer letter was even written— was that someone had already attempted the western route to land, and succeeded.

[Friday, 12 October.] The Admiral broke out the royal banner, and the captains two flags with the green cross. . . . Once ashore they saw very green trees and many ponds and fruits of various kinds.

With the banners and the appropriate personnel from the ships— the official observers, including the royal secretary Rodrigo de Escobedo, perhaps the official interpreter, probably a few sailors armed with swords and arquebuses to act as guards—the Admiral was rowed ashore. Ashore . . . to discover America.

Except, of course, Colón did *not* discover it. (And of course, it was not "America" then, but that's another, later question.) Whatever may have been in the Admiral's mind—and the idea of discovery, as we have seen, was only one possibility—we can say with assurance that no such event as "discovery" took place.

For one thing, that first island, and the chain of islands of which it was a part, and the two continents to which it was adjacent, were quite well known to the millions of people who inhabited them and who had discovered them on behalf of the human species tens of thousands of years before. The landfall island itself, as we may surmise from archeological scholarship, would have been first inhabited sometime around A.D. 900.

For another, the landmass that is today known as North America, to which the Bahamian islands are geologically and biologically related, was discovered and temporarily settled by Europeans at least as early as A.D. 1000. There is now no question whatsoever that Norse explorers, presumably sailing from their colonies in Greenland, came upon Baffin Island, Labrador, and Newfoundland, all parts of North America, in the eleventh century and established settlements for at least several years in all those places. The evidence for this is copious, available from several different kinds of sources, and increasing with each year's investigations. The most completely studied site, at L'Anse aux Meadows in northern Newfoundland, has provided incontrovertible evidence of European (surely Norse) occupation in the eleventh century, and several other sites, from Michigan to the coast of New England, offer corroborative clues at least of exploration if not of settlement. If "discovery" means sighting and landing by Europeans, then it is Leif Eiriksson who should most likely be honored, and it is October 9, selected by modern Scandinavians as the landfall date, that should be celebrated. (If it means simply sighting the land, the honor probably goes to Bjarni Herjolfsson, who reported this land on a trip out from Greenland in 986.)

But there is in addition a body of strong and generally persuasive evidence—sufficient probably to convince on any other question—that indicates any number of other sightings of, perhaps even landings upon, North America in the years before 1492. Henry Harrisse, a tough-minded nineteenth-century historian, listed no fewer than twenty claimed voyages and sightings, and since then other possibilities have been offered, with varying degrees of evidence. It is known from letters patent and other court records that Portugal sent at least eleven missions westward in search of new islands and fabled lands between 1431 and 1486, and the figure is most likely higher although only the ashes of the fire that destroyed the Portuguese archives in 1755 hold the truth. Some Portuguese historians also claim a voyage to North America in 1492–95, and a landfall before Colón's, by João Fernandes of the Azores (known as *il lavrador*, the farmer, and hence the label "Labrador" on later maps), although the only unambiguous record of his is for a voyage of 1499–1500 during which unspecified northern lands were found.

It is also known that ships out of Bristol attempted to find the mythical island of Brasil out in the Atlantic from at least 1480 on, and it is now held to be virtually certain that fishing ships from that port were catching cod off the coasts of Newfoundland from 1482 on—ships that found, according to the John Day letter of 1498, what "is assumed and believed to be the mainland" during that period. It seems likely that ships from other parts of Atlantic Europe—especially Brittany, Bordeaux, and Galicia, which were certainly fishing in those waters by 1500—had discovered these coasts at about the same time as the Bristol ships.

If the landfall of Admiral Colón was not in any true sense a discovery, why did it take on such importance—to his contemporaries, as soon as they heard the news, to all the generations down to ours these five hundred years later? What is different about this particular encounter with the unknown lands of the West that makes it stand out from the others and, ultimately, declare itself such a significant turning point in the history of the world?

First, perhaps most important, it was an official, royal mission of the King and Queen of Castile, León, Aragon, Sicily, Granada, etc., etc., which happened to be one of the most powerful princely establishments in Europe. This was not a casual fishing trip out of Brest with no more authority than that of the captain and his backers, nor a furtive excursion out of Bristol by a ship hoping to avoid local customs inspectors and the hated taxes of the crown.

Second, it was a carefully documented voyage, both by its Captain General in his daily log and, at least at points of historical moment, by the royal observers brought along for the purpose, particularly the royal secretary, whose independent verifications, although they do not exist today, would have served to establish authenticity. It returned to Europe, moreover, with tangible evidence—including human specimens of the like not seen before—of having achieved at least some exotic goal.

Third, it achieved not only a way *out* but a way more or less *back*, which other voyages could follow. Unlike sailors who declared that they had seen land when blown off course, or who had no certain way to know their location when they accidentally came upon some island, these mariners had kept as careful a record as they could of the directions to sail, the winds and currents, the weather, the shoals and reefs, and the other trivia that allowed their feat (except for its landfall) to be—it is, fittingly, the hallmark of science—replicable.

Fourth, its news was broadcast throughout Europe and, thanks to the printing press, quite swiftly, too. If other journeys had in fact succeeded in reaching new lands, they did not tell the world about it except through the scuttlebutt of unreliable sailors, and so they did not etch themselves in any significant way on the plate of history. It is entirely possible that one of the Portuguese missions did raise the shore of North America, perhaps even bring proof of it back to

Lisbon, and the discovery was kept secret by a Portuguese monarchy that did not wish to alert rival nations to new-found treasures it intended to exploit for itself. But such a voyage would have no more historical resonance than the noise of an anchor hitting ocean-bottom.

Fifth, the Columbian voyage had far larger purposes from the beginning than simply locating good fishing grounds or finding the long-lost St. Brendan's Isle, or even establishing a trading outpost like Portugal's El Mina on the Gold Coast of Africa. It was hoped to be, as it turned out to be, the start of a long, elaborate, and overt process of trade, conquest, colonization, and exploitation, something of which, if successful, the world would be forced to take note.

And finally, it was achieved by a power, and in a larger sense a culture, that wanted—even, as Braudel has written, *needed*—the means to expand to foreign shores and find relief from the inbred despondency and institutional decadence to which it had for so many decades been a victim. Norway in the eleventh century cared almost nothing for its outpost in Iceland, even less for its farther colony in Greenland, and even less than that for some dubious settlement (if it knew about it) on the shores of Vinland; it was not a kingdom that had any particular use for colonies, or extensive trade through icy waters, or even the sort of products, so similar to the ones already at hand, those far-off regions could supply. But Western Europe, by the fifteenth century, certainly did need such an outlet, or thought it did, and it intended to exploit it in any way it could. This is the sense in which it is rightly said that if there hadn't been a Columbus there would have been someone else very much like him, and not too many years later; if there hadn't been this landfall in the Bahamas there would have been another somewhere on the edge of the two vast continents whose secrets it could no longer keep to itself.

So it does not matter that, as his longboat touched the white sands of the small cove and his long-dreamed destination, Cristóbal Colón, Admiral of the Ocean Sea, was *not* about to discover America. What matters only is that here was the occasion with which Europe chose to begin its declared and demonstrable relations with that new part of the world it had found—to begin that process of exporting the discoverers, exploiters, adventurers, refugees, runaways, and settlers, and the disquieted culture that bore them, and importing the ores, jewels, medicines, exotics, foodstuffs, and timbers, above all the ideas and dreams and possibilities, it encountered.

"Discovery" as such is irrelevant. This exact moment rings down the corridors of time not because one foreigner comes to a tiny Bahamian island but because thus begins the European conquest of the world. This new land, as the Admiral could see from the *Santa María* longboat, was enclosed in a sea of luminescent emerald, ringed with bright coral sands, and covered with a dark conifer forest of "very green trees, many streams, and fruits of different kinds . . . the whole of it so green it is a pleasure to gaze upon." And there, standing at its edge, was a small crowd of "naked people," their quiet dignity and beauty impressive even from that distance, "with very handsome bodies and very good faces . . . of good-sized stature and of good faces well made." The invaders might very well be excused, as they set foot upon it, for thinking that this land was the province of Eden.

Chapter Four

Europe

II

"The Earth Shall Quake Before Them"

"THE land is as the garden of Eden before them, and behind them a desolate wilderness; yea, and nothing shall escape them.

"The appearance of them is as the appearance of horses; and as horsemen, so shall they run.

"Before their face the people shall be much pained; all faces shall gather blackness.

"The earth shall quake before them; the heavens shall tremble."

Thus the prophet Joel.

That this island was an intimation of Paradise probably occurred to Colón, as no doubt to his shipmates, and in years to come the suggestion would harden into a certainty, at least in the Admiral's case. That they had left behind them a "desolate wilderness" would be more than any of them would say, even those who had come from the spare scrub-brown hills and harsh sandy soils of the Andalusian coasts and knew the meager and uncertain harvests they bore. And yet there is a sense in which "desolate" was hardly an exaggeration, and not by comparison only: behind them lay a Europe that in thought and deed was estranged from its natural environment and had for several thousand years been engaged in depleting and destroying the lands and waters it depended on, and justifying that with one or another creed or conviction.

When Colón set foot on his landfall island he brought this ecological heritage with him, of course, and in ways of which he would
have had no understanding, of course. It was as certainly a part of
his cargo as his lombards, as inevitably one of the possessions of a
fifteenth-century European as the Bible and the sword—and ultimately deadlier.

The vastness and richness and beauty and variety of nature in the
Americas came to have an immense effect on Europe's environmental
sensibilities in the centuries ahead—an *eastward* impact, as it were
—if only because it opened up more than eight times the space of
Europe itself and introduced a thousand important species of biota
that Europe had never known before. But at this point more important was the ecological character and history of Europe and the lessons
from that heritage that were brought to these new lands—the *westward* impact, so to speak—because it wasn't so much that Europe
discovered America as that it *incorporated* it and made it part of its
own special, long-held and recently ratified, view of nature.

The tapestry that was Europe's view of nature was made up of many
strands, those strands of many threads and weaves, and their patterns
complex and various and not always beautiful. It is a subject whose
literature is vast indeed, for the relation of humans to their surroundings has been a preoccupation of societies since the earliest, and the
discourses in this genre in the last few decades alone make up an
impressive library by themselves. But it is possible to draw out the
broader themes of that literature, to see the most pronounced designs
of that tapestry, and thus to get some notion of the ideas and attitudes that made up the ecological consciousness of fifteenth-century
Europe.

We must begin, alas, with Europe's fear of most of the elements
of the natural world—a fear based, as it always is, on simple ignorance, a benightedness among the learned sectors of Europe as well
as the illiterate majority, that is shocking indeed as we look at it
today.

The Church offered no encouragement for any investigation into
the foreordained ways of God's creatures, much less the established
workings of His trees and rivers and soils, and it was sufficient for
most people to know that God created them, blessed them, and then

gave humans "dominion over" them.[1] Common lore, as we know it from the bestiaries and herbals of the time—which, being extremely popular, have come down to us in a large number of manuscripts as well as printed editions—was not much better, filled with either mundane and stereotypical views (lambs are meek, lions brave, wolves crafty) or fanciful and erroneous ones (toads suck cows' milk at night, woodpeckers are dangerous predators, beech trees deflect lightning, crushed rosemary leaves tied to the right arm "shall make thee light and merry"). Medieval poetry was not more sophisticated, treating the natural world with arch and ritual formulas by which "soft zephyrs" from the "dark woods" are always wafting over "murmuring waters," and one is certain to find passion in winds, love in roses, pity in streams, anger in storms, and violence in the ocean. All this platitude and misinformation about the real world was glued together with nonsense about the monstrous and fantastic world, and held to with the same level of credulity by even the most inquiring minds of the day: Laurence Andrew's very popular bestiary *The Noble Life & Natures of Man, of Beasts, Serpents, Fowls & Fishes That Be Most Known*, for example, the first printed work on animals in the English language, lists with equal credulence 144 known animals, 8 entirely unknown, and 21 strictly mythological.

It is hardly surprising that the European mind, mired thus, should fear what it did not comprehend and hate what it knew as fearful. Nature in the broad—its storms and floods, its harsh seasons and pestilences and famines—as well as in the particular—its rodents and roaches, its wolves and werewolves—represented for most people an antagonistic, oppositional world. The familiar was daunting enough, but the unusual and the distant and the unknown were scarier still, at times nothing less than terrifying, as we know from the fairy tales of the era, and this was particularly true of those places that remained the most remote: the mountains and the forests of the wilderness. As Lucretius had taught in his classic *De rerum natura*, earth "is filled full of restless dread throughout her woods, her mighty mountains and deep forests."

Mountains were places of dread. They were "regarded as physically unattractive" and "distasteful," as Keith Thomas points out in his illuminating study of European responses to nature, and "early modern travellers usually found mountainous country unpleasant and dangerous," likely as not to be "the home of uncivilized people."

Look at the depiction of mountains in all medieval and most Renaissance paintings: they are not the serene and majestic substantialities of beauty they were to become for the Romantics and in general are for us; they are distorted and jagged crags and precipices, diabolic, almost alive, dark and always barren but for a twisted tree or two, home only to fierce and wild creatures. Leonardo probably knew more about real mountains than any man of his century, and actually visited the Alps to study them, and yet in his *Madonna of the Rocks*—which he finished, incidentally, just two years before Colón stepped ashore in the New World—the bizarre monoliths of the grotto are scraggy and bare and somehow eerie, the mountainous shapes of the background like some unreal part of a forbidden desert: we are made to feel the stark, frisson-of-fear contrast with the beatific family group in the foreground. "Hideous" is the word that comes to mind, and indeed that is the adjective more than any other that characterizes the descriptions of such landscapes, over and over again: "hideous," says Thomas More about the wild Zapoletes who live in the mountains east of his Utopia; "hideous," says William Cambden about the "craggy mountains" of Wales; "hideous," says Chief Justice Roger North about the hills of northern England; "hideous," says James Howell about the Alps.*

Forests were worse. To be sure, actual mammals of some fierceness dwelled there, particularly in the heavily wooded areas of northern Europe; Marc Bloch in *Feudal Society* remarks that "wild animals that now only haunt our nursery tales—bears and, above all, wolves —prowled in every wilderness, and even amongst cultivated fields." No doubt also human outcasts and squatters and hermits of some unpleasantness inhabited the forests, as well as various criminals, outlaws, and bandits of the kind that the Robin Hood legends grew up about. But the imagination, of the adult as well as the child, made of the forest a place of many more fantastic terrors and dangers than those: it became the home of satyrs and centaurs (it is from the name

---

*It is often remarked that Petrarch climbed a mountain in the early fourteenth century and found it an experience of great pleasure. It is less often noted that he seems to have been the first person to have felt that way about a mountain at least since the early Greeks. It is almost never added that he immediately felt guilty for feeling pleasure and by some happenstance turned to that passage in his pocket St. Augustine that told him he should be ashamed "for not ceasing to admire things of earth" instead of the human soul. He learned his lesson: "As I descended, I gazed back, and the lofty summit of the mountain seemed to me scarcely a cubit high, compared with the sublime dignity of man."

of Pan, god of the satyrs, that we get the word "panic"); of devil-spawned monsters and hell-creatures (e.g., dog-heads, cyclopes, dragons) that abduct women and devour children; of whole races of accursed near-human peoples who are animalistic and savage (it is from *silva*, Latin for "woods," that we derive the word "savage"); and of the figure that recurs more than any other in medieval lore, the Wild Man—a huge, powerful, hairy figure, carrying a wooden club, with large genitals exposed, draped with strands of rank foliage, mute and therefore without reason, possessed of the secrets of nature, slave to natural desires and passions uncontrolled, always lurking there, over there, in the arboreal darkness—and as well in the dark, repressed corners of human desire and anxiety and fear.

But forests and mountains—and with them deserts, jungles, even islands—need not be populated to be fearsome. It was enough that these places were wild: *that* was the trigger to the terror. For "wild" is, etymologically, "willed," that is, self-willed, unruled, unmanage-able, out of control, uncivilized (as in Spanish, where "wilderness" is *falta de cultura*), and one is there lost, confused, be*wild*ered. It represents for the European mind that part of nature, and that part of human nature, where the hard-learned, hard-won constraints of "civilization" do not operate, where nothing is predictable and there-fore everything awaits. It was that place to which the covenant-breakers and cursed are sent by the Old Testament God, into "the great and terrible wilderness" (in the Hebrew text, incidentally, the word is *tohu*, or "chaos," as in the primordial darkness before Cre-ation), and to which sinners go to purge themselves of their natural evils. It was that place so alien to human contemplation that it is seldom even mentioned, only very rarely painted or drawn, and al-most never directly described for most of the period from the collapse of Rome to the sixteenth century. And it was that place so unrea-sonably fearsome that, as Keith Thomas notes, "the encroachment of wild creatures into the human domain was always alarming," even if it was nothing more than a bee flying into a cottage or a robin tapping at a window, either enough to send strong men to bed; the English House of Commons chose to reject a bill in 1604 because a jackdaw flew through the chamber during the speech of its sponsor.

This separation from the natural world, this estrangement from the realm of the wild, I think, exists in no other complex culture on earth. In its attitude to the wilderness, a heightening of its deep-seated antipathy to nature in general, European culture created a frightening distance between the human and the natural, between the deep silent rhythms of the world and the deep recurrent rhythms of the body, between the elemental eternal workings of the cosmos and the physical and psychological means of perception, by which we can come to understand it and our place within it. To have regarded the wild as *sacred*, as do many other cultures around the world, would have been almost inconceivable in medieval Europe—and, if conceived, as some of those called witches found out, certainly heretical and punishable by the Inquisition.*

It is but a short step from the fear of the wild to the love of the tamed and from there to the imperative of human domination and control of the natural world—hence the images of the subjection and mastery of the untamed landscape that are so frequent in late-fifteenth-century culture.

It is there in such celebrations of urban form as Piero della Francesca's *Ideal Town*, an entirely lifeless human construct without a single blade of grass or shadow of tree, dominated by that most controlling of all inventions of Renaissance art, perspective. It guides such assertions of human control over the physical world as the cityscapes and atlases then much in vogue, especially in the *mappemondes* that became the focus of the cartographical craze of the time, some 280 of them produced between 1472 and 1600. It permeates such popular works of adventure as the illustrated romances showing Christian Crusaders "victorious" over the bestial heathens or the imagined victories of Alexander the Great over the "wild men" and monsters of Persia and India.

But of all the images of control, the most pervasive and most

---

*I have not forgotten St. Francis of Assisi. He is in a sense the exception that proves the rule, and there is no doubt that his feelings about the immanence of God in every living creature (not, however, in God's inanimate products) became, particularly for later hagiographers, an important part of his Christian image. Nonetheless, his saintliness in this regard is less than perfect: we have the story of his rebuking a disciple for cutting the feet off a living pig to feed a colleague, but the rebuke is not for pain or cruelty, only for having failed to apologize to the pig-herder for having damaged his property. Moreover, the record is clear that Francis's influence in the Church was negligible: his Minorite order was solidly Aristotelian and pragmatic by the fourteenth century, having moved far beyond his "sentimentality" to animals; those of his followers who clung to his beliefs, the Fraticelli, were denounced as heretics and burned at the stake even in his lifetime.

Nor have I forgotten the pagan traditions—as, for example, among the Celts—that kept various kinds of worship of nature alive for centuries under the very nose of the Church, durable enough to be cited repeatedly as evidence of Satanism during the periods of the inquisitions and witch-hunts in the sixteenth and seventeenth centuries. But these were decidedly minority and largely rural strains, found for the most part in the northern Germanic and Nordic states, and never very influential, at least in mainstream culture.

revealing is that of the formal Renaissance garden, whose style was perfected and popularized in the last third of the fifteenth century and reached its peak in the middle of the next with such careful artworks as the gardens of Compton Wynyates in England (1520) and Tivoli in Italy (1549). Here it is the hand of man and not the grace of nature that is ever-present: bushes and small trees trimmed in rigid geometric shapes to look like wedding cakes or perfume bottles, closely clipped hedges along geometric walks, blocks of flower beds in uniform colors, carefully edged lawns, and artfully distributed statues, benches, fountains, pools, and bridges. (No chance that there should be such a thing as "an unweeded garden that grows to seed," as Hamlet will later say with typical disgust, where "things rank and gross in nature possess it merely.") If we know this to be the fifteenth-century style, it is almost not a surprise to see in Giovanni Bellini's *Allegory of Earthly Paradise*, painted no more than a year or two before Colón's First Voyage, an extremely stylized garden, more like a porch in fact, paved in geometric tiles with a single small potted tree in the center, surrounded by a low apertured wall and dominated by a kind of raised throne, an Eden that stands in marked contrast to a background of "wild" nature, complete with bare, forbidding mountains and peasant grottoes. It is the ultimate vision of mastered, if totally artificial, "nature."

Such a concept of mastery is not exclusive to early modern Europe, to be sure—the historical record suggests that the attempt to dominate nature began long before, with those ancient societies that became dependent on controlling animal herds and building water-control systems for agriculture and creating the monotheisms that would justify it. But it had seldom developed to this degree—"a compulsion," as the medieval historian John Block Friedman has put it, "of Western man to civilize what is rude and to dominate what is wild"—or so overtly entailed the unbridled hubris of human purpose and human right to possession and use: as Samuel Purchas put it in one of his diatribes justifying colonialism, "to tame nature where she is most unbridled," and "subdue her to the government and subjection which God over all blessed forever hath imposed on all servicible creatures to the natures of man."

The roots of this attitude are essentially biblical, found in that creation myth which is central to any society. The Hebraic Yahweh, so little a part of nature that He actually spends most of His time using its elements to wreak vengeance on His flock, creates humans in His image and as His surrogate, "to have dominion over" all the animals of the earth, and to "replenish the earth, and subdue it"; this is reiterated enough times to make it obvious what the proper hierarchy of creatures was and who was to get the chief benefit of it all. Keith Thomas's careful study of the importance of this thought for the English refers to "the breathtakingly anthropocentric spirit in which Tudor and Stuart preachers interpreted the biblical story," as with the Jacobean bishop who declared that "the creatures were not made for themselves, but for the use and service of man," or those divines who said the world would be annihilated after Judgment Day since it had been made for humans' use and would have no further purpose after their departure.

There was one other important source of such hubris, as we have seen: what was not authorized by God was sanctioned by the principles of humanism and science then being propounded with such vigor, all of them shot through with notions of human dominance, of what no less a figure than Bacon called "that right over Nature which belongs to [humans] by divine bequest." The humanist Ficino had it plainest: "Man . . . perfects, corrects, and improves the works of lower nature. Therefore the power of man is almost similar to that of divine nature. . . . How wonderful is the cultivation of the soil all over the earth, how marvelous the construction of buildings and cities, how skillful the control of waterways!" Or, as the medievalist A. R. Hall has put it, "The world . . . existed simply to be cooked, or distilled, or mutilated in man's service."

From these elemental patterns in Europe's tapestry of nature—ignorance and fear, separation and hostility, dominance and exploitation—a discernible image emerges: of a world more mechanistic than organic, more artificial than intrinsic, more corporeal than numinous, from which intimacy, sacredness, and reverence have all but vanished (it would be the achievement of the next five centuries to eliminate them entirely) and in which something colder, duller, and more lifeless presides instead.

As to the rest of what we know of Europe's ecological heritage, it can be seen written across the face of the land. With some significant exceptions, it is a record of deforestation, erosion, siltation, exhaustion, pollution, extermination, cruelty, destruction, and despoliation, all done either in the name of utility and improvement for the betterment of society or, as often, in ignorance of natural systems and the human connections to them.

The landscape of Europe had of course been a victim of this process—in ecological terms, *drawdown* beyond *carrying capacity*—for a long time: what it has meant to be "civilized" since the time of the Myceneans has entailed the increasing domination and control of the natural world. The Greek empires destroyed the once wooded hills and flowing streams of the Mediterranean through deliberate fires and urban encroachment, careless herding and overgrazing, ignorant planting and relentless cultivation; Plato wrote of visiting shrines dedicated to spirits of springs and streams where there were only dry crevices in the land. The Roman successors carried the devastation as far north as Britain, as far west as Iberia, and south into the Sahara, turning lands into granaries for their ever-growing cities and so heedlessly overdeveloping, overharvesting, and overgrazing that millions of square miles of European soils were soon exhausted and the imperium collapsed of its own inability to feed itself. During the long centuries of Christian dominance thereafter, environmental destruction was only intermittent, there being no cohesive empire to achieve it, but even then the rapacious use of nature went unchecked: England, for example, was significantly deforested as early as the eleventh century, with probably no more than 20 percent of it still wooded (and not more than 2 percent virgin) by the time of the Domesday Book in 1086.

Thus the legacy given to fifteenth-century Europe was straightforward: it was right and "natural" for human societies to fell trees, clear brush, "recover" fens and marshes, till soils, plant crops, graze herds, harness beasts, kill predators and "vermin," dig canals and ditches, and in general make use of the bounty of nature that a benevolent Lord had provided for them. Increasingly from the twelfth and especially the fourteenth century on, they did just that with a vengeance. For it was indeed a struggle, a battle experienced in hostile and violent terms, an unending campaign by which, as Marx would later say approvingly, "man opposes himself to Nature . . . in order to appropriate Nature's products."

All the works of human agency were permitted to impose themselves upon the European landscape with as much force as necessary to satisfy human needs. Cities, for example, began to be of substantial size in the fifteenth century (London had perhaps 75,000 people, Rome 55,000, Venice 80,000) and as always put a heavy burden on the surrounding countryside for their food and fuel and building materials; it has been calculated that a city of 3,000 in the eleventh century needed at least 3.3 square miles of developed land outside its walls on which to support itself, and the same probably could suffice a hundred years later, although the dimensions would expand exponentially as the city grew larger. Canals and artificial waterways and engineered streams, too—begun in about mid–fourteenth century, well-developed by mid-fifteenth—extended the human range, sometimes with quite astonishing boldness and ingenuity over plains and up hillsides, so that, as Fernand Braudel notes, "even the most unpromising stretches of water were everywhere exploited." Land was appropriated for crop cultivation and livestock herding on any conceivable terrain to feed or clothe a constantly needy population, the breakup of traditional manorial landholdings and the new inducements of capitalist trade encouraged the clearing and occupation of new acreage wherever anyone, peasant or prince, could get away with it. All in all, there was an enormous alteration of Europe's geography and natural systems in the fifteenth century; or, as Braudel chooses to put it from the alterers' perspective, "The slow toil of winning back [sic] land from water—from rivers, lagoons and swamps—from forests and heathland, tortured Europe incessantly and condemned it to superhuman effort." Superhuman indeed.

The costs were naturally great. The fossilized soils of western Europe were not especially fertile to begin with and were normally low in phosphorus, calcium, and certain other basics, and nowhere outside the western Russian steppes and the eastern Balkans were there any areas of that rich black soil upon which abundant grain crops (as in the American prairie) in particular depend. Cultivated lands were harvested over and over, often with four and five crops a year, and although fallow systems and manuring were in general use everywhere, yields were perennially inadequate, harvest failures frequent, and crop efficiencies low, and agriculture in general, as Braudel sums it up, "was an industry that was always in difficulty." Lands set aside for livestock grazing became progressively barren, with the soils compacted and ground cover depleted, and in many parts of Europe it was the custom simply to move herds of cattle and sheep into new areas when the old were exhausted; Spain in particular was devastated by the great herds of Merino sheep, nearly 3 million in all, that were permitted to forage great tracts of land in Andalusia and Estremadura in ever-widening circles for decade after decade from the mid–fifteenth century on. In the aftermath of both overfarming and over-grazing, the thin soils gave themselves quickly to erosion by both wind and water, and despite subsequent reclamation in the nineteenth century the legacy still can be seen today throughout the Mediter-ranean basin and in much of France and Germany.

But no alteration of the landscape was so profound or purposeful as the erasure of the European forests. There are no statistics on this destruction—the medieval age was not one to think that way—but considerable circumstantial evidence points in the same direction, and it is not even a matter of much controversy. Europe's was a civilization literally made of wood: wood was used to build its houses, ships, mills, machinery, plows, furniture, plates, pipes, tools, carriages, even clocks and (at times) watches; wood and charcoal provided the fuel for heating and cooking in homes and shops, castles and cottages, and in all industries from bakeries and glassworks to ironworks and arsenals. (An average fifteenth- or sixteenth-century ironworks, Braudel figures, consumed something like 5,000 acres of trees in two years; this rate eventually caused such fuel shortages that sometimes mills were forced to work only one year out of four or five.) All the great forests with which it had been blessed—an essential energy resource denied, incidentally, to the civilizations of the Middle East and much of Asia—were steadily and recklessly depleted to serve that civilization, and by the sixteenth century there were virtually no old-growth areas, no natural ecosystems, left.

It has been estimated that Europe in 1789 used up about 200 million tons of wood a year; extrapolating back to 1500, with a smaller population and fewer industries, we might guess at a yearly con-sumption of 60 to 80 million tons a year, which works out to an astonishing 1 ton of wood per person per year. Thus we can give credence to the record of a fourteenth-century terra-cotta factory near Dijon that employed 423 woodcutters to cut down the forest of Lesayes and 334 drovers to transport the timber to the ovens. And to the accounts of great clusters and rafts of wood regularly being sent down and occasionally choking the larger rivers of Europe—especially the Vistula, Danube, Rhine, Loire, and Marne—for use in the cities and especially the naval yards at the river mouths. And to the estimate that the great forest of Orléans south of Paris was reduced by half—from 120,000 to 60,000 acres—in the single century after

1520. There was, says Braudel pointedly, "a whole community whose profession it was to exploit, to utilize and to destroy" these forests, and, he adds in the same approving vein, "the forest was worth nothing unless it was used."

Devastation on this scale did not escape the notice of contemporaries, whatever their feelings about it, since at least local shortages and subsequent price raises were frequent. In Spain, which had to import wood from northern Europe as early as 1500, the writer Antonio de Guevara said ruefully in the 1520s that the fuel in Medina del Campo was more expensive than what it was cooking in the pot. Local ordinances and eventually royal decrees and acts of parliament were promulgated from at least the late fifteenth century (the first of England's many forest acts was passed in 1483), all attempting to put limits on both the numbers and kinds of trees to be felled and some of them encouraging the planting of new trees (especially "useful" trees) to replenish the crop. But these were futile, no more than wood chips in the wind, and they did virtually nothing to stop the unceasing deforestation of Europe in a sure, steady sweep from the Mediterranean littoral on up into the Low Countries and eastward through Germany to the Caucasus. Even King James I of England, who was concerned to halt that sweep and had issued decrees to check it, was forced to say, in some despair, "If woods be suffered to be felled, as daily they are, there will be none left."

Of course, forests were not the only living entities that came to be seen as exploitable resources in the late medieval world. It had long been assumed that animals, too—"made for man" and "subjected to his government and appointed for his use," in the words of an English churchman—were destined to provide humankind with food and drink, clothing, transport, labor, sport, and amusement. It has even been said that it was to this invaluable resource, and primarily to the ox and the horse as domestic animals, that Europe owes the very fact of its civilization. One might add that it owes to this also a considerable part of its ability to have spread its civilization over less favored peoples without large domesticates in both the Americas and the Pacific.*

It was not so much in its exploitation of animals, however, as in

---

*It has been estimated that because of its animals of transport and burden fifteenth-century Europe had a source of power five times as great as that of China. If one considers the almost total absence of large domesticated animals in the New World, it might be said to have had as much as twenty times that of the Americas.

its treatment of them that the medieval world truly revealed itself. This is vividly demonstrated by sports that were so popular then: bullfights in Iberia, where a dozen or more animals would be slaughtered in a single afternoon in a single corrida; bear-baiting in northern Europe, where a large, hungry animal would be staked and chained to the ground, its forefeet free for clawing, and set upon by a series of trained, vicious dogs; cockfights throughout western Europe, where a succession of birds, wings clipped and feet equipped with razor-sharp spurs to open flesh wounds, would fight to the death for eight, ten, sometimes fifteen hours at a stretch.

And above all, hunting. This was an activity so popular and common throughout the whole of Europe—among all cultures and all ranks of people, among the ignorant and the learned, commoners and kings, women and children as well as men—that it cannot fairly be called a mere sport, although it was far more than a fashion and only slightly less than a sacrament; it was for many, particularly in the aristocracy, nothing less than what Keith Thomas calls "an obsessive preoccupation." Recitation of the kinds and numbers slaughtered, and the pleasure taken therein, would be dreary, but it is pertinent to suggest the scale: Henry VIII, early in the sixteenth century, on more than one occasion had two to three hundred deer rounded up from his royal forests, penned, and set upon by his hunting dogs; an admiring observer of a wild-bird hunt wrote that "sometimes they take a pretty feathered army prisoners, two or three thousand at one draught and give no quarter"; the Duke of Henneberg in 1581 is credited with shooting "no fewer than 1003 red deer" in a single afternoon, and the elector of Saxony and his party killed 1,532 wild boar on one hunt in 1585.

Along with ferocity in the hunt for "sport" went rapaciousness in the hunt for food. Flesh played a much larger part in the diet of medieval Europe than anywhere else in the world, and so the everyday stance toward animals was also very different: the pig, the partridge, the perch were not so much living animals as potential dinners. Hunting and fishing for consumption were major industries throughout the subcontinent while they hardly existed as such elsewhere, and their practitioners were not bothered, except in rare local instances, with concepts of limits or overkill.

Thus the Mediterranean, once an abundant source of fish, was badly depleted by the fifteenth century ("only limited resources," in

Braudel's words) in types of species and numbers of catches. The Baltic, though more bountiful, had been so heavily overfished since the eleventh century that herring were essentially exterminated there by the fifteenth. In England, species such as barbel, bream, dace, and flounder were sharply reduced, in some areas eliminated, by over-fishing. And the right whale, in which the eastern Atlantic once abounded, had been so depleted by the sixteenth century that there-after only occasional sightings were made in the eighteenth and the mammal was extinct by the nineteenth.

Add to this the number of wild species hunted as predators in order to protect domesticated herds and flocks, and the toll rises significantly. Wolves, for example, were virtually eliminated in Eng-land by the thirteenth century (some few were said to last in the Yorkshire moors until the fifteenth) and gone from many parts of France by the early sixteenth century; bears also were extinct in the wild by the thirteenth century. Polecats and martens were driven into the remotest corners of northern Europe; foxes, weasels, hedge-hogs, and stoats all had bounties on them; crows and ravens and rooks were always fair game for farmers anywhere; and in England a series of official acts of Parliament from the early sixteenth cen-tury mandated that local parishes regularly had to see to the ex-termination of one or another species held to be undesirable. After his lengthy recitation of such practices, Keith Thomas is moved to say: "It is easy now to forget just how much human effort went into warring against species which competed with man for the earth's resources."

Indeed, it is not fanciful to see *warring against species* as Europe's preoccupation as a culture, the source of its food as well as its fur-niture, its energy as well as its sport, its urban space as well as its agricultural sprawl, its images for the nursery as well as for its pulpits. Disturbing as it may appear from our vantage, a sense of enmity and opposition, as in the more familiar kind of war, seems to have char-acterized the thought and action of much of fifteenth-century Europe, especially in those dark decades when the inadequacy of nature's yields brought famines and the malignancy of nature's spirits brought plagues. The diaries and letters and memoirs of the day are astonishing to our sensibility in their almost universal failure to praise—indeed their persistent refusal even to take much notice of—the beauties of the natural world, either sunset or vineyard, waterfall or hawk flight, and in their obsession instead with images in nature of violence and morbidity, fear and disgust.

It is fair to ask, should this really be so astonishing? One could argue that all cultures, to some degree, "war against" their environment to achieve the necessities of life, and no society can live without having some impact on, or even doing some violence to, the natural world: it is called survival. Is there something about the attitudes and practices of Europe that make it so different?

The answer would seem to be yes. We know too little about other societies of the world in either a comparable stage of development or contemporaneously in the fifteenth century, and even less about their ecological habits and beliefs, but the general scholarly agreement is that Europe of the late medieval era can be seen to be distinct in a number of important ways.

For one thing, it seems that its fundamental regard for nature was more hostile and antagonistic than was true of any other developed civilization. Other cultures were not uniformly so benign that they never misused their environments: China, for example, permitted its population expansion under several dynasties to lead to the clearing of forests and extermination of certain wild species; the Mayans permitted deforestation that eventually led to erosion and crop failures that in turn caused the downfall of Teotihuacan. But nowhere else was the essential reverence for nature seriously challenged, nowhere did there emerge the idea that human achievement and material betterment were to be won by *opposing* nature, nowhere any equivalent to that frenzy of defiance and destruction that we find on the Western record. Even China at its most statified, when it embarked on some fairly elaborate engineering projects to press back the wilderness, adhered religiously to its idea of "working with nature" and what it saw as carrying out the wishes and designs inherent in a particular river or mountain or waterfall.

"Religiously" is of course the key word. However misused and distorted, the central religions of neither the Asian nor the American civilizations permitted a separation from, or an attitude of dominion over, the natural beings and patterns of the nonhuman world. On the contrary, the religions of India, for example, most particularly Buddhism and Jainism, taught a compassion for all living things and an interweaving of humankind into the unity of nature; the wilderness of mountain and forest was not fearful there but holy (hence the image of the guru on the mountain ledge), and reverence for one or another Himalayan peak or range played a part in every local form of worship throughout that subcontinent. Of the Chinese beliefs, Taoism was perhaps most unqualified in its reverence for the natural world and the requisite place of humans in the sacred "web of life," but all of them expressed some of that; all of them expressed also a veneration for wilderness, as is seen so plainly in the traditional silk and scroll paintings, an art form well established from the sixth century on explicitly to celebrate and appreciate those places of the landscape that Western artists felt to be so fearsome. (Kue Hsi, in his eleventh-century "Essay on Landscape Painting," put forth the common wisdom that humans in general, artists in particular, "take delight in landscapes" because "the din of the dusty world and the locked-in-ness of human habitations are what human nature habitually abhors"; in contrast, "haze, mist and the haunting spirits of the mountains"—and he goes on to extend this specifically to streams, rocks, trees, and the like—"are what human nature seeks, and yet can rarely find.") And Japan's Shintoism was an explicit nature-worshipping religion, with shrines to the gods and goddesses of mountains, springs, forests, even storms, and ceremonies (still practiced today) such as the decoration of sacred rocks and communal prayers for the passage of the moon across the nighttime sky; wilderness, again, was a manifestation of the divine rather than the lair of the devil.

Europe's technophilia, its unchecked affection for the machine, also distinguished it among world cultures. The reasons for it are deep and tangled, but one can certainly say that Europe was more adept at turning technology to its own uses, and turning its institutions to the service of that technology, than any other society; in the judgment of Lewis Mumford, only Europe saw fit "to adapt the whole mode of life to the pace and capacities of the machine." Even those civilizations (Chinese, Persian, Japanese) that demonstrated a certain proficiency for mechanical inventiveness did not evolve an elaborate abstract system of rationality to go with it—we call it science—and thus did not develop a culture of technology, a self-propelling and self-reinforcing mode of thought that created its own purposefulness and momentum. Only Europeans, once learning of firearms from the

Chinese, went on to perfect them with such ferocious skill that in the space of little more than a century they had far surpassed all other cultures in armaments; only Europeans, too, borrowing again from many other cultures, refined and perfected the technology of ocean navigation so as to become the supreme naval power in the world by the middle of the sixteenth century, Chinese and Ottoman accomplishments notwithstanding.

Europe was also, as we have seen, uniquely a culture in flux, with its institutions and traditions in turmoil during the fourteenth and fifteenth centuries, and far less stable and conservative in its religious customs or political systems than those ancient, encrusted regimes of long-sanctioned rule and unquestioned authority of the kind found in Mesoamerica or China or the Muslim East. It was a society in which rootlessness and restlessness became adventure and curiosity, in which there was little room for constraints and limits and restrictions, in either the physical or the intellectual world. It would have been unlikely for such a culture to have achieved, for example, the power of ocean navigation and *not* to follow it with overseas possession and settlement; it could not have done as the Chinese, who launched several voyages of exploration as far west as the Persian Gulf and the east coast of Africa from 1405 to 1433 and, after some initial trading, decided there wasn't really anything out there superior to what they had at home and thereafter restricted their adventures to modest commercial traffic within the China Sea.

Finally, there was Europe's special emphasis on material acquisitiveness and resource accumulation, usually obtained at the sacrifice of the natural world. Perhaps, as some historians think, this was a response to the difficulties of survival on a relatively small land area—compared at least to the huge spaces of the Ming Dynasty, say, or Muscovy—under continual pressure from a population whose growth was encouraged by Church and prince alike. Perhaps, as Braudel suggests (when he ponders "whether Europe was somehow of a different human and *historical* nature from the rest of the world"), this is a result of its "particular social structures," which were encouraged always to expand and accumulate "on a larger scale and on a more secure footing than elsewhere—more often than not with the state's blessing." But surely the chief reason for this was the power of the still young but increasingly vigorous capitalist system, moving into vacuums left by medieval institutions, the likes of which existed nowhere else: more materialist, for sure, than any other economy, more expansionist, more volatile and energetic, more linked to growth and progress, and almost everywhere without the kinds of moral inhibitions found in the world's other high cultures. William Woodruff, in his *Impact of Western Man*, a path-breaking study some two decades ago, provides a neat summary:

> No civilization prior to the European had occasion to believe in the systematic material progress of the whole human race; no civilization placed such stress upon the quantity rather than the quality of life; no civilization drove itself so relentlessly to an ever-receding goal; no civilization was so passion-charged to replace what is with what could be; no civilization had striven as the West has done to direct the world according to its will; no civilization has known so few moments of peace and tranquillity.

So it was a very special civilization that was about to set foot on the sands of that small Edenic island in the Caribbean, a most proficient civilization in material terms, capable of immense energy and immense impact, but still dispirited and adrift, turmoiled and beset, sickened by gloom and suffering—and, above all, not quite grounded in the living earth, not quite at ease with itself in the circularity of nature, not quite able to accommodate its limitless genius to the limited world in which, perforce, it lived. A powerful civilization, though, a great people and a strong.

"Blow ye the trumpet in Zion, and sound an alarm in my holy mountain; let all the inhabitants of the land tremble.

"A day of darkness and of gloominess, a day of clouds and of thick darkness, as the morning spread upon the mountains: a great people and a strong: there hath not been ever the like.

"A fire devoureth before them; and behind them a flame burneth; the land is as the garden of Eden before them, and behind them a desolate wilderness; yea, and nothing shall escape them. . . .

"The earth shall quake before them; the heavens shall tremble."

Thus, again, the prophet Joel.

Chapter Five

1492–93

ADMIRAL Colón spent a total of ninety-six days exploring the lands he encountered on the far side of the Ocean Sea—four rather small coralline islands in the Bahamian chain and two substantial coastlines of what he finally acknowledged were larger islands—every one of which he "took possession of" in the name of his Sovereigns.

The first he named San Salvador, no doubt as much in thanksgiving for its welcome presence after more than a month at sea as for the Son of God whom it honored; the second he called Santa María de la Concepcíon, after the Virgin whose name his flagship bore; and the third and fourth he called Fernandina and Isabela, for his patrons, honoring Aragon before Castile for reasons never explained (possibly protocol, possibly in recognition of the chief sources of backing for the voyage).* The first of the two large and very fertile islands he called Juana, which Fernando says was done in honor of Prince Juan, heir to the Castilian throne, but just as plausibly might have been done in recognition of Princess Juana, the unstable child who eventually carried on the line; the second he named la Ysla Española, the "Spanish Island," because it resembled (though he felt it surpassed in beauty) the lands of Castile.

It was not that the islands were in need of names, mind you, nor

---

*The story of Isabella's pawning her jewels to raise money for Colón's explorations is pure fiction, based solely on a suggestion put out by both Fernando and Las Casas that the queen "was even ready to pledge her jewels for the cost of the expedition," an offer we may confidently believe was never taken up. The main source of funds was rather Luis de Santangel, *escribano de ración* (in effect, treasurer of the royal household) for King Ferdinand and a wealthy businessman in his own right, who may have put up some of his own money but was also responsible for securing a loan from the coffers of Santa Hermandad, the royal police force, of which he was one of the treasurers. (The Santa Hermandad's primary banker seems to have been Abraham Senior, a Jew, but its dealings with the crown were handled by Santangel, a *converso*, and Francisco Pinelo, or Pinelli, a Genoese banker and friend of Colón's.)

indeed that Colón was ignorant of the names the native peoples had already given them, for he frequently used those original names before endowing them with his own. Rather, the process of bestowing new names went along with "taking possession of" those parts of the world he deemed suitable for Spanish ownership, showing the royal banners, erecting various crosses and pronouncing certain oaths and pledges. If this was presumption, it had an honored heritage: it was Adam who was charged by his Creator with the task of naming "every living creature," including the product of his own rib, in the course of establishing "dominion over" them.

Colón went on to assign no fewer than sixty-two other names on the geography of the islands—capes, points, mountains, ports—with a blithe assurance suggesting that in his (and Europe's) perception the act of name-giving was in some sense a talisman of conquest, a rite that changed raw neutral stretches of far-off earth into extensions of Europe. The process began slowly, even haltingly—he forgot to record, for example, until four days afterward that he named the landfall island San Salvador—but by the time he came to Española at the end he went on a naming spree, using more than two-thirds of all the titles he concocted on that one coastline. On certain days it became almost a frenzy: on December 6 he named six places, on the nineteenth six more, and on January 11 no fewer than ten—eight capes, a point, and a mountain. It is almost as if, as he sailed along the last of the islands, he was determined to leave his mark on it the only way he knew how, and thus to establish his authority—and by extension Spain's—even, as with baptism, to make it thus sanctified, and real, and official.* (One should note that it was only his *own* naming that conveyed legitimacy: when Colón thought Martín Alonso Pinzón had named a river after himself, he immediately re-named it Río de Gracia instead.)

This business of naming and "possessing" foreign islands was by no means casual. The Admiral took it very seriously, pointing out that "it was my wish to bypass no island without taking possession" (October 15) and that "in all regions [I] always left a cross standing"

---

*Only a little more than a third of the names (24) were inspired by any natural feature. The rest came from religious figures or saints' days (11), general feelings of holiness or beauty (8), heavenly bodies (4), animals (4), specific people (3), Taino words (5), and miscellaneous —sometimes quite mysterious—inspirations (9), such as La Amiga ("Girlfriend") and Cabo de Cinquín ("Fifth").

(November 16) as a mark of Christian dominance. There even seem to have been certain prescriptions for it (the instructions from the Sovereigns speak of "the administering of the oath and the performing of the rites prescribed in such cases"), and Rodrigo de Escobedo was sent along as secretary of the fleet explicitly to witness and record these events in detail.

But consider the implications of this act and the questions it raises again about what was in the Sovereigns' minds, what in Colón's. Why would the Admiral assume that these territories were in some way *un*possessed—even by those clearly inhabiting them—and thus available for Spain to claim? Why would he not think twice about the possibility that some considerable potentate—the Grand Khan of China, for example, whom he later acknowledged (November 6) "must be" the ruler of Española—might descend upon him at any moment with a greater military force than his three vessels commanded and punish him for his territorial presumption? Why would he make the ceremony of possession his very first act on shore, even before meeting the inhabitants or exploring the environs, or finding out if anybody there objected to being thus possessed—particularly if they actually owned the great treasures he hoped would be there? No European would have imagined that anyone—three small boatloads of Indians, say—could come up to a European shore or island and "take possession" of it, nor would a European imagine marching up to some part of North Africa or the Middle East and claiming sovereignty there with impunity. Why were these lands thought to be different?

Could there be any reason for the Admiral to assume he had reached "unclaimed" shores, new lands that lay far from the domains of any of the potentates of the East? Can that really have been in his mind—or can it all be explained as simple Eurocentrism, or Euro-superiority, mixed with cupidity and naiveté?

In any case, it is quite curious how casually and calmly the Admiral took to this task of possession, so much so that he gave only the most meager description of the initial ceremony on San Salvador, despite its having been a signal event in his career. He recorded merely that he went ashore in his longboat, armed, followed by the captains of the two caravels, accompanied by royal standards and banners and two representatives of the court to "witness how he before them all was taking, as in fact he took, possession of the said island for the

King and Queen." He added that he made "the declarations that are required, as is contained at greater length in the testimonies which were there taken down in writing," but he unfortunately didn't specify what these were and no such documents survive; we are left only with the image of a party of fully dressed and armored Europeans standing there on the white sand in the blazing morning heat while Escobedo, with his parchment and inkpot and quill, painstakingly writes down the Admiral's oaths.

Fernando Colón did enlarge on this scene, presumably on the authority of his imagination alone, describing how the little party then "rendered thanks to Our Lord, kneeling on the ground and kissing it with tears of joy for His great favor to them," after which the crew members "swore obedience" to the Admiral "with such a show of pleasure and joy" and "begged his pardon for the injuries that through fear and little faith they had done him." He added that these goings-on were performed in the presence of the "many natives assembled there," whose reactions are not described and whose opinions are not recorded.*

> [Friday, 12 October.] I, in order that they might be very friendly towards us, because I knew that they were a people who could better be freed and converted to our Holy Faith by love than by force, gave to some of them red caps, and glass beads which they hung on their necks, and many other things of small value, in which they took so much pleasure and became so much our friends that it was a marvel.

Once safely "possessed," San Salvador was open for inspection. Now the Admiral turned his attention for the first time to the "naked people" staring at him on the beach—he did not automatically give them a name, interestingly enough, and it would be another six days before he decided what he might call them—and tried to win their favor with his trinkets.

---

*Morison, concluding his fairly fanciful description of this scene, suggests its true nature: "Never again may mortal men hope to recapture the amazement, the wonder, the delight of those October days in 1492 when the New World gracefully yielded her virginity to the conquering Castilians." This the watching Indians would have known, as they did come to know it, as rape.

> They all go around as naked as their mothers bore them; and
> also the women, although I didn't see more than one really young
> girl. All that I saw were young people [*mancebos*], none of them
> more than 30 years old. They are very well built, with very
> handsome bodies and very good faces; their hair [is] coarse,
> almost like the silk of a horse's tail, and short. They wear their
> hair over their eyebrows, except for a little in the back that they
> wear long and never cut. Some of them paint themselves black
> (and they are of the color of the Canary Islanders, neither black
> nor white), and some paint themselves white, and some red, and
> some with what they find. And some paint their faces, and some
> of them the whole body, and some the eyes only, and some of
> them only the nose.

It may fairly be called the birth of American anthropology.

A crude anthropology, of course, as superficial as Colón's descriptions always were when his interest was limited, but simple and
straightforward enough, with none of the fable and fantasy that characterized many earlier (and even some later) accounts of new-found
peoples. There was no pretense to objectivity, or any sense that these
people might be representatives of a culture equal to, or in any way
a model for, Europe's. Colón immediately presumed the inferiority
of the natives, not merely because (a sure enough sign) they were
naked, but because (his society could have no surer measure) they
seemed so technologically backward. "It appeared to me that these
people were very poor in everything," he wrote on that first day,
and, worse still, "they have no iron." And they went on to prove
their inferiority to the Admiral by being ignorant of even such a basic
artifact of European life as a sword: "They bear no arms, nor are
they acquainted with them," he wrote, "for I showed them swords
and they grasped them by the blade and cut themselves through
ignorance." Thus did European arms spill the first drops of native
blood on the sands of the New World, accompanied not with a gasp
of compassion but with a smirk of superiority.

Then, just six sentences further on, Colón clarified what this inferiority meant in his eyes:

> They ought to be good servants and of good intelligence [*in-
> genio*]. . . . I believe that they would easily be made Christians,

superiority

because it seemed to me that they had no religion. Our Lord pleasing, I will carry off six of them at my departure to Your Highnesses, in order that they may learn to speak.

No clothes, no arms, no possessions, no iron, and now no religion —not even speech: hence they were fit to be servants, and captives. It may fairly be called the birth of American slavery.

Whether or not the idea of slavery was in Colón's mind all along is uncertain, although he did suggest he had had experience as a slave trader in Africa (November 12) and he certainly knew of Portuguese plantation slavery in the Madeiras and Spanish slavery of Guanches in the Canaries. But it seems to have taken shape early and grown ever firmer as the weeks went on and as he captured more and more of the helpless natives. At one point he even sent his crew ashore to kidnap "seven head of women, young ones and adults, and three small children"; the expression of such callousness led the Spanish historian Salvador de Madariaga to remark, "It would be difficult to find a starker utterance of utilitarian subjection of man by man than this passage [whose] form is no less devoid of human feeling than its substance."*

To be sure, Colón knew nothing about these people he encountered and considered enslaving, and he was hardly trained to find out very much, even if he was moved to care. But they were in fact members of an extensive, populous, and successful people whom Europe, using its own peculiar taxonomy, subsequently called "Taino" (or "Taíno"), their own word for "good" or "noble," and their response when asked who they were. They were related distantly by both language and culture to the Arawak people of the South American mainland, but it is misleading (and needlessly imprecise) to call them Arawaks, as historians are wont to do, when the term "Taino" better establishes their ethnic and historical distinctiveness. They had migrated to the islands from the mainland at about the time of the birth of Christ, occupying the three large islands we now call the Greater Antilles and arriving at Guanahani (Colón's San Salvador) and the end of the Bahamian chain probably sometime around A.D. 900. There

---

*One point, never considered by the Admiral, was how slavery could be justified legally after he had taken possession of the islands. An act of possession automatically made the inhabitants Spanish subjects in theory, and naturally as such they could not, according to law, be enslaved by other Spaniards.

they displaced an earlier people, the Guanahacabibes (sometimes called Guanahatabeys), who by the time of the European discovery occupied only the western third of Cuba and possibly remote corners of Española; and there, probably in the early fifteenth century, they eventually confronted another people moving up the islands from the mainland, the Caribs, whose culture eventually occupied a dozen small islands of what are called the Lesser Antilles.[*1]

The Tainos were not nearly so backward as Colón assumed from their lack of dress. (It might be said that it was the Europeans, who generally kept clothed head to foot during the day despite temperatures regularly in the eighties, who were the more unsophisticated in garmenture—especially since the Tainos, as Colón later noted, also used their body paint to prevent sunburn.) Indeed, they had achieved a means of living in a balanced and fruitful harmony with their natural surroundings that any society might well have envied. They had, to begin with, a not unsophisticated technology that made exact use of their available resources, two parts of which were so impressive that they were picked up and adopted by the European invaders: *canoa* (canoes) that were carved and fire-burned from large silk-cotton trees, "all in one piece, and wonderfully made" (October 13), some of which were capable of carrying up to 150 passengers; and *hamaca* (hammocks) that were "like nets of cotton" (October 17) and may have been a staple item of trade with Indian tribes as far away as the Florida mainland. Their houses were not only spacious and clean— as the Europeans noted with surprise and appreciation, used as they were to the generally crowded and slovenly hovels and huts of south European peasantry—but more apropos, remarkably resistant to hurricanes; the circular walls were made of strong cane poles set deep and close together ("as close as the fingers of a hand," Colón noted), the conical roofs of branches and vines tightly interwoven on a frame of smaller poles and covered with heavy palm leaves. Their artifacts and jewelry, with the exception of a few gold trinkets and ornaments, were based largely on renewable materials, including bracelets and necklaces of coral, shells, bone, and stone, embroidered cotton belts, woven baskets, carved statues and chairs, wooden and shell utensils, and pottery of variously intricate decoration depending on period and place.

*"Antilles" is the Anglicized (and plural) version of the name the Portuguese gave to the island they expected to discover, and assumed Colón had indeed discovered, the long-lost fabled Antillia, the Island of the Seven Cities.

Perhaps the most sophisticated, and most carefully integrated, part of their technology was their agricultural system, extraordinarily productive and perfectly adapted to the conditions of the island environment. It was based primarily on fields of knee-high mounds, called *conucos*, planted with *yuca* (sometimes called manioc), *batata* (sweet potato), and various squashes and beans grown all together in multicrop harmony: the root crops were excellent in resisting erosion and producing minerals and potash, the leaf crops effective in providing shade and moisture, and the mound configurations largely resistant to erosion and flooding and adaptable to almost all topographic conditions including steep hillsides. Not only was the *conuco* system environmentally appropriate—"conuco agriculture seems to have provided an exceptionally ecologically well-balanced and protective form of land use," according to David Watts's recent and authoritative *West Indies*—but it was also highly productive, surpassing in yields anything known in Europe at the time, with labor that amounted to hardly more than two or three hours a week, and in continuous yearlong harvest. The pioneering American geographical scholar Carl Sauer calls Taino agriculture "productive as few parts of the world," giving the "highest returns of food in continuous supply by the simplest methods and modest labor," and adds, with a touch of regret, "The white man never fully appreciated the excellent combination of plants that were grown in conucos."

In their arts of government the Tainos seem to have achieved a parallel sort of harmony. Most villages were small (ten to fifteen families) and autonomous, although many apparently recognized loose allegiances with neighboring villages, and they were governed by a hereditary official called a *kaseke* (*cácique*, in the Spanish form), something of a cross between an arbiter and a prolocutor, supported by advisers and elders. So little a part did violence play in their system that they seem, remarkably, to have been a society without war (at least we know of no war music or signals or artifacts, and no evidence of intertribal combats) and even without overt conflict (Las Casas reports that no Spaniard ever saw two Tainos fighting). And here we come to what was obviously the Tainos' outstanding cultural achievement, a proficiency in the social arts that led those who first met them to comment unfailingly on their friendliness, their warmth, their openness, and above all—so striking to those of an acquisitive culture—their generosity.

"They are the best people in the world and above all the gentlest,"

Colón recorded in his *Journal* (December 16), and from first to last he was astonished at their kindness:

> They became so much our friends that it was a marvel. . . . They traded and gave everything they had, with good will [October 12].
>
> I sent the ship's boat ashore for water, and they very willingly showed my people where the water was, and they themselves carried the full barrels to the boat, and took great delight in pleasing us [October 16].
>
> They are very gentle and without knowledge of what is evil; nor do they murder or steal [November 12].
>
> Your Highnesses may believe that in all the world there can be no better or gentler people . . . for neither better people nor land can there be. . . . All the people show the most singular loving behavior and they speak pleasantly [December 24].
>
> I assure Your Highnesses that I believe that in all the world there is no better people nor better country. They love their neighbors as themselves, and they have the sweetest talk in the world, and are gentle and always laughing [December 25].

Even if one allows for some exaggeration—Colón was clearly trying to convince Ferdinand and Isabella that his Indians could be easily conquered and converted, should that be the Sovereigns' wish—it is obvious that the Tainos exhibited a manner of social discourse that quite impressed the rough Europeans. But that was not high among the traits of "civilized" nations, as Colón and Europe understood it, and it counted for little in the Admiral's assessment of these people. However struck he was with such behavior, he would not have thought that it was the mark of a benign and harmonious society, or that from it another culture might learn. For him it was something like the wondrous behavior of children, the naive guilelessness of prelapsarian creatures who knew no better how to bargain and chaffer and cheat than they did to dress themselves: "For a lace-point they gave good pieces of gold the size of two fingers" (January 6), and "They even took pieces of the broken hoops of the wine casks and, like beasts [*como besti*], gave what they had" (Santangel Letter). Like beasts; such innocence was not human.

It is to be regretted that the Admiral, unable to see past their nakedness, as it were, knew not the real virtues of the people he confronted. For the Tainos' lives were in many ways as idyllic as their surroundings, into which they fit with such skill and comfort. They were well fed and well housed, without poverty or serious disease. They enjoyed considerable leisure, given over to dancing, singing, ballgames, and sex, and expressed themselves artistically in basketry, woodworking, pottery, and jewelry. They lived in general harmony and peace, without greed or covetousness or theft. In short, as Sauer says, "the tropical idyll of the accounts of Columbus and Peter Martyr was largely true."

No iron, it is true, and little gold; but something the Europeans might have had even more use for.

Saturday, 13 October. The island is very big and very level; and the trees very green, and many bodies of water, and a very big lake in the middle, but no mountain, and the whole of it so green that it is a pleasure to gaze upon.

It is perhaps only natural that Colón should devote his initial attention to the handsome, naked, naive islanders, but it does seem peculiar that he pays almost no attention, especially in the early days, to the spectacular scenery around them. Here he was, in the middle of an old-growth tropical forest the likes of which he could not have imagined before, its trees reaching sixty or seventy feet into the sky, more varieties than he knew how to count much less name, exhibiting a lushness that stood in sharp contrast to the sparse and denuded lands he had known in the Mediterranean, hearing a melodious multiplicity of bird songs and parrot calls—why was it not an occasion of wonder, excitement, and the sheer joy at nature in its full, arrogant abundance? But there is not a word of that: he actually said nothing about the physical surroundings on the first day, aside from a single phrase about "very green trees" and "many streams," and on the second managed only that short sentence about a big island with a big lake and green trees. Indeed, for the whole two weeks of the first leg of his voyage through the Bahamas to Cuba, he devoted only a third of the lines of description to the phenomena around him. And there are some natural sights he seems not to have noticed at all: he did not mention (except in terms of navigation) the nighttime heavens, the sharp, glorious configurations of stars that he must have seen virtually every night of his journey, many for the first time.

Eventually Colón succumbed to the islands' natural charms as he

ɟw could he not?—and began to wax warmly about how
ɟds are very green and fertile and the air very sweet"
ɟ), with "trees which were more beautiful to see than any
ɟ that has ever been seen" (October 17) and "so good and
ɟmell of flowers or trees from the land" (October 19). But
his ɟ riptions are curiously vapid and vague, the language opaque
and lifeless:

> The other island, which is very big [October 15] . . . this island
> is very large [October 16] . . . these islands are very green and
> fertile [October 15] . . . this land is the best and most fertile
> [October 17] . . . in it many plants and trees . . . if the others
> are very beautiful, this is more so [October 19] . . . here are
> some great lagoons . . . big and little birds of all sorts . . . if the
> others already seen are very beautiful and green and fertile, this
> one is much more so [October 21] . . . full of very good harbors
> and deep rivers [October 28].

You begin to see the Admiral's problem: he cares little about the
features of nature, at least the ones he doesn't use for sailing, and
even when he admires them he has little experience in assessing them
and less acquaintance with a vocabulary to describe them. To convey
the lush density and stately grandeur of those tropical forests, for
example, he had little more than the modifiers "green" and "very":
"very green trees" (October 12), "trees very green" (October 13),
"trees . . . so green and with leaves like those of Castile" (October
14), "very green and very big trees" (October 19), "large groves are
very green" (October 21), "trees . . . beautiful and green" (October
28). And when he began to be aware of the diversity among those
trees, he was still unable to make meaningful distinctions: "All the
trees are as different from ours as day from night" (October 17),
"trees of a thousand kinds" (October 21), "a thousand sorts of trees"
(October 23), "trees . . . different from ours" (October 28), "trees
of a thousand sorts" (November 14), "trees of a thousand kinds"
(December 6).*

---

*However pallid that is, it must be said in Colón's favor that he did not exhibit any signs
of discomfiture at either the dense woods or the "soaring mountains" (none actually higher
than 3,000 feet) he encountered—"groves of trees, the most beautiful I have seen" (October
14), for example, and "very beautiful mountains in the manner of Sicily" (October 28)—
although, to be sure, he did not actually venture close to them, preferring to let his men do
the interior exploration and seldom himself leaving the safety of ship or longboat.

Such was his ignorance—a failing he repeatedly bemoaned ("I don't recognize them, which gives me great grief," October 19)—that when he did stop to examine a species he often had no idea what he was looking at. "I saw many trees very different from ours," he wrote on October 16, "and many of them have branches of many kinds, and all on one trunk, and one twig is of one kind and another of another, and so different that it is the greatest wonder in the world how much diversity there is of one kind from the other. That is to say, one branch has leaves like a cane, and another like mastic, and thus on one tree five or six kinds, and all so different." There is no such tree in existence, much less "many of them," and never was: why would anyone imagine, or so contrive, such a thing to be?

Colón's attempts to identify species were likewise frequently wrongheaded, usually imputing to them commercial worth that they did not have, as with the worthless "aloes" he loaded such quantities of. The "amaranth" he identified on October 28 and the "oaks" and "arbutus" of November 25 are species that do not grow in the Caribbean; the "mastic" he found on November 5 and loaded on board to sell in Spain was gumbo-limbo, commercially worthless. (On the other hand, one of the species of flora he deemed of no marketable interest—"weeds [*tizon*] in their hands to drink in the fragrant smoke" [November 6]—was tobacco.) Similarly, the "whales" he spotted on October 16 must have been simply large fish, the "geese" he saw on November 6 and again on December 22 were ducks, the "nightingales" that kept delighting him (November 6; December 7, 13) do not exist in the Americas, and the skulls of "cows" he identified on October 29 were probably not those of land animals but of manatees.

This all seems a little sad, revealing a man rather lost in a world that he cannot come to know, a man with a "geographic and naturalistic knowledge that doesn't turn out to be very deep or nearly complete," and "a limited imagination and a capacity for comparisons conditioned by a not very broad geographic culture," in the words of Gaetano Ferro, a Columbus scholar and professor of geography at the University of Genoa. One could not of course have expected that an adventurer and sailor of this era would also be a naturalist, or necessarily even have some genuine interest in or curiosity about the natural world, but it is a disappointment nonetheless that the Discoverer of the New World turns out to be quite so simple, quite so inexperienced, in the ways of discovering his environment.

Colón's limitations, I hasten to say, were not his alone; they were of his culture, and they would be found in the descriptions of many others—Vespucci, Cortés, Hawkins, Juet, Cartier, Champlain, Ralegh—in the century of discovery to follow. They are the source of what the distinguished English historian J. H. Elliott has called "the problem of description" faced by Europeans confronting the uniqueness of the New World: "So often the physical appearance of the New World is either totally ignored or else described in the flattest and most conventional phraseology. This off-hand treatment of nature contrasts strikingly with the many precise and acute descriptions of the native inhabitants. It is as if the American landscape is seen as no more than a backcloth against which the strange and perennially fascinating peoples of the New World are dutifully grouped." The reason, Elliott thinks, and this is telling, may be "a lack of interest among sixteenth-century Europeans, and especially those of the Mediterranean world, in landscape and in nature." This lack of interest was reflected in the lack of vocabulary, the lack of that facility common to nature-based peoples whose cultures are steeped in natural imagery. Oviedo, for example, setting out to write descriptions for his *Historia general* in the next century, continually threw his hands up in the air: "Of all the things I have seen," he said at one point, "this is the one which has most left me without hope of being able to describe it in words"; or at another, "It needs to be painted by the hand of a Berruguete or some other excellent painter like him, or by Leonardo da Vinci or Andrea Mantegna, famous painters whom I knew in Italy." Like Colón, visitor after visitor to the New World seemed mind-boggled and tongue-tied trying to convey the wonders before them, and about the only color they seem to have eyes for is green—and not very many shades of that, either.[2]

Monday, 15 October. And so I departed when it was about 10 o'clock with the wind southeast shifting to the south, to go to the other island, which is very big, and where all those men that I am taking from San Salvador make signs that there is a lot of gold and that they wear it in bracelets on their arms and their legs and their ears and their noses and their chests. . . . I do not wish to delay but *to discover and go to many islands to find gold. And since the people make signs that they wear it on their arms and their legs, and it is gold because I showed them some pieces that I have, I cannot fail with Our Lord's help to find out where it comes from.* *

One measure that Colón could make, and did so frequently, was the utilitarian: if he was not up to describing natural beauty or distinguishing trees, he was a master at determining the potential use and value of all that he saw, even when (as so often) he was deluding himself. Nature for him was all one form of treasure or another, whether aloes, mastic, spices, cinnamon, nutmeg, dyes, or medicines, or gold and silver and pearls—it hardly mattered as long as it could be sold in Europe. "Columbus's attitude to nature," says the Italian scholar Antonello Gerbi in his authoritative study *Nature in the New World*, "is strictly subordinated to his ambitions," ambitions largely of riches; or, as the Spanish scholar Ramón Iglesia has put it somewhat more starkly, Colón was nothing more than "a businessman" describing resources for potential markets.

Colón did not dissemble much about this raw utilitarian approach to nature in which all scenery is potential wealth, the more beautiful the more valuable: "Such handsome verdure and so very different from ours, and I believe that there are in it many plants and many trees which are much valued in Spain for dyes and for medicinal spices [October 19]. . . . To have seen it, especially the pines, he had felt inestimable happiness and delight, because as many ships as were wanted could be built here [November 25]. . . . He marveled greatly at seeing so many and such lofty islands . . . and he says that he thinks there are immense riches and precious stones and spices in them [November 14]." And then, most tellingly: "I had ordered [the crew] to treat [the Tainos] well and make them lose their fear, that something profitable might be had, since it didn't seem the land could

---

*It is important to note that the Admiral was sailing south and southwest (*into* the winds), as he had done and would continue to do except for a few days off the coast of Cuba. If his goal was the Orient, as he finally said on October 21, his normal route would have been due west or northwest, and indeed the winds were favorable for that direction many times during these weeks, yet he never took that course. When he left Cuba on December 5, the winds were north, northeast, and then east, encouraging a route southwestward around Cuba and then westward to Cathay or Mangi—and Colón instead headed straight into them, to the east, for Española.

be anything but profitable, by its beauty [December 12]." Where beauty, therefore treasure and profit: here was a true son of Renaissance materialism.

But the treasure that Colón wanted most of all—and kept convincing himself he was on the verge of discovering—was gold. Following the Admiral on his three rather cursory days on San Salvador and then on his fruitless rounds of one Bahamian island after another, one feels it was nothing less than an obsession. There were 16 references to gold, some of them lengthy, in the two weeks he spent on these first islands, another 13 during his coasting of Cuba, and finally no fewer than 46 during his scant five weeks on Española. (The word *oro* is used in these references 23 times in the outislands, 19 times along Cuba, and 98 times in Española.) It was the one constant of his *Journal*, the one recurrent goal, and on some days he seemed hardly able to get it out of his mind.*

The fixation was evident from the start. On his second day, tiring of the gifts of cotton and parrots and "other trifles" the Tainos lavished on him, he "worked hard to know if there was any gold," and finally noticed that "some of them wore a little piece" in their noses; in the next breath he somehow understood the islanders to say that to the south "there was a king there who had great vessels of it and possessed a lot." Never mind that for the next eight weeks he did not find more than scattered tiny bits of gold jewelry ("so little it amounts to nothing at all," October 22), he interpreted every sign, every conversation in tongues he knew not, as telling him that on the next island

> there is a lot of gold [October 15] . . . there is a mine of gold [October 16] . . . Samaot is the island or city where the gold is [October 16] . . . [on another island] there were mines of gold and pearls [October 28] . . . in Bohio there was an infinite amount [November 4] . . . [in Veneque] he had news, as he understood, that there was much gold [November 13] . . . [on a] neighboring island . . . very much gold was produced [De-

*The same obsession can be seen also in Colón's postils in his library, where in every book he commented on the regions of and traffic in gold and underlined almost every reference to it. And although various geographical allusions and theories were also underlined, particularly those relating to the size of the earth, the references to gold are underlined two and three times.

cember 18] . . . [on other islands there was] more gold than earth [December 22].

One might even say the Admiral was driven by this quest, and at times he was even apologetic about it: "There may be many things that I don't know, for I do not wish to delay but to discover and go to many islands to find gold" (October 15); "I will not delay here any longer . . . [or] go to the town . . . so as not to delay much, since I see that there's no mine of gold here" (October 23).

No mine of gold on Conception, none on Fernandina or Isabela, and none even on Juana, which had seemed so full of promise. The Taino captives on board said there was gold just over there (or so Colón wished to interpret them, though they had no language in common and communicated only in signs), but no one they met along the shore seemed to know where it was. Frustration mounted.

The Admiral then ordered that there should be no trading with those who came out to the ships in their canoes with cotton skeins and "other little things," in order that "they might surmise that the Admiral wanted nothing but gold" (November 11). Still no treasures appeared. Hearing tales of people who "gather gold on the beach by candles at night" (November 12), Colón headed off on a long journey to the southeast, but as he went along not only was there no gold to be found, there were not even any people: all fled their villages at the first sight of the three white men's ships. Frustration mounted still further.

By the middle of December, after two full months of exploring the islands, Colón had found no more than the smallest traces of gold, nothing more than a few grains worn as decorations, and he seemed on the verge of despair: "The breezes were like April in Castile," he reported on December 13, grasping at atmospheric straws, "the nightingale and other little birds were singing as in that month in Spain. . . . They saw many mastic trees and aloes and cotton trees," he went on, but—one feels it was painful to record—"gold they found not."

Even the golden trinkets and little pieces Colón did find, given to him freely by the obliging Tainos if he did no more than admire them, were never enough in themselves: each one in his eyes betokened vast mines and hoards of gold somewhere else, *beyond*, in the river farther east, in the interior, on the next island, around the next promontory.

Gold, there must be gold here, there *had* to be—and when, at one point, the Tainos saw how joyous the Admiral became with their little gifts of gold ("they rejoiced much to see the Admiral merry"), they reassured him that farther inland "there was a great quantity of gold . . . and told him that there he would find as much as he might want" (December 26).

Alas, they had no idea, and it would be a few years before they found out, that there was in truth no such quantity.

Sunday, 21 October. I sought here to fill up all the containers on the ships with water . . . and afterwards I will depart for another very large island that I believe must be Cipango according to the description of these Indians whom I carry. . . . But in any case I am determined to go to the mainland and to the city of Quisay [Quinsay] and to present Your Highnesses' letters to the Grand Khan, and to ask for a reply and come home with it.

It was on October 17, after nearly a week in the islands, that Colón first declared that he was somewhere in "the Indies" (all earlier references being clearly Las Casas's words), and not until October 21 did he put forth the idea that he was somewhere in the vicinity of the Grand Khan. It was patent by then that he was not actually in Marco Polo's Orient of marble and gold nor in the fabled islands of monsters and treasures, but he must have been genuinely perplexed as to where he really was. Under the circumstances he no doubt figured that a vague unspecified "the Indies" would do for his crew, and his journal.

But it did present something of a dilemma. How was he going to justify this expensive voyage to the Spanish court and the financiers who had put up the money, some of it personally to him, if there was nothing here of the "Pearls, Precious Stones, Gold, Silver," etc., he was sent to find?

His first thought was that he might be in the vicinity of the Grand Khan, that one of these large islands, in fact, was part of the Chinese mainland, and so twice he sent missions inland to make contact with what he hoped would be the court of Quinsay. The reports back not only were negative but must have convinced him that such an idea was fanciful, for after no more than a week he gave up the search for the Chinese ruler—the last reference is on November 1—and soon merely suggested that the cities of the Grand Khan "doubtless will be discovered" (November 12).

His next thought was that if he wasn't on the mainland he must be among the thousands of outislands in the China Sea—"all these islands of India," he decided on November 12—and that it would be simplicity itself on the *next* voyage to visit the court of the Khan, for "from here to *tierra firme* [the mainland] was a journey of ten days" (October 28). All very well and good, but what then had that left him for *this* voyage? No king, no palace, no great cities—and no gold—*but* the Admiral finally perceived now that these islands were not nearly so poor as they seemed to be at first, and in fact held hidden wealth, hidden possibilities for Spanish grandeur. The Admiral thus began to discover "a thousand kinds of fruit . . . and all should be very profitable" (November 4), trees "that he recognized . . . to be mastic" (November 5), a "very fine" cotton tree that "gives fruit the year round" (November 6), "tremendous quantity of mastic . . . a great quantity of cotton . . . an endless quantity of aloes" (November 12), not to mention magnificent harbors, lofty hills, "immense riches and precious stones and spiceries" (November 14), and of course, just over the next hill, gold mines of great munificence. After a month in the islands, in fact, Colón made but one more glancing reference to the Grand Khan and did not mention China or its ruler again, even dropping the use of "Indies" entirely until the journey home.*

It is not at all clear what Colón believed now in his heart of hearts, and it is possible that he did not even try for certainty. In the summary letter he sent to the Sovereigns at the end of the voyage, he regarded it the better part of wisdom to have it both ways. He reported confidently that "I reached the Indies" and it was a place not far from the continent "over there belonging to the Grand Khan." But he also asserted that the numerous islands he had found, in spite of their apparent meagerness, "are more richly supplied than I know or could tell"—not only was Española the "best district for gold mines" and

---

*Although Colón ceased to use "*Indios*" for the island natives after the middle of December—the passages in his own words, not Las Casas's paraphrases, use "folk" (December 21, 24) and "people" (December 24, 25; January 10) after December 16—that appellation would prove to be the most enduring of all, to the great regret of all subsequent scholars, the great confusion of all subsequent students, and the great outrage of all subsequent descendants of the various original people of the Americas.

near "another island" where "there is countless gold" but the whole region was full of "spice and cotton, as much as Their Highnesses shall command," and mastic and aloes and slaves and rhubarb and cinnamon, "and I shall find a thousand other things of value."

So much for the Grand Scheme. He had not reached Asia, if that's what he had sought, but only the route thereto "over there"; he had not found much treasure to speak of, only uncertain promises of it everywhere; and there was no mainland of any kind, eastern or southern, only a string of small, green islands. The rest of his life—with three more journeys and some seven years in these islands—would be spent trying to justify this strange, uncharacterizable discovery: to himself, to his Sovereigns, to his countrymen, to Europe.

Monday, 5 November. At dawn, he ordered the ship and the other vessels to be pulled out ashore [for cleaning and pitching], but not all at the same time, so that two should always remain in the place where they were for security; although he says that these people were very safe. . . . He says further that this harbor of Mares is among the better ones in the world and has the best breezes and the most gentle people, and because it has a cape of high rock, where a fortress could be built, so that if that trade became a rich and great thing, the merchants would all be protected there from other nations, and he says that Our Lord, in whose hands are all victories, leads the way to all things that will be done in His service.

One of the alternative possibilities for future Spanish glory in these none too promising islands suggested itself to Colón almost from the first. On his third day of exploration—a Sunday at that—he had set out to see "where there might be a fortress [built]" and in no time at all found a spit of land on which "there might be a fortress"— and from which "with fifty men they [the Tainos] could all be subjected and made to do all that one might wish" (October 14). Now, during the second leg of exploration along the north coast of Cuba, this grew into a full-blown fantasy of a colonial outpost, complete with a rich trade and merchants. And so Colón went on, rather like a young boy playing soldiers, turning various pieces of landscape into military sites: Puerto de Mares on November 5, a harbor for "a store and a fortress" on November 12, another harbor where "a fortress could be erected" on November 16, a place where "a town or city and fortress" could be built on November 27—until finally, as we shall see, misfortune enabled him to translate his fancy into reality.

Now there was no particular reason to go about constructing fortresses—"I don't see that it would be necessary, because these people are very unskilled in arms" (October 14)—but that was the way his architectural imagination, suffused with his vision of colonial destiny, seemed to work: a spit of land, a promontory, a protected harbor, and right away he saw a fort. Such was the deeply ingrained militarism of fifteenth-century Europe, in which fortresses represent edifices more essential to civilization even than churches or castles.

It may have been that Colón began his explorations with nothing more than an idea of establishing some sort of entrepôt in these islands, a fortress-protected trading post rather like the one the Portuguese had established, and Colón had perhaps visited, on the Gold Coast of Africa, at El Mina. But as he sailed along the coast of Cuba he seems to have contrived something even grander, not just a trading port but an outright colonial settlement, an outpost of empire where Spaniards would settle and prosper, living off the labor of the natives ("Command them to do what you will," December 16) and the trade of the Europeans.

On November 27, toward the end of his sojourn along Cuba, Colón put into a large "very singular harbor" which he named Puerto Santo (today known as Puerto Baracoa, about a hundred miles from the eastern tip of the island) and was nearly speechless at its tropical splendor: "Truly, I was so astounded at the sight of so much beauty that I know not how to express myself." The vision of conquest, however, loosened his tongue, and at great length, too:

And Your Highnesses will command a city and fortress to be built in these parts, and these lands converted; and I assure Your Highnesses that it seems to me that there could never be under the sun [lands] superior in fertility, in mildness of cold and heat, in abundance of good and healthy water. . . . So may it please God that Your Highnesses will send here, or that there will come, learned men and they will see the truth of all. And although before I have spoken of the site of a town and fortress on the Rio de Mares . . . yet there is no comparing that place with this here or with the Mar de Nuestra Señora; for inland here must be great settlements and innumerable people and things of great profit; for here, and in all else that I have discovered and have hopes of discovering before I return to Castile, I say that all Christendom will do business [*dad negociaçion*] with them, but most of all Spain, to which all this should be subject. And I say that Your Highnesses ought not to consent that any foreigner trade or set foot here except Catholic Christians, since this was the end and the beginning of the enterprise [*proposito*], that it was for the enhancement and glory of the Christian religion, nor should anyone who is not a good Christian come to these parts.

It may fairly be called the birth of European colonialism.*

Here, for the first time that we know, are the outlines of the policy that not only Spain but other European countries would indeed adopt in the years to come, complete with conquest, religious conversion, city settlements, fortresses, exploitation, international trade, and exclusive domain. And that colonial policy would be very largely responsible for endowing those countries with the pelf, power, patronage, and prestige that allowed them to become the nation-states they did.

Again, one is at a loss to explain quite why Colón would so casually assume a right to the conquest and colonialization, even the displacement and enslavement, of these peaceful and inoffensive people 3,000 miles across the ocean. Except, of course, insofar as might, in European eyes, made that right, and after all "they bear no arms, and are all naked and of no skill in arms, and so very cowardly that a thousand would not stand against [*aguardariá*] three" (December 16). But assume it he did, and even Morison suggests that "every man in the fleet from servant boy to Admiral was convinced that no Christian need do a hand's turn of work in the Indies; and before them opened the delightful vision of growing rich by exploiting the labor of docile natives." The Admiral at least had no difficulty in seeing the Tainos in this light: "They are fit to be ordered about and made to work, to sow and do everything else that may be needed" (December 16); "nothing was lacking but to know the language and to give them

---

*With the attention to the various forms of his name, the Admiral must have realized that both in Castilian and in Florentine Italian *colon* is a cognate of many words having to do with colonization. The policy, in his mind, may have been simply the inevitable and divinely wrought result of the person sent to make it come true.

orders, because all that they are ordered to do they will do without opposition" (December 21).

Missed in the dynamics of the assumed right of colonialism was an extraordinary opportunity, had it only been possible for the Christian intruders to know it, an opportunity for a dispirited and melancholy Europe to have learned something about fecundity and regeneration, about social comeliness and amity, about harmony with the natural world. The appropriate architecture for Colón to have envisioned along these shores might have been a forum, or an amphitheater, or an academy, perhaps an auditorium or a tabernacle; instead, a fortress.

> *Sunday, 9 December. This day it rained and the weather was wintry as in Castile in October.... The island is very big, and the Admiral says it would not be surprising if it is two hundred leagues around.... This harbor at its entrance is a thousand* pasos *wide, which is a quarter of a league.... Facing it are some plains [vegas], the most beautiful in the world, and almost like the lands of Castile; rather, these are better, for which he gave the name to the said island la Ysla Española.*

Rain and cold were no doubt fitting companions for the Admiral's mood, which must have been dark indeed as he came to his sixth and (what would turn out to be) last island, Española. For after two months of exploration, there was virtually nothing to show for it, and the whole voyage was likely to be written off by the Sovereigns, and history, as a foolish and expensive profligacy. The Indians were singularly uncooperative, most of them running away as soon as they saw the European ships put in. The weather was rotten and the seas so high and winds so strong that Colón dared not leave his harbor here for days on end. And to top it off, Martín Alonso Pinzón had abruptly deserted the fleet two weeks before, with no explanation and not so much as a by-your-leave, taking the *Pinta* off to the east as the Admiral was sailing on a tack north of Cuba—and what if *he* were the one to find gold and pack on sail to get back to Palos and win all the glory? Island plains, however beautiful—one so lovely that Colón would name it, tellingly, Valle del Parayso—were surely scant recompense.

The depleted fleet finally resumed its coasting after five days of this miserable weather, putting into this harbor and that along the north coast of Colón's Ysla Española.* And then, finally, on December 17, *gold*, or at least enough of it for a gold leaf "as big as a hand" and some small pieces, and signs that there would be more, "and the Admiral believed that he was very near the source, and that Our Lord would show him where the gold came from." The next day the local *kaseke*, "a youth of about 21 years," came on board with two more pieces of worked gold ("I believe that they are very near to where it comes from, and that there much exists") and thereafter the crew bartered on shore for a little more. A few days later, farther along the coast, the Admiral was presented with a belt and mask with large features of hammered gold—a present, so he was told, from a *kaseke* of great power, Guacanagarí, who said that if the Admiral would visit him "he would give him all that he had" (December 22)—and the sailors bartered for still more "good pieces of gold," apparently in considerable quantity (and given "as freely as those who gave a calabash of water"). Colón could not but decide "for certain that in these regions there was a tremendous quantity [*grandissima cantidad*]" of gold, and "he could get it, he imagined, for nothing" (December 23). So, at last, the justification for all the hardship, all the peril, seemed to be at hand.

The Admiral was in a most expansive mood. "Your Highnesses may believe," he wrote on December 24, "that in all the world there can be no better or gentler people":

> Your Highnesses should take great joy because soon they will become Christians and be instructed in the good customs of your realms, for neither better people nor land can there be. . . . All are of the most singular loving behavior and speak pleasantly, not like the others [unspecified] who it seems when they speak are making threats; and they are of good stature, men and women, and not black. . . . And the houses and villages are so

---

*The choice of name is notable. At first Colón's comparisons had stressed the distinctive exoticism of the islands—"as different from ours as day from night" (October 17) and "so different from ours that it is marvelous" (October 21)—but now, as the possibilities of colonization grew on him, he began to find everything quite like Europe and things became "similar in nature to those in Spain" (December 6) and "just like the land of Castile" (December 7). Finding and stressing similitude is a psychological precursor to claims of ownership, Gerbi argues in his *Nature in the New World*, and "recognition is already an act of conquest and subjugation."

pretty [*hermosos*] and with government in all, such as a judge
or lord, and all obey him so that it is a marvel. And all these
lords are of few words and very attractive manners; and their
commands are for the most part effected by signs of the hand,
so soon understood that it is a marvel.

So expansive indeed, that he ordered that these people be entertained
on board the ships ("more than a thousand persons had come to the
ship" by canoe, and "more than five hundred came to the ship swim-
ming for want of canoes") and after due celebration he even decided
that he would sail on that night to visit Guacanagarí, just down the
coast, and see what his promises of gold were all about. It was Christmas Eve.

The wind was light and the seas calm—as "in a porringer," the
Admiral noted—and the clear skies above showed the crescent of a
new moon low on the horizon, as the two ships, the *Niña* in the
lead, made their way slowly along the coast. There having been
"two days and a night that he hadn't slept"—probably because he
had stayed awake to palaver and trade with the Tainos who had
flocked aboard, and no doubt because there was a good deal of pre-
Christmas revelry by his crew—the Admiral decided "to lie down
and rest" a little before midnight. As it turned out, though, he was
not the only one in need of sleep: the seaman whose task it was to
steer the ship on the middle watch also decided to take a nap and
turned the tiller over to a gromet, even though he well knew that it
was a practice the Admiral "had always strictly prohibited during the
entire voyage, come wind or come calm."

Not long after midnight, with the gromet at the helm and the
Admiral asleep, the *Santa María* hit a coral reef a few miles from the
shore and "went upon it so gently that it was hardly felt." The boy
"gave tongue," the Admiral leapt from his bed, the sailors whose
watch it was ran on deck. Colón gave orders for the longboat to
carry an anchor astern to try to ease the ship off, but once set free
of the flagship the sailors in the longboat unaccountably made for
the *Niña*, sailing nearby—perhaps to alert it to the grounding and
enlist its aid, or perhaps, so the Admiral says, "they cared for nothing
but to flee to the caravel" (though if that was really the case he
inexplicably did nothing thereafter to chastise or punish the deserters).
In any case, the ship was quickly fixed firmly on the reef, her stern

swung around so that the whole beam drove against the coral, and each wave lifted her up and down on the hard, sharp extrusions of the rock. Within hours "the planking opened" and she took in so much water that she was listing hopelessly into the surf. The Admiral ordered his flagship abandoned and watched in the light of the dawn as she began to break up and sink.*

Having realized that he must be only a few miles from where he had been told he would find Guacanagarí's town, Colón sent the fleet marshal, Diego de Arana, to ask the *kaseke* for help. Guaca-nagarí, it was reported, wept at the news and immediately "sent all the people of the town with very big and many canoes" to help the Europeans offload the sinking ship, and they "cleared the decks in a very short time."

> He himself together with his brothers and his relations were so diligent both on the ship and guarding what was taken to land that all was well cared for. From time to time he sent one of his relatives to the Admiral, weeping, to console him and tell him not to grieve or be annoyed, because he would give him whatever he had. The Admiral assures the Sovereigns that in no part of Castile would better care have been taken of all the goods, so that not a lace-point was missing. He [the *kaseke*] caused all our goods to be placed together near the palace, until some houses that he gave us where all might be put and guarded had been emptied. He stationed armed men around everything to keep watch through the night; and he and the whole town were weeping.

There seemed to be nothing for it but to begin the colonial strategy immediately: there were something like sixty men or more with but a single small caravel at their disposal, so obviously some would have to be left behind and become the willy-nilly beachhead of the imperial project. Colón gave "orders to erect a tower and fortress, all very

---

*Just why the Admiral was sailing on a dark night along Caribbean coasts he well knew to be extremely dangerous remains a mystery, another mistake of the "great mariner" and one for which he paid dearly. It has, however, provided subsequent archeologists, amateur and professional, with years of fascinating scavenging, although with very little authentic to show for it. The Institute of Nautical Archeology of Texas A&M has conducted extensive preliminary research in its hunt for the *Santa María*'s remains, but so far without success.

well done, and a great moat, not that I believe it to be necessary for these people. . . . But it is right that this tower should be built, and that it be as it should be, being so far from Your Highnesses, that they may recognize the skill [*insenio*] of Your Highnesses' people and what they can do, so that they may obey them with love and fear." There can be no irony in this, yet when Colón returned eleven months later the tragic nuance of those words would be all too clear: by then "these people" had certainly seen what the Spanish colonists could do.

In spite of what he recorded as "the anguish and pain which he had received and kept from the loss of the ship," Colón took considerable consolation from the prospect of establishing his new colony, which he named La Navidad in honor of the Day of Nativity on which its inadvertent founding took place. Naturally he thought he detected God's hand in all this—he "recognized that Our Lord had caused the ship to run aground there, in order that he might found a settlement there" (December 26)—and even declared that "it is the best place in all of the island to make a settlement" (January 6), despite the fact that it was a patently poor harbor, fully exposed to northern storms, perhaps as ill chosen a spot as could be found along that coast. Using the timber salvaged from the *Santa María*, and with the help of the willing Tainos, in a few days the Spaniards had constructed the essential buildings of the village. The first structure erected by Europe in the New World was a fortress.*

Colón took even greater consolation, it seems, from the gold nuggets and gifts that Guacanagarí lavished on him day after day: a big mask "which had great pieces of gold in the ears and the eyes and in other parts" and other "good ornaments" that the *kaseke* "put upon the Admiral's head and neck" (December 26), "a great plate of gold" he hung on his neck (December 28), "a great gold mask" (December 29), "two great plates of gold" (December 30), and finally, a pledge

---

*The location of La Navidad is not known for sure, although several archeological searches have been made in recent years, beginning with that of Dr. William H. Hodges, a medical missionary with an archeological flair, at En Bas Saline, Haiti, in 1958. Extensive fieldwork has since been conducted there by the University of Florida—including topographic maps, an electric-conductivity survey, close-grain scavenging and excavation, and microscopic analysis and dating—but the exact site of the European fortress, and of Guacanagarí's village, still is not fixed. The bones of a European rat have been found through these excavations; though it is not quite certain when it arrived, it would be perfectly in keeping that the first European animal to land in the New World was a rodent "pest," introduced accidentally.

in just ten days' time of "a statue of pure gold as large as the Admiral himself" (January 2). And by now the Admiral realized that the divinely selected colony would have a true purpose, one but for the shipwreck he might never have been able to exploit: to collect as much of this abundant gold as possible from the simple islanders before he brought back a relief ship. "He hopes in God that on his return, which he intends to make from Castile, there would be found a barrel of gold that those left behind would have obtained by barter, and that they would have found the mine of gold and the spicery" (December 26).

> *Thursday, 27 December. At sunrise the king of that land [Guacanagarí] came to the caravel and told the Admiral that he had sent for gold, and that he wished to cover everything with gold before he went away; rather he asked him not to go. . . . At this juncture there came [certain Indians with news] that the caravel* Pinta *was at a river at the end of that island. . . . Now the Admiral undertook with the greatest speed to get ready for the return to Castile.*

Originally, so he tells us (October 19), Colón had planned to return to Castile sometime in April, when, he presumably knew from his earlier travels, the North Atlantic would be past its winter storm season. But now, after the wreck of the *Santa María* and with news that the *Pinta* was not far away, he apparently decided to sail back immediately. It was a risky decision and most unseamanlike—as he would soon discover, when he was blown off course and almost capsized by two fierce storms in February and March—that leads one to assume that the Admiral's need was dire. Yet all he ever said, a few days later, was that he intended to head back home "without detaining himself further," because "he had found that which he was seeking" (January 9) and intended "to come at full speed to carry the news" (January 8).

Strange locutions, those, and never explained: what, after all, *had* he found, and why exactly did he have to go at full speed, and why was he determined to set sail into the Atlantic in midwinter? There is a likely answer, but since it is never stated outright we are forced to tease it out from the few suggestions the *Journal* offers.

It was on the day that news came that Pinzón and the *Pinta* were

farther down the coast of Española that the Admiral first decided to
depart, and it was three days after he finally met up with Pinzón on
January 6 that he spoke of having found "that which he was seeking."
Could it be that on his detour *Pinzón had actually found* "the mines
of gold" in the interior of Española, and had first conveyed that and
then demonstrated it to the Admiral? Certainly he had put in at some
harbor closer to the interior mountains of Española, where there were
in fact gold nuggets to be found—Colón confirmed this on the Second
Voyage—and where several of the rivers actually do wash gold dust
down from the mountains—as Colón confirmed on January 8, when
he explored one such river and called it Rio del Oro because its sand
was "all full of gold, and of such quality that it is marvelous." Certainly Pinzón had been there for at least ten days, probably twenty
(as one of the Tainos told the Admiral), time enough to make friends
with the natives and, even more likely, explore the interior and find
some likely goldfields. Might not this proof of the awaited "mines
of gold" have been exactly the goal Colón was seeking all along (so
much for "a route to China" and the Grand Khan) and impressive
enough so that, far from disciplining Pinzón and his crew for desertion, as he originally had planned, "for having done wrong by having
parted company without permission" (January 3), Colón chose instead to do nothing, telling Pinzón he "wished to forget" (January
6) his treachery and would overlook the desertion "to give a good
end to this voyage" (January 8)? Might not it have been quite true,
as the Admiral was told, that Pinzón had found "a great quantity of
gold and many mines," his "caravel bartered much gold," and "in
the island Española they gather pieces of gold as large as grains of
wheat" (January 6)? Might not this signal discovery, in fact, be the
reason the Pinzóns, "and others who followed them with insolence
and greed," judged, as Colón complained, "that everything already
belonged to them, unmindful of the honor that the Admiral had done
and shown them" (January 8)?

And if so, might that not be the reason Colón wanted to get back
to Castile in such unseemly, such unseamanly, haste, so that the crafty
Pinzón might not go off by himself again and, supported by all his
friends from Palos, claim to Castile that *he* was the one who really
found all that was worth finding in the islands? And also the reason
Colón never came right out and gave Pinzón due credit for his crucial
discovery, instead burying it in such confusing prose that most historians to this day have concluded, quite wrongly, that there was

scant gold on Española and Pinzón, the deserter, had no part in finding it anyway.

> *Sunday, 13 January. He sent the boat [barca] ashore on a fine beach to obtain yams to eat, and they found some men with bows and arrows with whom they stopped to talk, and bought from them two bows and many arrows, and asked one of them to go and speak to the Admiral in the caravel, and he came; of whom he [the Admiral] said that he was very ugly in appearance, more than the others that he had seen. . . . He had the Indian given food, and gave him pieces of green and red cloth and little beads of glass, of which they are very fond, and sent him back ashore and told him to bring gold if he had it, which he believed from certain little things of his that he wore. When the boat reached the shore there were behind the trees a good fifty-five naked men with very long hair, as the women wear it in Castile. On the backs of their heads they wore plumes of feathers of parrots and other birds, and each one carried a bow.*

Whatever the reasons for his haste, the Admiral certainly made his way along the remainder of the island's coast with great alacrity, and little more than a week after he met up with Pinzón, the two caravels were off on the homeward leg. Only one notable stop was made, at a narrow bay some 200 miles east of La Navidad, where a party Colón sent ashore discovered, for the first time, some Indians with bows and arrows.

The Admiral having given standing orders that his men should buy or barter away the weaponry of the Indians—they had done so on at least two previous occasions, presumably without causing enmity—these men in the longboat began to dicker with the bowmen with the plumes. After just two bows were sold, the Indians turned and ran back to the cover of the trees where they kept their remaining weapons and, so the sailors assumed, "prepared . . . to attack the Christians and capture them." When they came toward the Spaniards again brandishing ropes—almost certainly meaning to trade these rather than give up their precious bows—the sailors panicked and, "being prepared as always the Admiral advised them to be," attacked the Indians with swords and halberds, gave one "a great slash on the buttocks" and shot another in the breast with a crossbow. The Tainos grabbed their fallen comrades and fled in fright, and the sailors would have chased them and "killed many of them" but for the pilot in charge of the party, who somehow "prevented it." It may fairly be called the first pitched battle between Europeans and Indians in the New World—the first display of the armed power, and the will to use it, of the white invaders.

And did the Admiral object to this, transgressing as it did his previous idea of trying to maintain good relations with the natives so as to make them willing trading partners, if not docile servants? Hardly at all: now, he said, "they would have fear of the Christians," and he celebrated the skirmish by naming the cape and the harbor de las Flechas—of the Arrows.

It was not the first time (or the last) that Colón was able to delude himself—it may indeed have been a European assumption—that violence can buy obedience. Twice before, he had used a display of European arms to frighten the Tainos, to no purpose other than instilling more fear and awe than they already felt: once on December 26, when he had a Turkish longbow, a gun [*espingarda*], and a lombard demonstrated, at which occasion the people "all fell to earth" in terror and the *kaseke* "was astonished"; then again on the eve of his departure from La Navidad, when he ordered a lombard fired from the new fortress out at the remains of the *Santa María* so that Guacanagarí, when he saw "how it pierced the side of the ship and how the ball went far out to sea," would then "hold the Christians whom [Colón] left behind as friends" and be so scared "that he might fear them." Strange behavior at any time; toward this softhearted *kaseke* and his kindly people, almost inexplicable.

Wednesday, 16 January. He departed three hours before daybreak with the land breeze from the gulf which he called Golfo de las Flechas. . . . He . . . turned to the direct course for Spain northeast by east. . . . After losing sight of the cape that he named San Theramo *on the Island Española, which was sixteen leagues to the west, he made twelve leagues to the east by north, accompanied by very fine weather.*

Thus ended that most portentous event, the first encounter of the Old World with the New, though the representatives of neither one would have known to call it that, any more than they could have begun to imagine its consequences. The depleted fleet, now with about fifty crewmen and perhaps two dozen Taino captives,* both ships taking on water, set their prows to the north and to the latitude where the Admiral believed he would find the westerlies that would take him back to Spain.

January was an especially fitting month for this crossing, for it is the month named for the god Janus, in ancient times the god of the doorway, and hence of beginnings, of both time and place, of which there has never been a more consequential example. It was after that same god that the first king of Italy was named, the great-grandson of Noah, so it is said . . . and the founder of Genoa.

---

*The number of captives Colón mentioned in the *Journal* adds up to thirty-one, but four escaped and three were put ashore; we do not know how many started the Atlantic crossing, nor does the Admiral ever say, but Martyr says ten. The number of Europeans is equally uncertain, since it is not clear how many were left behind at La Navidad: the *Journal* says thirty-nine, as does Fernando, Martyr and Oviedo say thirty-eight, and Andrés Bernáldez has forty. All the rest returned safely.

Chapter Six

1493-94

Friday, 15 March. Yesterday after sunset he sailed on his course until daylight with a light wind, and at sunrise found himself off Saltes; and at the hour of noon with a flood tide he entered by the bar of Saltes within the harbor whence he had departed on the third of August the preceding year; and so he says that now he ends his writing except that he proposed to go to Barcelona by sea, in which city he had news that Their Highnesses were, and thus to give them a report of his entire voyage that Our Lord had permitted him to perform.

It was a grueling homeward journey—two terrible storms during which the *Niña* and the *Pinta* became separated again, half of the crew of the *Niña* detained when they put into the Azores, Colón forced to dock in Portugal for repairs and tell his news to King João before reaching Spain—but by mid-March, 224 days after he had left it, Cristóbal Colón was back in the port of Palos. Back in triumph, with news that there were indeed populated islands far out into the Ocean Sea, with proof that there were winds both easterly and westerly to carry one there and back, with artifacts of gold and other supposed treasures from these lands, and with six (or seven or nine, depending on the account) bronze and painted natives of that region, all that remained after two months on small, leaky ships in the storm-swept North Atlantic. Now to tell the world.

Sometime during the early weeks of the return voyage, before the weather turned bad, Colón started writing a summary letter to the Sovereigns to tell them of his great discoveries; he completed it off the Azores on February 15 and mailed it, probably from Lisbon on March 4, to the court at Barcelona. It is, as one would expect, a self-serving letter, full of exaggeration (Cuba, for example, said to be "larger than England and Scotland together" when it is barely half as big) and of fable (reports of amazon women, people born with tails, and the de rigueur people "who eat human flesh"), and even in several places of outright duplicity (as when he claims to "have taken possession" of "a large town [*una villa grande*]" called La Navidad, with nary a word about the shipwreck). But it fairly throbs with great promises of all kinds of wealth, "great trade and profit," streams and "great mines of gold," spices and cotton and mastic and aloes and "a thousand other things of value," harbors beyond compare, lands "rich for planting and sowing and for livestock of every sort," and "all are more richly supplied than I know or could tell." And it offers what must have been a fascinating, tantalizing (although not very detailed) picture of a world beyond imagining: "very fertile to an excessive degree," beautiful with "trees of a thousand kinds and tall [that] never lose their foliage," "little birds of a thousand kinds," and "marvelous pine groves, and extensive meadow country . . . and a great variety of fruits"; and the people simple and untainted, who "all go naked, men and women, as their mothers bore them," without weapons or iron or even private property, it seems, "well-built people of handsome stature" and "keen intelligence," but "timid beyond cure" (this he says four times), exceedingly generous and friendly, "so artless and so free with all they possess, that no one would believe it without having seen it."

It is not hard to suppose what must have been the reaction of Ferdinand and Isabella to this letter—commonly known as the Santangel Letter, after the royal officer to whom it was addressed—when it arrived in Barcelona sometime in mid-March. The monarchs, undoubtedly pleased that something so auspicious had come from so unpromising a voyage, immediately summoned their admiral to court for further information and set about plans for a second fleet, far larger, to be sent out even before the summer was over. Their avidity for the new realms Admiral Colón had found for them and for the opportunity, as he put it in the letter, for "the turning of so many peoples to our holy faith, and afterwards for material benefits," was reflected in the haste with which they sent word to Rome in order to have the discovery sanctioned by the pope. By mid-April a copy of the Santangel Letter is known to have been in Rome (it was mentioned in a Venetian chronicle of April 18), and on May 3, His

Holiness Alexander VI, who owed much to the favors of Ferdinand
and Isabella over the years, issued a papal bull confirming Spanish
ownership of all lands so far, and all to be, discovered by *dilectus
filius Christophorus Colon*.

But the conventional idea that the news contained in this letter
immediately set Europe on its ear is false. A small edition, in Castilian,
was printed very quickly in Barcelona in late March or early April,
probably for private distribution by the court—so small, in fact, that
only one copy survives. Not long after, in early May, an edition
translated into Latin (*De insulis inuentis. Epistola Cristoferi Colom*)
and published in Rome as an eight-page pamphlet enjoyed a certain
popularity, even the equivalent of best-sellerdom, with two more
Latin printings in Rome and five others in Basel, Paris, and Antwerp
before the year was out; there were also three editions translated from
the Latin into quite atrocious Tuscan verse, by one Giulano Dati,
the first in mid-June. But from the scarcity of these copies we may
assume that their print runs were small and their contents of interest
primarily to scholars (eight of the twelve editions were in Latin) and
that most of Europe remained serenely oblivious of their existence
and their news. Certainly there was no intellectual explosion, nothing
that "caused Europe to realize that the perimeters of their world were
changing" and "to reevaluate their concept of the world" (as a recent
study has put it). For in the first place, as the archivist Rudolf Hirsch
of the John Carter Brown Library has argued, the popularity of these
editions was confined "to limited groups of readers, and little intrigued the general public"; moreover, no one, even among cosmographers and scholars, knew exactly how to incorporate this new
information, and it was another decade—in some quarters, many
decades—before there was any clear idea that Colón's discovery of
some distant islands in the Ocean Sea was any more significant than,
say, the discovery of the Azores or the Canaries. Even among the
learned, interest in the discoveries apparently faded fast, and over the
next seven years there were only seven more printings, two in Latin
in 1494, two in Tuscan in 1495, one in Castilian and one in German
in 1497, one more in Tuscan in 1500, and from then on, nothing at
all.

In the first flush of the news at the Spanish court, however, the
successful admiral stood very high in the Sovereigns' esteem. In mid-
April they received him at court, an event whose details, surprisingly

enough, are quite sketchy—there is no official court record extant, nor are we even sure of the exact date—but it must have involved a certain pomp, given the noteworthiness of the occasion, not to mention a certain drama, given an entourage from the *Niña* said to consist of six Indians, several seamen, parrots in cages, "rats" (*hutias*) and dogs on leashes, chests of presumed treasure, and gold nuggets and artifacts.[1] On May 20 they not only endowed him with a coat of arms but permitted him to display on it a likeness of the castle of Castile and lion of León, paronomastic elements of the royal standard. A week later they reaffirmed the conditions of their original agreements of the year before:

> And we, considering the risk and danger to which you have exposed yourself for our service in going out to search and discover the said islands, and that to which you will now subject yourself in going to seek and discover the other islands and mainland, whereby we have been and hope to be greatly served by you, and in order to confirm a benefit and favor upon you, confirm by these presents to you and to your said sons, descendants, and successors, one after the other, now and for evermore, the said offices of Admiral of the said Ocean Sea, which you have found and discovered, and of viceroy and governor of the said islands and mainland.

The following day, May 29, they issued formal instructions for the Second Voyage of discovery and gave their Admiral explicit power not only over the outfitting and operation of the voyage but over all activities in and profits from the "Islands and Mainland, discovered and to be discovered in the Ocean Sea in the region of the Indies." (With such honors, we may assume that the monarchs either had not discovered yet that his various "treasures" of aloes and mastic and spices were worthless detritus or else, as long as the gold was real, didn't care.)

Colón was at the apex of his power: never again was he to be so highly regarded at court, never again to be taken so seriously as a strategist or mariner. The king and queen even agreed in substance to his particular ideas about future colonization, as he had delineated them the previous month in a memorial on "the Settlement and Government" of the islands of the Indies, the formal working-out of those Fortress Thoughts he had been brooding on in the Caribbean. The memorial is quite a remarkable document and is undeservedly ignored, inasmuch as it was the first statement of the colonial strategies and policies of empire that were eventually to carry Europe to every cranny of the earth. For one thing it assumed an unchallenged European sovereignty, the islands to be "won and managed" by the 2,000 Spaniards who were to be sent out, with no thought of any prior or conflicting claims from any such potentates as the princes of Cipango or the Grand Khan, figures who as a matter of fact were never referred to again by either Colón or the Sovereigns. Nor did it give any thought to the rights, or conditions, of the Indians themselves—other than that there should be priests sent out to convert them—automatically making the native population into a kind of historical cipher without legal or political corporeality. Then, too, it was almost entirely concerned with establishing the means of exploitation and trade, providing no suggestion of any other purpose for settlement or any other function for government. Above all, as we might by now expect, its overriding concern was for gold, with nearly two-thirds of the document given over to the process by which the governor (Colón himself, of course) and local officers would control the gathering, melting, storing, selling, and shipment of the metal. (In one interesting and self-revelatory paragraph, Colón even acknowledged the obsession gold inspires, arguing that "owing to the greed for gold, everyone will prefer to seek it rather than engage in other necessary occupations," and proposing that for part of the year there should be a ban on mining so that there may be "an opportunity for performing other tasks.")*

Thus it was that Spain, leading the other nation-states into the imperial lists, was to cart its government and culture almost piecemeal

---

*One is only slightly surprised to find, at the end of a letter so single-mindedly materialistic, the signature that Colón used here for the first time and would continue to use for the rest of his life:

·S·
·S· A ·S·
X M Y
: Xρ̄o FERENS /

The first part of it is entirely mysterious, no doubt cabalistic, and it has defied all attempts at deciphering for the last five centuries; the last part, though, a mixture of Greek and Latin, is simply the name of the Admiral as Christ-bearer.

onto foreign soils, imposing its rules (and settlements) on any other piece of solid land where it could maintain its hold quite without regard to whatever native cultures or natural conditions might exist there; as Colón put it, no doubt without a moment's reflection, the settlements of the Indies were to be governed "according to the custom and practice of Castile." It was an arrogance ill becoming the princes and people of a state so steeped in militarism, religiosity, exploitation, and dominance, but it must be said that it expressed those characteristics with some precision; hence the Spanish colonial legacy of conquest, conversion, cumulation, and control.

That long process began with Colón's Second Voyage.

The Second Voyage was no ragtaggle three-tub affair: this was now the Beginning of Empire, and the Sovereigns provided no fewer than seventeen ships, fully equipped and provisioned for a six-month round-trip sail, with seamen "the most expert and most dependable of their craft" and somewhere between 1,200 and 1,500 colonists— including, this time, five *religiosos* specifically charged with the work of conversion; several hundred *hidalgos* out to extend the Reconquista to new lands and new wealth; a large band of soldiers complete with cuirasses, crossbows, arquebuses, and cannon; two of the surviving Indian captives to serve as interpreters; a few craftsmen, farmers, miners, and assayers; and assorted adventurers out to fill their chests with the vast gold riches the Admiral promised. A lavish enterprise, indeed, and at least some of the vast sums required for it came from wealth confiscated from Spanish Jews, if we judge by royal orders of May 23, 1493, the very day Ferdinand and Isabella authorized the Second Voyage, imposing new injunctions on Jewish property unclaimed or left with *converso* friends.* Interestingly, there were still no women, which meant that the crown had not yet decided on a policy of fixed settlement and was intending for its men to use the island women as they might; there is no suggestion of Spanish women being proposed for Caribbean colonization before 1497, no actual evidence before 1502.

Despite the importance of this voyage, it was remarkably under-chronicled. The Admiral apparently kept a journal, used by Fernando

---

* Meyer Kayserling has estimated that the confiscated wealth amounted to about 6 million maravedis ($42,000 in gold-standard dollars, or some $480,000 today), three times the cost of the First Voyage.

for his biography, but it was apparently never copied and was subsequently lost; the court sent out no official chronicler for the occasion, the only royal official being, typically, a comptroller to keep
close track of the share of gold to be collected for the Sovereigns.
Luckily there are three short accounts, no more than letters really,
which together give some idea of the outward leg to Española, the
initial attempts at settlement, and the Admiral's subsequent explorations of Jamaica and the southern coast of Cuba: a 1494 letter by
a fleet surgeon, Dr. Diego Alvarez Chanca; a 1495 letter by a Ligurian
nobleman, Michele de Cuneo, who may have been a boyhood friend
of Colón and accompanied the fleet as a simple adventurer; and some
letters by Guillermo Coma of Aragon, translated into Latin and published by his friend Nicolo Scillacio in Pavia in late 1494 or early
1495. Serviceable as these are, however, we miss the distinct voice of
Colón himself that Las Casas accustomed us to, with its intimate
insights into his complex character, and it is not until the Third
Voyage in 1498 that we once again have a taste of his direct record.

The Second Voyage marks the first extended encounter of European
and Indian societies, the clash of cultures that was to echo down
through five centuries, and its record reveals all the hallmarks of that
profound sweep of time. Attitudes before only hinted at toward the
people of nature as well as the world they lived in become much
clearer now, and the essential unsuitability of European culture for
the task on which it was embarking becomes, sadly, even clearer still.

> [*Sunday, 3 November. Dominica.*] *Lookouts with the best
> vision engaged in a contest of long-range observation,
> announced from the masthead of the flagship that land was
> sighted. Now they call out that they see the peaks of the
> mountains, now the green of the forests, and suddenly seven
> islands hitherto unknown loomed into sight. . . .*
>
> *These islands are inhabited by* Canabilli, *a wild,
> unconquered race which feeds on human flesh. I would be
> right to call them* anthropophagi. *They wage unceasing wars
> against gentle and timid Indians to supply flesh; this is their
> booty and is what they hunt. They ravage, despoil, and
> terrorize the Indians ruthlessly.—Coma*

On the very first day the fleet sights the Indies we have the *Can-
abilli*, those dreaded people who, Colón told the Sovereigns, ate

human flesh, also known as Canibales, Canibas, and most commonly Caribas, the Indians from whom all languages of Europe get the word—and their first supposed examples of—"cannibalism." It opens us to a subject of great fascination, one that manifests the mind of Europe as few others do.

The Caribas, or Caribs—to anthropologists they are usually "Island-Caribs" to distinguish them from a quite different mainland people who were endowed with the same name—apparently called themselves Kalinas (or Killinagos), for "Carib" and all its derivatives were the words the Tainos used (or so Colón heard) to describe them. They were newcomers to the islands and the sea that eventually bore their name, having moved into and occupied the Lesser Antilles from Grenada up to Guadeloupe sometime in the early fifteenth century, conquering but intermingling with and taking on many of the customs of the native Igneris. Little is known about them, in spite of their great notoriety, for it is almost impossible to isolate Carib archeological sites from earlier and later Indian sites, and little anthropological work was ever done in their region. And in time these people were as hard hit by European conquest and disease as the rest of the island populations, so much so that there were only a few deracinated pockets of them left for study by the nineteenth century.

What *is* known about them, though—or at least should be known, given the available facts—is that they were *not*, contrary to the persistent European image, either fierce or warlike—or cannibals.

The myths surrounding the Caribs are almost entirely fabrications born in the fable-heated mind of Cristóbal Colón. And he, as it turns out, was a singularly unreliable source—a man who could not possibly have known anything substantive about Carib culture, who almost certainly never once set foot on a single Carib island in all his years in his Indies, and who probably never did meet a single Carib in the flesh (so to speak) except for a few women and children whom he ordered taken on board as captives, *two and a half years* after this initial sighting of Dominica.

That seems strange to say, for all the ink Colón himself and those around him had to offer on the true nature of the Caribs, but the facts are fairly straightforward. On the First Voyage, Colón never met or saw any Caribs, nor did he claim to have; he manufactured in his mind the idea of their fierceness, choosing to hear the Tainos, in a language of which he knew nothing, disclosing that picture for him, and those people he did see then with bows and cudgels who he said first were Caribs, or "at least they must be their neighbors," were in fact an eastern branch of his "gentle Tainos," with no particular reputation for violence. Now, on the Second Voyage, Colón seems to have decided *in advance*—although he could have had no possible way to know it, save the supposed information of his Taino captives—that the islands he came to were populated by Caribs, and this is clearly what he conveyed, complete with suggestions of great ferocity, to Coma and the other correspondents traveling with him. Yet on Guadeloupe, the one and only Carib island his fleet anchored at on this voyage, the natives "as soon as they saw us, instantly ran to the mountains" (Cuneo)—hardly evidence of much ferocity, that—and the only other Indians Colón could have seen, fourteen teenage "boys and girls" he ordered to be kidnapped, were said not to be Caribs at all but their unfortunate captives.

Colón did encounter some direct resistance a few days later, as we shall see, and of course assumed—as did his contemporary chroniclers, and as nearly as I can tell most historians down to the present—that those who showed such hostility to the white men must be Caribs. But this was on Santa Cruz (St. Croix), which was apparently not then or ever a Carib island—it is thought that the Caribs settled no farther north than Guadeloupe, more than 200 miles away—and its residents were probably part of those same bow-armed eastern Tainos the Admiral had met at the Cabo de las Flechas on the First Voyage. His mistake here is one that would be repeated again and again: whenever the people of an island were submissive or at least nonhostile, the Spanish declared that they were the Tainos, or good Indians, and whenever they were deemed to be hostile or at least defensive, they were said to be the warlike Caribs, the bad Indians. And that was very largely the level of Europe's understanding of the island populations for the century of their contact.

The idea of fierce and hostile Caribs, in short, was never more than a bogey, born of Colón's own paranoia or stubborn ferocity and spread to his comrades, to the chroniclers of Europe, and to history. Certain sixteenth-century sailors did come to grief when landing on those islands—given the fierce reputation of the white man by then, it is not surprising that the Caribs were less than hospitable—but the historical record for that century actually emphasizes the friendliness of the islanders and the passivity of their behavior. Father Raymond

Breton, a French priest who lived among the Caribs in the mid-seventeenth century, expressed exasperation at their lack of aggressiveness: "I would complain much more readily," he wrote, "of their gentleness toward me."

And their rapacious cannibalism? That, similarly, from all the *real* evidence we have, seems to be a myth. Colón himself never saw or recorded any evidence of the eating of human flesh, although he was always in search of it, and on only two occasions did his men report even the vaguest signs of it: once during a visit to an abandoned Guadeloupe village, where Dr. Chanca said "the neck of a man was found cooking in a pot" and in the huts bones from which the Indians "had gnawed everything that could be gnawed"; and later, on the return visit to the island in 1496, when, Fernando says, it was reported that they found "a human arm ready for roasting on a spit."* In both instances the evidence is extremely flimsy—it is hard to think that European seamen would be able to distinguish a disembodied neck or arm as distinctly human, and not from a monkey, say, or a dog, and in any case there is no evidence that they were to be *eaten* or that the bones had been "gnawed" rather than (as in certain other Indian cultures) cleaned and preserved in ossuary fashion as religious artifacts. Both seem to be simple examples of people who, when primed with dark presuppositions, find what they expect to find.

That is all there is. There is no further support for the legend of Carib cannibalism in any of the firsthand accounts of the Caribs over the next century, no reliable description of the dismemberment, cooking, or eating of human bodies, even (as is found occasionally elsewhere) for ceremonial reasons. The only suggestive story is one from Father Breton in which he describes Carib meat-eating; but he may not actually have been a firsthand witness, he was not able to say whether the flesh being eaten was human, and his assertion that the Caribs *told* him they were eating human flesh is vitiated by the fact that the incident happened when he first arrived on Guadeloupe and did not yet know the language. Las Casas, who had considerable experience in the islands over several decades, said flatly that the Caribs were not cannibals, and a nineteenth-century scholar, William Sheldon, reviewing all the literature, said that he could find no believable evidence of cannibalism. Archeologists have uncovered

*For some reason Keen translates this as "a human hand roasting on a spit" and Morison as "a man's arm was found all dressed to roast on a spit," but the original Italian is perfectly clear: *"un braccio di uomo, posto arrosto in uno schidone"*—no hand, no dressing.

isolated human bones at presumed Carib sites, though these could just as easily be from pre- or even post-Carib cultures, but there is nothing—tooth marks or knife incisions, for example—to suggest the bodies had been used for food. Father Breton, who eventually did learn the Carib language, said that he knew of no words connected with ceremonies of cannibalism, nor have subsequent ethnographers come up with any signs of such a ceremony, which is hardly possible if in fact it was a frequent and important rite. Robert Myers, a recent scholar in this area, has said that "neither archeological nor linguistic data support the existence of cannibalism" and argues: "Available data do not allow an absolute conclusion, but all the evidence is weak, circumstantial, and largely second-hand. If the Caribs were on trial for cannibalism, they would be acquitted." The anthropologist W. Arens, in his wide-ranging *The Man-Eating Myth*, says that he was "unable to uncover adequate documentation of cannibalism as a custom in any form for any society" and adds that "there is little reason to assume that the very aborigines whose name now means man-eaters actually were so."[2]

Why then was such a myth perpetrated and then perpetuated with such intensity that the cannibal became the dominant image for Europeans of the people of the Indies, indeed eventually of the whole New World? As, for example, on a 1532 map from Basel, perhaps illustrated by Hans Holbein the Younger, where a few grand and elaborate buildings stand for the Middle East, and a band of cannibals, cheerfully chopping up and spit-roasting various arms and legs, stands for America. Why did Chanca and Amerigo Vespucci and Sebastian Münster and a great many subsequent chroniclers dwell on the man-eaters, slavering over the details? As in the account by Peter Martyr, in which it was said that when cannibals capture children,

> they geld [them] to make them fat as we do cock chickens and young hogs, and eat them when they are well fed; of such as they eat, they first eat the entrails and extreme parts, as hands, feet, arms, neck, and head. The other most fleshy parts they powder [salt] for storage, as we do pieces of pork and gammons of bacon.

The simple answer is that for centuries Europe had read about strange tribes of man-eaters in the nether regions of the world—anthropophagi were standard in the highly popular "reports" of world travelers such as John Mandeville and were fixed, like the Wild Men, in the forefront of the pantheon of monsters—and any knowledgeable man would have expected to meet them in such a place as the Indies, might indeed have interpreted any sign, however slim, as proof of their existence. Something about the idea of such people fascinated Europe for centuries: it was such a flagrant violation of the Lord's natural law, by which "higher" orders were expected to eat "lower" ones only ("The imperfect creature falls to the use of the perfect," as Francisco de Vitoria says); it showed the certain handiwork of Satan himself, whose rites were well known to contain such travesties of Christian ceremonies (i.e., the Eucharist); and it violated the canons of Europe's civilization, by which humans could be roasted *alive* and killed, as happened daily throughout the countries of the Inquisition, but were not supposed to be killed and then roasted *dead*.＊

A more complex answer, especially important for Colón, is that reports of cannibalism provided the means of justifying the enslavement and deportation of those creatures so clearly beyond the pale of God's favor that they could rightfully be regarded as beasts. As we have seen, the idea of slavery of the island peoples grew in the Admiral's mind on the First Voyage as he found fewer and fewer other lucrative excuses for his Grand Scheme, until by the end he could promise the Sovereigns "slaves, as many as they shall order." Now, on the Second Voyage, the idea seems to have developed into an almost full-blown policy even before the first landfall, according to which any islander confronted is said to be a Carib and therefore enslavable—and even those who are first held to be Taino captives of the vile cannibals become "the said Canibales" to the Admiral just a few months later so that they can ultimately be sent back to Spain

---

＊One of the ironies of European revulsion at cannibalism is that it appears to have been a practice by no means unknown in Europe itself. Among the instances of it reported with some authority: in 1476, in Milan, the unpopular tyrant Galeazzo Maria Sforza was dismembered and eaten by a crowd; in 1572, after the St. Bartholomew's Day Massacre, Huguenot body parts were sold at auction and reportedly eaten in Paris and Lyon; in 1617 the body of Marshal d'Ancre was eaten in France. In times of severe hunger, the eating of human flesh was acceptable, at least for some—Fernand Braudel mentions a 1662 record of a famine in Burgundy during which "some people ate human flesh," and cannibalism is suggested (and occasionally admitted) in any number of sixteenth- and seventeenth-century accounts of ships at sea that run out of food. Montaigne asserts in "On Cannibalism" that both Catholics and Protestants ate each other during the sixteenth-century Wars of Religion, but he does not pretend to offer proof of it, perhaps because it seemed so believable.

as slaves. (It is amazing how many islanders at first thought to be gentle Tainos turned out on closer inspection to be ferocious Caribs and were hauled in chains to the Spanish ships.)

An even more complex explanation for the tenacity of the myth of man-eaters is that it permitted the denigration, and thus the conquest and exploitation, of peoples whose lands were seen as increasingly desirable in European eyes. It is always convenient to regard foreign populations as inferior, more convenient still to regard them as animalistic, or bestial, especially when you have decided to enslave or eliminate them; how positively fortuitous, then, to discover that they are all anthropophagi and provide evidence of their inferiority —indeed, their unhumanness—three times a day, with every meal. Thus the theme that was to play repeatedly through the sixteenth century, here in a version by the Spanish historian Gómara, who wrote that "there, on those islands and new lands, some men ate other men, and . . . all of them were idolatrous; and [Ferdinand and Isabella] promised, if God should grant them life, to get rid of that abominable inhumanity and to uproot idolatry from all the lands of India which might come under their power."

So the cannibals, invented by those who had need of them, served their multiple purposes for the next several centuries, of which they remained of course unaware. It is appropriate that Shakespeare should have given them in the mind of Europe a local habitation and a name: the Carib, having become cannibal, became Caliban, "a savage and deformed slave," a despised creature of nature—"Thou earth, thou!" Prospero spits at him, the ultimate calumny, it seems, for Europe— and a "thing of darkness" fit only for usurpation and enslavement, serving "in offices that profit us." He is in fact that Wild Man who had always lurked on the edges of Europe's consciousness, now come to life in what is, but not for him, the brave New World.

[Thursday, 14 November.] Santa Cruz. While we were lying at anchor we saw coming from a cape a canoe . . . on which there were three or four Carib [sic] men with two Carib women and two Indian slaves . . . and we having the flagship's boat ashore, when we saw that canoe coming, quickly jumped into the boat and gave chase to that canoe. While we were approaching her the Caribs began shooting at us with their bows in such manner that, had it not been

for the shields, half of us would have been wounded. But I must tell you that to one of the seamen who had a shield in his hand came an arrow, which went through the shield and penetrated his chest three inches, so that he died in a few days.

We captured that canoe with all the men, and one Carib was wounded by a spear in such a way that we thought he was dead, and cast him for dead into the sea, but instantly saw him swim. In so doing we caught him and with the grapple hauled him over the bulwarks of the ship where we cut his head with an axe. The other Caribs, together with those slaves, we later sent to Spain.—Cuneo

Eleven days later, at Salt River on the island Colón called Santa Cruz, came the second pitched battle of the New World, and the first known deaths. That the casualties were equally shared belies the future.

The Admiral's fleet had not for nothing shipped out boatloads of soldiers, laden with European arms and an abiding belief in the savagery of the Caribs, and here, at the very first opportunity, entirely without provocation, they went after the natives. The European longboat, according to Dr. Chanca, carried some two dozen men, fully armed, and the Indian canoe held "not more than four men and two women," but the idea of a fair fight would have had no meaning in these circumstances. "Caribs"—who in fact these were not—were fit for slavery, or death. A culture familiar with violence, extending its Reconquista, could hardly be expected to have doffed its past just because it was up against naked people armed only with bows and arrows.

But still . . . still there is something ominous here:

They were captured and led before the Admiral [Coma wrote]. One of them was wounded seven times and his entrails were hanging out. Since it was thought that he could not be cured, he was cast into the sea. But keeping above water and raising one foot, he held on to his intestines with his left hand and swam courageously to the shore.

This affair terrified the Indians who were brought along as interpreters, for they were afraid that the Caribs might escape and undertake to [inflict] a more barbarous torture. Accordingly they insisted that the Caribs should be done away with. Therefore, the wounded Carib was caught again on shore. His hands and feet were bound more tightly and he was once again thrown headlong. But this resolute savage swam more furiously, until he was struck several times by arrows and perished.

It is perhaps fitting that this vengeance was wrought at the spot where we may mark the first time that Cristóbal Colón anchored at—but did not, as legend has it, "set foot upon"—the soil of what is now held to be, by extension, the territory of the United States.

The trail of Spanish violence throughout the Second Voyage from this point on is not well recorded, for none of the correspondents seems to have paid much attention to the coercive nature of this invasion—any more, indeed, than they would have thought of it as an invasion. There are suggestions, here and there, however. Cuneo, with complete casualness, described an encounter between the Admiral's longboats and some Indians in Jamaica:

When we wished to land they threw stones at us; wherefore the boats had to come back to the ships. We then equipped the boats with shields, crossbows and lombards and went toward the shore; and again they did the same to us. Then we, with those crossbows, immediately killed 16 or 18 of them, and with the lombards five or six. This happened past vespers or thereabouts; later we returned to the caravels.

Later, with similar nonchalance, Fernando described how the crew went ashore on Guadeloupe, "looting and destroying all they found," and he told of an instance on a deserted island off Española, when, "as they were leaving that island they killed eight seals which were sleeping in the sand. They also killed many pigeons [no doubt gulls] and other birds, for as that island is uninhabited and the animals are unaccustomed to men, they let themselves be killed with sticks." He made no mention that this slaughter was intended to provide food; it is likely that this was, for the Spanish, sport.

The apex of European violence on this voyage was the rounding up and transshipment of Indians to be sold as slaves in Cádiz. This practice, begun here in the outer Antilles, was apparently of Admiral

Colón's devising, fulfilling the promise made in the Santangel Letter but without any known authorization from the Spanish crown. The details are sketchy, but the fleet did take several dozen Caribs—or Carib-captives, it hardly mattered—and sent them back with the first returning ships in February 1494, along with a memo of Colón's proposing a regular shipment of humans from the Indies in exchange for cattle and supplies from Castile: "Payment for these things could be made to them in slaves, from among these cannibals, a people very savage and suitable [*dispuesta*] for the purpose, and well made and of very good intelligence . . . better than any other slaves." The Sovereigns were distinctly cool to the prospect—"This . . . has been postponed for the present," they wrote back that summer, "until another voyage has been made from there, and let the Admiral write what he thinks about it"—but that seemed to deter Colón not a bit. On the next fleet returning to Spain, in February 1495, he rounded up no fewer than 1,600 Tainos from the interior of Española—these the gentle Tainos, "no better people" in the world—and had them brought back under guard to the ships, where 550 of them, "among the best males and females," Cuneo says, were loaded in chains. And the others?

> Of the rest who were left the announcement went around that whoever wanted them could take as many as he pleased; and this was done. And when everybody had been supplied there were some 400 of them left to whom permission was granted to go wherever they wanted. Among them there were many women who had infants at the breast. They, in order the better to escape us, since they were afraid we would turn to catch them again, left their infants anywhere on the ground and started to flee like desperate people; and some fled so far that they were removed from our settlement of Isabela 7 or 8 days beyond mountains and across huge rivers; wherefore from now on scarcely any will be had.

Left their infants anywhere on the ground: does that not wrench? And at that, they may have been better off than those on the ships. Cuneo reports that "about 200 of those Indians died" and "we cast them into the sea," and half of those remaining were sick, and "very much fear cold, nor have they long life."

True, standards about slavery and human life were different in that age. Still, it is hard to fathom from what depths Europe could justify such wholesale deportation and death of fellow humans, and then go on to establish it as an enduring part of the economic life of the Americas for centuries to come.

> [*Thursday, 28 November. La Navidad.*] *At dawn next day, they repaired to the island in which . . . the Admiral had left some Christians in the previous year when he returned to Spain to the Sovereigns. . . . After eight days at sea, during which they explored everything on their course, they reached the Christians' harbor with feelings of joy and ineffable solicitude. For they were anxious to find their comrades safe and sound and then to hear about the customs of the Indians and about the trade with them. But the outcome was very different from what they had hoped.*
>
> —*Coma*

When the Admiral's mighty fleet finally put into its destination, the little presidio of La Navidad that Colón had involuntarily established the year before, it found a scene of devastation: neither the fortress nor any of the other buildings remained standing, the corpses of Spaniards were lying on the ground, "miserably deformed and corrupted," and not one of the forty-man garrison was alive. The reasons may have been multiple—there are suggestions of the Spaniards' fighting among themselves over gold and women, of their cruelty to the Tainos and attacks in revenge—but Coma's explanation is probably truest: "Bad feeling arose and broke out into warfare because of the licentious conduct of our men towards the Indian women, for each Spaniard had five women to minister to his pleasure" and "the husbands and relatives of the women, unable to take this, banded together to avenge this insult and eliminate this outrage (no race of men being free from jealousy), and attacked the Christians in great force."

About the sexual contact between the early Europeans and the women of the islands much has been written but very little is known. Colón himself makes no mention of the matter on the First Voyage, in part no doubt because he is writing directly to Ferdinand and Isabella, for the latter of whom at least sexual details would have been inappropriate; he does speak several times of naked women, even of those who "have very pretty bodies" (December 21), but with no salacious connotation. It is assumed by certain writers that great orgies took place on that expedition, the sailors being a month out of port and the Tainos people of "the most singular loving behavior" (December 24) who "gave everything they had" (October 12), but there is no direct evidence of this. One piece of evidence argues against it: it is thought that the strain of syphilis that proved so infectious in Europe after 1494 originated in the Caribbean, and yet at least the crew of the *Niña* returned to Palos on the First Voyage with no signs of the ravages of syphilis (which should have been evident by then) and in fact, as the Admiral himself attested, in remarkably good health.[3]

Far from being sexually available and willing, the women of the islands seem rather to have been naturally resistant to European advances. The first account we have of sexual intercourse between members of the two cultures—by the Italian nobleman, Cuneo, at Santa Cruz—is most revealing:

> While I was in the boat I captured a very beautiful Carib woman, whom the said Lord Admiral gave to me [!], and with whom, having taken her into my cabin, she being naked according to their custom, I conceived desire to take pleasure. I wanted to put my desire into execution but she did not want it and treated me with her finger nails in such a manner that I wished I had never begun. But seeing that (to tell you the end of it all), I took a rope and thrashed her well, for which she raised such unheard of screams that you would not have believed your ears. Finally we came to an agreement in such manner that I can tell you that she seemed to have been brought up in a school of harlots.

It is every rape fantasy ever penned, dripping with ugly macho triumph. One longs to know the young woman's version.

Such resistance, and such retaliation as the men around La Navidad demonstrated, did not seem to make any significant impact on the preconceptions lodged in European minds and myths, however. There, the idea of the people of nature as sexually active and indiscriminate was firmly fixed—as firmly as, and often mingled with, the idea of cannibalism. One of the reasons for the popularity of the accounts published as Vespucci's is their frequent descriptions of a lusty Indian society:

They marry as many wives as they please; and son cohabits with
mother, brother with sister, male cousin with female, and any
man with the first woman he meets. . . . The women as I have
said go about naked and are very libidinous; yet they have bodies
which are tolerably beautiful and cleanly. . . . When they had
the opportunity of copulating with Christians, urged by excessive lust, they defiled and prostituted themselves.[4]

Here, as in many similar accounts in the centuries to follow, Indian
sexuality exerted a complex and powerful pull on the European psyche, opening as it did the image of free, unbridled, and natural sexual
activity and thus triggering a combination of responses having to do
with the permissible and the taboo, the liberated and the repressed,
the desired and the feared, the human and the animal. And if the
resolution of those troubling responses took the form of rape and
exploitation, as it seems so often to have done, that too was well
lodged in the European psyche, the masculine attitude toward the
feminine, the acquisitive toward the desired, the dominant toward
the weak, the civilized toward the natural: the women of America
were as much a part of the bounty due the conquering Europeans as
the other resources in which it luxuriated.

What was thus implanted in the next few decades of European
contact was not merely a future population of *mestizos* but attitudes
toward sex and women that were every bit as exploitative and in-
strumental as those toward nature: Mother Earth and earth mother
were all one, and all to be used.

> [*Monday, 8 December. Isabela.*] *We stayed 10 days in the*
> *neighborhood, and on December 8 left that place [La*
> *Navidad] because it was unhealthy on account of the*
> *marshes which are there, and we went to another location*
> *still in the island, in an excellent harbor where we landed;*
> *and there we built 200 houses which are small like our*
> *hunting cabins and roofed with thatch.—Cuneo*

If La Navidad was a poor choice for Europe's first city in the New
World—poor harbor, "marshes" (mangrove swamps), exposure to
winter storms—it was at least inadvertent. When the Admiral abandoned that site, however, and moved eastward some seventy-five

miles to establish a town he called Isabela (after the queen, of course), the selection was entirely purposeful—and equally ill chosen. Whatever he may have known about the sea, Colón was singularly ignorant about the land, and almost willfully blind about settings that would be suitable for colonial outposts.

To begin with, Isabela had, Cuneo to the contrary, a very poor harbor, wide open on the north and northwest and so shallow that the larger ships of the fleet had to anchor more than half a mile offshore. The nearest fresh water was a river a mile away, a deficiency Colón later attempted to correct not by moving the town to the river but by ordering the construction of a canal to move the river to the town. The soils were poor and hardly suited to the European crops whose seeds the fleet brought over—especially not to such European "essentials" as wheat, chickpeas, beans, onions, and lettuce—and there was little rainfall in any case. And the pestiferous lowland marshes nearby may have helped breed the infectious diseases that soon laid much of the colony low.

In short, a most unfortunate seat of empire—and most perplexing, for it would have been no trouble to send a longboat to find, or ask the Tainos to direct them to, one of the excellent ports not far away. Yet that is where the Admiral offloaded his seventeen ships, his 1,500 companions, his two dozen horses, his innumerable cows and pigs and chickens, and his ambitions. There he established his colonial capital for the next three years, there he ordered the building of the proper signifiers of his rule, which Coma tells us were "a mighty fortress with lofty battlements," a "noble church bursting with the furnishings sent by Isabella," a storehouse, and a residence for himself, one of the few buildings made of stone, which he deigned to call, Coma swears, "the royal palace"—naturally because it would serve for the Sovereigns if they should "visit this well-favored land and behold the islands won for them so far from home."

As we might expect, the clouds of disaster shrouded that site as persistently as the clouds of the tropical afternoons: illness and debilitation, crop failure and famine, disorder and mutiny, repression and autocracy, uprising and retaliation. The history of Isabela is somewhat longer, but no happier, than that of La Navidad. And when Colón returned to Spain after two unfortunate years of governance, early in 1496, the first capital was quickly abandoned in favor of Santo Domingo, on the south shore of the island. According to Las Casas, the local Indians long afterward regarded the place as haunted by the ghosts of the departed Spaniards, whose awful cries in sickness and starvation, they insisted, still rang in the deserted streets. And at least one man swore that he once encountered there two rows of elegantly dressed *hidalgos* in the streets whose heads, when they made their customary gesture of greeting, came off with their hats, and whose bodies then vanished into air.*

[*Tuesday, January 20, 1494. Isabela.*] *After we had rested for several days in our settlement it seemed to the Lord Admiral that it was time to put into execution his desire to search for gold, which was the main reason he had started on so great a voyage full of so many dangers. . . . Therefore the Lord Admiral sent two captains with about 40 men, well armed, and with two Indians who were acquainted with that island to a place called Cibao, in which he had found that according to Ptolemy there must be plenty of gold in the rivers. . . .*

[The Indians] presented our captains with a certain amount of gold which included 3 big pieces, viz. one worth 9 castellanos,† another of 15 castellanos and the last of 12, which included a piece of rock. This gold they brought to the Lord Admiral telling him all that we have related above, as seen or heard. With this he and all of us made merry, not caring any longer about any sort of spicery but only of this blessed gold.—Cuneo

The Sovereigns might talk of religious conversion and the Admiral might talk of settlement and building, but the real purpose of colo-

---

*This same site was visited, on the eve of the Columbian Quatercentennial in 1891, by a United States naval expedition on the ship USS *Enterprise*, under Commander G. A. Converse, in search of "the ruins of the city of Isabella [*sic*]." The party of men that landed found the entire area deserted "within a mile and a half of the ruins" and saw nothing more than "various small, ill-defined heaps of stones, remnants of walls built of small unhewn stones, evidently laid in mortar, pieces of old tiles and pot-sherds, some of the latter glazed, and fragments of broad, roughly made bricks. . . . The trees, matted roots and trailing vines overspread the ground. . . . We overturned all the cut blocks of stone and examined them carefully in the hope of finding some mark or dates, but without success, and it is our belief that nothing of the kind exists."

The government of the Dominican Republic, in whose territory the site now resides, has promised "an archeological reconstruction" of Isabela in time for the Quincentennial celebrations.

†A *castellano* was worth 435 maravedis, or about $3 in pre-Depression U.S. dollars, equivalent to about twenty-five days' wages for a common laborer.

nization, after all, was "this blessed gold," and none of the men on the Second Voyage had the least doubt about it. Up to and including the new governor of Española, who lost no time in dispatching crews into the interior to track down those mines of gold that Martín Pinzón—poor Martín Pinzón, who had died just days after landing back in Palos—had proven to him on the First Voyage were certainly to be found.

The treasure turned out to be somewhat more elusive than the Spanish adventurers expected, however. High in the metamorphic intrusions of the Cordillera mountains that cut through the middle of Española there were indeed considerable deposits of gold, but the terrain was difficult and the auriferous rocks almost impossible to discern without special equipment or training, of which the new colonists seemed to be in oddly short supply. Most of the gold that could be found initially was in the beds of the rivers that washed down from these mountains or in the nearby floodplains, but the business of locating and then working placer mines required not only time but intensive labor, and the *hidalgos* were little inclined to expend much of either. Some quantity of nuggets could be found in various nooks and crannies, some of the gold-bearing rivers were comparatively easy to work, and with each new village there was more of the most accessible form of gold, the Taino jewelry and artifacts and trinkets that could be bartered away for next to nothing—and all that served to make the search for gold the driving preoccupation of the entire settlement for its first year. Cuneo, whose frankness at least is refreshing, tells of one trip on which the Lord Admiral himself led some five hundred men into the Cordillera plains, and although they were for some reason "not too well fitted out with clothes" and went through "20 days with terrible weather, bad food and worse drink," not a man was discouraged: "Out of covetousness of that gold, we all kept strong and lusty."

In the event, while they did not find any mines of gold, the Spaniards did amass enough so that the Admiral could send back what was said to be 30,000 ducats' worth (about 104,000 grams, or $70,000 at pre-Depression values) on the first return trip to Cádiz in early February, just a few weeks later. That was probably not quite the amount of treasure for which the Sovereigns had manned and outfitted a seventeen-ship flotilla, but it could at least be said to hold promise for the future, and to it Colón added some "cinnamon," pepper, sixty parrots, and an unspecified number of Indian captives, twenty-six of whom survived.* And enough to keep the hunt continuing apace, everyone from artisan to *hidalgo* still filled with dreams of great riches.

But lust for gold exacts its price. Predictably, it made men impatient with the necessary quotidian tasks of settlement—as when the Governor decided that he wanted a gristmill built and ended up complaining, in Fernando's words, that "in this project, as in all others, he had to stand over the workmen and urge them on, because they all shirked work." Nor were the noblemen of Castile much taken with the idea of work in the first place: they were soldiers largely, products of a crusading society, accustomed to military conquest, the parceling of newly won lands, and the division of booty; at one point, according to Peter Martyr, Colón complained that "the Spaniards which he took with him into these regions were given rather to sleep, play, and idleness, than to labor." It was this ingrained attitude, plus the illnesses that forced hundreds of men to their beds for months on end, that must have produced what the Governor chose to call "a mutiny" sometime very early in the year. Its nature is not well described, but according to Fernando, it was led by men who "had embarked on the voyage with the idea that as soon as they landed they could load themselves with gold and return home rich" and who were "disgruntled at having to work on the construction of the new town"; it doesn't seem to have amounted to very much, either, though a number of Spaniards did try to seize some ships in the harbor to sail them back to Castile, and when they were discovered they were held prisoner on the flagship and sent back on the next return fleet.

The Governor—to call him the Admiral at this point is to overlook his landward responsibilities, which many of his admirers naturally prefer to do—was not entirely innocent in the fomentation of such a rebellion. In addition to his high-handed and autocratic manner, he was after all responsible for having spun the stories of the "abun-

---

*Possibly this was the shipment that also sent back syphilis. No direct account of this return leg exists, but we do know that many of those shipped home had already fallen sick in Isabela and may well have been carrying the virus. Syphilis makes its first certain epidemic appearance in Italy in late 1494 or early 1495 during the Franco-Italian wars, and it is possible that Spanish soldiers, fighting against the French, carried it there. It is also possible that Spanish women contracted the disease from the Indians Colón left at court in 1493, or these newly shipped back in 1494, and transferred it thence to either Spanish soldiers or Italian travelers.

dant gold" and "great mines of gold and other metals" that had enticed
the hundreds of Castilian knights to this enterprise in the first place.
And he had no very clear ideas about how to inspire order in his
colony, or impose it where it could not be inspired—not in the capital,
and certainly not in the interior, where a thousand men or more were
trekking over the lands at their whim, armed and hungry, in search
of gold, with little compunction about using force to try to get it
(one Alonso de Hojeda, for example, is known to have cut off the
ears of two of the aides of a *kaseke* whom he accused of stealing some
Spaniards' clothes). What force Colón exerted to establish order,
although it had its precedents in Castilian rule, seemed ineffective in
the colony; Cuneo wrote that any Spaniard who was found secreting
gold away so that Colón and the crown could not exact their shares
"was well whipped" and "some had their ears slit and some the nose,
very pitiful to see," but it still did nothing to halt the thefts: "As
you know, the devil makes you do wrong," and "As long as Spain
is Spain, traitors will never be wanting."

> [*Friday, 25 April. Isabela.*] *I will tell you of the voyage
> on which I went with the Lord Admiral to go and find
> other islands and mainland. You must learn how on April
> 25 we sailed from our settlement with three caravels . . .
> and with us we had, between good and bad, 98 men.*
> —*Cuneo*

After the Admiral had dispatched the bulk of the fleet—twelve of
the seventeen sails—back to Spain in February 1494 and imposed
what authority he could over the disgruntled men of Isabela who
remained, he seems to have lost all taste for the messiness of government and started itching for the simplicities of the sea—specifically, to renew his search for the presumed mainland, or whatever
lands of treasure he hoped would be nearby. In his stead he installed
his youngest brother, Giacomo (known to the Spanish as Diego), a
shadowy figure of whom little is known other than that he had no
qualifications for such a responsibility of leadership except his fra-
ternal relationship, an example of Colón's repeated inability to pick
capable men on whom to depute power, relying instead on family
ties. (This unfortunate trait was manifested first at La Navidad, where
Colón had installed Diego de Arana, the cousin of his Cordovan

mistress Beatriz, as leader of the colony, a task for which he was manifestly unfit, as the complete loss of garrison and men might suggest.)

This trip of exploration is of some minor interest in that it was the first to discover Jamaica, the first to range the southern coast of Cuba (where for the second time Colón "took possession" of his "Juana," erecting another cross), the first to sight flamingoes and pilot fish and, we are assured, the tracks of lions and griffins. But it is of no real geographical significance and is important largely for the peculiar and revealing incident of what is known to historians as the "Cuba-no-island" oath.

On June 12, when the Admiral's three ships were almost at the westernmost end of Cuba, he decided that the entire crew should declare under oath that the coast they had been sailing along for the past four weeks was *not* that of an island at all but in fact "the mainland of the commencement of the Indies," and that if they went on, "land would be found where there are civilized people of intelligence who trade and know the world." And it was no casual oath, either: the Admiral made it clear that each man and boy among them had to take it, dispatched a notary public to write down their sworn statements, and decreed that all were "under a penalty of 10,000 maravedis and the cutting out of the tongue for every time that each one hereafter should say contrary," with an extra hundred lashes for gromets or "a person of such condition."

Confront this curious event any way we might, it still perplexes. True, Colón and his men at this point were weary, hungry, weak, and wanted to call their expedition to an end and go back to Isabela, and this would provide a legitimate excuse for their return—but they could easily have agreed to this lie informally, without all the notarized rigmarole. True, too, the Admiral must have been getting nervous again about justifying this second expensive voyage, inasmuch as there was all too little treasure found on Española, and on Cuba and Jamaica none at all—but a million men swearing to Cuba-no-island would still have hardly been enough to convince the hard-headed Spanish court. And true, according to the affidavit of the oath, Colón wanted very much to assure that "after having finished the said voyage no one might have cause, with malice, to speak ill of, and belittle the things which merit great praise"—but as he might reasonably have figured at the time, he was far more often belittled (ridiculed even) for this preposterous oath, even by his friend Cuneo (it "was only a very big island," he later wrote).

Was this perhaps another of Colón's self-serving attempts to delude not only his crew but, through them, the sponsors in Castile and even more the already restless colonists in Española? Or was this perhaps an outright *self*-delusion, born in a mind unsteadied by a recent illness—even Morison admits he was "mentally disturbed because he had found no certain evidence of being in the Orient"—and needing the ratification of the crew in order to become convincing, a sort of outward confirmation of inward dreams much as that other don, from La Mancha, might have sought?

It is impossible to tell. All one can say is that, in spite of the Admiral's continued insistence that Cuba was part of some Asian mainland, even as late as the summary letter of the Fourth Voyage in 1503, it would have taken a true madman to have actually believed such a thing for very long. No fewer than five maps drawn in Colón's lifetime, including the beautiful world map made around 1500 by Colón's sailing mate Juan de la Cosa ("*Maestro de hacer cartas*"—i.e., cartographer—on this very voyage), unquestionably show Cuba as an island, and as early as 1501 Peter Martyr reports that "there are many who affirm that they have sailed around Cuba."

> [*Wednesday, 24 September. Española.*] *They sailed to the eastern end of Española and from there to an island that lies between Española and San Juan and that the Indians call Amona.*
>
> *From that point on the Admiral ceased to record in his journal the day's sailing, nor does he tell us how he returned to Isabela. He relates only that because of his great exertions, weakness, and scanty diet he fell gravely ill in crossing from Amona to San Juan; he had a high fever and a drowsiness, so that he lost his sight, memory, and all his other senses.—Fernando*

Illness overtook the men of the Second Voyage from their very first days onshore at La Navidad, and it was unabating thereafter. At Isabela at one point in 1494 Dr. Chanca estimated that "one third of our people have fallen sick," and Fernando reported that "most of them were weak and ill, with certain diseases caused by the thinness of the air, which did not agree with them." Syphilis was probably one of the culprits, possibly malaria as well, but as near as we can tell from the meager symptomatic evidence the principal disease was probably bacillic dysentery, transmitted by unsanitary latrine facilities, and ignorance.

Disease was compounded by a general state of dietary deficiency and in some cases starvation that left the Europeans weak and vulnerable; this fact seems almost unbelievable in retrospect, if we consider the bountiful menu they had before them: cassava bread, sweet potatoes, corn, peppers, peanuts, fish of all kinds, clams, conches, turtles, papayas, pineapples, plums, pears, and so on and on. But very little of this cornucopia, apparently, would the Spanish eat—although eventually they became accustomed to, indeed dependent on, the cassava the Tainos prepared for them—and very seldom would they fish and almost never would they hunt. The bizarre refrain of hunger and malnutrition would be almost ceaseless during these early years of settlement, until the colonists finally determined which *European* crops would grow in the new lands. (One reason for the malnutrition may also be Spanish ignorance—they never learned "the way nor the time to sow," Cuneo says—which he explains as the result of the feeling that "no one wants to live in those countries.")

The Admiral's own stretch of ill health began in December, when he came down with some unspecified disease—probably dysentery —that laid him low until mid-March. It seems to have recurred in late April on the voyage to Cuba, when, Fernando says, "he was seriously indisposed" for eight days; during that time he was obviously neither eating nor sleeping well, and at one point he claims that he "had not undressed and slept a full night in bed" for the last four weeks. Just five months later, after a summer of grueling and unrewarding coasting along Cuba, when food was often scarce and he "sometimes went eight days with less than three hours' sleep," an even graver sickness befell him. The fleet then decided to return right away to Isabela, where they arrived on September 29. The Admiral had to be carried ashore, where, Fernando says, "he lay ill for more than five months."

Thus began a history of serious ailment that would bedevil the Admiral for the rest of his life—that would at times make him completely incapacitated and at times, all evidence suggests, bring him very near to the realms of madness.

No one is sure precisely what Colón was suffering from, and everything from syphilis to gout has been proposed. It is known, however, that a small percentage of those who contract dysentery are persistently and recurrently plagued by a specific triad of related diseases —arthritis, uveitis, and urethritis (inflammation of the joints, the eyes, and the urinary tract, respectively)—that is called Reiter's syndrome after the twentieth-century doctor who first diagnosed it. We do not know anything at all about the Admiral's urinary tract, fifteenth-century delicacy being what it was, but we do know something about the other symptoms. His illness on his return to Isabela was diagnosed by Dr. Chanca as "gout," which would have been the way to describe a severe inflammation of the legs and feet, and he had recurrent bouts of arthritis of the spine and lower limbs, sometimes so severe as to immobilize him throughout the remaining years of his life, and was in fact "much afflicted" by it on his deathbed. Blindness, which he says struck him during his September bout, was also recurrent, accompanied by retinal bleeding on both the Third and Fourth Voyages, at one time afflicting him so severely that he was not able to disembark and set foot on the mainland that he had so long been searching for.

Reiter's syndrome, then, following dysentery, is the most reasonable diagnosis of Colón's medical symptoms. Little on the record connects it specifically to outright mental disorders, but I am persuaded that we can lay much of the Admiral's somewhat bizarre, at times quite demented, behavior in the years ahead to this most devitalizing disease.

The figure of the Admiral, in what should have been the days of his triumph, lying ill and helpless for months on end in his "royal palace" while the affairs of his fledgling colony deteriorated around him, is one that appropriately calls forth compassion. Compassion, though, we may be sure, was not the emotion that engaged the Spaniards among whom he lay: it was not a feeling that the traditions of the Reconquista would have much bred in the hearts of its *hidalgos*, where the freight of medieval machismo would in any case not have left much room, and it was certainly not their response to this foreigner who had enticed them to a vile, infectious, inhospitable wilderness with promises of wealth where there were only baubles.

Not that compassion was a sentiment to which the Admiral was much given or would have inspired by example. For the two score men who had perished at La Navidad, companions at sea and heroes in the adversity he had caused, he expressed not a single emotion when discovering their awful fate the year before, if we may believe all our chroniclers. No sorrow, anguish, despondency, no word in elegy, no pause for obsequies or requiems; only, according to Fernando: "The Admiral went ashore and felt much grief *at the sight of the ruins of the houses and the fort.*" In that bosom little capacity for empathy, and the only pity it ever seemed capable of—though this in extenso—was for himself.

It is said, by Las Casas among others, that what perplexed the Tainos of Española most about the strange white people from the large ships was not their violence, not even their greed, nor in fact their peculiar attitudes toward property, but rather their coldness, their hardness, their lack of love.

Chapter Seven

1495–1500

FOR THE last six years of the fifteenth century, Cristóbal Colón served as the governor and viceroy of the island of Española, a man of the sea tragically lost on the land he found and named, swept by currents of human politics he could not chart and winds of human passions he could not tack, still unable to find *querencia*, to know a home, to sink his roots. Although he would spend two years back in Spain and return on one more voyage during this time, his life was essentially taken up with the difficulties, many of them of his own manufacture, of overseeing the first implantation of Europe in the lands he still thought of as the Indies. It was not a happy time, not for the Governor, not for the island, and at the end of it he returned to Castile in many ways a broken man, racked by his continuing illness, in the eyes of the Spanish Sovereigns an embarrassment and in the eyes of the Spanish public a disgrace.

Nonetheless, by inadvertence as much as by design, those six years reveal much of the character of the entire imperial experience, not alone of Spain but of all the colonizing nations of Europe that were to follow. They were years of violence and subjugation, and of that cruelty of human to human that created what comes to be known as La Leyenda Negra—the Black Legend—by which the Spanish were castigated for much of the sixteenth century. They were years of environmental despoliation and waste, of the ignorant and destructive transplantation of one culture, and agriculture, heedlessly upon another. They began with great misfortunes, great misadventure, and great ignorance, and ended with great fortunes, great adventure, and the great vision not only of a new hemisphere but of a new world.

One might now wish that those years had left a different record, provided a model of cultural contact befitting both sides. But Europe, this medieval Europe becoming modern, was not equipped for such a role; it was, as J. H. Elliott has pointed out, a culture imbued with "its own unique status and position in God's providential design," and, he asks, "how can we expect a Europe so conscious of its own infallibility . . . even to make the effort to come to terms with a world other than its own?" In any event, it did not.

As soon as he was recovered enough from the illness that kept him bedridden until early 1495, Colón set himself to try to bring some order to a colony that had only descended into worse chaos under the inept misrule of his brother Diego; and he now had beside him for the job another brother, Bartolomé (as it was in Spanish), who had arrived in Española the previous June and whom he made, on dubious authority and to the displeasure of the colonists, *adelantado*, in effect coruler of the island.* Their task was considerable.

While the Admiral was off exploring Cuba, the colonists, whom he had ordered "to patrol the country and reduce it to the service of the Catholic Sovereigns," had taken to their role a little too ardently, rampaging through the island worse than before, searching everywhere for gold, begging or stealing food, kidnapping boys to serve as slaves and women as concubines, beating and maiming at will, raping and pillaging at ease. "Each one went where he willed among the Indians," Fernando reported—and he was hardly one to play up the deficiencies of his countrymen—"stealing their property and wives and inflicting so many injuries upon them that the Indians resolved to avenge themselves on any that they found alone or in small groups." Hence, on his return, "the Admiral found the island in a pitiful state, with most of the Christians committing innumerable outrages for which they were mortally hated by the Indians, who refused to obey them."

But the Governor's response, if perhaps typical, did not augur well: he chose to punish the victim. On March 24, 1495, he assembled two hundred soldiers in full armor (equipped with arquebuses, crossbows, lances, pikes, swords, and twenty vicious dogs) and another twenty mounted cavalry (whose horses, the likes of which the islands had never seen, were often enough to send the Tainos flying in fear),

*The title, fittingly, was borrowed from the Reconquista and meant, literally, "lord of the march" (from *adelantar*, "to advance").

and marched out of Isabela to subdue the recalcitrant natives and tame the countryside. In the valley of the Vega Real, about ten miles south—a valley that Las Casas said the Spaniards had considered "some sort of Paradise" the year before—the little army encountered a force that Fernando solemnly gives as "more than one hundred thousand Indians" (probably a tenfold exaggeration) and, having divided in two, descended upon them with such ferocity that they "fled in all directions." No pity now for the "gentle Tainos," who might just as well have been Moors: the soldiers mowed down dozens with point-blank volleys, loosed the dogs to rip open limbs and bellies, chased fleeing Indians into the bush to skewer them on sword and pike, and "with God's aid soon gained a complete victory, killing many Indians and capturing others who were also killed." Of the valley that was Paradise they made a desert, and called it peace.

And this was government for Española, based largely upon raw force and exercised primarily at the whim of the Governor and his brother. When Colón wanted to capture the recalcitrant *kaseke* Caonabó, whom he described as "the principal king of the island," he dispatched a commander who gave the Taino leader some polished steel handcuffs and leg irons and persuaded him to wear them, just as, he said, did the great King of Spain; once shackled, Caonabó was dragged away from his village and led back to Isabela, thrown in jail, and then shipped to Castile—dying en route, Martyr says, for "anguish of mind." When Bartolomé wanted to punish six Tainos who had buried some Christian icons in a field and pissed on them, he had them arrested, "tried," and publicly burned at the stake; what he did not know was that the Indians had put the Christian gods in their fields and blessed them in traditional fashion, the better to fertilize their crops. When Colón learned that some Indians had taken Spanish property—their sense of ownership being quite different from that of the Europeans—he ordered their noses and ears clipped, and when he subsequently learned of three more "thieves" he decided to have them beheaded. Forts were established in every major settlement across the island—at least seven of them by 1500—but it was the gallows that was the real symbol of colonial rule: gallows, usually several of them, marked every Spanish town, and before the decade was out no fewer than 340 of them stretched across the Vega Real.

Then to force were added two other branches, so to speak, of colonial government: tribute and slavery.

The tribute system, instituted by the Governor sometime in 1495, was a simple and brutal way of fulfilling the Spanish lust for gold while acknowledging the Spanish distaste for labor. Every Taino over the age of fourteen had to supply the rulers with a hawk's bell full of gold every three months (or in gold-deficient areas, twenty-five pounds of spun cotton); those who did were given a token to wear around their necks as proof that they had made their payment; those who did not were, as Fernando says discreetly, "punished" —by having their hands cut off, as Las Casas says less discreetly, and left to bleed to death. (A most gruesome engraving, printed in a seventeenth-century edition of Las Casas's *Brevísima relación*, shows a Spanish axeman cutting off the hand of one naked Taino while two others, handless, stare in terror, a third is having his eyes or nose cut, and Spanish troops in the background, using dogs and pikes, round up more victims for the chopping block.) Now a hawk's bell is not such a large affair—say about as big as a good-sized thimble—but the Tainos had never found (or cared to find) all that much gold on their island, and what there was had to be laboriously panned from the gold-bearing streams or uncovered by trenches dug in alluvial plains and mountainsides. There was no way that they could meet their quotas, even dredging all the known auriferous areas, nor any way that their sparse cotton plants could supply enough spools to provide a substitute. The system was quite simply, in Las Casas's words, "impossible and intolerable."

Slave labor was also instituted almost as soon as Colón succeeded in pacifying the island. The residents of Isabela, we may remember, were allowed to "take as many as they pleased" before the return voyage of February 1495, and within a few years slavery had more or less replaced the faltering tribute system as a means of wresting wealth from the land. Before the decade was over Colón installed it formally through the institution known as *encomienda*, a new variant of an old Castilian principle by which the Governor could give, or "commend," certain Indians to various colonists (*encomenderos*) to use as they might choose (for tribute or forced labor), in return for which the masters' only obligation was to provide their charges with instructions on becoming good Christians. It was not *called* slavery, to be sure, and indeed the Indians were supposed to be paid pittances, but that was a provision no one much bothered to enforce, and the institution was essentially indistinguishable from outright slavery; Las

Casas would call it "a moral pestilence . . . invented by Satan." It was to prove an enduring legacy of Colón's administration, however, for it was made an official policy on Española in 1502, sanctioned by the crown in 1503, and thereafter taken by the conquistadors on their invasions of Mexico, Peru, and La Florida.

The slave trade itself, it might be noted, was treated ambivalently by the Spanish crown during this period. A royal letter of April 12, 1495, permitted Colón to sell Indian slaves in Andalusia ("You must sell them as seems best to you"), but it was countermanded four days later ("because we wish to consult about the matter with lawyers, theologians, and specialists in canon law, to see whether they can be sold in good conscience"), and in June the Sovereigns ordered Indians in Spain set free and no more brought. This did not prevent the Admiral himself, however, from shipping some thirty Indians back with him when he returned to Castile in June of the following year, or Bartolomé from consigning an additional three hundred that summer, or occasional slave shipments from being sent back by enterprising captains thereafter, apparently with no punishments exacted by the crown. Ultimately, of course, it was the trade not in Indian but in African bodies that marked these islands, but that vast and far more devastating trade did not begin until around 1505, and was not the fault—at least not directly—of the Admiral's.

Such government as this, however, designed by the Governor to conquer and control the Taino population, apparently had little effect in controlling the Spaniards now on the island, some 630 of them in 1495, perhaps as many as a thousand by 1500, and none too savory a lot. They were more *canalla* than *hidalgo* now, for most of the gentlemen had chosen to return to Castile, and those left behind, like those who could be attracted out, came largely from the lower rungs of Spanish life, some of them, Fernando reported, with clipped noses and ears, sure signs of convicted robbers in Castile as in Española. These men—those at any rate who were not sick month after month—were allowed to roam through the countryside in search of their beloved gold, with or without *encomiendas* of their own, and it is hardly surprising that they spread with them the worst traits of conquistadorian cruelty and avarice. Or indeed, their own kind of government: "They made a law among themselves," Las Casas tells us, "that for one Christian whom the Indians killed, the Christians should kill a hundred Indians." He was not exaggerating.

Las Casas, who came out to Española in 1502 and was himself an *encomendero* for eight years before taking his religious vows, i[s] chief source for the descriptions of the almost unbelievable a[b] committed by his fellow colonists, and one is led to assume that [th]ey applied with no less veracity to the earlier years as well. He was, as we know, a committed partisan of the Indians when he wrote these descriptions, but there is no reason to doubt his accuracy, and all that he recounts has the indisputable ring of truth to it: "I saw all the above things," he repeatedly assures us, and, "All these did my own eyes witness."

The Spaniards, Las Casas reports, "made bets as to who would slit a man in two, or cut off his head at one blow; or they opened up his bowels. They tore the babes from their mother's breast by their feet, and dashed their heads against the rocks. . . . They spitted the bodies of other babes, together with their mothers and all who were before them, on their swords." For more formal retribution they would hang chosen Tainos from a gallows frame, "just high enough for their feet to nearly touch the ground, and by thirteens, in honour and reverence for our Redeemer and the twelve Apostles, they put wood underneath and, with fire, they burned the Indians alive." Once, when Las Casas was accompanying a contingent of Spanish troops, they came upon a group of Tainos sitting around the plaza of their village. Having sharpened their swords earlier that morning on whetstones in a riverbed, the soldiers were eager to test them out, and the occasion somehow offered itself:

> A Spaniard, in whom the devil is thought to have clothed himself, suddenly drew his sword. Then the whole hundred drew theirs and began to rip open the bellies, to cut and kill those lambs— men, women, children and old folk, all of whom were seated, off guard and frightened, watching the mares and the Spaniards. And within two credos, not a man of all of them there remains alive. The Spaniards enter the large house nearby, for this was happening at its door, and in the same way, with cuts and stabs, begin to kill as many as they found there, so that a stream of blood was running, as if a great number of cows had per- ished. . . . To see the wounds which covered the bodies of the dead and dying was a spectacle of horror and dread.

Nor was Las Casas the only observer. Fernández de Oviedo, who was later the official historian of the Indies and a great partisan of

Spanish imperialism, nonetheless tells quite similar horror stories—
of one *kaseke* the Spaniards named "Quemado" ("Burnt One"), for
example, "because in fact and quite without cause they burned him,
because he did not give them as much gold as they asked him
for"—and his conclusions are equally harsh. The New World, he
wrote in his *Historia general*, was a victim of the "conquistadors,
who would more accurately be called depopulators or squanderers
of the new lands," and of the "private soldiers, who like veritable
hangmen or headsmen or executioners or ministers of Satan, [cause]
various and innumerable cruel deaths . . . as uncountable as the
stars."

At the end of his long life, Las Casas would look back at this early
period of pillage and murder in the Indies—"cruelty never before
seen, nor heard of, nor read of"—and write, in his will, this anguished, unforgiving prophecy:

> I believe that because of these impious, criminal and ignominious
> acts, perpetrated unjustly, tyrannously, and barbarously upon
> them, God will visit His wrath and His ire upon Spain for her
> share, great or small, in the blood-stained riches, obtained by
> theft and usurpation, accompanied by such slaughter and anni-
> hilation of these people—unless she does much penance.

No convincing evidence of Lordly wrath and ire served to illicit such
penance during his lifetime—he died in 1566, when Spain was taking
out nearly $8 million in blood-stained riches a year—but the proph-
ecy was accurate nonetheless. Spain did end up paying, in the next
century and the centuries to follow, for the manner and severity of
its conquest, and left a legacy, no less for itself than its colonies, that
was, like the legend, mostly black.

It is almost impossible to assess the toll that all of this took upon
Taino society, except in the crudest way, but suffice it to say that it
was devastating indeed, and ultimately fatal.

Murders, official and otherwise, the hard life of tribute and slave
labor, starvation, suicide, and the severe social dislocations caused
by the uprooting of families and communities, accompanied by forced

resettlement onto *encomiendas*, exacted many thousands of victims. Las Casas offered this summary:

> In this time, the greatest outrages and slaughterings of people were perpetrated, whole villages being depopulated. . . . The Indians saw that without any offence on their part they were despoiled of their kingdoms, their lands and liberties and of their lives, their wives, and homes. As they saw themselves each day perishing by the cruel and inhuman treatment of the Spaniards, crushed to the earth by the horses, cut in pieces by swords, eaten and torn by dogs, many buried alive and suffering all kinds of exquisite tortures, some of the Princes, particularly those in Vega Real . . . decided to abandon themselves to their unhappy fate with no further struggles, placing themselves in the hands of their enemies that they might do with them as they liked. There were still those people who fled to the mountains.

He then supplies, as a telling, sad example, the story of the *kaseke* Guacanagarí, the loyal friend of Colón's through whose efforts the cargo of the *Santa María* was saved and the first settlement built at La Navidad, who was forced to flee "from the massacres and cruelty of the Christians" and "died a wanderer in the mountains, ruined and deprived of his state."

It was on tribulations such as these that Las Casas and the other earlier historians tended to dwell—"war, slavery, and the mines," as Las Casas said—and out of this that the first English and Dutch propagandists constructed the Black Legend. But in recent years a new school of scholars has begun to emphasize a quite different cause of Indian devastation: the microbes and viruses that the Spanish introduced into what epidemiologists call a "virgin-soil population," which spread such diseases as measles, influenza, typhus, pneumonia, tuberculosis, diphtheria, and pleurisy, any one of which could bring death to the vulnerable Taino population—and then, in 1518, the even deadlier smallpox. These would have been little understood by contemporary chroniclers, given the state of Renaissance pathology, and probably seldom identified as the causes of the widespread morbidity, but the consensus is now that they were the real killers, of the Tainos and the Caribs in the Antilles and, later, of the mainland populations. "It was their germs," as Alfred Crosby sums it up, "not these imperialists themselves, for all their brutality and callousness, that are chiefly responsible for sweeping aside the indigens."*

Whatever the causes, the eventual destruction was catastrophic. We must enter the world of historical demography here in order to assess it properly, and that is a somewhat uncertain one, relying as it must on incomplete records, unprofessional estimates, and often nothing more than middens and mounds; a somewhat controversial one as well, stirring as it does impassioned arguments between those who like to think of the Americas as essentially empty continents and those who wish to show that they were substantially populated. For a long time in this century it was assumed that the population of the Caribbean islands in 1492 could not have been much more than 200,000 or 300,000, and estimates by Las Casas among others of "more than three million" were discounted as the reckless exaggerations of amateurs. In recent years, however, considerable scholarly interest has been focused on the population issue, thorough searches of contemporary records have been undertaken, and a more reliable count has been arrived at.

In the case of Española, for example, by far the most populous of the islands, we now know that in 1496 Bartolomé Colón, acting while his brother returned to Spain, authorized a headcount of Indian adults, presumably in order to keep track of the tribute system, and came up with a figure of some 1.1 million. Inasmuch as this did not count children below fourteen, the aged, *kasekes*, and some others —estimated at perhaps another 40 percent of the population—and covered only that half of the island in Spanish control, a more accurate figure for the whole of Española would be something closer to a little more than 3 million. Moreover, the Bartolomé survey was taken four years after the initial contact with European pathogens and two years after the imposition of the debilitating European rule, so we may assume that the population of 1492 was even larger than that. The

*One reason that the Indian populations, in the Caribbean as elsewhere, were so vulnerable to diseases of any kind is that, to an extraordinary extent, the Americas were free of any serious pathogens. The presumed passage of the original Indian populations across the Bering Strait tens of thousands of years before served to freeze to death most human disease carriers except a few intestinal ones, it is thought, and there were apparently none established on the continents previously, so in general the Indians enjoyed remarkably good health, free of both endemic and epidemic scourges. As Henry Dobyns says in his examination of aboriginal North American populations, *Their Numbers Become Thinned*, "People simply did not very often die from illnesses" before the Europeans came.

two leading researchers here, Sherburne Cook and Woodrow Borah of the University of California at Berkeley, have calculated the rate of population decline *after* 1496, extrapolated from that a curve going back to 1492, and come up with an estimate of the original island population at just under 8 million people.

That makes the next figures we have almost unbelievable. Spanish surveys of Española taken in 1508, 1510, 1514, and 1518 all show the same rough picture, of a population then *under 100,000* and declining precipitously. The most detailed census, the *repartimiento* of 1514, listed just 22,000 adults (which Cook and Borah expand to 27,800 to include those officially uncounted): *from 8 million to 28,000 in just over twenty years.* That is more than decimation, it is a carnage of more than 99 percent, something we must call closer to genocide, and within a single generation. By 1542, according to Las Casas, who was there at the time, only 200 Tainos remained on Española, probably the last of that people anywhere in the islands. Within a decade or two of that, they were extinct. Dark indeed, the legend.*

But it would be a falsification of history to let the matter rest there. It is important to realize that there is not a single European nation which, when the opportunity came, did not engage in practices as vicious and cruel as those of Spain—and in the case of England, worse—with very much the same sort of demographic consequences. The Spanish, for all their faults, at least thought it right to convert, and in many cases to marry, the Indians, regarding them on a plane of humanity, capable of receiving Christian precepts and European civilization, above that generally accorded by other colonizers. And it was they, it must be remembered—or some among them, such as Las Casas—who ultimately exposed the darkness of the record and raised the protests in the highest circles, leading to a series of reforms, beginning with the Laws of Burgos in 1512 and going on to the New Laws of 1542, which mitigated at least the worst abuses of colonial rule. Had there not been such a public outcry, in fact, there would likely have been no Black Legend, since it was this that the Protestant nations used as the ammunition for their propaganda war against

---

*A recent scholar has reported that there are estimated to be a thousand people in eastern Cuba as of 1989 who exhibited Indian "characteristics," at least some of whom claim to be descendants of the original Tainos. A cultural survival, possibly, but unlikely to be a genetic one.

Spain, to disgrace its reputation in Europe and challenge its hegemony in the Americas.

As heedless as they were of the people of the islands, the Spanish invaders were even more careless, and nearly as destructive, of the islands themselves.

It was the Admiral's design all along, and it seemed only natural to the Sovereigns, to export Castilian life to the Indies and to turn Española, as its name suggested, into a Spanish island, with Spanish livestock, Spanish crops, Spanish food and drink. We can tell, by the extent of provisioning records and the commentaries of the early travelers, that no thought was given to whether the foreign life-forms belonged in the islands, whether they would prosper, whether they would damage the native species: it simply was assumed that anything the Europeans wanted to grow would and should grow. An appreciation of the differences of natural environments and the fragility of established ecosystems was not, apparently, for all their classical learning and Renaissance scientism, something the minds of Europe took with them abroad; as long as there was land there, neither native populations nor native species were regarded as any barrier to implantation. "The European," in Crosby's words, "immediately set about to transform as much of the New World as possible into the Old World."*

The first species that Colón chose to import were those that made up the staples of the Mediterranean diet (psychologically, anyway) —chickpeas, wheat, wine, and olive oil. The wheat and chickpeas withered in the heat—"at the most [they] grow nine inches," Cuneo noted in his letter, "then all at once they wilt and dry"; the vines produced sparse and stunted grape clusters out of which no liquid could be pressed; the olive trees wouldn't take at all. (The general

---

*Europe itself of course had seen the evidence of the dangers of environmental tampering: the natural history of that continent is replete with instances of the introduction of foreign species producing severe environmental consequences. A minor example, close to home: Colón's own father-in-law introduced the European hare to the Madeiran island of Porto Santo, where he was the governor, sometime in the mid–fifteenth century. That animal, as is its bent, multiplied so rapidly that it took over the entire island within a single year, eating every green thing upon it, starving out the native animals that had depended on that greenery for survival, removing ground cover and exposing soils to severe wind and rain erosion, and eventually turning it into a virtual desert. The settlers there had to move to Madeira until the rabbit population, as in all population blooms, overstressed its environment and experienced crash and die-down.

response to that was well expressed by the Spanish cleric who argued some years later that since these forsaken lands couldn't produce the wine necessary for the celebration of the Lord's sacrament, He obviously hadn't meant their inhabitants to become Christians in the first place.) Other European plants did rather better—cauliflowers and cabbages, melons, cucumbers, and radishes—but the attempt to change the environment to suit the European diet was never successful, and instead the colonists decided to rely on imports from the homeland; hardly any thought was given—I know of none on record—to trying to change the diet to suit the environment. This was in large part responsible for the recurrent famines that affected Europeans on Española from the start: not that there was not enough food—that couldn't be, with the productivity of the *conuco* system —but that it wasn't *Castilian* food and Ysla Española wasn't Spain. Even during those periods of famine when they came perforce to depend on Taino food grown and supplied by Tainos amid all the hardships, the Spanish absorbed only the smallest elements of it into their regular diets, regarding it as somehow, well, *foreign*.

Despite this spotty beginning, the Spanish, under Colón and well into the sixteenth century, introduced a whole range of European animal and plant species, intentionally and inadvertently, with severe and ultimately near-ruinous effect. It hardly mattered whether the new species were benign or malignant: the more they adapted themselves to their new environment the more they displaced the native species, the more they altered and eventually transformed the long-stable ecosystem of the islands.

Take, for instance, the large European mammals that were brought over on the Second Voyage. Nothing of the kind (nothing larger than a small dog) lived in the Caribbean, no competing species of any sort, so there were no established diseases to threaten them and, with the exception of sheep and goats, they bloomed spectacularly. Cattle reproduced so successfully on Española that, it was said, thirty or forty stray animals would multiply to three or four hundred in a couple of years; horses did so well—a lucky thing for the Castilian *caballeros* there—that the original twenty had multiplied to at least sixty or seventy within a decade and by 1507 imports of horses were forbidden; pigs were so numerous by 1500, just seven years after the first four pairs were introduced, that according to Las Casas they were called *infinitos*.

All these voracious animals naturally dominated and then destroyed native habitats, rapidly and thoroughly, with human help and without. The record is inadequate, since none among the colonists, even those who would take on the job of describing native species for audiences at home, ever noted the extensive alteration of the environment that was taking place literally beneath their feet. Las Casas, however, does mention that a certain grass common in Española at the turn of the century had vanished just forty years later, a victim of the hungry herds, and we may presume there were many similar floral die-outs. Crosby, without specifics, considers that the spread of these large species "doubtlessly had much to do with the extinction of certain plants, animals . . . and even the Indians themselves" who lost out "in the biological competition with the newly imported livestock."

Typical of this process was the *ranchero* system that Colón imported wholesale from Castile—complete with roundups, lassos, open ranges, branding, and cowboys on horseback—and installed with herds of 500 head or more (and by the 1520s, according to Oviedo, some of 8,000 or more). These stocks were let loose everywhere, in fields abandoned because of depopulation, in valleys cleared of forest cover, in native *conuco* farms, even on steep hillside slopes; everywhere they depleted the native grass species, compacted the tropical soils, and stripped the ground cover that had resisted soil erosion. Thus here, in its very first New World outpost, Europe implanted a system, and endowed a legacy, that would go on to mark indelibly both of the continents it was to conquer—and would produce a red-meat–dependent society that almost automatically ensured environmental destruction.*

In addition to the invasive animals, the plants introduced by the Spanish had a deleterious effect. These included the ones established accidentally—such aggressive pioneer species as daisies and dandelions and nettles that moved into any open space and crowded out the weaker native species—as well as those that were deliberately introduced and fostered, such as sugar, brought in from the Canaries, which took immediately to the Caribbean climate and was rapidly

---

* Another destructive effect of the *ranchero* system was that it depended on Spanish private *ownership* of Caribbean lands. This *repartimiento* land-grant system, begun by Colón in 1498 (and reaffirmed a year later), meant not only the rapid displacement of Tainos who were said to be encroaching on private property, but the creation of a Spanish elite class, here and subsequently on the mainland, that effectively denied land ownership to indigenous populations and produced the dangerous inequities that have stained Latin societies to this day.

installed in all lands not given over to food and livestock. Again, though we know with precision what invader species established themselves in the islands, we have a very imperfect record of the species that were lost: none of the contemporary chroniclers noted them, and despite the "obviously . . . spectacular biogeographical phenomenon going on right under their noses," they "did not understand it," Crosby says, and certainly did not take the trouble to write about it.

Not just the *kinds* of plants but the *system* of planting: the European style of intensive agriculture, particularly row-style plantation agriculture that the Spanish established everywhere, was the worst sort to introduce to a tropical ecosystem. It was done by plowing, which laid soil to waste far more severely than the Indians' planting stick and hoe; it used monocultural open-field planting, which exposed the surface soils to wind and water erosion far more drastically than the Tainos' careful *conuco* planting; and it required (along with fuel and shelter needs) the cutting and almost complete clearing of the heavy evergreen forests that were the stable, old-growth vegetation throughout the Caribbean.

The inevitable results of this were noticeable within a few decades. Soils were quickly eroded by the torrential rains and fierce winds of what the Tainos called *hurricana*, with attendant loss of nutrients and organisms; rivers began to silt up and in some cases went completely dry; estuarine habitats were destroyed by siltation and estuarine animals disappeared; and with the loss of the dense tree cover the whole hydrology, and thus the whole climate, of the area was slowly altered, at considerable cost to both land and water species. Interestingly, Colón himself was astutely aware of this last point, realizing the importance of the forests for local climate: he had noted on his trip to Cuba in 1494 that "in the Canary, Madeira, and Azore Islands . . . since the removal of forests that once covered those islands, they do not have so much mist and rain as before," and again in 1498 wrote of the Cape Verde Islands that they "have a very misleading name, for he never saw a single green thing, everything was dry and sterile." This wisdom, however, had no influence on the agricultural policies he permitted in Española, in which deforestation played a major part.

Just two decades after the tenure of Governor Colón, in 1518, Alonso de Zuaso wrote to a friend at the Spanish court, "If I were to tell you all the damage that has been done, I should never make an end. . . . Although these islands had been, since God made the earth, prosperous and full of people lacking nothing they needed; yet . . . they were laid waste, inhabited only by wild animals and birds, and useless indeed for the service either of God or of Their Highnesses." Las Casas would add, some years later, of Española: "It was the first to be destroyed and made into a desert." But not the last.

In the midst of all of this, early in 1496, the Governor decided to return home. Not, surely, because he looked upon the works of his government and found them good, for even he, so often seeing what he wished, could not blink away certain bitter truths: the Spaniards on the island, lords and louts alike, cared little for the Colóns' discipline and seemed to wander and plunder at will; the supplies of gold promised to the Sovereigns were still rather meager even after two years of working both placer mines and miners to the full; sicknesses as persistent as dysentery and as debilitating as syphilis continued to weaken and kill off his colonists; the Tainos were dying in such numbers that there weren't enough laborers to maintain either the mines or the fields; not one Indian had as yet been converted to the Catholic faith, though conversion was as high on the Admiral's agenda as it was on the Sovereigns'; and worst of all, everyone on the island, like all those who had returned to Castile, had nothing but malediction to bestow upon the man who had served the Sovereigns, as he said, "with unheard of and unseen devotion" for all these years and had begun that Second Voyage with such high hopes. Thus it was only natural that Colón thought it perhaps best to get back home, away from this pestilence, and see what could be done to arrange for a third voyage of exploration—something to get him to sea again, something that, after all, he really *did* know how to do.

The return trip when it came, in March 1496, seemed to carry the stain of the island with it. Onto two tiny ships (one of them the *Niña*, that enduring little caravel) the Admiral was forced to load what is recorded as thirty Indians—most of them prisoners from Isabela, including the *kaseke* Caonabó and his shiny shackles—and 225 Spaniards, the lucky ones to escape from Española, where, Las Casas says, the only oath the colonists had was "*¡Así Dios me lleve a Castilla!*"—"As God may take me to Castile!" When we remember that the *Niña* came out on the First Voyage with no more than two dozen men or so, the appropriate complement for such a ship, it seems incredible that it was now jammed with *five times* as many people: where could they have been put? What foul conditions must they have had to endure? What foul conditions must they have been escaping?

And the famed navigator at the helm of this little fleet only compounded the difficulties of that sardinity when, for some reason forgoing the northerly route that he had taken so successfully on his First Voyage, he set sail directly eastward, ran straight into the contrary trade winds, and spent an entire month without getting any farther than Guadeloupe, only 700 miles from Isabela. Running low on food, they put into Guadeloupe to get some cassava bread from the islanders (this was the island of the fierce cannibals from the outward journey, mind you, yet it didn't seem to trouble the Admiral in the least), and they descended upon a seaside village, took the Indians' cassava dough, "and made enough bread to satisfy their needs." This, together with fresh water, wood, and two more Indian slaves from the island, was stocked on the ships, which then continued on to Spain, still fighting the same contrary winds. They finally arrived in Cádiz more than seven weeks later, having spent three months on a journey that should have taken no longer than four weeks. We do not know how many died aboard, though among the dead was Caonabó, but it is mentioned that those who did survive were severely emaciated and had "faces the color of lemon or saffron"—and those the Europeans.

And now something very strange: the Admiral of the Ocean Sea, Governor of the Indies, discoverer of the lands hitherto unknown to Europe from which shall come profit and glory beyond reckoning, suddenly decided to dress himself in the humble gray habit of a Franciscan monk. Las Casas, who recorded this, did not explain why; Andrés Bernáldez, in whose house Colón stayed for the first few months after this return voyage, also recorded it and also did not explain, either; Fernando, who would have seen his father thus dressed on his subsequent visit to the court, mentioned it not at all.

What can it mean? One can only assume that something having to do with genuine feelings of penitence dictated these simple coarse robes of a mendicant—contrition perhaps at the abject conditions of his colony, remorse at his inability to control it, sorrow at the failure of his Grand Scheme to find the promised treasures. But it may also have had to do with a recognition that his viceregency was held in disrepute by the subjects of his island, and particularly those who had returned to spread the stories of its meager riches and abundant torments in and around the Spanish court. (Morison in fact suggests that the habit may have been inspired by a simple desire for anonymity, since "he could no longer walk the crowded *sierpes* of Seville without being insulted by disillusioned seekers after wealth and glory.") In any case, this seems to have been Colón's consistent dress for the next two years in Spain—some of that time spent, appropriately, at the monastery of Las Cuevas in Seville—as he put to the Sovereigns his case for a third voyage of exploration, and waited . . . and waited . . . for their answer.*

Ferdinand and Isabella were of course none too happy with the news they had been receiving from their Indies—the colonizers disgruntled to a man, so many of them sick or dead, so little in the way of wealth and nothing in the way of conversion—and they realized that, capable admiral though their Colón might be, capable governor he was not. There is no record of any royal rebuke, no dressing-down or reprimand or withdrawal of privilege, yet there is nothing to suggest that Colón was accorded anything like the reception he received on his previous return. In fact there is no record of his meeting with the Sovereigns at all, but it must have been sometime in the late summer or early fall of 1496, for we know he set off in late July to join the court in Burgos with his usual retinue of half-naked Indians, parrots, exotic plants, and gold nuggets. Fernando suggests that "he was well received by the Catholic Sovereigns," who accepted his offerings "with rejoicing," and even goes so far as to say that "they granted him many favors and privileges in what related both to the Admiral's affairs and estate and to the better government and administration of the Indies"—though inasmuch as he somehow forgets to enumerate such remarkable rewards, and they are not mentioned elsewhere, we may suspect that they consisted largely of filial wishful thinking.

It is most likely that the Sovereigns in effect ignored the Governor

---

*The choice of Franciscan gray (and the color at that time *was* gray, not brown, as Las Casas said) was no doubt determined not by any particular attachment to St. Francis's teachings—certainly neither to the saint's reverence for nature nor to his commitment to poverty—but rather by Colón's earlier association with the monks of La Rábida. A theory has been advanced that he was even a third-order Franciscan, but there is no specific evidence for that.

of the Indies for most of the next two years, and delayed his petition for the next voyage of discovery, being concerned not so much with the state of the Indies as with the state of Europe. Spain at this moment was at war with France, trying to consolidate its victories on the Italian peninsula, and the prime task as the Sovereigns saw it was to achieve a circle of alliances around France through a series of royal marriages with the Hapsburgs, the English, and the Portuguese. That all this took an immense amount of money and an extraordinary number of ships (some 130 ships, complete with 25,000 soldiers, had sailed in Prince Juan's wedding fleet in September 1495) rather disinclined the monarchs from indulging the Lord Admiral in any elaborate or expensive venture of exploration. But eventually, by mid-1497, they were persuaded to let him take a small provisioning fleet out to Española, and they provided him with six small ships and a promise of 2.8 million maravedis (about a sixth of what must have been spent on the previous voyage).

Thereafter began a long period of haggling and tape-cutting before the money was actually sprung from the royal coffers, and then another long period of finding, provisioning, and manning the ships—and the latter achieved only because *this* time, in order to get the necessary complement, the crown promised pardons to all criminals who would agree to "go with the said Admiral to Española" and stay for a year or two. Finally, in the spring of 1498, the preparations were complete, and on May 30 of that year the Third Voyage was begun.

In the two years of his wait, though Colón almost certainly did not know it, two other skillful mariners had taken to the world's oceans and spectacularly continued the process of European expansion he had begun. On June 24, 1497, when Colón was probably again with the court at Burgos, negotiating the terms for the next voyage, Giovanni Cabotto, sailing for King Henry VII of England and using the English form of his name, John Cabot, sighted the coast of what we may assume to be northern New England and thus inaugurated the long and fitful series of contacts between northern Europe and northern America that would culminate in the Virginia and Plymouth settlements more than a century later. And on May 20, 1498, as Colón's six ships were being outfitted in Seville for the journey to the Indies, Vasco da Gama, sailing for King Manoel I of Portugal, actually arrived in the real Indies, putting into the port of Calicut, on the southwestern coast of the Indian subcontinent, where he was received by the local rajah with proper Oriental pomp and grandeur, and thus inaugurated the highly fruitful sea route to Asia that would anchor the Portuguese empire for the next three centuries.

Wednesday, 1 August. He ran five leagues down the coast to the west and reached a point at which he anchored with all three vessels, and they took on water from springs and streams. . . . He says they found aloes [again, wrong], large palm groves and lands of great beauty, "for the which let infinite thanks be given to the Holy Trinity."

It is called the Third Voyage, and was indeed the Admiral's third trip to the Indies, but it was a paltry thing, nothing more than an extended detour, without even a return crossing under his command: it lasted (aside from the overlong ocean passage) a bare three weeks, from this landfall on the island Colón named Trinidad on August 1, to the departure from the island he named Alto Velo and passage to Española on August 22. (And it consisted of only three ships, the other three having been sent directly to Española with provisions for the hard-pressed and probably starving colonists.)

In the surviving *Journal* abstract—once again made by Las Casas, although he, too, realized the scantiness of this trip and provided us with a very short form of it—the Admiral apologized several times for this hasty reconnaissance. The reasons he offered were many, but only two have the ring of sincerity: first, that he had three shiploads of supplies for Española that "were perishing" in the holds; and second, that he had lied to his crew about where he was going, not daring "to tell them in Castile that he was setting out with the intention of discovering, lest they set up obstacles and ask more pay than he could give."

In view of this limited duration, it is perhaps surprising that the voyage encompassed two quite remarkable events—both born in the increasingly troubled mind of the Admiral (still suffering the weakening effects of his Reiter's disease), one of which turned out to be an accurate and prophetic geographical theory (far more so than he then understood), the other pure, though revealing, cosmological fantasy.

[Tuesday, 13 August. Paria.] The Admiral seems to have gone about 30 or 40 leagues at most since leaving the Boca

del *Dragon* [off *Trinidad*]. . . . *He observed that the land stretched out wider and appeared flatter and more beautiful down toward the west. . . . He therefore came to the conclusion that so great a land was not an island but a continent; and, as if addressing the Sovereigns, he speaks thus:*

"I have come to believe that this is a mighty continent which was hitherto unknown. I am greatly supported in this view by reason of this great river [the Orinoco] and by this sea which is fresh. . . . And if this is a continent it is a wonderful thing and will be so regarded by all men of learning."

A *continent*—and hitherto unknown! Was this more self-delusion, the Admiral convincing himself that here in what the natives called the land of Paria he had actually achieved the object, as he put it in the first entry of this *Journal*, "of discovering new land, not already discovered" and with a new route "to the south . . . to see if there were islands or lands there"? Was it because he knew that this time he had to justify himself, had to "find islands and lands wherewith God might be served and Their Highnesses and Christendom gratified," that is to say, provided with treasure? Was this an instance of seeing-what-he-wished-to-see, a sort of Paria-no-island?

Quite possibly there was self-persuasion here; it would certainly not be surprising. Only this time the Admiral really *had* found a continent—it was the land that became known as South America, and he was the first known European to "discover" it, just six years to the week after he first set sail from Palos.

The actual landfall had taken place a week earlier, on August 5, somewhere on the southern coast of the Paria peninsula in what is now Venezuela, when the Admiral sent his boats ashore to what he then assumed was one more of those interminable Caribbean islands. It was not until the following week when he experienced the heavy discharge of the Orinoco River into the Gulf of Paria that he began to reason that such an outflow meant a large river, which could come only from a large landmass, and that the "island" back there might be a peninsula, and the peninsula attached to . . . *tierra firme*, a continent! The more he thought of it the more convinced he became: "I am also supported by the statement of Esdras in Book 4, Chapter

6, which says that six parts of the world consist of dry land, and one part of water"; and come to think of it, "I am supported by the statements of several cannibal Indians whom I captured on other occasions, who declared that there was a mainland to the west of them"; and there were others, too, "in the islands of Santa Cruz and San Juan, who said that there was much gold on the mainland." Yes, there would be doubters, but remember, "there was no one in my own time who believed that a man could sail from Spain to the Indies."

Very well, a continent. But *what* continent?

Was this some lower appendage of Asia, unknown to Marco Polo, a vast southern part of what the ancients (and Esdras once again) had asserted was the one contiguous Island of the Earth that stretched from Europe to China?

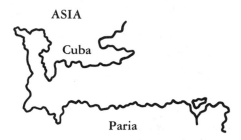

If so, there was no passage to India here, no way to explain how Polo had sailed from the east coast of China (as Colón knew he did) back to India.

Or was this an insular continent *off* Asia, separate from the mainland that began at Cuba, an entirely new landmass, perhaps that famous Terra Australis, the Southern Land, where some said there had to be much gold because it was so hot?

If so, then the ancients and the Holy Church were wrong about the single Island of the Earth and this was some kind of *orbis alterius* that the theologians had proved was impossible.

Or was this something else entirely, something with no relation to Asia at all, something that might really be called . . . a new world?

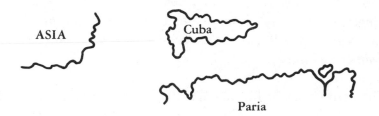

If so, it was almost unbelievable, and all that he had claimed about his islands being in the China Sea and Cuba a part of Asia would have to be publicly denied and discarded.

We can imagine the confusions that must have been aswirl in the none too healthy mind of the Great Discoverer: he was opening questions here that were as profound and disturbing in their cosmological implications as any that the mind of Europe could have conceived. They were questions so deep that he may never have worked them out entirely—although he eventually came to something close to the last version—and indeed they were to perplex the best scholars and finest cartographers of Europe for decades to follow, even after many more transatlantic voyages. Mapmakers were still offering variations on all these themes (especially the latter two) well into the sixteenth century.*

Thursday, 16 August. He sailed northwest by north 26 leagues on a flat sea, "thanks be to God," as he always used to say. . . . Here again he exhorted the Sovereigns to esteem this business highly, since he had demonstrated that

---

*Certain cartographers came up with a pretty good notion of the truth fairly early on—Waldseemüller in 1507, the 1512 Stobnicza, the 1512 Reisch, and the later Mercators—but the idea of two separate new continents was very slow to be established even among the specialists. In the 1560s as great a cartographer as Giacomo Gastaldi was hedging his bets: one of his maps shows two large landmasses in the ocean separate from a very nearby Asia, but another has the northern continent as a seamless part of Asia.

there was gold in these lands, and he had seen
innumerable minerals which have to be extracted with
intelligence, industry and labor . . . and he has brought
Their Highnesses a lump of virgin copper of six arrobas'
[twenty-five pounds], lapis lazuli, gum arabic, amber, cotton,
pepper, cinnamon, an abundance of dye-wood, aromatic
gum [estoraque], white and yellow sandalwood, flax, aloes,
ginger, incense, myrobolans of all kinds, the finest pearls,
and reddish pearls, which Marco Polo says are worth more
than the white.

The perplexities of his new discoveries must have tormented the
Admiral during these days at sea, since they were questions for him
not of abstract cosmology alone but of his own worldview, his self-
worth and reputation, even his very self-identity. In the midst of
that, the only certainties were those of wealth, and the commodities
of that he seems to have loaded on in considerable quantity, although
just how it fitted on ships already heavily laden with cargo for Española is somewhat hard to see. It was not, as we might expect, of
any special worth, nor was it even what he said it was, except for
the cotton, dye-wood, and pearls.

It is noteworthy that here for the first time the Admiral had discovered pearls—at last—bought by barter from "some women . . .
who wore on their arms strings of small beads and among them pearls
or seed pearls (*aljofars*) of high quality." They told him, moreover,
that there were rich pearl fisheries "toward the west," and in this
case there really were, just off the island of Margarita, though in his
haste the Admiral failed to stop and locate them when he sailed right
by five days later. It was left to Alonso de Hojeda the following year
to find and get credit for the abundant pearls there, a fact that rankled
Colón so much that four years later he was still complaining to
Ferdinand and Isabella that Hojeda had "robbed me of the pearls and
infringed my rights as admiral" and should be punished.

The perplexities of mind could only have been exacerbated by the
recurrence of the Admiral's persistent sickness. In the *Journal* he
complained several times of the "grave illness" that had stayed with
him for the past two years in Spain, and on shipboard he again suffered
from "gout and insomnia" on July 14, "so much pain" and bleeding
from his eyes on August 4, "fatigue," bleeding, and "travails at sea

. . . without parallel" on August 13, and shortly thereafter, believing "he had almost lost his eyesight owing to lack of sleep, as a result of the long and continued watches," he cursed his eyes and said, "May it please Our Lord to free me from them." Whatever his affliction, it was surely compounded by his inability to sleep and the anxieties of his career; if it was Reiter's syndrome, it would also have caused painful inflammation in the joints of his arms and legs, and perhaps his spine, probably a painfully inflamed urethra and penis at times, and conceivably incipient mental dislocation.

Then, on August 17, Colón decided that the "great continent" he had found was, in truth, "the Terrestrial Paradise"—"for all men say that it is at the end of the Orient, and that it is." No trumpets were called out here; no grand ceremony made; the Admiral was exceedingly calm about it, in fact made no further mention of it in the *Journal*. (Fernando, in his recounting of the *Journal*, chose to ignore it entirely.) Yet this was obviously a discovery beyond all discoveries, putting in the dark any islands of gold or even realms of the Khan: here is the Earthly Paradise, the Garden eastward of Eden, God's chosen home for all life on earth, denied to humankind since Adam.

But if he was somewhat modest about his discovery in the *Journal*, the idea nonetheless clearly stirred and roiled in him in the weeks to follow. By the time he was ready to spell it out, in his summary letter to the Sovereigns two months later, it fairly exploded, page after page, in a very long and muddled mishmash of theology and astronomy and geography and fantastic lore, rambling, repetitive, illogical, confusing, at times incoherent, self-serving, servile and vainglorious all at once—and quite loony.

"I am completely persuaded [*muy assentado*] in my own mind that the Terrestrial Paradise is in the place I have said," he asserted, because the people of Paria are "whiter than any others I have seen in the Indies" and "are more intelligent and have more ability [*ingenio*], and they are not cowards"; they had plenty of gold, just as the Bible said was to be found in the land of the first river out of Eden; and they lived just above the Equator, where the best authorities had always argued Paradise would be found; and they called their land Paria, the name an obvious form of *Paraíso*. As if that were not enough, the Admiral also, as Las Casas rendered it, "experienced such freshness in the land, such green and pleasant trees, such mildness and amenity of soft airs, so great and so impetuous a confluence of sweet streams of water, and in addition, the goodness, generosity, simplicity and mansuetude of the people; so what else could he judge or conclude, save that there or thereabouts divine providence had placed the Terrestrial Paradise?"

All of that evidence, however, paled to insignificance in the face of the one irrefutable discovery Colón made. Taking citings of the North Star and finding night after night that it cut a peculiar and abnormal circle, he became convinced that the earth was not perfectly round, but rather in this hemisphere "it has the shape of a pear, which is all very round, except at the stem, where it is very prominent, or that it is as if one had a very round ball, and on one part of it was placed something like a woman's nipple [*una teta de muger*], and that this part with the stem is the highest and nearest to the sky, and it is beneath the equinoctial line and in this Ocean Sea at the end of the East (which is what I call the place where all the land and islands end)." Because Paradise was to be known by "the mildness of the sky, or in its height toward the sky," and Paria was marked by "the mild climate that is there, and this in turn comes from its being the highest land in the world," this is obviously the very extremity of Terrestrial Paradise, "by which it might be understood that it was there." And so on and on, for pages.

All of this was written in apparent sobriety, in an official report to the Sovereign Rulers of Castile, León, Aragon, Sicily, Granada, etc., the most eminent royal couple in all Christendom and notoriously hard-minded to boot. It is astonishing to imagine Admiral Colón sitting in his governor's chambers on Española, the chaos and sadness of the island all about him, and solemnly dipping pen into inkwell hour after hour to render this vision of a hemisphere rising in the shape of a woman's breast until it culminates in Paradise—and actually planning how Spain will go about the job of colonizing it. It staggers the mind, and sorrows the heart.

Paradise, in Christian terms, as Colón well knew, was a highly charged image. There is about it, of course, the idea of abundance, and peace, and health, and simple happiness, the ample uncomplicated life of naked, prelapsarian people without rulers, without laws, without crime or war or greed or avarice or hierarchy or private property. But there is also intertwined with that the sense of tragedy, of inevitable loss, the guilt and shame of the forever outcast . . . and a lingering, unquenchable pride in the heart of the rebellious species that was destined to seek knowledge, to experience good and evil,

and ultimately to survive in its own way, now subduing with Abel
its own beasts of the pasture, now cultivating with Cain its own
plants in the field. Humankind is forever damned, forever stained
with sin, and waits until the Millennium to recapture the lost Paradise;
but in the meantime, it achieves nothing less than *civilization*, its own
prideful way to conquer the world, its own assertion of godhead.
And now here again all of this exact tension in the European soul,
this deep historical drama of sin and guilt and technology and conquest, was about to be played out across the lands and among the
people of the newly found world, which was, in fact, as close to
Paradise as noncelestial existence has. As, I believe, the Admiral of
the Ocean Sea had now come unconsciously to realize, without knowing exactly how or what it meant, without even knowing he had come
to that realization; and when that thought took expression it came
out, because of his cultural vocabulary, in biblical terms wrapped
around with astronomical cant.

There is a recurrent theme among the myths of many of the Indians
of the Americas that might be described as one not of Paradise Lost
but of Paradise Now: in effect, of peoples having ascended from a
dark Other World, a world of sorrow and evil, into the present Edenic
garden, peoples not fallen but risen, not damned but blessed, not
inherently sinful but inherently salubrious. Such a belief might change
a culture's view of the world around it quite substantially.

> [*Wednesday, 22 August. Alto Velo.*] *He departed thence
> . . . and eventually with some difficulty owing to the strong
> currents and breezes, which here are continuous and
> contrary, he made this harbor of Santo Domingo on Friday
> the last day of August, the same year 1498.*

So to all effects ended the Third Voyage, in the harbor of Santo
Domingo, a town settled in the Admiral's absence, which was to
become—largely, one might say, because its site was chosen not by
Cristóbal but his brother Bartolomé—the permanent capital of the
Spanish Indies and the oldest continually occupied city in the Western
Hemisphere. Its founding was notable in that it was the first city of
the New World to be stamped with the orthogonal grid system, that
imperial gift of Alexander the Great, picked up by the Romans and
used on Castilian soil as elsewhere, whose primary feature is that it
establishes streets and blocks "by ruler and compass," as the planners

said, without regard for the natural contours and features of the land, the springs and streams and marshes and woodlands, or the denizens thereof; that gift, described by Lewis Mumford as "an essential part of the kit of tools a colonist brought with him," which would become the single most important concept in town planning throughout the future settlement of the Americas.*

The island, not surprisingly, was in much the same mess it had been in when Colón had left it two and a half years before; Fernando put it somewhat mildly when he said Colón "found all at sixes and sevens," Martyr somewhat more accurately when he wrote, "He found all things confounded and out of order."

The tribute system had now given way to the forced labor of the *encomienda*, but the Tainos were fleeing and dying in the same numbers and the Spaniards operating the placer fields complained that they did not have enough workers. Spanish dissatisfaction with the Colóns' rule and the island's conditions had broken out into open rebellions—"all the families of the island were infected with a disorderly and rebellious spirit," Fernando wrote—the most serious led by Francisco Roldán, whom the Admiral had selected as the *alcalde mayor* (chief justice), and who now had gathered several hundred Spaniards and Indians to his cause; in trying to put it down, Bartolomé had led a punitive expedition across the island after him that succeeded only in further killings and alienation of the Indians in the way. No serious religious conversion had gone on, and the one poor and self-effacing friar still working at it had only a "mere handful" of recruits. Death and disease had taken a steady toll, and of the Spanish population, bolstered with the new arrivals to perhaps seven or eight hundred, "one hundred and sixty," Fernando reports, "were sick with the French sickness."†

Faced with this, Colón once again proved as an administrator what

---

*The grid system, though begun by Bartolomé, was not fixed until 1502, when, after a devastating hurricane, Santo Domingo was rebuilt on the west bank of the Ozama River. Fernando, incidentally, says that Bartolomé named the city in honor of his father, Domenico, but this is highly unlikely, with the reputation the Colón family then enjoyed on Española. Besides, there already was a Santo Domingo to name the city for, the thirteenth-century Castilian founder of the Dominican order, and it is most likely that the settlement was begun around August 4, his feast day, in 1496.

†Soldiers in the French army had contracted syphilis on their invasion of Italy in 1494–96, and the Spanish subsequently liked to name the dread disease after the French, as did the Italians, naturally, and the English as well; the French, of course, called it the disease of Naples; the Poles afterward called it the German disease, the Russians called it the Polish disease, and so on.

a good sailor he was: he tried to ignore everything. He set himself up in grand style in a stone house in Santo Domingo, apparently devoted most of his attention to managing his own personal estate, which he put together around the capital and in the Vega Real district, and, it seems, amassed a good deal of money. The details of his wealth are not clear, but the Admiral himself says that by 1500 he had "four millions [maravedis, presumably]," which would be the rough equivalent of $28,000 pre-Depression dollars, plus "a little more from the tithes," or the tenth part of the Sovereigns' share of all production, amounting to between $1,500 and $12,000 a year, depending on the amount of gold shipped. If it was anything like $30,000, as it may well have been, it was a substantial fortune for those days and might have been part of the reason the Lord Governor was so roundly hated by his colonists.

Whether or not such accumulation occupied the Governor full-time, he certainly showed little interest in or capacity for the settling of the various unrests, Indian or Spanish, that beset the island. (He also had, it must be said, very little support for it: he could muster "less than seventy men to go out against the rebels," Fernando wrote, "and of these less than forty could be relied on." Fernando gives an exceedingly long account of the dispute with the rebellious Roldán, mostly a tale of ineptitude, delay, and the Governor's increasing humiliation, until in the end—some *thirteen months* after his return to the island—he capitulated entirely, reestablished Roldán as *alcalde mayor* (for life!), rewarded the rebels with "houses and grants of land," and allowed as many as wanted to return to Spain to sail on the next available ships. One gets the sense again that Colón was not much suited to this task of running a colonial outpost and that all he really wanted was to get out as fast as he could, back to the comparative safety of the sea. "For six months I had been ready to leave to come to Their Highnesses," he wrote in a letter to the court at the end of his tenure there, "and to escape from governing a dissolute people who fear neither God nor their king or queen, being full of folly and malice"—some of whom, he went on, "did not deserve [baptismal] water before God and the world." And the Tainos, he complained, were no better: "a people warlike and numerous, whose customs and religion are very different from ours"—and, mark this well—"who live in hills and mountains without fixed settlements." So much for the gentle Tainos, now become Wild Men.

Reports of Española's continuing troubles would certainly have reached Ferdinand and Isabella by early 1499: Colón sent back two ships with disgruntled colonists as well as his I-have-found-Paradise letter in October 1498, and other unauthorized ships were no doubt putting into various island ports and picking up the news by now. They could not have been awash with confidence in their twice-failed Admiral, especially now that he seemed to be suffering from a severe unsoundness of mind. So they authorized a trusty servant of the crown, Francisco de Bobadilla, Comendador of the Order of Cala-trava, to replace Colón and establish order. In the middle of the following year, July 1500, he left Castile to become the new "Gov-ernor of the Islands and Mainland of the Indies." What did *not* reach the Sovereigns before Bobadilla's departure—though it perhaps might not have changed their minds—was news of the first discovery of significant and extensive deposits of gold in Española, sometime around Christmas 1499: at last the famous mines that Colón had been talking about all these years. "That day," the Admiral wrote in triumph, "I learned there were 80 leagues of land and mines all over it."

It is astonishing that this event has attracted so little attention from Columbus historians, inasmuch as it did more to vindicate his entire Grand Scheme, in his eyes as in the Sovereigns', than anything else in his career, and ultimately brought them all a considerable amount of wealth while the fields were played out over the following two decades. Those poop-deck pundits who like to think of Colón as being eternally at sea of course seldom bother with such sordid details, most of them following Morison's lofty assertion that "the much-publicized 'mine of gold' " had not been found "for none there was." But one wonders what they thought their hero was talking about, when, in his letter to Juana de Torres in October 1500, he referred to "the good news about the gold," "so much gold has been found," and even, outright, "the discovery of gold in Española." (Morison was so perplexed by this last reference he even scolded the Admiral: "Gold was discovered in Hispaniola in 1492. He must mean new measures for extracting gold.")

The new discoveries were of the substantial deposits of gold in veins all along the north slope of the Cordillera Central, about 50 miles south of the abandoned Isabela and some 80 miles northwest of Santo Domingo, and if the auriferous veins really did cover 80 leagues (and we discount Colón's usual exaggeration), that would be something like 250 miles, representing as extraordinary a single find as Europe had ever known. And as rich: Colón reported that "some have collected 120 castellanos a day, others 90, and it has gone as high as 250"—a nice day's take, if one considers that 120 castellanos would represent about $363, roughly what a sea captain might be paid in a year (the captains of Colón's ships on the Fourth Voyage earned the annual equivalent of 110 castellanos) and four times as much as the annual pay of an ordinary seaman or even a ship's carpenter. *In a day.* It was in truth a strike of El Doradan proportions: according to the incomplete (and official, therefore surely underrepresented) records we have of the crown's share of gold, between 1504 and 1519 it produced an average of roughly 150,000 castellanos ($450,000) a year at the minimum; Las Casas, who was there at the time, claimed that the annual production from 1502 to 1509 was more like 450,000 castellanos ($1,360,000). The lower figure would represent the equivalent of about a *ton* of gold a year, the upper closer to three; since the average imports of gold for the entire century and a half of American production (from both continents) came to 1.2 tons a year, the Cordillera field can obviously be seen as a significant cache, and not a single of the lucky colonists, nor their beleaguered leader, doubted it for a moment.

For Colón, at least, it came not a moment too soon. In his Torres Letter he describes his mood on that Christmas Day in 1499:

> I was suffering great affliction and attacks from the evil [*malos*] Christians and the Indians, and was about to give up everything and escape with my life, if I could, [when] Our Lord miraculously consoled me and said, "Be of good cheer, be not dismayed nor fear. I shall provide for all. The seven years, the term of the gold, are not passed, and in this and in the rest I shall grant thee relief."

It is hard to know what this fevered mysticism is all about, but so it came to pass. It was exactly seven years after the first real suggestions of gold treasure and the divinely chosen founding of La Navidad that the Cordillera strike was announced. "Gold is most excellent," Colón wrote just three years later. "Gold is treasure, and with it, whoever has it may do what he wants in the world, and may succeed in taking souls to Paradise."

. . .

On August 23, 1500, Comendador Bobadilla arrived in the harbor
of Santo Domingo to take up his duties as the new governor of the
Indies. (Colón partisans, including Fernando, of course, try to argue
that Bobadilla went to Española as inquisitor and judge, not governor,
but the royal authorizations of May 21 and May 29 leave no doubt
that he was intended to replace Colón as governor as well, if not in
full accordance with Colón's original agreement with the Sovereigns
at least in full accordance with their current mood.) And what should
be his first sight, and first confirmation of the sad viceroyalty of his
predecessor, but the bodies of seven Spaniards hanging from the
gallows in the town square. Going ashore, he confronted Diego Colón, who told him that the Admiral was off suppressing a rebellion
in the Vega Real, the *adelantado* was in charge of another armed
force upcountry, the seven corpses were rebels who had just been
caught and tried, and five more Spaniards were scheduled to be hanged
the next day.

The worst suspicions were confirmed: the Colóns had turned Española into one long rebellion, and now they were ruthlessly slaugh-
tering good Castilian men at will. Bobadilla was no sentimentalist—
a tough, loyal knight, he had been put in similar circumstances before
and come away roundly feared, ofttimes sued, and once nearly
assassinated—and he immediately moved into the Governor's house,
clapped Diego in jail, and sent for the other brothers to come take
their punishment. The Admiral returned within weeks, the *adelantado* shortly thereafter, and, according to Fernando, the eldest brother
"advised them that in order to serve the Catholic Sovereigns and not
cause disorders they should surrender to Bobadilla peacefully." This
they did, and Bobadilla brought them before a hearing at which the
pent-up dissatisfactions of six years of misrule and misfortune, not
appeased by six months of gold strike, were given vociferous vent.
Charges of the most condemnatory kind were leveled at the Colóns,
and in the end Bobadilla seemed to have no choice but to order the
brothers sent back to Castile to stand trial. He had all three placed
in irons, led to the waiting ships among jeering, taunting crowds—
"Admiral of the Mosquitoes," they were calling Colón then—and
dispatched forthwith to Cádiz. "This island," noted one Fray Juan
de Trasierra, who had come out with Bobadilla's fleet, "has been
liberated from King Pharaoh."

It was a terrible blow to the proud servant of Castile, and it rankled. "Suddenly," he recounted three years later,

> when I was expecting the arrival of ships to take me to your royal presence, bearing triumph and great tidings of gold, in great joy and security, I was arrested and cast into a ship with my two brothers [in fact, Bartolomé was on a companion ship], shackled with chains and naked in body, and treated very badly, without being brought to trial or convicted. . . . All that was left to me and my brothers has been taken away and sold, even to the cloak that I wore, without hearing or trial, to my great dishonor.

The tone of self-pity, so typical of the Admiral's writings, is here sharpened to a strident perfection, and with it went a martyr's touch. For according to Fernando, the captain of the homeward ship offered to remove the Admiral's chains, unworthy and unnecessary appurtenances, as soon as they left the harbor, but proud Colón refused: "He had been placed in chains in the Sovereigns' name, he said, and would wear them until the Sovereigns ordered them removed."

Tennyson captures the Admiral's tone quite well:

> *Chains for the Admiral of the Ocean! chains*
> *For him who gave a new heaven, a new earth,*
> *As holy John had prophesied of me,*
> *Gave glory and more empire to the kings*
> *Of Spain than all their battles! chains for him*
> *Who pushed his prows into the setting sun,*
> *And made West East, and sailed the Dragon's mouth,*
> *And came upon the Mountain of the World,*
> *And saw the rivers roll from Paradise!*

And so, early in October 1500, very nearly eight years to the day from his momentous landfall on Guanahaní—how much, how vastly much, had happened since then—Cristóbal Colón completed his Third Voyage, and his viceroyalty of the Indies . . . in chains.

Chapter Eight

1500–06

"IF RESENTMENT against the world is new for me," Colón wrote in the Torres Letter, with the manacles still fastened to his wrists, "its practice of maltreating me is very old. A thousand battles have I had with it, and all have I resisted until now, when neither arms nor counsels [*avisos*] avail me. Cruelly it has cast me down into the depths."

It was in those depths, in spite of appeals and entreaties and petitions to the crown, even in spite of one last, long, troubled voyage to his Indies, that the Admiral of the Ocean Sea spent the last years of his life. When he took to his bed, in Valladolid, on the day before he died, so much done but so much left undone, he still believed he had been grievously wronged by his sovereigns and the world.

Upon landing in Cádiz, Colón was taken, still in chains and accompanied by an unnamed jailer, to the Carthusian monastery of Las Cuevas in Seville, where he had stayed under the care of his friend Fray Gaspar Gorricio on his last visit to Castile. And there he remained a prisoner for more than five weeks, in what must have been considerable anguish of soul if not pain of body, before he finally heard from Ferdinand and Isabella, who on December 12 ordered him released and brought to the court in Granada. The delay was not intended as punishment—the monarchs would later write, "We were much distressed by your imprisonment,"* and "As soon as we were aware of it we gave orders for relief"—and was more likely the result of the royal preoccupation with their version of affairs of state, that is, the prosecution of wars on the Italian peninsula and the

---

*Next to the words "much distressed" in the Paris Codex copy of this letter is a drawing of a hand with a pointing index finger, in red ink, put there, we may assume, by an aggrieved Colón.

wedding of Catherine of Aragon to England's Prince Arthur. When
they finally received him at court, on December 17, they were apparently quite polite and conciliatory, giving him a reception of such
sympathy that we might well suppose they were mindful of the report
delivered to them a few months previously by a Fray Francisco Ruiz,
a colleague of Bobadilla's, about the considerable gold rush then
taking place in the Cordillera—which Colón, too, would not have
forgotten to mention.

It is possible that they were impressed as well by the fact that their
servant had provided for them what Colón had now decided to call
(still not quite precise about its geography) an other world—"*otro
mundo*," something unknown to Europe and the ancients, consisting
not only of new islands of which the public now knew but of *a new
continent*, never seen before, vast and full of riches, and there for the
continued glory of Spain. He had first used the phrase on August
10, 1498, in his journal, when in one of his supplications to the
Sovereigns he reminded them that he alone had found new territory
for Spain, "and Your Highnesses have won these vast lands, which
are an other world [*que son otro mundo*] in which Christendom will
have so much enjoyment and our faith in time so great an increase."
He used it again in his summary letter of that voyage on October
18, again arguing that "no princes of Spain ever gained territory
outside their borders save now, when Your Highnesses have an other
world here, by which our holy faith can be so greatly advanced and
from which such great wealth can be drawn." And once again, in the
Torres Letter of October 1500, he reminded the Sovereigns that "I
have placed under the sovereignty of the king and queen, our lords,
an other world, whereby Spain, which was reckoned poor, is now
most rich."

Ferdinand and Isabella had every right originally to be skeptical
of this story of a new continent and its great riches, accompanied
as it was by visions of God speaking directly to the Admiral and
the certain discovery of Terrestrial Paradise at the tip of a woman's
breast and the like. But they took it seriously enough to authorize
at least four independent exploratory voyages to Paria in 1499 as
soon as they heard the news (by Alonso de Hojeda, with the company of one Amerigo Vespucci; by Vicente Yáñez Pinzón, Martín
Alonso's younger brother; by Diego de Lepe, a Pinzón relative;
and by Peralonso Niño, an officer of the *Niña* on the First Voy-

age*), and at least four more the following year; all these ventures returned with treasure of various kinds, mostly pearls, and confirmation of the extent of Colón's Otro Mundo. The Sovereigns were extraordinarily closemouthed about news of this continent, however, perhaps because they wanted to exploit it entirely on their own before the rest of Europe got wind of it, or perhaps because they were afraid it might fall within Portugal's sphere of influence (as indeed a part of it did) and did not want to stir up their ally. No quickly printed and widely circulated letters announced the new land to the world —the Admiral's overheated letters being no doubt too embarrassing to put before the literate European public—and it remained largely unknown, at best a subject of conjecture, until the pirated Vespucci accounts asserting the existence of "what we may rightly call a new world" began circulating after 1503.

However cordial the Sovereigns' reception, it did not content the Admiral; he wanted, as always, more. He felt that he had been unjustly deprived of his viceroyalty on Española and wanted to be renamed governor there, with similar privileges for his son Diego upon his death, and he wanted to be sure that he and his heirs had their full share of all the riches that would come out of the Other World. Ferdinand and Isabella seem to have been somewhat aloof and off-putting on these scores, and so for the next several years Colón was almost obsessed with the ardent—and, for a man in poor health, arduous—presentation of his case. His suit took the form of two manuscript "books," quite disparate and in some ways incongruous, and both for some reason almost always ignored or short-shrifted by conventional historians in spite of the revealing and striking picture of the Admiral they afford.

The first was the *Book of Privileges*—or, as on its title page (in the version known as the Paris Codex), *Cartas Previlegios Cedulas y otras Escrituras de Dõ Xp̃õual Colon, Almirãte Mayor del Mar Oceano*

---

*One great historical error should be cleared up here. In Peter Martyr's account of the Peralonso Niño voyage, his name is given as "Petrus Alphonsus (called Nignus)," and this turns up in the pirated *Libretto* edition as "Pietro Alonso, called the Negro [*el negro*]," from which certain later readers have contrived the idea that Peralonso was a black man, a Moor of Spain, and written that a black man was therefore on the original voyage of discovery. It is entirely a fabrication and should not be allowed to deceive schoolchildren any longer; if a black sailor is wanted, there is a Diego el Negro listed as a gromet on the flagship of the *Fourth Voyage*, and he might have been African.

Visorey y Governador de las Islas y Tierra Firme—which was begun probably in 1497 and assembled in final form apparently during most of 1501, and at least four copies of which were authorized by Colón in January 1502.[1] There, in forty-four documents, most of them apparently copied for Colón on his previous stay in 1497, he collected all the evidence he could find for his claims to titles, rewards, benefits, and revenues from the crown, both for himself and for his posterity, including the original Capitulations, various letters from the Sovereigns, and the royal permission for him to create a *majorat* (estate) for his sons. The case is fairly convincingly made, despite the inclusion of repetitive and sometimes irrelevant documents (such as the Torres Letter), although it should have been obvious to Colón that on certain matters the Sovereigns never would (and never did) budge, no matter how many elaborate arguments one might compile. What is most noticeable, however, is the tone of martyrdom and victimization that increasingly characterized Colón's writings ("Had I despoiled the Indies . . . and given it to the Moors, I could have been shown no greater enmity in Spain") in his later years. Perhaps it is best to regard it as the sad and somewhat desperate cry, at times even a whine, of one who still has not found a home after all these years, nor thus a way to pass his heritage to his children, and who, with his final days now in sight, knows only how to plead as victim—in monkish robes, in chains—for the crown to provide for his children what he could not for himself.*

In the end, the Sovereigns did bend somewhat under Colón's importuning, but never to his satisfaction. They reaffirmed his right to be called Admiral of the Ocean Sea and have this title devolve upon

---

*Of note is Document 30, authorizing Colón to create a *majorat*, where his estate is specifically assigned by the crown to his son Diego and not to "*your other sons* who are able to inherit." This is perhaps a scribe's error, although Colón took exceeding pains over these documents, but that plural "other sons" seems to suggest that he had other offspring besides Diego ("legitimate") and Fernando (not), possibly one or more with his wife, Felipa, during those shadowy years of 1481–85 in Portugal and Porto Santo. This surmise is reinforced by two other perplexing references. The first is from February 14 in the *Journal* of the First Voyage, in which he referred to "two sons whom he had at Cordova" whom he would "leave orphaned" if he should be lost at sea—Diego, of course, would certainly be orphaned, but not Fernando, whose mother lived in that city; could this refer to still another child? Later he wrote that he "left wife and children, whom I never saw again," when he left Portugal, suggesting that Diego had siblings then. (Cecil Jane says this suggests also that he was *married* when he left Portugal, and hence was married when he took up with Beatriz de Arana later on, and thus felt so guilty about her in his will, where he gave her an inheritance "for the satisfaction of my conscience, because this matter weighs heavily upon my soul.") If there were indeed other children, however, they are lost to history.

his male descendants, as indeed it did into the twentieth century, but they refused to reinstate him as governor or viceroy or even to consider his going back to assume any office in Española; to seal this, they named Nicolás de Ovando, Comendador de Lares, their new governor, in September 1501. They were also willing to reaffirm Colón's claim, as set out in the original Capitulations, to *one-tenth* of the revenues from the Indies (which they interpreted as meaning one-tenth of the crown's one-fifth, no matter what Colón wanted to make it mean) and *one-eighth* of the profits from any expeditions he may have sponsored himself, but they resolutely denied him the *one-third* of the revenues he had lately decided were due him, since they themselves were now taking only one-fifth and were little inclined to permit the troublesome Admiral to siphon off more than they. And they were even willing to see that Colón's money and property on Española, confiscated by Bobadilla, were returned to the Admiral after all his debts on the island were paid, although they arranged that most of it would be divided up "into ten parts, nine to be for us and one for the said Admiral," as they put it in their decree of September 1501.

If the *Previlegios* thus seemed to have at least some effect upon the Sovereigns, nothing of the kind can be said of the second manuscript Colón prepared, the bizarre *Book of Prophecies* (*Libro de las profecías*). This was assembled over the course of the Admiral's first two years back in Castile, with much of the same motive but in this case to convince the Sovereigns of the cosmic importance of his ventures on their behalf and the eternal significance of their results. The work was apparently never finished—at least no finished copy exists—and it is the version that Colón put aside when he started preparations for the Fourth Voyage in March 1502 that we have today, a manuscript of eighty-four folios, a small part in Colón's own hand and the rest, it seems, by brother Bartolomé, son Fernando, and Fray Gaspar Gorricio. It, too, is a jumble of documents, this time commentaries by Church Fathers (calling on "forty-four books of the Old Testament" and "four Evangelists with twenty-three epistles") and medieval authors, along with some fragments of Spanish poetry (probably not by Colón, though he did say in one letter to Gorricio that he intended to put it into verse one day), all prefaced by a long, rambling introduction.

The *Profecías* shows Colón at his millennial, apocalyptic height, at times not coherently so, wrapped up in astrology and mysticism and almost indecipherably complex cosmology. It gives full vent to that ample strain that we have already seen in Colón's soul, as in the soul of much of Europe at the time, the crusading Xp̄o FERENS side of him that is symbolized in the signature he had now adopted. That impulse may well have played a part in his original determination to sail in search of new lands, as some scholars argue ("Columbus's apocalyptic vision of the world," writes Pauline Moffitt Watts, "and of the special role he was destined to play in the unfolding of events that would presage the end of time was a major stimulation for his voyages"); it obviously grew in importance as the years went by (as evidenced in the 1492 *Journal*, the Torres Letter, and his 1498 will); and here it became positively an obsession, justifying the Admiral not merely to his Sovereigns but to all of Christianity, now and to come.

This strain has always been an acute embarrassment to most Columbus hagiographers, since it is so at odds with the scientific Renaissance rationalist they like to depict as the forerunner of European conquest, and for the most part they have chosen to ignore or forgive it as a passing "mental hallucination" (Justin Winsor), a temporary "dark and sordid stupor" (Filson Young), or a clever ploy by which Colón hoped to convince the gullible queen that he was "the chosen man of destiny to conquer an Other World" (Morison). So discomfiting is this aspect of the Discoverer, in fact, that it was not until 1892 that the *Profecías* was first published (in Italian, in the classic *Raccolta* edition Cesare de Lollis prepared for the Quatercentennial) and not until 1982 that it appeared in the original Spanish; and not until 1991 will it appear in English.

The essential argument of the *Profecías*, amid the morass of biblical quotation and medieval theology, is simple: Cristóbal Colón was chosen by the Lord as the divine instrument to fulfill the ancient prophecies that would rescue Christianity before the Apocalypse— and that was only 155 years away, as we remember—namely, to spread Christianity to the unblessed heathen populations around the world, and to provide the gold for financing the crusade to recapture the Holy Sepulcher from the infidels. That was why He led Colón, His Christ-bearer, to the new lands, the Otro Mundo, where by divine coincidence there existed both so many heathens and so much gold. For not only did He endow the Discoverer with rare mundial talents—

He has bestowed the marine arts upon me in abundance and that which is necessary to me from astrology, geometry, and arithmetic; he has given me adequate inventiveness in my soul and hands capable of drawing spheres and situating upon them the towns, the rivers, mountains, islands, and ports, each in its proper place—

but far more important, He has offered celestial inspiration, a "light, which comforted me with its rays of marvelous clarity . . . and urged me onward with great haste continuously without a moment's pause," because "in this voyage to the Indies, Our Lord wished to perform a very evident miracle" through his humble servant Colón. (Or as Colón expressed it the year before, in the Torres Letter, "Of the New Heaven and Earth which Our Lord made, as St. John writes in the Apocalypse, after He had spoken it by the mouth of Isaiah, He made me the messenger thereof and showed me where to go.")

Most of the evidence for this divine purpose for His chosen servant was naturally to be found in the Bible, and Colón's selections therefrom are copious, but the prophecy was supported as well by two eminent nonbiblical sources. The first was Seneca, who predicted in *Medea* that "the years will come, in the succession of the ages, when the Ocean will loose the chains of things, and a huge land lie revealed"—this, obviously, the discovery of the Indies. The second was Joachim of Fiore, a twelfth-century Calabrian abbot who foretold that "he who will restore the ark of Zion will come from Spain"— this, obviously, the reconquest of Jerusalem.* And the man who achieved the former, the *Profecías* wanted to prove, was destined for the latter: "In the execution of the enterprise of the Indies . . . what Isaiah said was completely fulfilled and that is what I wish to write here, that it may be firmly set in Your Highnesses' minds, so that you may rejoice when I tell you by the same authorities that you are assured of certain victory in the enterprise of Jerusalem if you have faith."

---

*Morison takes Colón to task for this, saying that Joachim predicted "this man would be Christian, not necessarily a Spaniard." What the abbot actually said, however, was that this Christian was to *depart from*, sail from, Spain, so the prediction actually fits doubly. The apocalyptic Joachimite tradition was very strong in fifteenth-century Spanish Franciscanism, largely through the works of Arnold of Villanova, which were well known in those circles, and it was probably Colón's closeness to the Minorites that provided both the inspiration and the sources for much of the *Profecías*.

It seems doubtful that the Sovereigns ever bothered to read the *Profecías*, more doubtful still that two such down-to-earth strategists would have been persuaded by its millenarian passion even if they had. However much they might have fancied a crusade to free Jerusalem—and Colón had reminded them that even before his First Voyage "I pledged to Your Highnesses that all the gain of this my enterprise be spent in the Conquest of Jerusalem, and Your Highnesses laughed and said that it pleased them, and that even without this profit they had that desire"—they were not about to go up against Suleiman the Magnificent and the might of the Ottoman Empire to achieve it. Only in the mind of a man like Colón could such a bizarre idea not merely take root but flourish and positively blossom, occupying him for more than a decade and prompting him now, just released from chains, to set forth such an elaborate, probably blasphemous case as the *Profecías*.

Bizarre though it was, to disparage it as simple madness or dismiss out of hand the apocalyptic vision and religious zeal that gave rise to it would be a mistake. For it was an authentic expression of that deeply embedded millenarianism we have seen in medieval European culture, and Colón would not be the only colonist motivated by this passion in the subsequent conquest of the New World. The apocalyptic vision, with its holy biblical foundation and ecclesiastic elaboration, provided many with the essential justification for—the overarching *rightness* of—the Christian mission of expansion, and it was appealed to as often by the Puritan English and the evangelical French as by the Catholic Spanish in the decades to come. "God will prevail against them, it is said," St. Augustine wrote in a passage that Colón was careful to include in his book, "and he will wipe out all the gods of the peoples of the earth, and they will adore him, each one from its own place, all the peoples of the islands, and indeed not only the peoples of the islands, but all peoples." What could that mean but conquest?

It seems clear that the monarchs did not pay much attention to these two strange manuscripts that Colón worked so hard on, and indeed throughout this period there is an underlying sense that they wanted rather to have done with the dickerings over the Indies and to dispatch their Admiral as soon as possible on some lengthy exploration that would take him far away from court. And here they operated with quite unusual alacrity: just sixteen days after Colón proposed his Fourth Voyage, on February 26, 1502, they gave their royal assent, along with such repeated suggestions as "You should leave at once without any delay whatsoever" and "You must set sail with your vessels as speedily as may be" and the like. Only two stipulations did they make to safeguard their interests, whatever the Admiral had in mind: first, "you are in any case to choose some other route" than "to go by way of Española," so as to avoid any further difficulties there; and second, if treasure is found, "you must draw up an account of all this in the presence of Our Notary and Official whom We are commanding to go with you for this purpose, so that We may know everything that the said Islands and Mainland may contain."

On May 9, less than two months after it was authorized, the Fourth Voyage set sail from Cádiz, four smallish caravels and 143 men and boys, including for the first time Colón's son Fernando, then thirteen, as well as his brother Bartolomé.* Although in later years one seaman reported that Colón "always called this, his fourth and last expedition, *el alto viaje*"—the high voyage—there was very little high about it, unless perhaps the winds and the casualties. It covered at least 6,000 nautical miles and discovered practically nothing the Europeans perceived as valuable, no grand civilizations (though it came within 200 miles of the Mayan culture in the Yucatán) and no passage to India (though it came within 40 miles of the Pacific Ocean); it did not find much gold, and its attempt to establish a settlement where the best nuggets were taken was a disastrous failure; it alienated, through kidnapping, treachery, bombardment, and warfare (and, Fernando admits, "innumerable outrages"), almost every one of the peoples it came in contact with on the mainland and in the islands; and in the end all four ships were lost, the captain and crew were marooned on Jamaica for an entire year, at least thirty-two crew members died and a half-dozen deserted, and the rest of them endured long periods of starvation and disease. Only an admiral practiced in deception, one is tempted to think, could regard that as "high."

Wednesday, 29 June. Having come to off the harbor [of Santo Domingo], the Admiral sent Captain Pedro de

---

*The crew (apart from officers and "gentlemen") had in fact more boys than men—fifty-seven to forty-two, suggesting the difficulty of getting seasoned *marineros* any longer to sail under the great Admiral.

Terreros, captain of one of the ships, to explain to the Knight Commander [Ovando, the governor of Española] that because he had to replace one of his ships and also because he expected a great storm, he wished to take shelter in port. . . . The Knight Commander, however, would not permit the Admiral to enter the port. . . . The Admiral being forbidden the harbor, anchored as close as he could under the land in order to save himself [from the storm]. . . . By his skill and good judgment he managed to keep the fleet together till the next day, when as the storm gained in intensity and night came on with deep darkness, three ships were torn from their anchorages, each going its own way; and though all ran the same danger, each thought the others had gone down. —Fernando

The first thing one is struck with on this voyage is Colón's continual battle (as rendered in his summary letter and Fernando's later account) with the dreadful weather that he seemed to encounter in every month, in every latitude, right from the start. The trip out was uneventful, but Colón ran into a violent hurricane as soon as he approached Santo Domingo—he had no business in waters that far north and had been forbidden to go there besides—that he described as a "dreadful tempest" that put every vessel "in desperate straits, with nothing to look forward to but death."* Surviving that, he made it to the coast of Central America, off modern Honduras, but, wonder of wonders, "the terrifying hurricane had pursued me, so that I saw neither the sun nor the stars," and he encountered "wind and a terrible current" that he beat against almost fruitlessly for a whole month (which in his telling becomes "88 days"), during which "the storm in the heavens gave me no rest" and "rain, thunder and lightning continued without ceasing, so that it seemed like the end of the world." Thereafter, along the coast of Veragua (modern Panama), there was more of the same, "great violence of sea and sky," "furious wind and current," and "cruel weather":

---

*This was the storm that by coincidence (some said divine) also hit a large fleet sailing from Santo Domingo with Comendador Bobadilla, all his records, and significant amounts of gold (including one nugget said to be worth more than $10,000), sinking a score of ships with the loss of some five hundred lives. Only one ship (according to Fernando, along with Las Casas our only source for this, and not altogether reliable) made it through the storm to Spain, and that was the one carrying the 4,000 pesos ($12,000) that Bobadilla had restored to the Admiral's account.

The tempest returned and wearied me so much that I knew not where to turn . . . and for nine days I was lost, without hope of life. Eyes never beheld the sea so high, angry and covered with foam. . . . There I was held, in an ocean turned to blood, seething like a caldron on a mighty fire. Never did the sky look more terrible: for one whole day and night it blazed like a furnace, and the lightning broke forth with such fury that each time I wondered if it had destroyed my spars and sails; the flashes came in such fury and frightfulness that we all thought the ships would be consumed.

Putting in at Veragua finally, at a place he named Belén, he still found no succor, for the "next day the tempest returned" and "the river suddenly rose very high and turbulent, parting my cables and breast-fasts [lines to shore], and all but carried my vessels away; certainly they were in greater danger than I had ever seen them before." And on it went, month after month.

There is no doubt that the gallant admiral ran into some very unfortunate weather during this season in the Caribbean, but what is striking is that in his mind it seems to be so purposefully malevolent, as if a plot designed by a nature wanting to torture his already painfully racked soul. This is not an entirely new element in Colón's response to nature—he had been set upon by "terrible" tempests and "terrifying" tidal waves on earlier voyages—but never before had he found nature to be at once so single-minded and so violent, so evil, so "cruel." Never before had Colón so fixed himself in opposition to the climatic forces that, as every mariner knows, are the inevitable lot of the sea. And if there was any other kind of weather dealt to him, it impressed him not: always he recorded the storms, rarely the calms.

There are other glimpses, too, of the responses to nature of both Admiral and men on this voyage, rather more insightful than we have had since the very first reactions on the First Voyage. At one point, for example, during a few days of unaccustomed calm, the ships were surrounded by sharks, and Fernando (who composed this not as a youth but when a savvy fifty) reported, "We were frightened, especially those among us who pay attention to signs and omens"; so, he said, "we made such a slaughter of these sharks with hook and chain that we were unable to kill any more"—a wanton carnage, and without food as a motive, although afterward "all did shark the honor of eating it" since they had run out of meat rations. At another point, for amusement, seamen in one of the ship's boats took a harpoon on a line and hooked "a ray as large as a medium-sized bed" as it lay sleeping on the surface, then held on as "it drew the boat through the harbor as swiftly as an arrow," much to the amazement of the rest of the crew looking on—until "eventually the fish died and was hauled aboard with tackling gear used for raising heavy objects." On still another occasion, after the local Indians had made a gift to the Admiral of a wild "boar" (actually a Caribbean peccary) that had "run at everybody on deck, including the dog," the Admiral decided to contrive a "novel and pretty sport" for the amusement of the crew:

> An archer had wounded an animal which seemed to be a monkey, except that it was much larger and had the face of a man [perhaps a spider monkey]. He had pierced it with an arrow from neck to tail, and since it was ferocious, he had to cut off an arm and a leg. The boar, on seeing the monkey, bristled and fled. When I saw this, I ordered the [monkey] to be thrown to where the pig lay. When it got up to the pig, although on the point of death and still with the arrow in its body, it coiled its tail about the hog's snout and held it very firmly, and with its remaining hand seized the boar by the head, as if an enemy.

This, Fernando reported, "provided fine sport." A society that could raise the killing of hapless bulls to an art form could certainly be expected to find amusement here; it is only a little disconcerting to realize that these words of the Admiral's appeared in an official document directed to the royal couple, whom Colón assumed would be as amused as his common seamen.

Not all was fear and cruelty, to be sure, and it would be unfair to suggest that, but many other episodes reveal equally characteristic attitudes. There is the prevalent distaste for, the uncomfortableness with, the view of nature in the raw, variously seen as "dark" or "wild" or "rude," and by contrast an admiration for all those places where the imposition of the human hand, in husbandry or habitation, is made manifest; coming into one harbor Colón decided to name it Portobelo, Fernando wrote, "because it is very large, beautiful, thickly populated, and surrounded by cultivated country," and especially because it is "well tilled and full of houses only a stone's throw or a crossbow shot apart, all as pretty as a picture, the fairest thing one ever saw." There was also the tendency to turn every element of the foreign landscape into some part of Europe, to make it fixed and known and familiar, catalogued and controlled by the European eye, even when it was novel and bizarre and heretofore unknown: the mammee apple became a "pomegranate," the manatee a "calf," large lizards were classified as "crocodiles," and cougars as "lions" or "leopards."

In one respect only did European myopia not come into play on this voyage: that utilitarian view of nature so typical of the earlier voyages was almost completely absent. Neither the Admiral nor his son paid attention now to "tall trees" or dye-wood or mastic or spices or aloes ("This country contained nothing worthy of mention" is a typical entry of Fernando's), not even to the Indians they met as potential fodder for the slave trade. The reason was simple: the Admiral had become a specialist, and all his attention was now on gold, whether of plate or necklace or nugget—"gold everywhere," as he said, hopefully, "gold without limit."

> *Sunday morning, 14 August. . . . The natives of this country are much like those on the other islands, but their foreheads are not so broad and they do not appear to have any religion. They speak different languages and generally go naked except for a cloth about their genitals. . . . They tattoo their arms and bodies by burning in Moorish-style designs that give them a strange aspect. Some display painted lions, others deer, others turreted castles [?!], and others a variety of other figures. . . . When they adorn themselves for some festivity, some paint their faces black or red, others draw stripes of various colors on their faces or put on a beak like an ostrich, and still others blacken their eyes. They do this to appear beautiful, but they really look like devils.*
> *—Fernando*

Nothing shows so well Europe's perception of the natural world as its reaction to the natural people living in it—and thereby hangs an inquiry of some complexity. We arrive here at a realm of myths and myopias and misunderstandings, of uncertain realities and certain fancies, imposed dreams and received nightmares, that comprised the European image of the American for at least the next two centuries, an image that might best be thought of as the confusing and shifting combination of the *Noble Savage* and the *Savage Beast*.

Both concepts surely dwelt within the mind of the Discoverer, and they could be brought to the fore to serve first one purpose, then another, according to the conceit at hand. But the former was the image predominately conveyed in the Santangel Letter of 1493, easily the most widely read—and at least, among the educated, the most widely influential—of any of Colón's works in Europe. Here the subcontinent for the first time had a firsthand, face-to-face description of people actually living in that Paradise, or Arcadia, or Elysian Fields, envisioned by the ancients: they "all go naked, men and women, as their mothers bore them"; they do not have weapons "nor are they capable of using them"; they are "well-built people of handsome stature" and "of a very keen intelligence" but "wondrous timid"; they have no religion and "know neither sect nor idolatry"; "they are so artless and free with all they possess, that no one would believe it without having seen it," and "whether the thing be of value or of small price, at once they are content with whatever little thing of whatever kind may be given to them." How sharply must those descriptions have struck the morose and troubled European soul, concepts of innocence and generosity and pacifism that could have cut like beacons through the dark night of late medieval Europe.

The idea of splendid innocence also shone through the works of Amerigo Vespucci—or, that is to say, the reports bearing his name that were fabricated from his letters with such success from about 1503 on. "Vespucci" was far more lavish and colorful than Colón, far more salacious and erotic, and certainly far more inventive—none of which, the historian reports with regret, did anything to diminish his popularity—and his heavily fictitious tales were the most widely read accounts of the New World for at least the first four decades after its discovery.* Vespucci's Indians, living somewhere along the Atlantic coast of South America, were like Colón's, "entirely naked,

---

*"Vespucci" had 12 editions and reprints (in Latin) from 1502 to 1504, then 17 more in vernaculars in 1504–06, another 21 before 1510, and 10 more in the next decade. Compared to his 60 editions and reprints, Colón had but 20 (19 of them of the Santangel Letter), Cortés had 18, and the others (Martyr, Magellan, Cabral, etc.) had 30. Moreover, 37 editions of Vespucci were in vernacular languages, as against 10 of Colón's.

the men like the women without any covering of their shame," but they had several crucial additional features: they have "no laws and no religious faith, they live according to nature"; "there is no possession of private property among them, so everything is in common"; "they have no king, nor do they obey anyone, each one is his own master"; "there is no administration of justice, which is unnecessary because in their code no one rules"; "they live in communal dwellings"; "they mate with whom they desire and without much ceremony" and "are a very procreative people"; and they are a people of great longevity . . . and do not suffer from infirmity or pestilence or from any unhealthy atmosphere." It is true that they are "assuredly" cannibals, are also "warlike" and "very cruel to their own kind," and wear ornaments in their lips and cheeks, "a brutal business," but that sort of exotica was the kind of thing one might expect of strange new peoples and was not to be seen as detracting substantially from their wondrous libertarian society.

These Vespuccian themes were immediately picked up by the diligent Peter Martyr at the Spanish court, whose accounts, beginning with the pirated *Libretto* edition of 1504, were particularly influential among scholars and the literati and were now given elaborate supportive details (though supplied entirely by hearsay, inasmuch as Martyr never saw the New World). Of Española he wrote:

> The inhabitants of these islands have been ever so used to live at liberty, in play and pastime, that they did hardly [boldly] away with the yoke of servitude which they attempt to shake off by all means they may. And surely if they had received our religion, I would think their life most happy of all men, if they might therewith enjoy their ancient liberty.
>
> A few things content them, having no delight in such superfluities, for the which in other places men take infinite pains and commit many unlawful acts, and yet are never satisfied, whereas many have too much and none enough. But among these simple souls, a few clothes serve the naked; weights and measures are not needful to such as know not skill or craft and deceit and have not the use of pestiferous money, the seed of innumerable mischiefs.
>
> So that if we should not be ashamed to confess the truth, they seem to live in that golden world of which old writers speak so

much: wherein men lived simply and innocently without enforcement of laws, without quarreling Judges and libels, content
only to satisfy nature, without further vexation for knowledge
of things to come.

And of the Indians of Cuba he wrote:

It is certain, that among them, the land is as common as the sun
and water: and that Mine and Thine (the seeds of all mischief)
have no place with them. They are content with so little, that
in so large a country, they have rather superfluity than scarce-
ness. So that (as we have said before) they seem to live in the
golden world, without toil, living in open gardens, not en-
trenched with dikes, divided with hedges, or defended with
walls. They deal truly one with another, without laws, without
books, and without Judges. They take him for an evil and mis-
chievous man who takes pleasure in doing hurt to others.

It is an extraordinary picture, and must have been extraordinarily
attractive to a Europe which, as Martyr repeatedly suggests, is mired
in the "mischiefs" of what we can see as early capitalism and nascent
statism. So attractive, in fact, that it entered very quickly into European culture and became lodged in political discourse as the very
image of the newer, better world that Europe might become. Not
by accident did the classic, defining work of utopian literature,
Thomas More's *Utopia*, appear in 1516, just two decades after Europe
first learned of the Indian societies of the Americas, nor is it an
accident that it is specifically located in and was inspired in large part
by the New World presented so effectively by Vespucci. (Similar
seventeenth-century works, such as Francis Bacon's *New Atlantis*
and Tommaso Campanella's *City of the Sun*, we may note, also have
American inspirations.)

For the Noble Savage is not, as sometimes supposed, an ancient
and common part of Europe's mythical heritage. Visions of the
Golden Age and Arcadia and the like go back a long way, but the
images are often blatantly fanciful (houses made of sugar-and-spice,
for example) and the inhabitants usually undefined stick figures, nothing more specific than Adam and Eve, or Brahmin sages and Ethiopian
kings, or endlessly happy children. (Nor is this a frequent theme:

one diligent researcher found only sixty-five mentions of such creatures in all the literature from the Hebrews to the fifteenth century.)
The specific elements of the Edenic society are not found in the works
of classical authors or early Christian theologians, not even in the
radical sectarian dissidents of the fourteenth and fifteenth centuries,
whose images of the Good Polity are essentially, in the words of a
recent study by Germán Arciniegas, "built on air . . . poetic abstrac-
tions without consequence."

This is of marked importance because it is the description of the
Indian of the New World in the early accounts, beginning with the
Santangel Letter and running for three decades thereafter, that basically created the idea of the Noble Savage in Europe and provided
for European political thought the underlying characteristics of the
free commonwealth. The idea of political liberty—masterlessness, a
society without kings, hierarchies, laws, parliaments—really began
here; so too the idea of equality—social parity, shared property,
without mine or thine; the idea of social harmony—communal ease,
peaceful concord, sodality, without judges and lawyers; and the idea
of abundance—enoughness, living on the fruits of nature, without
wants, without toil. Right from the start these were the impressions
that made the New World stand for "the land of liberty," the land
of Possible Paradise; as the decades went on, they became every bit
as important and ubiquitous in Europe as potatoes and tobacco, two
other borrowings from the same soil. When Europeans (particularly
north Europeans) actually began to settle in that New World in the
seventeenth and eighteenth centuries, they were taking back to it
these ideas and ideals, expecting to see them flourish in the colonies
they implanted there, a process that of course culminated in the
revolution that for the first time asserted just these values to the world
and sought to build a new nation upon them. Full circle.

But this positive impression of the New World, important as it
was for Europe, was not the only or even the principal one: for the
Noble Savage existed always intertwined with the Savage Beast, and
it was the latter whose images gradually predominated, particularly
in the minds of those who went to the new lands and dealt with the
Indians face to face.

Cristóbal Colón in this sense was quite typical. We have seen how
he lost interest entirely in the gentle Tainos, so easy to subjugate,
and contrived out of wish and myth the fierce Caribs who must be

enslaved or slaughtered; we have seen how he conquered and ruled the Indians by force, killing fellow beings with no more compassion than a butcher for his beasts. Now, on this last voyage, when he spoke of the Indians at all it was with contempt. Those who did not take kindly to his building a colonial outpost in their midst he called "very wild," and he decided on impulse to capture their *kaseke*; those who he decided ate human flesh he said had "brutish faces" betraying their practice; those whose language he could not understand he dismissed as "savage people." And when in the midst of the people of Jamaica, on whose hospitality he and his crew of more than a hundred had depended for an entire year, whose gifts of food and drink were all that kept the indolent and sickly foreign band alive, he wrote that he was "surrounded by a million savages full of cruelty and our enemies." By the end he seems to have quite forgotten the sweet marvelousness of those people of Guanahani, whom he now decreed to be, with all their kind, like the Wild Men who "live in hills and mountains."

This same cast of mind is evident in a great many other chroniclers of the Indians, and if their writings were not at first as popular as those of the Noble Savagists, they were actually more numerous and in the end more influential. Not surprisingly, they emerged as soon as anything of real value was seen in the new lands that were inconveniently in the hands of the natives, and after 1519, when Cortés uncovered the immense wealth of Mesoamerica, they fairly proliferated: those Indians who looked like Noble Savages when there was nothing but Guanahani to conquer came quickly to look like Savage Beasts when the treasures of the two vast continents became apparent and the stakes involved Mexico and Peru. Then, in official document and personal letter alike, with only the occasional exceptions from a man such as Las Casas, we hear again and again of the sinister nature of these foul creatures.

Here is a Dominican monk, Tomás Ortiz, writing to the Spanish Council of the Indies in mid–sixteenth century:

> They are more given to sodomy than any other nation. There is no justice among them. They go naked. They have no respect either for love or for virginity. They are stupid and silly. They have no respect for truth, save when it is to their advantage. They are unstable. They have no knowledge of what foresight

means. They are ungrateful and changeable. . . . They are brutal. . . . The older they get the worse they become. About the age of ten or twelve years, they seem to have some civilization, but later they become like real brute beasts. I may therefore affirm that God has never created a race more full of vice and composed without the least mixture of kindness or culture.

Thus the kindly cleric; here the great humanist and nationalist Juan Ginés de Sepúlveda:

Compare then those blessings enjoyed by Spaniards of prudence, genius, magnanimity, temperance, humanity, and religion with those of the little men [*hombrecillos*, the Indians] in whom you will scarcely find even vestiges of humanity, who not only possess no science but who also lack letters and preserve no monument of their history except certain vague and obscure reminiscences of some things on certain paintings. Neither do they have written laws, but barbaric institutions and customs. They do not even have private property. . . . How can we doubt that these people—so uncivilized, so barbaric, contaminated with so many impieties and obscenities—have been justly conquered?

And, he concluded, Indians were as different from Spaniards as cruel people are from mild, as monkeys from men.

The recurrent bestial theme is revealing: "They live like proper beasts," said Cuneo; "stupid wild insensate asses," said Gómara; they "commit bestial obscenities," said Oviedo; nothing but "wild beasts," said Garcilaso de la Vega. It comes from that hallowed Christian tenet that those who live closest to nature are by nature beasts and therefore *less than human* in the divine hierarchy called the chain of being. This of course ties in with the Wild Man again, the hairy savage of the woods—and indeed, a woodcut in a 1505 edition of the "Vespucci" *Mundus novus* shows a classic Wild Man figure, bearded, heavy bow instead of club, naked wife beside, to represent the new-found Indians. It ties in, too, with the European degradation of nature: "America is today inhabited," wrote the French historian André Thevet in 1558, "by marvelously strange and savage peoples . . . living like irrational beasts *just as nature has produced them*."

It was not wholly a cynical device-of-empire thus to denigrate the

Indian into the Savage Beast, though it certainly played an important part in the ideologies that Europe used to justify its conquest and exploitation of the New World. It was, in a still deeper sense, a response to the unresolved burden of guilt that was (and was felt to be) an inherent part of the cast-from-Eden mythology of Christianity, made all the heavier for the medieval soul by the official castigations of St. Augustine, and sharpened by jealousy and resentment toward the prelapsarian peoples living without such a burden in apparent fertility, ease, simplicity, safeness, freedom, harmony, and uncorruptedness. The resulting tensions, then, could be resolved, as Europe's perception of nature had always permitted, only by being played out against—literally against—the natural world and its natural peoples. This is a matter of some complexity, but I would suggest that the only way the people of Christian Europe ultimately could live with the reality of the Noble Savage in the Golden World was to transform it progressively into the Savage Beast in the Hideous Wilderness—and then progressively work to destroy it.

Wednesday, 9 November. We left Portobelo [Veragua] and sailed eight leagues eastward, but the next day were forced back four by a contrary wind, and so put in among some islets near the mainland. . . . We remained there until 23 November, repairing the ships and mending our casks; then we sailed eastward to a place called Guiga (which is also the name of another place situated between Veragua and Ciguare). . . .

We did not tarry there, and on Saturday, 26 November, we put in a little harbor that the Admiral named Retrete [closet] because it was so small that it would not hold more than five or six ships.—Fernando

We have it on Fernando's authority, and his alone, that the purpose of the Fourth Voyage was to search for a strait to India, a notion that more gullible historians have accepted readily.* It is more likely,

---

*The strait-searching idea comes up also in the summary account to the crown by its agent, Diego de Porras, and one testimonial in the *Pleitos* about Colón searching for the Spice Islands. But there is no mention of it in the royal instructions for the voyage, certainly nothing about a passage to India, and there is nothing about it in Colón's summary letter, the *Lettera Rarissima*.

however, that Colón's true purpose was to determine the dimensions, or at least the northern coastline, of the new continent that he had discovered and that other Spanish captains had begun coasting and trading along as if it were their own; this after all was tangible (not like the elusive strait and the ever-distant Quinsay), and a place likely to be rich with gold and pearls, and had best be secured by right of discovery by the Admiral himself. This is borne out by the actual route of the small fleet, which sailed west only at the start and as soon as land was sighted, off Honduras, kept its headings east and south for the whole next year, no matter how severe the winds, just as they were now doing through this November stretch: this was the way to fill in his knowledge of the coastline from where he had left it on the Third Voyage, but it was no way (in fact was quite the opposite) to find a passage to India.

That he deceived his son about it, and would on occasion seek to deceive the wider world, is hardly surprising: as long as he put it about that Cuba-no-island was a part of mainland Asia, and that all he was doing was searching for the strait, presumably he would have this whole area to himself, and then he would know the extent of his new continent, claim this Tierra Firme for himself, and, by San Fernando, make it *his* land to rule and profit from, without any Bobadillas or Ovandos to take it from him. (Colón was so touchy about having it all to himself that back in Santo Domingo at the end of this voyage he confiscated the charts that the pilots and even the crown's notary had made along the way, including a book of one Pedro Mateos "which contained all the sierras and rivers . . . and the Admiral afterward took it from me.")

There is also one significant confirmation that the Admiral had given up the idea of a strait to Asia by this time and had begun to realize the true dimension of his discovery, in a remarkable and little-noticed document in the *Book of Privileges*. In Document 43 (undated but presumably late 1501 or early 1502, certainly not later), Colón's dictated account of his discoveries actually used the phrase *"Indias Occidentales"*—*West* Indies—for the first time, and added, "the said West Indies which were unknown to all the world" until he "miraculously found them through his great skill and knowledge of the sea." *West* Indies: this was an extraordinary geographical conception, and something quite new to the world. It shows that Colón was aware that da Gama had discovered some other Indies, the old Indies, and that his were unrelated, even hemispheres apart. If they were both part of the same Asian landmass, then da Gama's of course would lie farther west and Colón's to the east, and his would then be the *East* Indies. But no, these new lands were the West Indies; they lay in the west—that is, in the Western Hemisphere—and were half a world away from India. To underscore this, Colón emphasized that they were previously "unknown to all the world," thus obviously not part of China or Malaysia or India, places long known to geographers. This was truly an Other World, newly found, to the west, and Colón now clearly recognized it.

And it was just here, along the coast of Veragua during this month of November, that Colón could claim for a certainty the correctness of his new geographical vision, the third of the choices that had presented themselves on the last voyage. Here, at the harbor of Retrete, where Rodrigo de Bastidas's caravels had put in sometime during the previous year (and whose charts Colón's captain had been given during the brief stop at Santo Domingo), the Admiral could fill in the last gap of the geography that delineated the entire northern coastline of his Tierra Firme from 60 degrees to 85 degrees west. The vast stretch—1,800 miles long (and even then only less than half the real northern rim of the continent)—was certain proof that, as he had been saying, it *was* a continent; that it bore no relation to the descriptions of Marco Polo's China and was geographically quite different in both configuration and latitude from what China was presumed to be (as, for example, on the Behaim globe) was certain proof that it was *not* Asia.

The final piece of evidence to certify the Admiral's new concept, if more was needed, was provided sometime in mid-November by the Indians along the coast. The Admiral conveyed it—in convoluted form, to be sure, framed by a mind still suffering from a racking illness and the toll of the long hard spate of weather he'd just been through—in the so-called *Lettera Rarissima* he sent to Ferdinand and Isabella at the end of this voyage in July 1503. It is nothing less than the final confirmation of his Otro Mundo.

First, he says, he is absolutely certain that a province called Ciguare "lies just nine days' journey by land to the west," approximately 200 miles from where he has put in on the Veragua coast. (A few pages later he says that the mines of Veragua run "westward 20 days' journey"; the discrepancy is not resolved, but no matter.) Second, this

Ciguare is a civilized place where "there is gold without limit" and "the people wear coral on their heads," "all know of pepper," "are accustomed to do business in fairs and markets," "wear rich clothing, and have fine houses," and—surely the key mark of a civilized society—"they are accustomed to warfare." Third, this Ciguare is on the coast of a large body of water, possibly another sea, and "it seems that the lands have the same bearing with regard to Veragua that Tortosa has to Fuenterrabia [the one a port on the Mediterranean, the other on the Bay of Biscay, a distance of 210 miles], or Pisa to Venice [from the Tyrrhenian Sea to the Adriatic, a distance of 150 miles]," in other words, a country across some large mountains no more than a few hundred miles away. And finally, "they tell me, too, that the sea encompasses Ciguare and that it is a journey of ten days to the Ganges River," meaning perhaps 2,000 miles or so to the real Indies.

There is only one way to make sense of this. Veragua must lie on the *east* side of a landmass that is about 200 miles wide, and Ciguare lies on its *west*, and in between are mountains like the Pyrenees or the Apennines. Ciguare must be a civilized place, but it cannot be China (nor does he try to confound "Ciguare" into "Cathay" or somesuch) because it lies on the west coast of a large body of water, which China did not. From there, sailing west, one would somehow bypass China and eastern Asia—lying presumably to the north—and reach the Ganges in Hindustan in a ten days' sail. The landmass of Veragua–Ciguare, therefore, must be a large peninsula at the top of this new continent here in the Otro Mundo that lay between Europe and Asia. Thus, "the lands here which are now subject to Your Highnesses are more vast than all other in Christian possession"—a continent, moreover, that had not only great civilizations in it but vast amounts of gold, and Terrestrial Paradise (he threw this in again, for good measure) to boot. That, in sum, is how he now imagined the world.

Can it be an accident that this was almost exactly the configuration of the Western Hemisphere represented on the first printed map of the New World, by Giovanni Matteo Contarini in 1506, just four years later; on the Johannes Ruysch map of 1507; and quite similar to the Piri Re'is map of 1513 that was labeled as having been based on a chart taken by the Turks from "the Genoese infidel Colon-bo"?

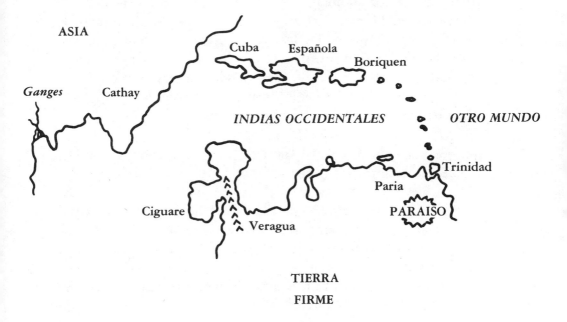

ASIA

Cuba Española

Boriquen

Ganges   Cathay

INDIAS OCCIDENTALES   *OTRO MUNDO*

Trinidad

Paria

Ciguare

PARAISO

Veragua

TIERRA

FIRME

Does that not suggest a congruence of geographical ideas whose ultimate source could only be the man who sailed all along these coasts
and confiscated his pilots' maps thereof?[2]

All this seemed to be—in fact it was—a feat of such great proportions that Colón imagined a Voice from Heaven coming to congratulate him at Veragua one night, as he lay "with a high fever and
very fatigued," saying:

The Indies, so rich a portion of the world, He gave thee for
thine own, and thou hast divided them as it pleased thee, for He
gave thee the power to do so. Of the barriers of the Ocean Sea
which were closed with such mighty chains [a reference to the
Seneca prophecy in the *Profecías*: how well-read this Voice], He

gave thee the keys, and thou was obeyed in many lands, and thou hast gained an honorable fame throughout Christendom. What more did He do for the people of Israel when He brought them out of Egypt? or for David when He made him from a shepherd into the king of Judea? . . . Thus have I told thee what thy Creator hath done for thee and so does for all men: now He hath had me reveal the rewards for thee of those toils and dangers thou hast endured in the service of others.

Appropriately, the Lord's garlands of praise and comfort for His humble servant's achievement.*

The achievement here was so clear, in spite of the miasma the Admiral's mind had become—it was a new, rich continent between Europe and Asia—that one wonders why it should have eluded conventional historians of so many persuasions for so many years. True, there have always been some, such as Henry Vignaud, who realized that the Admiral did not believe his continent was part of Asia, and a great many contemporaries of Colón, both historians and cartographers, who decided that the two continents were indeed separate no matter who had discovered what. But the standard historical line has been that Colón always thought he was in some part of Asia and never realized to his dying day that he had found a new continent: "He was convinced until the very end," as Björn Landström puts it typically, "that he had reached India, and did not realize that he had discovered a new world."

It is hard to explain. My suspicion is that most historians have not bothered to look beyond the First Voyage and have been taken in by the falsifications put forth in the initial *Journal* and the Santangel Letter—put there, we presume, to induce the Sovereigns to sponsor a second trip for their new admiral; they may also have been misled by the interpretations of Fernando and Las Casas, which ignore this discovery of a continent in order to keep intact their notion that their hero was all along aiming for Asia and really thought he had reached it. It is also possible that later scholars either ignored such writings

---

*The Voice is also remarkable for the blatant reminder it delivers to the Sovereigns: " 'The privileges and promises that God bestows, He doth not revoke; nor doth He say, after having received service, that such was not His intention, and that it is to be understood in a different manner. . . . All that He promises He fulfills with interest; this is his way.' "

as the *Previlegios* and the *Lettera Rarissima* or dismissed them as the products of a man not entirely in control of his faculties; earlier chroniclers of the sixteenth century, moreover, would probably not have been privy to these later writings, which were directed specifically to the Sovereigns and kept more or less private. (The *Lettera* was published in Italian, in Venice, presumably in a small edition, in May 1505, but it was not widely circulated and was not translated into any other language, the first Spanish version apparently not appearing until the late seventeenth century; the *Previlegios* and *Profecías* were not intended to be, and were not, published.)

Nonetheless, in spite of all the difficulties, the record is ample and remarkably clear. There is no doubt about this extremely important fact: Admiral Colón claimed to have found a new continent, surmised its dimensions, calculated its rough geographic position, and asserted as much, more than once, to his royal patrons. In the pithy summary of the Columbus historian John Boyd Thacher, "He knew that between the country of the Great Khan and the shores of Europe lay great continental lands and that he—Christopher Columbus—and none other was their discoverer." And this time he was right.

> *The Eve of St. John's Day [Friday, 23 June 1503]. The water in our ship rose so high that it was almost up to the deck. With great toil we continued in this state until daybreak when we made a harbor in Jamaica named Porto Bueno. . . . The next day we sailed eastward to another harbor, named Santa Gloria, that was enclosed with reefs. Having got in, since we were no longer able to keep the ships afloat, we ran them ashore as far as we could, grounding them close together board and board.—Fernando*

Thus, ignominiously, ended the Fourth Voyage of Cristóbal Colón, Admiral of the Ocean Sea: shipwrecked and marooned on the north shore of Jamaica, at least 200 miles from the nearest Spanish ship of rescue. The "High Voyage" brought low.

For all his navigational skill, about which the salty types make such a fuss, and all his fortuitous headings, about which they are largely silent, Admiral Colón could be a wretched mariner. The four voyages, properly seen, quite apart from bravery and fortitude, are replete with lubberly mistakes, misconceived sailing plans, foolish disregard of elementary maintenance, and stubborn neglect of basic safety—all characterized by what can best be called a kind of *ecohubris*, the assertion of human superiority over the natural realm. Almost every time Colón went wrong it was because he had refused to bend to the inevitabilities of tide and wind and reef or, more arrogantly still, had not bothered to learn about them; the very same reckless courage that led him across the ocean in the first place, and saw him through storm and tumult to return, lay behind his numerous misfortunes.[3]

The Fourth Voyage is a perfect case in point. Led by some purpose he did not explain, he started out by sailing where he was explicitly forbidden by the monarchs to sail and ended up in a terrific hurricane. (His explanation, as Fernando retailed it, that one of his caravels was unseaworthy and he wanted to replace it at Santo Domingo, is unsupportable: that ship was part of a fleet that had just completed a very fast and smooth transoceanic journey, and it was to survive for the next two years when two others failed, ending up, with the flagship, marooned in Jamaica.) Then, in the grip of some purpose we cannot fathom, he went into storm after storm, ranged against the "cruel weather" and "raging sea" and "terrible current," even beating into a headwind so severe that he did not get 200 miles in a whole month. Next, driven by some urgency that has no rationale, he refused to stop to take the most elementary precautions to keep his ships seaworthy. Experienced in Caribbean waters, Colón would have known by now how necessary it was to protect against the inevitable, crippling shipworms of those waters by beaching, careening, cleaning, and if necessary retarring any wooden ship after a few months at sea; this was indeed a procedure he had ordered several times on the First Voyage. But despite countless opportunities, and plenty enough good weather, Colón apparently careened his ships only once (three of them, it seems, in October 1502 and one in December), and that was after more than six months in the water, when it was probably too late; by January 1503 it was obvious to him that "my vessels were unseaworthy," and still he did nothing for them. One he abandoned at Belén, the next at Portobelo, and the last two, "more riddled with holes than a honeycomb," he beached forever at Santa Gloria. That is irresponsible behavior for any admiral, indeed any traveler of the sea.

. . .

Colón and the remains of his crew were rescued from Jamaica by a ship from Española in June 1504, after a year that ended the Admiral's career with mutinies, pitched battles, starvation, sickness, fear, unaccountable indolence, unprincipled trickery on the part of the Admiral, great hospitality on the part of the Jamaica Tainos, considerable heroism on the part of several of his crew, and extreme good fortune. It is not surprising that in his *Lettera Rarissima* he said not a word about it. What he did say, however, gives some picture of his tortured soul as he lay marooned at Santa Gloria:

> I am wholly ruined, as I have said. Hitherto I have wept for others; now, may Heaven have pity on me, may earth weep for me! Of things material I have not a single blanca for an offering; of things spiritual I have even ceased observing the required forms here in the Indies. Alone in my trouble, infirm, daily expecting death, surrounded by a million savages full of cruelty and our enemies, and thus deprived of the holy sacraments of Holy Church, how forgotten will be this soul if here it part from this body! Weep for me, whoever has charity, truth and justice!
>
> I did not come on this voyage to gain honor or wealth, that is certain, for already the hope of all of that was dead. I came to Your Highnesses with honest purpose and true zeal, and I do not lie. I humbly beseech Your Highnesses that, if it please God to remove me from here, you will help me to go to Rome and on other pilgrimages. May the Holy Trinity guard and increase Your lives and high estate.

After a month's rest in Santo Domingo, Colón set sail for Spain with son and brother and twenty-two others in a chartered ship whose name we do not know, his last experience on the gray expanses that were all he ever knew for a home, and he arrived on November 7 at Sanlúcar de Barrameda, some fifty miles down the coast of Andalusia from Palos, where his momentous travels had begun a little over twelve years before.

No chronicler seems to like talking much about the last year and a half of the Admiral's life—Fernando, for example, gave it but a single paragraph—and indeed nothing in that time accords well with any picture of the Great Discoverer resting comfortably on his laurels of fame and fortune.

For one thing, he was almost totally ignored by the court and the Sovereigns on whose mercy he had just thrown himself so abjectly in his final letter. Isabella, it was true, was sick and died only three weeks after Colón reached port, but Ferdinand, though he appointed Colón's son Diego to his personal guard, showed no interest in hearing what the Admiral might have to tell him about the Fourth Voyage. It was not until May of the following year that the King finally granted an audience to Colón and, though there is no record of what transpired, it manifestly did not win Colón any of the extra privileges that his gift of a continent and Otro Mundo he might reasonably have hoped would inspire.

For another, he seems to have been absorbed now in pressing the petty arguments of his *Previlegios*, hoping to win this trivial honor and that improbable fortune, concerned with enlarging whatever he had been granted. Where he might well have spent his time setting out his new geographical conceptions in coherent form, for his government as for the rest of Europe, he was occupied only in the minutiae of securing the rewards for himself and his children to which he felt entitled.

And to hear him tell it, you would think that he truly was "ruined" and "without a single blanca," not even a roof for his head, as he put it in the *Lettera*. But the fact is that he then possessed a very considerable fortune. The operations of his large *mayorazgo* in the Vega Real on Española (a ranch and most probably several gold mines), overseen by his Genoese factor, Rafael Cattaneo, were thought to bring in at least $12,500 a year (according to Colón's own estimate in his 1506 will) and eventually should be worth between $30,000 and $60,000 a year (according to his maximum calculations in his 1498 will); he had established some extensive trading agreements with Genoese merchant-bankers supplying Española, whose trading licenses he controlled as admiral regardless of his governancy, and at one point around 1504 he claimed to have no less than $180,000 in assets on the island for use as collateral for such cargoes; he had been given a chest of coins of some kind to carry home from Santo Domingo on this last voyage, and he had already gathered a considerable amount in gold nuggets and gold jewelry in Veragua; presumably he had the gold cargo from the single ship that was said to have escaped the 1502 hurricane off Española, and we do have a record that some $3,300 of gold was sold on his behalf in 1503–04; and he received one-tenth of all the crown revenues in gold from the island, which may well have averaged something like $15,000 a year during this period. There's no way around it: Admiral Colón, for all his poor-mouthing, was a very wealthy man for his time, and his absorption in privileges and profits ill became him.[4]

Then, too, Colón was still in the throes of that persistent illness, presumably in considerable pain of body and possibly considerable torment of mind. On the last voyage his arthritic affliction had clearly passed into something far more serious—"I was sick and many times lay at death's door" is a typical reference—with symptoms still consistent with Reiter's syndrome. Moving about was so painful that he had what he called a "doghouse" built for him on the poop deck so that he wouldn't have to climb up from his cabin below, and almost assuredly he never left the flagship, never set foot this time either on the soil of his new continent. (He claimed in the *Lettera* that "on a mountain" he saw a "tomb as large as a house," but Fernando was clear that it was actually Bartolomé who made this trip.) The *Lettera* is shot through with his mental anguish, never more painfully so than in the Voice of Heaven passage, which even he suggests was inspired by fatigue and fever; but he was not ashamed to pass it along with all its bombast to the Sovereigns, and his continued pleadings during this time suggest that the Voice persisted with him.

This does not, obviously, add up to the portrait of an honored and noble admiral such as the hagiographers would like us to be left with; no wonder Morison says simply that, after the last voyage, "it were well had the rest been silence."

In the fresh April spring of 1506, Cristóbal Colón followed the court from Salamanca to Valladolid, in the heart of ancient Castile, where he moved into a one-story house not far from the Church of San Francisco (although there is no reason to suppose it was the house now celebrated as the Casa de Colón in calle Cristóbal Colón) and took to his bed. On May 19, in the presence of two citizens of Valladolid, seven servants (hardly poverty, that), and a notary, he dictated and signed a codicil to his previous will, making his son Diego his principal heir, providing small inheritances for his brothers Bartolomé and Diego and his son Fernando, asking for a chapel to be built in the Vega Real if there were money enough, and providing for his mistress Beatriz "so that she may be able to live honestly."[5]

On the following day, the celebration of the Feast of the Ascension, Colón drew around him his sons, his brother Diego, a few shipboard comrades, and his servants, underwent the last sacraments of the Church, and, Fernando avers, said these last words in echo of none less than Christ himself: *"In manus tuas, Domine, commendo spiritum meum"*—Into thy hands, Lord, I commend my spirit.

Not more than a mile away from the house in which the Admiral of the Ocean Sea departed on the final tide lies the house of a Spanish novelist who, almost a century later, may have called upon the Admiral's ghost to inhabit the immortal character of the man who lived only to wander the world, ever restless, ever rootless, ever deceived, brave and chivalric and absurd, indomitable and credulous and not entirely sane, the great knight known to the world as El Caballero de la Triste Figura. And though no authentic portrait of Colón exists—none was done before the 1550s, as near as we can tell—those of the sixteenth century, presumably the nearest to accuracy, are unified in showing a man of great somberness and sadness, a Knight of the Sorrowful Countenance indeed.[6]

No reliable record comes down to us of the weather on that Wednesday in late May 1506—but then no reliable record comes down to us of anything much about the day of the death of the Great Discoverer. There was no notice taken of his passing in the daily chronicle of the city of Valladolid, which covered many minutiae, or in the official record of the Spanish court, though it was sitting only miles away; no contemporary historian noted the occasion, not even Peter Martyr, who was in Valladolid around that time, certainly by the end of the following month. In fact the first public notice of the departure of Cristóbal Colón in the Spain he served does not come until ten years later, with the publication of Martyr's *De orbe novo*, in Alcalá, in 1516, and then it was quite glancing indeed: "Colonus being now departed out of this life, the king began to take care how those lands may be inhabited with Christian men to the increase of our faith." The Admiral of the Ocean Sea died unnoticed and unsung.

Indeed, the scope of the Admiral's achievement, the importance of those mysterious lands to the west, was very slow to dawn on Europe. The idea of an Other World, a *New World*, in a new hemisphere was simply so staggering that it could not be easily assimilated, even in many intellectual circles, or readily appreciated, even when Spanish wealth began to arrive from there by the shipload. The savvy Machiavelli, as late as 1513, could praise the skill and admire the exploits of King Ferdinand of Spain without once mentioning any of Colón's discoveries in the New World. Later still, a popular French cosmology published in five editions between 1539 and 1560 made no mention of the Americas or any new lands anywhere to the west of Europe; at least seven general histories printed in France between 1516 and 1549, including numerous editions of the popular *Mer des histoires*, failed to allude at all to the discovery or exploration of the New World. And the works that began to recognize the existence of a new hemisphere were not that numerous: Jean Bodin's 1566 bibliography of history, the most complete record of sixteenth-century scholarship, listed only three books on the New World, and in the entire period between 1480 and 1609 there were three times as many books published in France on Asia, twice as many on Turkey, as on any part of the Americas.

Slow, too, to emerge in Europe—and here the Discoverer was doubly neglected—was a *name* for these new-found lands. Colón generally referred to them as "the Indies," even after his idea of the Otro Mundo became fixed, and it was as "the Indies" that they remained in the official records of the Spanish government (supplemented later by "Nueva España" and the like) through the sixteenth and seventeenth centuries. Elsewhere, however, a new coinage slowly gained currency, by fits and starts, first in France, then in Holland, then in England—it was "America," which the mapmaker Martin Waldseemüller derived from the Latin name of that fellow whose *Quattro viaggi* talked about the discovery of the large southern landmass, and which he boldly printed on that continent when he put out his map of the world and his globe in 1507. It was by no means a universal designation—mapmakers often used "Mundus Novus" or "Terra Firma" or even "Terra Incognita" on continents both north and south, and Mediterranean writers avoided it altogether until midcentury—and even Waldseemüller ceased using it on his later maps. But it appeared with increasing frequency for the next three decades, and then in 1538 it was used for the first time for the northern as well as the southern landmass ("Americae") by the most illustrious cartographer of his century, Gerardus Mercator, and thereafter was well established, particularly in northern Europe. Only Las Casas was round in his denunciation of it: the new land, he said with some asperity, "ought to be called *Columba.*"*

It is perhaps the final ignominy surrounding the death of the Admiral, though of this too he was spared the knowledge, that history does not even know what became of his remains. He was buried at Valladolid, possibly in the Franciscan church near his house, and local legend has it that his remains are still there, though the church is now a pool hall. Documents, however, suggest that in 1509, by his son Diego's order, the body was removed from there to the Chapel of Santa Ana at Las Cuevas, the monastery in Seville. When Bartolomé Colón died in 1514 he was buried in the chapel, and then Diego, who had served for a time as admiral and governor in Española (with hardly more success than his father), followed him on his death in 1526. In the 1530s several royal ordinances approving the removal of Cristóbal's and Diego's bodies to Española were issued, and in 1539 and 1541, according to entries in the chapel's daybook, the urn or casket with Cristóbal's remains was removed and prepared for shipment to Santo Domingo. No sure record of this shipment exists, but it is assumed that both bodies were reburied before the high altar of the cathedral in Santo Domingo sometime in the early 1540s, and lay undisturbed until 1667, when they were rediscovered and given "a more decent interment." When France took control of Española in 1795, Madrid ordered that Cristóbal's remains be sent to safety in Havana; these were moved again after Cuba became independent in 1898 and shipped to Seville to be interred finally in the cathedral there in a tomb thought to be appropriate for the Great Discoverer.

Two decades before that, however, in 1877, a small lead casket was discovered and removed during the enlargement of the Santo Domingo cathedral, and when examined it was found to have two inscriptions with the name Cristoval Colon; in 1879 it was returned to the cathedral, and it lies there today in a tomb thought to be appropriate for the Great Discoverer.[7]

It is perhaps fitting that the bones of the man honored as the European discoverer of the Americas should lie, in a sense, on both continents. Fitting, too, that even in death he finds no home.

* "America" was never used by Vespucci himself, who died in 1512 probably without knowing of the coinage. His son Juan, in a 1526 map, avoided using the term even though it had some currency then; instead he named only provinces and coasts and left the continent unlabeled.

Chapter Nine

1506–1606

I

The Columbian Legacy

"I SAY that Don Christopher Colonus (as it is well known), being the first Admiral of this India, discovered the same in the days of the Catholic king. . . . The which gift and benefit was such that it is unto this day one of the greatest that ever any subject or servant hath done for his prince or country, as is manifest to the whole world. And to say the truth, this shall doubtless be so commodious and profitable unto the whole realm of Spain, that I repute him no good Castilian or Spaniard that does not recognize the same."

So, in 1526, exactly twenty years after his death, did the first official historian of the Spanish conquests, Gonzalo Fernández de Oviedo, write of the man who made them possible. He continued (as we may take it from an English translation of a few decades later):

Forasmuch as unto our time this great part of the world was unknown to the antiquity—insomuch that none of the writers of that age, nor yet Ptolemy in his Cosmography, or any other since him, have made any mention thereof, until the first Admiral Don Christopher Colonus discovered the same. A thing doubtless without comparison, much greater than that which is said of Hercules, that he first gave the entrance of the Sea *Mediterraneum* into the Ocean, which the Greeks could never do before him. . . . And certainly sir, if there had been an image of gold made in the praise and fame of Colonus, he had as well deserved it as any of those men to whom for their noble enterprise the antiquity gave divine honor, if he had been in their time.

A statue of gold for the Spanish admiral: what a fitting, what a wondrous idea. Yet so far from erecting such a statue, the Spanish took more than 350 years before establishing any memorial whatsoever to Colón. Then, although they chose indeed to build in granite and marble rather than gold, they nevertheless made up for past neglect with no fewer than six large and magnificent monuments in time for the 400th anniversary of the Discovery, in Seville, Barcelona, Huelva, Granada, Salamanca, and Madrid.

And therein lies the fascinating puzzle of the historical reputation of the Great Discoverer. To examine his treatment at the hands of subsequent centuries—to look at his life after his death, as it were —is to follow the peculiar gyrations of the Old World coming to terms with the presence of the New, a process of surprising complexity. Thus the image of Colón, effectively the symbol of that New World for Europe as he was its cause, shifted through successive European prisms. In the first century after his death he started as merely the sea captain who brought amazing tidings of some new islands to the west and their outlandish denizens, then became the forerunner of the Spanish conquerors who began to extract wealth from the Americas heretofore unknown in Europe, and finally turned into the tragic but indomitable hero whose genius was at last seen to have given "a fourth part of the world" to Europe. In the seventeenth century, as other European nations came to learn the full dimensions—and importance—of that fourth part, he was the goad for their explorations and the inspiration for their settlements, Cristóbal Colón now become Christopher Columbus. By the eighteenth century he had developed into a legend in the societies taking root in the New World, a kind of mythic symbol of their special fortuity; and in the supremely successful one that claimed and set out to occupy the northern continent, he became its very personification and the embodiment of its independence. But it was not until the nineteenth century, after the uncovering and publishing of dusty documents from the Spanish archives—including, for the first time, the *Journal* of the First Voyage—that the full story of Colón, and the full record of his triumphs and tribulations, began to be understood by a wide general audience and he came to attain anything like the standing in which he is held today.

It was then that the Discoverer was finally recognized with statues and monuments in growing numbers on both sides of his ocean— not a one of them, however, of gold. Even though, as Oviedo took pains to point out, "as a brave and wise sailor, and a courageous captain, he showed to us this New World, which is so full of gold that thousands of such statues could have been made out of the gold that is sent to Spain."

On October 11, 1501, a Portuguese ship under the command of Miguel Corte Real put into Lisbon after a successful voyage to territories in the northern Atlantic that were even then held to be a part of the same landmass "connected with the Antilles, which were discovered by the sovereigns of Spain." Its primary cargo: some fifty Beothuk Indians, taken from Newfoundland, who were regarded as having the "most bestial habits and manners, like wild men," although "exceedingly well-formed in their limbs" and thus "excellent for labour and the best slaves that have hitherto been obtained." The news, wrote the Venetian ambassador, "so pleased his majesty that it has made him desirous of sending ships again to said region, and of increasing his fleet for India, in order to conquer more quickly."

Corte Real was carrying on the unfortunate tradition of Indian enslavement and deportation begun by another Iberian ship captain in the Caribbean nine years earlier. This cargo would not, in the end, turn out to be a very serviceable commodity—the Indians did not last long, apparently, faced with Mediterranean elements and diseases— but neither that experience nor the similar ones of Colón and his numerous Spanish imitators did anything to discourage further kidnapping of Indians from the New World for at least a century more by captains of virtually every European nation: the Italian Verrazzano, for example, took a baby from its mother's arms near Cape Hatteras in 1524; the Portuguese Gomes "filled his ship with innocent people of both sexes" (said to number fifty-eight) from Maine in 1525; the Frenchman Cartier took two prisoners from the St. Lawrence in 1534, ten more in 1536, and two more in 1541; and the Englishman Frobisher took one Inuit in 1576 and three more (including a young mother and her baby) in 1577. Nor did it serve to end the Atlantic slave trade itself, which the Portuguese continued to carry on with African bodies instead of Indian in ever greater numbers as the sixteenth century went on, establishing themselves as the most thorough and successful practitioners of one of the most odious pursuits in the annals of modern Europe.

The history of the Beothuks is in many respects similar to that of the Tainos. A gentle and pacific people, who in fact had retired from the mainland to Newfoundland to live in peace and seclusion, they lived on fish, caribou, and seal, which were there in abundance. As soon as the Europeans came to Newfoundland—fishermen, hunters, explorers—the Beothuks were steadily displaced and eliminated, and the summertime cod fisheries from the mid–sixteenth century on took it as a matter of policy to hunt down and shoot nearby natives and despoil their villages. In the words of one British account, "Before we left the spot we set fire to three of their wigwams out of four," no reason given. But as it was to the south, the main killer was probably diseases, particularly the one that went into Beothuk legend as "the cough demon"—tuberculosis. After no more than a century or so, the island caribou and beaver had been hunted to extinction and the Beothuks were down to only a few hundred. By the twentieth century, they were extinct.

It is true that the totality of Colón's achievement, other than the initial discovery, was slow in being conveyed to Europe. After the extraordinary dissemination of the news of the First Voyage—nineteen editions between 1493 and 1500, in four languages—almost nothing more was printed about the subsequent voyages during the Admiral's lifetime: the Second Voyage was described in but a single small work, in Latin, published in Pavia in 1494; the *Lettera Rarissima* on the Fourth Voyage was printed in only one edition, in Italian, in 1505; and a pirated version of Peter Martyr's "First Decade," giving details of the first three voyages, was published in a single edition, also in Italian, in 1504.* As a result, the news that Colón had gone on to find an Otro Mundo, not to mention an Earthly Paradise, had sailed along much of its northern coast on two separate journeys, and had found gold and pearls in considerable abundance, was not generally known even to the literate European public; it remained largely the privileged information of a small circle of courtiers and navigators in Spain. Only with the Spanish publication of Martyr's work in 1511 did the story of Colón up to 1500 become known at all in Spain (and still only to that small part of the educated public

---

*Fernando implied that the *Lettera Rarissima* was printed in Spanish as well, but no copy is known.

versed in Latin); and only with the appearance of a popular omnium-gatherum called *Paesi novamente retrovati* in Italy in 1507, picking up the pirated edition of Martyr, was this transmitted to Europe at large. And not until 1516, when Martyr's "Three Decades" were published in Alcalá as *De orbe novo*, and then between 1521 and 1534, when these were reprinted in nine editions in five languages, did the story of all four voyages—and hence the considerable stature due the Admiral as the discoverer not only of a few islands but of the continent of the New World—become available throughout literate Europe at large.

It is *not* true, however, as received historical opinion has it even today, that Colón after his death was ignored by an ungrateful Spain and an unknowing Europe. Due and appropriate recognition was somewhat lagging, perhaps, but during the course of the sixteenth century he was given mention, as near as I can calculate it, in at least 142 individual printed works by 118 authors, appearing in a total of 385 editions and imprints, in nine different languages (Italian, Spanish, Portuguese, French, English, Dutch, German, Polish, and Latin) from Lisbon to Cracow and London to Naples.[1] Some of these made only glancing reference, often in connection with the introduction of syphilis, but many gave considerable space to Colón's voyages, a number of them with details of his early life and trials in Portugal and Spain. And at least two dozen of them were devoted wholly or in large part to the events and achievements of the Admiral's life— one, in fact, was a full-scale biography.

The image of the Discoverer right from the beginning was, if still in many ways indistinct, entirely eminent, and it became only more so through the century as more and more details (as well as myths) were added to it and more and more writers addressed themselves to the import of the New World. The first work to sketch his full life appeared ten years after his death, a *Polyglot Psalter* in 1516 by Agostino Giustiniani, who reckoned Colón as "this illustrious man, who if he had lived in the time of the Grecian heroes, without doubt would have been enrolled among the number of the gods." This assessment was repeated and then embellished in the next decades— Spaniards such as Oviedo were particularly prone to sing his praises as more and more bullion crossed the waters to Seville from Mexico and Peru—and by the end of the century the poor Genoese sailor had even become the glorified subject of elaborate epic poems. To follow that process is to see not only how the Columbian Legacy was transmitted to Europe but how the subcontinent developed its sense of what the Americas were and what they might become.

The groundwork for it all was laid within the first half-century after Colón's death, with six widely printed and influential works on the New World:

• Peter Martyr's "Three Decades" devoted a quarter of its pages to Colón's discoveries and his governance of Española until he was returned to Spain in chains, plus two dozen other scattered references; this was printed in no fewer than nineteen editions between 1504 and 1563, in Latin and seven vernacular languages, and was the first and for a long time the most important work on the New World. Martyr's account became the centerpiece—sometimes lifted in toto, since niceties of authorial ownership were not much observed in those years —for other important books on America in the first half of the century, including the versions of Montalboddo, Grynaeus, Münster, and Ramusio, which collectively passed on Colón's story in fifty-seven editions. It also was the work that more than any other influenced the champions of English colonization in the second half of the century—an important impact of the Columbian Legacy to which we shall turn in the next chapter—especially Richard Eden (who translated the "Three Decades" in 1555) and Richard Hakluyt (who reprinted a Latin edition in 1587).

Martyr was a phlegmatic historian, little given to embellishment or analysis—ignoring Colón's early life, physical description, and character entirely, and offering few details of the voyages themselves—but he was of no doubt as to the Admiral's heroism: "Whereas I have heretofore declared how Veragua was first found by Colonus, I think I should commit a heinous crime if I should defraud the man of the due commendations of his travails, of his cares and troubles, and finally of the dangers and perils which he sustained in that navigation." Nor did Martyr mince words about the importance of the discovery for Spain, and for Europe:

> To be short, therefore: all things do so flourish, grow, increase, and prosper that the last are ever better than the first. And surely to declare my opinion herein, whatsoever has heretofore been discovered by the famous travels of Saturnus and Hercules, with such others whom the ancients for their heroical feats honored

as gods, seems but little and obscure if it be compared to the Spaniards' victorious labors.

• Fracanzano de Montalboddo's ingenious collection of travel accounts, *Paesi novamente retrovati*, was extremely important in popularizing knowledge of Europe's New World ventures; the historian Boies Penrose has called it "one of the most important books ever published" and "the book par excellence by which the news of the great voyages and great discoveries—east and west—was disseminated throughout Renaissance Europe." After its original printing in Italian in 1507 it was quickly translated into German, Latin, and French and went through fourteen editions between 1508 and 1521 (tantamount to best-sellerdom), with printings apparently of some size, judging by the number of surviving copies.

Accounts of da Gama, Cabral, the Corte Reals, and others are to be found there, plus the fabricated "Vespucci" relation *Mundus novus*, and Martyr's "First Decade." Because the "Vespucci" claimed that he discovered South America on a 1497 voyage (which never took place), even a careful reader might not have credited Colón with being the first European there, in spite of Martyr's full account of the Third Voyage in 1498, when the Admiral did indeed discover Paria and decided it was a continent ("He supposes," as Martyr said, "it to be a Continent"). But there would be no doubt in anyone's mind that Colón was the man who first opened up the New World and that, as Martyr put it, "the ship masters and mariners ran over many coasts during these ten years [1492–1502]: but ever followed such as were first found by Colonus."

• Gonzalo Fernández de Oviedo, the advocate of the golden statue, was an *hidalgo* who spent three decades in the Americas and took the matter of its history very seriously; he provided the first accounts for the literate Spanish public of the full story of Spain's conquest of the New World. His *Sumario*, printed in Spanish in Toledo in 1526, was so well received—"a huge and immediate success," a modern historian has called it, with eleven editions before 1577—that he was made the official historian of the Indies for the crown. His *Historia general natural de las Indias*, which came out sporadically from 1535 to 1557 (and not in full until the nineteenth century), was similarly popular, enjoying nine editions, and parts were translated into French, Italian, English, and even Arabic.

Although he knew the voyages of Vespucci, the Pinzóns, and Magellan, and had firsthand experience of many of the conquistadors of Central America, Oviedo gave pride of place to Colón and a full treatment to his voyages, in serviceable if not very exciting (and rather meandering) prose, declaring he was "worthy of fame and glory" not only for discovering lands "so overflowing with gold" but "for having brought the Catholic faith to these parts." Indeed, Oviedo was the first writer to see Colón as a great and complex heroic figure, courageous in the face of adversity both at sea and on land, and was the first (from the hindsight of Mexico) to recognize his historical importance as the Discoverer, the "cause of everything that is known in these parts, and he taught it and discovered it for all those who enjoy it." He defended Colón the Governor in true *hidalgo* fashion for his harsh colonial rule ("You should know that it was needful, and is needful, that there should be a gallows in the town, and a [chopping] block, so that evildoers can be punished") and for having hanged those he saw as troublemakers ("Without obedience there is no rule . . . in these new lands"). So enamored of Colón was he that he said, upon witnessing the arrival of Colón's coffin in Santo Domingo in the 1540s, that he too wanted to be buried in the capital's cathedral, near the Admiral's tomb. He was.

• Francisco López de Gómara, in the generation after Oviedo, produced a *Historia general de las Indias* in Saragossa in 1552 that ended up going through a remarkable twenty-three editions and reprints in the next three decades plus several more thereafter; it was thus the most popular single work of history on the New World produced in the century.

Gómara was not quite so admiring in tone as Oviedo, and he set Colón's achievements more in the context of the subsequent discoveries of Cortés and Pizarro (in fact one English version of the *Historia*, in 1596, was devoted entirely to Cortés, without any mention of the Admiral). But he began with the acknowledgment that Colón had fulfilled the Senecan prophecy beyond *"ultima Thule,"* and spent some time on "what manner of man Chrystopher Colón was," including his early life, his stay in Portugal, and his difficulties with Ferdinand and Isabella ("whereby he was greatly tormented in his imagination"). The voyages were told with little detail, and not much drama was wrought from the specifics of the Admiral's career, as if Gómara was impatient to get on to the "wealth of gold and silver" that were to follow. But he was the one who coined that simplest, boldest, and perhaps most eloquent summary of the Columbian achievement: "The greatest event since the creation of the world (excluding the incarnation and death of Him who created it) is the discovery of the Indies."

• Sebastian Münster's *Cosmographia* was printed in no fewer than thirty-five editions between 1544 and 1576, in Latin and five vernaculars (including Czech); it was an immensely popular work and probably the most influential geographical compendium of the century. The earlier editions had almost nothing on the New World— as late as 1545, fifty years after the Discovery, Münster gave only desultory attention to "the new islands" and failed to mention a continent out there at all (although his maps from 1540 on do indeed show unmistakable continents)—but the later printings carried quite complete retellings of the Martyr and Montalboddo versions of the early voyages, including the first three of Colón. The English translation of Münster, Richard Eden's *A treatyse of the newe India* in 1553, was especially important, as we shall see; it was the first book devoted to America printed in England and the beginning of that nation's eventually powerful colonial ideology.

Münster's treatment of Colón—twenty-four of the eighty-four pages in the English edition devoted to the Americas—was quite complete, with the exception of the account of the last voyage. Matter-of-fact about his accomplishments ("He applied his mind to search unknown parts of the world" and "at the length found certain islands"), Münster grew fairly heated, by contrast, when it came to discussing Colón's meeting with the "Canibales" and "serpents of monstrous greatness," and even more so with the discovery of gold (there is "much gold" on Española, where "in the year of Christ 1501, they gathered within the space of two months 1200 pounds weight of gold"). All in all, it was what might be called a Germanic treatment, cooler in tone than such Spanish champions as Oviedo and Gómara, but even-handed and as comprehensive as a work based on the tales of others could be expected to be.

• Finally, Giovanni Battista Ramusio's collections, *Navigationi et viaggi*, provided (in the third volume) the definitive historical picture of the New World and its discovery, a rendition (out of Martyr by Oviedo, we may say) that would not really be surpassed in accuracy and comprehension until the eighteenth century. First printed in Ven-

ice in 1556, it had only three other editions in the sixteenth century—two in Italian, one in French—but it had a wide circulation
and, as the British historian David Beers Quinn has put it, "thereafter,
English, French, and German writers were to go to Ramusio as to a
treasure chest, plundering it for references and for texts to translate
into their own languages." It was also the book that provided both
the influential English editor Richard Hakluyt and the influential
French historian André Thevet with their basic knowledge of the
Americas. As did others by that time, Ramusio gave Colón his rightful
historical place as the heroic initiator of "the Indies," and devoted
the first tenth of this volume to the four Colón voyages, the chaotic
governorship of Española, and the Admiral's retreat into obscurity
in his last years.

It is evident, then, that by the middle of the sixteenth century any
literate European could have had a pretty good fix on the truth about
(as Richard Eden put it) "the newe founde lands": they were the
authentic discovery of the stubborn and heroic Cristóbal Colón (Colonus, Columbi, Columbus . . .), they were a genuinely *new* part of
the world heretofore unknown, they were endowed with unexpected
riches available for the taking (gold and silver, dye-wood and codfish,
not to mention cocoa, turkeys, and other exotica), and they were
populated by naked heathens whom armed Christians could easily
displace. Far from being ignored or forgotten, Colón was in general a figure of considerable renown, at least among those who would
have concerned themselves at all with the new explorations, probably a distinct minority of the reading public even then, but also
probably—as merchants, bankers, investors, princes, courtiers,
scholars, cosmographers, religious leaders, missionaries, and adventurers—an influential one.

*On June 7, 1542, Jean-François de La Roque, the lord of a number
of fiefdoms in France including one called Roberval (the name by
which, mistakenly, he has gone down in history), put into St. John's
Harbor, Newfoundland, with three ships from La Rochelle. With
perhaps two hundred passengers or more—including French lords and
a number of their ladies, soldiers, masons and carpenters, priests and
doctors, and a contingent of ex-convicts—he was on his way to establish a permanent colony on the St. Lawrence River that would*

truly inaugurate the French empire in the Americas, much as a similar voyage fifty years before had launched the now resplendent Spanish empire. Although charged by his liege, François I, with the tasks of conversion and civilization, those usual excuses for empire, La Roque and company had no doubt as to their principal mission: to find and subdue the immensely rich Kingdom of Saguenay, where the Hurons had assured the French that "il y a infiny or, rubiz et aultres richesses," and provide for France its Laurentian Mexico.

La Roque was a man of some intelligence and ability, although there is no record of his ever having been at sea before, but his principle of colonial governance seems to have been quite as crude as that of his Spanish predecessor on Española. On his way to his settlement, discovering that one of his well-born relatives on board was having an affair with a Norman peasant lad, he marooned both of them, along with the lady's maid, on a Laurentian island with a basket of provisions and a couple of arquebuses. (Miraculously, though her companions and a subsequent baby died in the wild, it seems that the demoiselle survived and was rescued two and a half years later.) At the settlement itself, which he chose to name France-Roy, La Roque was, by a contemporary account, "very cruel to his men [and] insisted on their living in peace according to his decrees, which he caused to be strictly kept." Strictly, indeed: "one day he had six of them hanged even though they were his favorites," and "he had several exiled on an island with irons on their legs for having been caught in a theft" amounting to a few pennies. "John of Nantes was layde in yrons and kept prisoner for his offence," according to another account, "and others also were put in yrons, and divers were whipped, as well men as women." "By which means," the report ended, without irony, "they lived in quiet."

In quiet, perhaps, but not in much comfort, and the tribulations of France-Roy seem to have followed a kind of sad parallel with those of Isabela five decades earlier. It was only September when La Roque sent two ships back to France for "victuals and other things," "seeing that provisions were failing from day to day" and "because of wheat, pork-fat, flour, cider, and wine there was none." Some kitchen-garden planting was done before winter set in, but the results were meager, and despite the abundant local wildlife of every kind the French apparently spent the bulk of the winter on short rations and near starvation rather than troubling themselves to hunt or forage. They lived *largely on the supplies of the local Stadaconans, who, "considering the poverty of [these] afflicted foreigners, deprived thus of all resources, . . . strove day and night to hunt wild game and to fish" to keep the colony alive. On toward spring, it seems, some of the men "were forced to go fishing or die of hunger, and had to gather hither and yon certain plants and roots to eat," but even that was done with such ineptitude that several of the colonists died from eating poison mushrooms. How many died from hunger was not related in the skimpy records we have, but the weakened settlement fell prey to diseases, chiefly scurvy, "and there dyed thereof about fiftie," a figure undoubtedly on the low side.*

No sign was ever found of the supposed Kingdom of Saguenay— La Roque may have realized in the end that it was all a myth built out of fanciful Indian fables and gullible French greed—nor any trace of promised riches. When spring broke, La Roque made one last fruitless search upriver, which achieved nothing more than the capsizing of a longboat and the drowning of at least eight men, and he then decided, because of "the intemperate climate of said country, and the slight profit," to abandon the unhappy colony. Sometime in July the last of the colonists piled into their one remaining ship for the voyage home and apparently made it safely back to French soil by mid-September.

Like Isabela, France-Roy crumbled and rotted into the soil, its prospect again the domain of the Stadaconans, and nothing remained when the next Frenchmen ventured up the river there sixty-five years later. There is no tradition, however, of lingering ghosts of white intruders whose heads come off with their hats.

The essentials being known—in varying degrees in various lands, and for the most part only among the literate, though some of it was starting to become the stuff of popular myth—it is not surprising that during the second half of the century Cristóbal Colón should begin to achieve the status of a full-fledged hero, in works both historical and literary.

One measure of that was the actual designation of Colón as "of historic stature" and his inclusion in the collection of short biographies of famous historical figures, *Elogia vivorum illustrium*, by Paolo Giovio, the bishop of Nocera, in 1551. ("*Hic enim ille est Christo-*

*phorus Columbus, stupendi alterius et nullis ante seculis cogniti ter-
rarum orbis repertor.*") Giovio owned a villa outside Como where
he collected portraits of famous people (and where, presumably sometime around 1552, he received or ordered a painting of the Discoverer), and this *Elogia* seems to have grown out of the interest in his
gallery. The first edition was popular—it had eight reprints and editions in four languages (including Spanish) by 1571—but it did not
in fact have a portrait of Colón; that apparently had to await an
edition put out in Basel in 1575 (with reprints in 1577, 1580, and
1596), containing a woodcut credited to Tobias Stimmer, said by the
publisher to be faithful to the original. This original portrait—which
we have no reason to think actually bears a resemblance to Colón,
done so long after his death—was subsequently copied for the Uffizi
Gallery in Florence, for Ferdinand I of Austria, and for a local Italian
princess, all in the 1550s—and incidentally, in 1784, for Thomas
Jefferson, who had it hung in his Monticello mansion.*

Another measure of Colón's stature was the somewhat unusual
presence of three epic poems about him written toward the end of
the century, all by Italians who not only saw Colón as a countryman
of theirs deserving special praise but also saw the Spanish empire he
founded as a Catholic bulwark against the onslaughts of the Reformation. The first was by Lorenzo Gambara, in 1581, a historical epic
in Latin that took four long books and 120 pages to tell, with fair
accuracy, the complete story of Colón's voyages (even including, for
example, some of the madder passages from the *Lettera*); this was
given a second edition in 1583, with the addition of a map and a
picture of the Virgin Mary, and a third in 1585—a surprising success
in Italy for a Latin poem on a Spanish navigator. The next was by

---

*This Giovian original is said, though without authentication, to be the one subsequently
owned by Count Alessandro de Orchi, with the inscription "COLUMBUS LYGUR NOV[I] ORBIS
REPTO[R]" at the top, and is variously reproduced. In addition to the Stimmer, other sixteenth-
century engravings are those by André Thevet (1584), Aliprando Caprioli (1596), and Crispin
de Pas (1598), all for collections of famous men, and by Theodore de Bry for his edition of
Girolamo Benzoni in 1595–96. At least eleven other paintings done in the sixteenth century
(the list is in John Boyd Thacher, *Christopher Columbus*, vol. 3) are said with varying authority
to be of Colón (including works attributed to Sebastiano del Piombo, Lorenzo Lotto, and
Girolamo Parmigiano), although it is difficult to assign exact dates to any of them, and there
is no reason to suppose any of them bears a likeness to Colón. (The Piombo is now generally
thought to be a portrait of some Italian gentleman, no connection to Colón; the inscription at
its top identifying it as Columbus is accepted now as having been added well after the painting
was done, probably well after Piombo's death.) But such an outpouring of portraiture hardly
suggests a forgotten figure.

Julius Ceasar Stella, a full-fledged classical epic, in Latin, complete with angels and Satan and interminable speeches, first published in London in 1585 and reprinted in Rome in 1590; Colón here is a Spanish Aeneas, founder of a glorious empire, and he bestrides his New World with complete disregard of the facts. Last came a work by Giovanni Giorgini in 1596, 24,000 lines' worth in Italian ottava rima, presenting Colón as a figure with all the classical virtues—he is pious, learned, skillful, wise, courageous, and loyal—who is not only a great navigator but a great soldier, diplomat, and conquistador, and who turns out to be the man who was responsible for the conquest of Mexico, with only a little help from Cortés and King Ferdinand.

As barometers of Colón's reputation, if not precisely as great works of epic art, these three poems—and a few lesser poems of the time*—are intriguing. But for literature it is necessary to turn to another Italian, Torquato Tasso, acknowledged as one of the greatest of Italian Renaissance poets, and his *Gerusalemme liberata*, which went through seven editions when it was first printed in 1581 (later translated into French, Spanish, and English in another six editions) and was long the most popular Italian narrative poem. It is a protracted work, in many cantos, and only two of the stanzas in canto XV have to do with the Discoverer, but they suffice to show his accepted standing at the time, at least to the literate Italian. In the 1600 English version:

> *A knight of Genes [Genoa] shall have the hardiment*
> *Upon this wond'rous voyage first to wend;*
> *Nor winds nor waves that ships in sunder rent,*
> *Nor seas unus'd, strange clime, or pool unken'd,*
> *Nor other peril nor astonishment*
> *That makes frail hearts of men to bow and bend,*
> *Within Albias' strait [Gibraltar] shall keep and hold*
> *The noble spirit of this sailor bold.*

> *Thy ship, Columbus, shall her canvas wing*
> *Spread o'er that world that yet concealed lies;*

---

*They include three epitaphs by a Bishop of Fano in 1574, an Italian ode of 1591 (Gabriel Chiabrera), and a "heroic poem" in 1602 (Giovanni Villifranchi); Spanish poems of 1566 (Luis Zapata) and 1589 (Juan de Castellanos); a French verse of 1574 (M. de Saint-Gelais); and two occasional English verses of 1563 (Robert Seall) and 1576 (George Gascoigne).

That scant swift Fame her looks shall after bring,
Though thousand plumes she have and thousand eyes:
Let her of Bacchus and Alcides sing,
Of thee to future age let this suffice,
That of thine acts she some forewarning give,
Which shall in verse and noble story live.*

The best measure of Colón's standing at this time, though it comes from a decidedly interested source, was the full-scale biography produced by his son Fernando—a singular honor for any public figure, even if endowed by one's son, and not to be repeated for Colón until the late eighteenth century. The work was originally composed, we may suppose, sometime in the 1530s, probably not long before Fernando's death in 1539, and in manuscript form was probably known to a number of contemporary Spanish historians, including Las Casas, in the following decades; it passed into the hands of Colón's heirs and was eventually sold by Cristóbal's grandson, Luis, to a wealthy Genoese patron who had it published in Venice in 1569 (and again in 1571), translated into not very distinguished Italian by one Alfonso Ulloa. The original manuscript is now lost.†

Fernando's *Historie* of course set out to paint in brightest colors the man he referred to from first to last as "the Admiral," devising for him a special calling from the Lord, a high-born Genoese pedigree and education, and a nearly divine genius for navigation and geography. But Fernando was a scholar of sorts, a highly educated man himself, with a library of some 15,000 books and manuscripts, and he had access to almost all of his father's papers (including the journals of the First and Third Voyages); he himself had been with his father

---

*Out of the tortured verse of Edward Fairfax, no match for the original, we may understand this to mean that Fame will find Colón no matter how far he sails and, rather than sing aloud, she has merely to give a hint of his great acts for history to remember them forever.

†This biography was influential even before publication, being circulated in at least one and possibly (customarily) more manuscript copies for at least three decades after Fernando's death, and possibly among a few close friends before that. We tend to forget from our vantage point how wide a circulation a manuscript could have in those days, and how widely known it might be, at least among scholars. Among the manuscripts that are known to have had currency in Spain in this era were also Las Casas's *Historia de las Indias*, another history of the Americas by Fernando's friend Hernán Pérez de Oliva, Juan López de Velasco's official chronicle of the Indies, Andrés Bernáldez's *Historia de los reyes católicos*, and Juan Ginés de Sepúlveda's initial treatise against the American Indians, all of them quite important documents, none published in book form until centuries later.

on the Fourth Voyage and had seen him intimately on land and sea, in glory and ignominy, for more than half a dozen years. Hence his work was indisputably valuable for its intimate and informed picture of the Admiral, and it was used by all subsequent scholars (sometimes verbatim) for both the fine-edge details and the chiaroscuros of Colón's life. It seems not to have been popular enough to have called forth a Spanish edition, as one might have expected, nor was it translated into other European languages until centuries afterward (in English not until the mid–eighteenth century); but its insights and intimacies were more revelatory than anything published by any other writer until the nineteenth century. Washington Irving deservedly called it "the corner-stone of the history of the American continent."

On July 30, 1578, Captain Martin Frobisher anchored with a fleet of fourteen English ships in a harbor off the south end of Baffin Island in the stormy and icy waters of the North Atlantic, ready to spend a month in finding, mining, and filling his barks and buses with as many tons of heavy black rock as they could hold. The rock, he knew, was rich with gold, for not only had he found spiders in this area on his previous voyage the year before ("which as many affirme, are signes of great store of gold"), but he had taken back some two hundred tons of it to London and saw it assayed as worth approximately £24 a ton (at a time when a captain of Frobisher's experience was probably earning around £5 or £6 a month, when hired). This voyage, then, would be the climax of his three-year challenge of the Labradorean arctic and its constant torments of sea and weather, not to mention of twenty years of piracy and plundering before that, and the delight with which he oversaw the extraction of some 1,350 tons of ore could not have been any less than that expressed by another brave seaman in the same month exactly seventy-five years before: "Gold is most excellent, gold is treasure."

The search for gold was still, nearly a century after its first discovery, the transcending motive impelling Europeans across the Atlantic waters, heedless of suffering and risk, and it would continue to be for a century more: not a Spaniard from Ponce de León to Menéndez, not a Frenchman from Laudonnière to Champlain, not an Englishman from John Rut to Newport, not a Portuguese from Corte Real to Gomes, but expected to find one land of El Dorado or another and make it rightfully his. "We Spanish suffer from a strange disease of the heart," Cortés is said to have informed the ambassadors of Motecuhzoma in explaining his need for another chestful of tribute, "for which the only known remedy is gold." He need not have been speaking of his countrymen alone.*

After staying a month along the Baffin Island coast, finding more than seven mines from which to load his ships, including one so rich with rock "that it might reasonably suffise all the golde gluttons of the worlde," Frobisher decided to return to England before winter set in, abandoning his plans to establish a colony. The voyage home endured another battle with the ice and storms of the north, but in late September the fleet, now down by two ships and some forty men from its complement just four months before, put into harbor at Harwich and nearby ports. The cargoes were offloaded and shipped on to Bristol and London, amid great excitement at the thought of England's newfound Mexico and those familiar assurances that there was more gold to come, for which Queen Elizabeth awarded Frobisher a chain of gold.

The stones were assayed, and assayed again, then cracked and crushed and smelted and examined again. "Not one stoane therof" was of any value. All 1,350 tons, collected at such price and labor, were, in commercial terms, worthless. From those black lumps—perhaps crystallized marcasite, or iron pyrite—"neither Gold, Silver, nor any other metall could be drawne," wrote the historian William Camden in his Annales a few decades later, and so they were "throwne away to repayre the high-wayes."

Such ignorance of the treasures of nature was not uncommon in those days—Verrazzano in 1524 returned from America with a cargo of spices and gold, which weren't, and the Canadian diamonds that Cartier displayed in Paris in 1542 were simple quartz crystals (making the phrase un diamont du Canada synonymous with worthlessness thereafter). But here several hundred men were involved, of many ranks and skills, including a number of professional miners, at least three assayers, and educated gentlemen and prosperous merchants, and up to the very end not one of them seemed to have any doubts

---

*Arthur Hawkins, in an introductory poem to George Peckham's A true report of the late discoveries in 1583, provided the English equivalent:

> The Metall [gold] heere is showne that with a quenchles fire,
> Inflames our thirsting hartes unstaunched in desire.

as to what gold was supposed to look like. The cost of that ignorance was at least £20,000, a considerable fortune, and the loss of some half a hundred lives.

The only gold to come out of it hung around Frobisher's neck.

Before the sixteenth century was out, therefore, Cristóbal Colón was established as a major figure in the expansion of Europe, a process that was itself coming to be understood (albeit slowly) as important in shaping, as it was in expressing, the character of that subcontinent. In fact, because he was by then the undisputed originator of the process, because more was known about him than any other navigator of the time, and because his was the style of colonization and exploitation followed in great part by all his successors, he came to symbolize more than anyone else the complex of ideas and myths and dreams that characterized that expansion.

Whatever Europe understood the New World to be—and it was many things, not all clearly assimilated yet—it was a *new* world, another half of the globe not known before, plainly different from Europe and even from the Orient, rich and large and mysterious, a place of new peoples, new vistas, new treasures, new species. ("Jesus! said I, have we here a new world?"—Rabelais) We can scarcely imagine what this could have meant at the time, but Europeans must have adjusted to it with as much bewilderment as fascination, as much dread as curiosity, as much trepidation as covetousness; it was not long before it came to take on mythic proportions as the land of the New, the Other, the Unknown, the Possible. It was for some a Paradise—Colón was joined in this fantasy by many other explorers and writers—where there was thought to be innocence and fertility and abundance such as Europe had never known, and where anyone might find regeneration and salvation. It was for others the land of opportunity, a new frontier from which to escape the sickness and violence and corruption and repression that made up daily life for the large majority of Europeans. It was for still others a treasure trove of gold and silver and who knows what manner of riches, where even the poor and the uncultured might become wealthy, and without considerable labor at that. And it was for some a vast and mysterious land of Nature, raw and powerful, strange and fearful, replete with wondrous sights and creatures, dangerous, plentiful, and irresistible.

Each of these visions, these concepts, was new to the European psyche—nothing like the Discovery had ever happened before, nothing would again—but as they took hold over the decades, and the centuries, they came to act as an inevitable impetus toward the west. And each was understood to be, at least on some level, the gift of the celebrated Spanish admiral, for as even the English explorer Humphrey Gilbert recognized, "by him it was in a manner first discovered, made knowen, and profitably communicated unto the Christian world, in the yeere of our Lord 1492."

Every age, of course, casts the heroes it needs. Out of the turmoil, poverty, repression, misery, and bewilderment that continued to bedevil Europe in the sixteenth century much as it had in the fifteenth—in some cases with even greater ferocity and anguish—the nascent modern culture created for itself a man who symbolized for the dark soul the bright new world, that bourne of escape and hope, of treasure, space, freedom, and rebirth. And as he effectively acquired symbolic life—interestingly, it would be as a symbol much more than as a real person that he persisted in history at least until the nineteenth century—he came in the mind of Europe to stand for the Explorer, the Discoverer, and the Hero, three parts of the same being but not necessarily the same thing at all.

As the quintessential Explorer, he personified the whole ambitious outward thrust of early modern Europe and its apparent determination to break out of the confines of the familiar, to make known the unknown, to defy the constraints of nature, to conquer all that was conquerable. Something about his very audacity—setting out across an unexplored ocean with three small ships and a few score ignorant sailors—appealed to the Renaissance imagination, and just at a time that risk-taking of all kinds, from investments by the new capitalist merchants to piracy and voyages to Canton, was becoming more and more a part of European life. Something, too, about his sheer adventurism—sailing into the new, time and again, each time challenging the limits—at a time when "venture" was coming into use to describe capitalist enterprises (so used in English first in 1584) and the explorer and the pirate and the conquistador became new folk legends alongside the knight and the saint. And something, finally, about his defiance—of the experts, of the past, proving that the old had to give way to the new—at a time when innovation and experimentation, in everything from the new science to the new religion, became the mark of a culture that could not help, as Marlowe's Tamburlaine has it, "still climbing after knowledge infinite."

What adds luster to this image, though, is that Colón not only sought but found: he was the Discoverer, the first to open up the prodigious golden riches of the Americas, the man who showed that the results of adventurism would be profit. To the English and the French, specifically, but to many Europeans elsewhere, he was the symbol of the Spanish overseas empire and the immense wealth and power it provided with every passing decade, making Spain the leading nation of Europe. However little the average person of Europe may have known about the details of bullion shipments, their impact would have escaped no one: it was the principal fuel that powered Spain's vast military forces across the fields and seas of Europe almost constantly for a century, the principal lever of the "price revolution" that increased costs in virtually every village in every country by some 400 percent in the course of the century. Stories about this unprecedented treasure—the fabulous gilded temples of Mesoamerica, the Golden Man of the Amazon, the inexhaustible silver mountain of Potosí, the Spanish fleets laden with gold coins and silver ingots—became very quickly the folklore of Europe, and even such a sober-minded chronicler as Richard Eden became nearly tongue-tied speaking of "what riches the Emperor hath gotten out of all the new found lands . . . yet speak I here nothing of pearls, precious stones, and spices. Neither yet of the great abundance of gold."

These two images of Colón blend into the one that probably more than any other became fixed in the European mind—by popular tales, one supposes, as much as by published epic—that of the early modern Hero, the individual triumphant, by courage and rationality, over great and unjust odds. Not so much out of Martyr, for he is scant in such personal matters, but out of Oviedo and Münster, and then with the elaborate wrenching details of Fernando, the idea grew of Cristóbal Colón as a kind of marvelous martyr: in the phrases of England's George Abbot, from his *Briefe Description of the Whole Worlde* in the last year of the century, Colón was undaunted by the initial rebuffs of Ferdinand and Isabella ("he found but small entertainment, yet persisting in his purpose without weariness and with great importunitie") and with diligence won them over; he then proved so dogged and valiant at sea (despite "the great indignation and often mutinies of his companie") that he was favored with the discoveries ("God did so bless him to the ende that his voyage might not prove in vaine") and treasures ("aboundance of gold and pearle"); in spite of his triumph ("with great treasure he returned unto Spaine,

bringing joyfull newes of his happie successe") he was not given all
the rewards that had been promised him; and ultimately after death
he was denied his due riches, his fame, and even his reputation ("the
Spaniards . . . labored to obscure his fame, envying that an Italian
or stranger, should bee reported to be the first discovered [sic] of
those parts"). Here we have the stuff of tragedy, or at least of tragic
pathos, and it was readily woven into a heroic tale by which Europe
could celebrate its new stature in the world and the unjustly treated
figure by whom it was first attained.

Never mind that indeed there was very little truth to it, that it was
constructed almost entirely out of Colón's own notoriously deceptive
words, and that it is a version he tendered in his later, most beset
and most paranoid years. No matter: it served the age; the images
persisted; it became the functional reality. Europe needed a hero for
its early modern age, a fitting embodiment of those strains of individualism and materialism and rationalism it could not escape; how
much better if he could be seen to triumph over ignorance and narrow-
mindedness and still fall victim to perfidy and callousness.

Some of the flavor of this is to be found in a rather execrable
broadside, the first poem about Colón in English, written by one
Robert Seall, a street-corner poet of mid-century England, in defense
of a third-rate ship's captain named Thomas Stukely, whose proposed voyage to America in 1563 had been squelched by the English
government:

> Columbus as I reed,
>   The space of many yeares;
> Was counted as unwise also,
>   As in writers appeers.
> His earnest sute denied,
>   Yet in the finall ende:
> His wurds & deeds did seem at length,
>   On reason to depend.
> The like assay [attempt] in hand
>   He did at last procure:
> Whose life and lucky viages [voyages],
>   Good fortune did assure.
> At thend [the end] in savety home,
>   At lenght [sic] he did retourn:
> And quenched all their mocking harts

> *Which erst did seem to burn. . . .*
> *And then the malice gon,*
> *The fire falleth down:*
> *And quenched quite as by this man*
> *Which was of great renowne.**

Colón as legend, then, passed in the sixteenth century as much into European folklore as into European history, made up of each chronicler's need, each prince's schema, each adventurer's sought-after justification, not necessarily for what he was but for what he could be made to do. Thus around him, as around perhaps no other similar figure, accrued the myths.

The myth of his tryst on Puerto Santo and the mysterious sailor who died in his house and left him with a map of the New World; of the rejection of his enterprise because the Spanish court and Salamanca council determined that the world was flat; of the years of importuning the Sovereigns and of the hardness of the Ferdinandian heart; of the eventual softening of Isabella's because of her . . . love? mystic identity? shared religious fervor? and of her pawning her jewels to finance the journey; of the mutiny on the First Voyage and his holding out alone against those afraid to go on; of the triumphal entry into Barcelona after the First Voyage; of the egg. Myths, all without substance.

The egg story is rather nice. As retailed by Girolamo Benzoni's *Historia del Mondo Nuovo*, Colón was being feted by the archbishop of Toledo after his return from the First Voyage, with "many noble Spaniards" in attendance, one of whom challenged him by arguing that if he had not found the Indies someone else would have done so sooner or later because Spain was full of "great men clever in cosmography and literature":

Columbus made no reply, but took an egg and had it placed on the table saying: "Gentlemen, you make it stand here, not with

---

* The Stukely story is complex and somewhat mysterious, but he seems to have been selected by a group of English entrepreneurs who wanted to help the French captain Jean Ribaut defend a fortress he had established in Florida, thereby creating a base from which English pirates could raid Spanish treasure ships on their way back from Mexico. For some reason Stukely seems to have told all this to the Spanish ambassador in London, who not unnaturally protested to the English government, then on good terms with Spain, forcing it to intervene to end the venture. A number of the entrepreneurs lost the money they put up for this voyage; one of them may have been the patron, if that is not too grand a word, of the Seall broadside.

crumbs, salt, etc. (for anyone knows how to do it with meal or sand), but naked and without anything at all, as I will, who was the first to discover the Indies." They all tried, and no one succeeded in making it stand up. When the egg came round to the hands of Columbus, by beating it down on the table he fixed it, having thus crushed a little of one end; wherefore all remained confused, understanding what he meant: that after the deed is done, everybody knows how to do it; that they ought first to have sought for the Indies, and not laugh at him who had sought for them first.

A nice story, but without a trace of truth to it: no record at the time of such an event, no mention even by a Colón who would have delighted in such a story; wholly improbable on the face of it for Spanish *hidalgos* to so insult the Sovereigns' hero to his face; and Cesare de Lollis has proven that it is a hoary Italian story that had been trotted out for at least a century to prove the genius of whichever path-breaker it was attached to.

The Barcelona entry story is even better, and each added detail of the jubilant throng and the graciousness of the queen and the honors given the Admiral serves only to make the vindication sweeter. There is in truth no record of any such thing, no mention of any Cristóbal Colón in the *Anales consulars*, the royal chronicle of events at court, or in any other contemporary account of such an occasion, including Colón's own. The only one of the subsequent historians of Spain anywhere near the city was Oviedo, who was fifteen years old at the time, and he makes no mention of any triumphal parade or carryings-on at court. But for Fernando, and even more for Las Casas, and then for most popular historians thereafter, the visit to the Sovereigns in Barcelona had to be a dramatic grand occasion of public celebration for the newly styled Admiral: not only must the entire city turn out for the procession of Indians and parrots and treasures, but the Sovereigns must show their humility (and gratitude) with a lavish reception at court and the bestowal of innumerable laurels. As Las Casas (who was 600 miles away in Seville) told it:

He having kissed their hands, they with most joyful faces ordered him to arise, and what was the supreme honour and favour among those which their Highnesses were accustomed to grant to very few Grandees, they ordered a stool brought and that he

should be seated in their Royal presence. . . . He showed the
things which he brought which had not been seen, bringing out
the large specimens of gold in beaten pieces . . . and likewise
what was the most precious treasure and to be thought most of,
he told of the multitude and simplicity, meekness and nudity
and customs of the people of these countries. . . . Having heard
all this and pondered upon it profoundly, the Catholic and most
devout Princes arose and knelt down upon the floor and having
joined their hands and raised them to Heaven, and with their
eyes filled with tears, they commenced to give thanks to the
Creator from the depths of their hearts: and as the singers of the
Royal chapel were there, in readiness and prepared, they sang
Te Deum Laudamus and the high minstrels responded, so that
it appeared that in that hour the celestial delights were opened
and manifested to them and they communicated *with* them. Who
can describe the tears which sprang from the Royal eyes and
from the eyes of many Grandees of those realms who were there,
and of all the persons of the Royal House? What joy, what
pleasure, what ecstasy bathed the hearts of all!

Not sufficient as terrestrial Hero, the Admiral has become a figure
upon which the celestial choruses also send their blessings, melting
the hearts even of the obdurate *hidalgos* of Spain. And all this devised
and perpetuated by his historical champions within a century from
that moment in Valladolid when, far from such glories, he com-
mended his soul to Christ.

It is not a statue of gold, no—but something even more durable,
more honorific: a myth, an *idea* . . . and a legacy.

Chapter Ten

1506–1606

II
England

LATE in the year 1606, one hundred years after the unrecorded death of Cristóbal Colón in Valladolid, three small English ships, not unlike those the Discoverer had commanded on his First Voyage, sailed down the Thames bound on a journey to the New World.

Their destiny was somewhere along the North American coast, between 34 and 41 degrees north, in that area the English were pleased to call Virginia, named for (and apparently by) the Virgin Queen, who most likely wasn't, and whose passing three years earlier England still mourned. Their mission was "to digg, mine and search for all manner of mines of goulde, silver and copper," to find a passage that would "soonest find the other sea" to Asia, and to establish a colony that would serve as the initial outpost for what was confidently hoped to be the island nation's expansion into the Americas, until then a province alone of the hated Spanish. Could the irony have escaped any of those on board that just behind them, in the Tower of London off to port, was imprisoned Sir Walter Ralegh, the very man who had sponsored the first English venture to Virginia twenty years earlier with exactly those same goals in mind, only to see them thwarted by that combination of cupidity and stupidity that marked nearly all of Europe's colonial forays, but who even now could write from that tower, about the land that had so absorbed his dreams, "I shall yet live to see it an English nation"?*

And could any of those on board have known that just behind them on the starboard side, in the elegant new Globe Theatre, a play called *Antony and Cleopatra* had only recently joined the repertory, its very first scene containing the line whose double meaning, and striking pertinence, would likely have been understood by many among them: "Then must thou needs find out new heaven, new earth"?

The little fleet—the flagship, *Susan Constant*, the smaller *Godspeed*, and a pinnace, *Discovery*—contained probably 140 or 150 men and boys, a hundred or so destined to stay on as settlers, including a council of seven to guide the intended settlement, only one of whom, Bartholomew Gosnold, had any experience at all in colonizing, and that was a failed venture in New England four years before. Of the ninety-three whose names we know, no fewer than fifty-nine have been identified as "gentlemen" of one sort or another: an inauspiciously high proportion of those who experience had shown were more likely to cultivate their tastes than their fields in America—as we may judge from the wardrobe of one of them, George Percy, who seems to have had five suits of silk, broadcloth, and velveteen, another of brocaded silk with taffeta facing and gold lace and buttons, and (coals to Newcastle) the requisite Dutch-made beaver hat. Particularly inauspicious in that, of the remaining colonists, there were no more than a dozen experienced laborers, four carpenters, a couple of masons, a blacksmith, a barber, two surgeons of uncertain quality, and a parson: there were no farmers, no stockmen, no botanists, none with a special knowledge of what was then called "natural history"; there were no assayers or goldsmiths, although the mistakes of Frobisher's mission were surely known to all; and there were no women, although a century of European colonization attempts had demonstrated by then how crucial they were to successful settlement. In spite of numerous precedents to guide them, including at least four failed ventures under their own flag, the English seemed to have learned nothing from the past.

And yet this was the fleet that was, after extraordinary tribulations,

*Also in that tower was the "Wizard Earl" of Northumberland, imprisoned for his connections to the Gunpowder Plot, who was the elder brother of a lordly member of the Virginia fleet, George Percy; a certain Peacock, in "for witchcraft"; Sir John Yorke and his lady, "for the play in his house in Yorkshire"; and one Mr. John Cotton, "for suspicion of writing a book."

to establish not only the first permanent English settlement in the New World but the basis of the empire that would supplant the fading dominion of Spain, implant itself throughout North America, and eventually span the world. It was, says the historian Matthew Page Andrews, "one of the most important voyages in world history."

As befits such a venture in the inaugural age of capitalism, the fleet was sailing on behalf not of the crown, as Admiral Colón had done, but of the recently founded Virginia Company, a private enterprise of mostly wealthy London stockholders, most of whom planned to accrue the benefits of overseas plantation without themselves having to set silk boot on foreign soil. Those investors were of no doubt as to the gains in the offing: they were granted, according to James I's royal patent that chartered their company, the right "to make habitacion, plantacion and to deduce a Colonie of sondrie of our people into that parte of America," so as to possess—the phrase is repeated six times within a few pages so that there will be no misunderstanding—"all the landes, woods, soile, groundes, havens, ports, rivers, mines, mineralls, marshes, waters, fishinges, commodities and hereditamentes whatsoever" found by their chosen delegates.

The company had prudently ordered that a set of instructions be delivered to the would-be colonists before their departure, assembled by the preeminent partisan of English colonialism, Richard Hakluyt. First among the advice he had to offer—how to search for minerals, how "not to offend the naturals," how and where to plant, and the like—was this: "When it shall please God to send you on the coast of Virginia, you shall do your best endeavour to find out a safe porte in the entrance of some navigable river." The name of the man selected by the company to be the captain of the inaugural fleet was, as if history was listening, Christopher Newport.

A seasoned mariner and navigator, Newport was then a man of forty-six, apparently with a full white beard, who had been active on the Atlantic at least since the days of the Elizabethan "sea dogs" (he is first mentioned on a 1581 West Indies voyage) and was a successful member of that £200,000-a-year industry of piracy, sponsored largely by London "privateer" merchants for more than a generation, which provided the experience, capital, and ships out of which England's overseas empire was eventually built.* He had sailed

---

*"Privateer" is simply the genteel name for a pirate, used when the thievery and looting is practiced against ships of a country with which one's own country is officially at war.

with Sir Francis Drake, prince of pirates, on the daring and celebrated raid on Cádiz that "pulled King Philip's beard" in 1587; had had a part in the capture of the Portuguese carrack *Madre de Dios* and its half-million pounds of treasure in 1592, one of the richest hauls of the age; and had gained a large fortune and lost his right arm in one of several pirate raids on Spanish ships and ports in the Caribbean in the following decade. By the time of this voyage Newport was as experienced an Atlantic commander as England could claim, "a Mariner," as one of his shipboard companions put it, "well practised for the westerne parts of America."

   The departure of the three ships during the night of December 19–20 was undertaken in some secrecy, unrecorded by any shoreside chronicler, probably to avoid any open confrontation with the embassy of Spain, which had long laid a general claim to the lands of the northern continent and had in fact enforced that with two ruthless onslaughts (in 1565 and 1572) against outposts the French had dared to establish. But the fact of an impending voyage was hardly a secret, for the doings of the Virginia Company were more or less of public record; an inspirational poem in honor of those daring enough to be on its first voyage had been printed in London, with some modest attention, only months before:

> *You brave heroic minds*
> *Worthy your country's name,*
>   *That honour still pursue,*
>   *Go and subdue,*
> *Whilst loit'ring hinds*
> *Lurk here at home with shame. . . .*

> *And cheerfully at sea,*
> *Success you still entice,*
>   *To get the pearl and gold*
>   *And ours to hold,*
> *Virginia,*
> *Earth's only Paradise,*

> *Where nature hath in store*
> *Fowl, venison, and fish,*
>   *And the fruitful'st soil*
>   *Without your toil*

Three harvests more,
All greater than your wish.

Michael Drayton of course had not been to Virginia, and had no special way to know of its paradisiacal nature other than a few promotional tracts of previous travelers that the Virginia Company had put around, but he captured well enough the spirit of the venture: words like "subdue," "ours to hold," and "nature hath in store" were the meat upon which the project fed. (Although "without your toil," a concept that may have enticed the high proportion of gentlemen on the fleet, would prove to be every bit as illusory as it had been for the Spanish *hidalgos* a century before.)

Sir Walter Ralegh* lay imprisoned in the Tower of London for crimes of blasphemy and treason, for which the only shred of substance was his being roundly hated by James I, who came to the throne on the death of Ralegh's onetime champion Elizabeth in 1603. But questions of blasphemy were taken seriously in England at that time, as they were throughout a Europe violently torn by contending and uncompromising forms of Christianity. Ralegh, when convicted in 1604 of being an agent of Catholic Spain and holding "the most heathenish and blasphemous opinions," was sentenced thus:

> *You shall be drawn upon a hurdle through the open streets to the place of execution, there to be hanged and cut down alive, and your body shall be opened, your heart and bowels plucked out, and your privy members cut off, and thrown into the fire before your eyes; then your head to be strucken off from your body, and your body shall be divided into four quarters, to be disposed of at the King's pleasure; and*
> *God have mercy upon your soul.*

The emotions—and the violence—stirred by the great contest between Protestantism and Catholicism had inflamed Europe by then for nearly a century, since October 31, 1517—then as now All Hallows'

---

*The spelling "Ralegh" was his favored (though not exclusive) version; the form "Raleigh" is not one he is ever known to have used.

Eve—when Martin Luther had posted his ninety-five theses on the door of the Wittenberg church. That spark leapt quickly into a flame, Luther's break with the papacy came soon after, and within just a decade cities and states throughout Europe had subscribed to one or another form of the new nonhierarchical, non-Italian Reformation. By 1560, the flame now become a conflagration, Protestantism had won over the population of maybe as much as half of Europe, was the state religion of national and local governments from Switzerland to Sweden and Scotland to Hungary, and was a significant force in most of the polities in between. All this within the span of an average lifetime.

Such a swift and sweeping transformation of a long-entrenched system could come about only because the Reformation was the clear expression—first theological and intellectual, in the end social and political—of those hallmarks of humanism, rationalism, materialism, and nationalism that characterized the early modern age. It was, indeed, the instrument by which that age in Europe was first made manifest. And England, by 1606, was capable in its name of condemning, and beheading, the heroes it had sung just decades before.

Why the English ships departed on their journey in the middle of December—hardly a propitious time for a foray into the Atlantic—remains a mystery, but since Newport made no log of this voyage, or none that survived, we do not have his explanation. (What we know about the voyage comes largely from accounts by two of the principals in the venture—the young nobleman and soldier George Percy, whose "Observations" were first printed by Samuel Purchas in 1625; and John Smith, pleased to call himself Captain, a blunt sort of reporter whose *True Relation* appeared as early as 1608 and was followed by another, fuller description, *A Map of Virginia*, four years later. Neither accounted for the wintertime departure.) Whatever the reason, the fleet paid for its boldness: it almost immediately ran into bad weather in the Channel, "where we suffered great stormes" for a full month, and it was forced to anchor along the English coast for dreary (and contentious) days on end. Not until early February was it even out of sight of England, and then set its course southward toward the Canaries—planning, as Colón had, a crossing with the southern trades—where it finally docked around February 21, a most unpromising two months' start.

The ocean crossing itself was apparently uneventful, though some-what slow, and it was not until March 24, 1607, that they raised Dominica, which young Percy asserted was the home of "Canibals, that will eate mans flesh." For the next month the fleet followed the course of Colón's Second Voyage with remarkable fidelity—Maria-galante, Guadeloupe (where the passengers were allowed ashore, as Colón's were), Nevis, Virgin Islands, Mona—and then turned north, along the Florida coast. In the early morning of April 26, after several days of heavy storms, God (according to Smith) "did drive them by his providence to their desired port, beyond all their expectations": it was the mouth of the Chesapeake Bay, the largest and finest harbor on the whole Atlantic coast and the exact spot that the colonial pro-moters in London had been saying all along would be the ideal lo-cation for a settlement. How Newport found it so unerringly, so directly, we do not know, though it is possible he had been there before on a presumed, but not recorded, voyage of 1604; somehow it is reminiscent of the directness, the calm certainty with which Colón on his Second Voyage sailed straight to Dominica, as if he somehow knew it to be, as he said it was, the easternmost island of the Indies.

As the Englishmen sailed into the enormous bay, past a promon-tory they would later name for Crown Prince Henry and along the wooded southern shores, they must have been overwhelmed by the luxuriousness of the nature that lay before them, more varied and more complex—and wild and untended—than even an experienced man such as Newport would ever have seen before. Yet where huge swamp junipers and loblolly pines dripped with moss, grapevines hung with heavy clusters along the shore, blue herons in the hundreds winged gracefully across the marshes, and passenger pigeons in flight were so numerous they darkened the sun, these men were inspired to record scarcely a word: Percy remarks offhandedly that "we could find nothing worth the speaking of" other than some meadows and "goodly tall Trees" (who does that sound like?) and the first fresh water they had seen in three weeks; Smith says nothing at all about their surroundings.

There before them, at any rate, was the land they had come to conquer, where they would indeed, at the cost of many thousands of lives and many hundreds of thousands of pounds, succeed in im-planting the first colony north of Mexico. (Spain did have a belea-guered garrison, it is true, at St. Augustine, with an estimated population of three hundred or so, but most of those were transient soldiers or Franciscan missionaries, not settlers.) More than that: they would implant the very special English idea of a colony, different from the Spanish; of a *plantation*, a complete imposition in miniature of the Old World society, with large numbers of permanent settlers whose purpose was not simply to strike it rich and return home but to stay and make a life; of a *commonwealth* that would largely set its own rules according to its own conditions, rather than be the endpoint of a large transatlantic bureaucracy with controls stretching back to king and pope; of a *community* that had a mission not of conversion but of displacement and that would supplant or eliminate, rather than take over and manipulate, existing native societies. When this colony took hold on the bank of the Chesapeake (the story of the next chapter)—it was to be called Jamestown, in honor of a monarch who cared very little for its fate—the world, and not just the American world, would be changed forever.

The man after whom the new settlement was named was the patron of a theatrical company in London known as the King's Men, whose chief playwright had only recently completed a play with special meaning for the new monarch, called Macbeth. *It was about the uniting of the crowns of Scotland and England, which James's ascendancy had just achieved; about a king named Banquo, from whom James considered himself to be descended; and especially about witchcraft, a subject close to James's heart and about which he had even written a learned treatise,* Demonology, *published in 1597.*

James not only believed deeply in witchcraft but believed deeply it was a profound evil that had to be extirpated with as much force and as little compassion as possible. In this he was hardly unusual for his era—though he seems to have seen in it a direct personal threat not all men, or rulers, felt—for the period of the sixteenth and seventeenth centuries in Europe, with all of its religious excess, is the high point of that form of repression known as the witch-hunt.

In southern Europe the witch-hunt was conducted, as it had been since the days of Ferdinand and Isabella, by the Catholic Inquisition. To the Spanish form of the Inquisition, which actually diminished somewhat in severity as the sixteenth century went on (in part because most of its targets had been expelled or eliminated by then), the Church added, in 1542, a Roman version, run by a Supreme Tribunal of

Cardinals, "with the power of apprehending and incarcerating suspected persons and their abettors, of whatever estate, rank or order,"
and executing them at will. Directed against all forms of heresy in
Catholic lands, and of course anything even hinting of Protestantism,
it reserved a special passion for rooting out and condemning suspect
witches by the uncounted tens of thousands and created an effective
reign of suspicion and terror in the lives of millions for more than a
century.

In northern Europe the prosecutorial zeal was no less ardent, though
not so institutionalized, and from all indications enacted with even
greater severity and intensity—perhaps "mania" is a better word—
by the new Protestant states, particularly the Germanic ones. Figures
are not easy to come by and must be treated with caution, but those
we have are suggestive: 72 people killed for witchcraft in one little
town, Ellingen, in the Main valley in the single year 1591; 274 witches
executed in one year in the prince-bishopric of Eichstädt; 43 women
and 11 men executed in the town of Obermarchtal, population about
700, in 1586–88; 63 witches burned in Wiesensteig in 1562; 133 executed in a single day at a convent in Quedlinburg in 1589; some
2,500 witches executed between 1611 and 1660 in Vaud. In all, according to the most sober estimates, it seems that at least 100,000 and
perhaps 200,000 people (80 to 90 percent of them women) were brought
to trial as witches between 1500 and 1700, most of them tortured into
confessions, and the great majority of those burned to death (or sometimes hanged) in ceremonies, often public, where agony was welcomed.

What was this witchcraft all about? It was, in essence, the name
given by the established authorities to the various surviving forms of
paganism, animism, and goddess-worship that still played a large part
in certain European belief-systems, particularly in rural areas, stem-
ming from roots deep in fertility cults and nature-worship from the
past that the Church had never been able to suppress. For more than
a century the Church had sought to identify such blasphemies with
witchcraft, and witchcraft with dark, satanic, sexual evil: witches,
according to the standard text, Malleus maleficarum, fly on broom-
sticks and he-goats to rites at which they worship the Devil, dance in
his celebration and kiss his genitals, and take their pleasure with Devil-
lovers of all sexes in the heaths and moors. And why were women so
involved in such satanic evil? "What is woman," the Malleus asks,
"other than the ruin of friendship, an inescapable punishment, a nec-

essary disaster, a fascinating evil, a natural temptation, a domestic
peril, a desirable danger, a universal evil in fine colors?"

It is all quite complex, but somewhere deep, the fierce and frenzied
responses of these times must be seen as symptoms of a troubled society
acting out both a recrudescent misogynism, inflamed now by the pres-
sures of its early modern transformation, and an ancient phobia against
the forces of nature and the earth goddesses (as in the quasi-Marist
and Diana cults of the era) that gave them expression. Woman, as the
creature closest to nature, and nature, as the fecund spirit of woman,
were somehow held to be malevolent allies against the rising powers
of the new, ordered, scientific world.

How now, you secret, black, and midnight hags,
What is't you do?

How did it happen that, 115 years after the *Santa María* longboat
first touched the sands of Guanahani, it was the small island nation
of England that started on the venture that was to make it the second
great colonizing power of Europe? What inspiration, what propul-
sion, led a land of certainly no more than 5 million people, with a
history more of insularity and inertia than of adventure, across the
Atlantic to establish a permanent place in the Americas?

The answer in most of the learned texts, ornated about with anal-
yses of the restlessness of an increasingly urban population and the
overflow of pent-up genius, normally comes down to something like
"historical circumstances," suggesting an inevitability perceived only
with the clarity of hindsight. But one can reduce that generality to
something more precise: namely, its gradual inheritance of the Columbian Legacy, conscious as well as osmotic, and with it a desire
as well as a capacity for overseas colonization, exploitation, and expansion very much like that with which the Spanish monarchy and
its Admiral had launched the first ventures to the West.

The Columbian Legacy was based initially on the friendly relationship that Spain and England, both experienced in Atlantic sailing,
enjoyed in the early decades after the Discovery. Official ties were
close: the Treaty of Medina del Campo in 1489 had established
the two as allies; Ferdinand and Isabella's daughter Catherine of
Aragon was wed first to Crown Prince Arthur in 1501 and to

Henry VIII in 1509, uniting the royal houses; relations between English and Iberian merchant and maritime interests were also long-
standing and firm. More than that, though, the legacy was possibly
transmitted via two direct—but not entirely proven—connections
from Cristóbal Colón himself.

The first of those is the ostensible visit by Bartolomé Colón to
London sometime between 1488 and 1492 to get support for his
brother's westward exploration; as the dutiful Oviedo told it, on
what authority we know not:

> Colón . . . worked, through his brother Bartolomé Colón, on
> King Henry VII of England (the father of the Henry VIII who
> is reigning now), trying to get him to sponsor and equip him
> for the exploration of these western seas, offering to give him
> great treasures in return, in the form of an increase in his kingdom
> and estates, of very large new realms and subject lands. The king
> took the views of his advisers and people entrusted to look into
> this, then laughed at what he said, and took his words to be vain.

There is no special reason to believe the story accurate—there are no
court records to support it, and Colón himself never mentions it—but
it seems nonetheless to have achieved the stature of truth in sixteenth-
century England, being included in Eden's translation of Gómara of
1555, again in Hakluyt's first major compilation, the *Principall navigations* of 1589, and in George Abbot's popular history of 1599.[1]

The second connection is a letter, addressed to an "Almirante
Mayor" assumed to be Colón, from one John Day, thought to be
an alias for Hugh Say, a member of a prominent London shipping
family, dating from around January 1498. It implies that by then,
before his Third Voyage, Colón already knew that sailors from Bristol
had found land to the west—"as your Lordship knows"—and that
the Admiral was in regular touch with sources providing him with
news of English voyages to Newfoundland and the fabled "Island of
Brasil," so that he had a picture of the northern continent that would
square with the version I have suggested he developed on his Fourth
Voyage. This in turn suggests that the English, both private merchants
and the crown, kept themselves fairly well informed of the whereabouts and discoveries of the Admiral and, after 1499, of the other
Spanish explorers as well.

If Henry VII did in fact receive and reject Bartolomé, he none-theless proved himself sufficiently interested in Atlantic discoveries to sponsor the next applicant, another Genoese mariner with ties to Colón named Giovanni Cabotto. Cabotto—later known as John Cabot—was living in Seville when Colón passed through in his days of triumph in 1493 and certainly heard the stories of the Discovery and presumably saw the captives and their artifacts, if he did not indeed meet and talk with his fellow countryman. We may surmise that he was not quite so credulous as the Sovereigns and their circle about the new lands being "the Indies," and that he eventually decided that, wherever it was Colón had landed, it certainly was not the fabled East; this would have given him the impetus to journey north and find a sovereign to whom he could suggest a voyage to the *real* Indies; and that he did sometime in 1495 or 1496 in London. This time Henry was receptive—according to Cabot's son Sebastian, the news of Colón's Discovery had created such "great talk in all the court" that "all men with great admiration affirmed it to be a thing more divine than human"—and in 1497 and again in 1498 he granted royal charters to John Cabot to find the passage to Asia.

No Asia was found, of course, or route thereto, and official En-gland apparently saw little value in exploring further the cold, rocky lands that were uncovered—especially after the failure of the second voyage, on which Cabot, as a contemporary historian wrote, "is believed to have found the new lands nowhere but on the very bottom of the ocean." Some private ventures were sent out between 1501 and 1505, and Sebastian Cabot went on a fruitless voyage in 1508–09, but with the accession of the dull-minded Henry VIII to the throne all interest in Western exploration ceased—it might in any case have seemed impolitic, threatening to involve the English in spheres already claimed by Henry's in-laws—and was not to be re-vived again in any serious way for another seven decades.[2]

In the meantime, the idea of what Colón had wrought, the strange new hemisphere lying there on the other side of the Atlantic, slowly began to take shape in the mind of the English public, oddly enough probably the last in western Europe to grasp its full meaning. (No copies of the Santangel Letter appeared in England, and a 1503 *Chron-icle* in London made no mention of the New World or its discovery in its section on world geography.) The concept of the Discovery appears first in a translation of Sebastian Brant's *Ship of Fools* in 1509, with credit given (as in the Giulano Dati versions of the Santangel Letter) to Ferdinand alone:

> *Ferdynandus that late was kynge of spayne*
> *Of lande and people hath founde plenty and store*

but the idea of America does not appear in print until somewhere around 1511, with credit now given to King Manoel of Portugal:

> it is named Armenica/there we sawe meny wonders of beestes and fowles yat we have never seen before/the people of this lande have no kynge nor lorde nor theyr god But all thinges is comune.

At about the same time two "interludes"—short dramatic works often performed after a banquet—were published that mention a "newe founde Ilonde" (*Hyckescorner*, c.1510) and "newe landes founde lately ben callyd America" (*Four Elements*, c.1517). These suggest that by then the idea of Western discoveries was common enough to be understood at a typical London high table.

In the following decades references to the New World in English were sparse indeed, and only two English exploratory voyages are known to have been undertaken there—John Rut's in 1527 and Richard Hore's in 1536—neither of which seems to have inspired any writings. (English ships out of Bristol were making annual summer voyages to Newfoundland for codfish and whale oil during this period, but no descriptions about those survive, either.) With the considerable outpouring of material from the mainland, it is fair to assume that the better-educated English audience would be familiar to some degree with the texts in Latin (the language of learning) or Italian (the language of culture), but not until 1553 was the first book about America printed in England, Richard Eden's translation of part of Sebastian Münster's *Cosmographia*, under the title *A treatyse of the newe India*.

This little book—about four inches by two and a half, and only some two hundred pages long—has aptly been called, by the modern historian Boies Penrose, "the foundation stone of English geographical literature," but it is more than that: it is the work that marks the start of the process by which, over the next half-century, the Columbian Legacy became embedded in English thought. All the essential elements are elegantly rendered in Eden's prose: a Colón, now become Columbus,* who is at first rebuffed ("the King and Queen laughed him to scorn") and then allowed to sail, returning home in triumph ("greatly magnified with innumerable glorious titles"); the new lands beautiful and rich ("rivers in which is found much gold, and a mountain whose sand is sparkled with gold," "pearls and gold and such other riches," etc.); the nature of Spanish colonization, with large-scale immigration ("twelve hundred men well appointed"), imported plants and animals, settlements ("the Admiral builded a city, which he compassed about with a wall"), slave labor and tribute; and the strange new peoples, some fierce (including "canibales," amazons, and giants), some friendly, all essentially "rude and barbarous," "beastly and fierce," "filthy and without shame." No one reading these pages could have failed to understand the extraordinary achievement that was Colón's, the glory that had been Spain's and might now be England's.

From the publication of the *Treatyse* in 1553 until the departure of Newport's ships for Virginia in 1606, there were no fewer than twenty books (in a total of twenty-eight editions) in English that made mention of Colón, out of no more than sixty-three works, including herbals and diaries, largely concerned with the New World.[3] Two of these had full descriptions of his life and voyages, and both were very popular—Martyr's *Decades of the newe worlde*, translated by Eden in 1555, with a large first edition handled by *four* publishers, reprinted in 1572 and 1576 and then somewhat condensed for an entirely new edition by Eden and his collaborator Richard Willes in 1577;† and George Abbot's *Briefe Description of the Whole*

---

*It is not clear why the English settled on this one Latinized version of Colón's name, but Eden's choice of it in his translation of Münster, where it appears for the first time in an English book, may have played a significant part. (Münster's Latin version, printed in Basel in 1550, from which Eden made his translation, has "Christophorus Columbus.") Although his next translation, of Martyr, used "Colonus" throughout, Eden was careful there to note that the explorer was "other wise called Columbus," and it is this latter name that subsequently appears in the works of Seall, Abbot, John Wolfe, and, providing the most important stamp of approval, Hakluyt. (Although Laudonnière, in Hakluyt's *Principall navigations*, is allowed to use "Christopher Colon," and Hakluyt himself in a later dedication of 1600 says "Christopher Colon, alias Columbus.") "Columbus" of course was the version brought to America by the English colonists, and so has remained to this day, but to the Spanish-speaking world, including the Admiral's ancestors named for him, the form is still "Cristóbal Colón."

†Eden's work may commemorate a further Anglo-Hispanic link, coming a year after the marriage of England's Queen Mary to Philip of Spain (who became the Spanish king in 1556) and, as the historian Elizabeth Baer thinks, being written "to flatter the new monarchs by glorifying the deeds of the Spaniards."

Worlde, originally 1599, with reprints in 1600 and 1605 and another six editions before 1636. The other works tended to make only passing references to the Admiral, as in Stephen Parmenius's learned *De navigatione* (1582)—

> *when spirited Cabot*
> *Approached these regions, following the wake*
> *Of great Columbus—*

or Humphrey Gilbert's *Discourse* (1576)—"which discoverie al the writers of our time ascribe (& that not unworthily) unto Christopher Columbus"—but the references suggest that many of Colón's achievements were well enough known to need no lengthy amplification. There was in these English works none of the incipient hagiography of the Mediterranean writers, no florid epics glorifying the Admiral, but by the end of the century the literate English public (and it was considerable*) would certainly have known at a minimum that it was Colón who discovered a new fourth part of the world across the Atlantic (despite the learned André Thevet's work giving credit to Vespucci as late as 1568), established a Spanish colony there among its savage denizens, and laid open its fabulous riches to the conquistadors.

As elsewhere in Europe, there was less concern among the English writers for the real Colón than for the image of him that was useful to their ends. As a figure of heroic stature and daring achievement, Colón was the symbol of choice: Cabot would not have done, though he was England's own, because almost nothing was known about him; nor the Bristol fishermen, though they were perhaps the real discoverers, because the only treasure they laid bare was cod. For some Columbus was the model of perseverance rewarded, the mythic figure (as Seall presented him in his awful poem) who returned in glory "and quenched all their mocking harts"; for others he was that goad and instigator who forced a reluctant nation overseas ("Had they not Columbus to stirre them up, and pricke them forward unto their Westerne discoveries?"—Hakluyt, 1598); for still others he was the brave adventurer driven by inspiration ("Columbus had none of

---

*One estimate, in Carl Bridenbaugh's *Vexed and Troubled Englishmen*, is that by 1640 "over half" of the males in London, and a third of those in "the counties," were thought to be literate; an observer of 1610 complained that "one of the diseases of this age is the multitude of Bookes, that doth so overcharge the worlde."

the Western Islands set foorth unto him, either in globe or card, [and] himselfe had neither seene America nor any other of the Islands about it . . . but only comforted himselfe with this hope, that the land had a beginning where the Sea had an ending"—Gilbert, 1576).

It remained for one Thomas Abbay to encapsulate this, in a dedication to John Smith's *Map of Virginia*: "Cannot this successfull example [of Colón] move the incredulous of this time to consider, to conceave, and apprehend Virginia, which might be, or breed us a second India? Hath not England an Izabell, as well as Spaine, nor yet a Collumbus as well as Geneua?" The answer: "Yes, surely it hath, whose desires are no lesse than was worthy Collumbus," and it would be the Virginia project in fact that would provide, though only in the fullness of time, that "second India."

The English, or at least the colonial proponents among them, were confirmed in their certainty of supplanting Spain in the New World by the fact that they had so decisively defeated the vaunted Spanish Armada at the confrontation in the English Channel in 1588. It doesn't matter that there was no such decisive defeat, that the number of pitched battles between the two sides was meager and the results inconclusive, that the exigencies of weather more than anything else kept the Spanish force from landing and caused its subsequent casualties in the North and Scottish seas. Nor does it seem to have mattered much that at least 10,000 men (most of them Spanish) were shot or butchered or drowned or died of disease and famine in less than a month. What remained after the Channel cleared and the great captains appeared before a grateful Elizabeth was the unshakable sense that on sea as on land the future lay in armaments, in military force however bloody.

It was the violent judgment of a violent age, and it infected every policy and program of the nations of Europe, not excluding those conducted in the name of the Prince of Peace. In the late night of Saturday, August 23, 1572, for example, the eve of the feast day of St. Bartholomew, the principal leaders of the Huguenot faction of France, Protestants but then enjoying a general truce with the Catholic sovereigns, were in Paris to participate in the designedly political marriage between the sister of King Charles IX, a Catholic of course, and Henry of Navarre, an outstanding leader of the Huguenots. At two in the morning the churchbells of the city unexpectedly rang out, the signal for a Catholic plan, hatched and endorsed by the royal house, to murder all the Huguenot leaders and their families at a single blow.

Armed bands, under the sanction of the king, went from house to house throughout the city, killing any and every Huguenot they could find, or believed they had found, women and children included. Encouraged, impromptu bands of private citizens entered into the butchery, murdering Huguenots and supposed Huguenots and looting their houses while the bodies lay bleeding on the floors. Decapitated heads were carried on pikes through the streets in torchlight parades as crowds cheered and applauded. As news spread, towns on the Parisian outskirts joined the massacre, and in days a large part of France was in a state of full internecine war.

Municipal figures suggest that at least 2,000 bodies were thrown into the Seine at one point in an effort to keep the streets clear, but estimates of the number of Huguenots killed must be chancy guesswork, as there are only the sketchiest of records. Modern scholarship has suggested ranges from 13,000 to 100,000, with some scholarly support for a figure around 40,000—and Paris had no more than 200,000 people in it at the time.

It was reported by the French ambassador to Spain that Philip II, a dark and dour man who dressed perpetually in black, and was undoubtedly inflicted with the insanity that ran in his family through several lines, laughed only once in his entire life. It was when he was told the news of the St. Bartholomew's Day Massacre.

By the time the Newport fleet lifted anchor in the Thames in 1606, the Columbian Legacy in one way or another had given England a fairly reasonable image of the New World. By then, after all, there had been at least forty-two European voyages to one part of the continents or another, fifteen of which had produced printed accounts in English; maps of the Americas had been published in England for a half-century (including the excellent world map by Edward Wright that Shakespeare referred to in *Twelfth Night*), providing geographic knowledge of at least the coast of the Americas from Baffin Island to the Strait of Magellan and on up the west coast to California; English sailors had explored and catalogued resources at sites from Newfoundland to the Amazon; English ships had returned with samples of

American treasures, real as well as illusory; and something was known about the strange new people of the new lands (and of the strange new flora and fauna), and these had even been depicted with an approximate accuracy in engravings by Theodore de Bry, from drawings by Jacques Le Moyne and John White, in 1590 and 1591.

For what that all meant, how that fitted into the English imagination, we have but to turn to the two greatest poets of the age. John Donne, who was closely connected to many of those in the Virginia Company and at one point planned to go to America as the company's official recorder, saw the New World in terms of the seduction of women:

> *Licence my roaving hands, and let them go,*
> *Before, behind, between, above, below.*
> *O my America! my new-found-land,*
> *My kingdome, safeliest when with one man man'd,*
> *My Myne of precious stones, My Emperie,*
> *How blest am I in this discovering thee!*

Shakespeare, similarly: in *The Merry Wives of Windsor*, Mistress Page is "a region in Guiana, all gold and bounty," which Falstaff declares his intention of extracting; in *Henry VIII* the king "has all the Indies in his arms, and more and richer," when he embraces his newest queen; and in *The Comedy of Errors* Dromio describes a woman as "like a globe: I could find out countries in her," and when asked, "Where America, the Indies?" answers: "O, sir, upon her nose, all o'er embellished with rubies, carbuncles, sapphires, declining [giving up] their rich aspect to the hot breath of Spain."

Englishmen might have had different emphases and often a multiplicity of goals when it came to the New World, but the poets conveyed the predominant priority: America as the succulent maiden to be seduced, deflowered, and plundered by a virile Europe, which shall bask in her treasures. America, in a phrase, as the land of *exploitation*.

That is a term not so much derogatory as explanatory, describing both the process by which the English (as the other people of Europe) experienced the New World and the attitude they took toward it. There is no reason to exaggerate this, but none to shirk it either: it was the desire for material enrichment—we might bluntly call it greed—that more than anything else impelled Europe across the Atlantic right from the start and sustained its interest for the next two centuries. All the talk about taking Christianity and civilization to the heathen, or building a City on the Hill for the perfection of the human spirit, or finding outlets for European creativity and imagination, even when genuinely meant, was just so much ancillary camouflage. This was understood at the time: Arthur Barlowe in 1585, for example, was frank that his voyage was to find out "how profitable this land"; Dionyse Settle in 1577 was similarly after what was "profitable," "needfull for our use," and would "satisfie his greedie appetite"; Eden in 1555 declared the New World abundant with "al these thyinges which [God] causeth the earth so plentifully to brynge foorth to owre use"; and Robert Harcourt in 1613 even confessed that discoveries were fueled by the Englishman's "greedy desire of Gold." And it is accepted historical opinion now: "The invasion of North America," writes the historian James Axtell, "was primarily an aggressive attempt to subdue the newfound land and its inhabitants, and to turn them to European profit," and the economist E. J. Hamilton echoes, "America was discovered, explored, and settled because powerful Europeans believed there would be a net gain." Few scholars challenge the opinion that this was an age, as it has been said, that in its expansion brought to perfection every deadly sin but sloth.

Let us, in far too brief a compass, look at some of the specifics of this expansion during that long period from, say, 1500 to 1700, when Europe's relationship with the New World was one of almost single-minded extraction, the high point of which, in the years from 1550 to 1650, we may appropriately term the Century of Exploitation.

It begins, of course, with gold and silver—the latter actually more important in the end, for all the poetry devoted to the former. The enormousness of this treasure, however we try now to measure it, is simply staggering, most of it accruing, except for the occasional losses in piracy, to the Spanish, who in the mines of Mexico and Peru had come upon the richest gold and silver deposits in the world. Hamilton's researches, though challenged on ancillary points in recent years, illuminate that bullionic side of exploitation very well: from 1503 to 1660, with a peak in the 1590s, Spain officially exported about 200 tons of gold and 18,600 tons of silver from the New World, worth perhaps (though such calculations are necessarily very rough) $1.25 billion in gold-standard American dollars. This represented a large and sudden increase in Europe's stock of precious metals, estimated generally at from *three to five times* the gold and silver then on hand, and in a period of maximum impact of less than a century (1570–1640); and as these riches moved through Spain, and from Spain to its creditors, its licensees, its trading partners, its armies, and its Hapsburg extensions, their velocity had a massive and pervasive effect throughout the entire European economy.

Economists and historians today debate with some heat to what extent American bullion was responsible for the dramatic changes in Europe during this period, but there is no question that it played a significant part in both the economic and the political dynamics that affected every land of the subcontinent. Consider just these: the "price revolution" that increased consumer costs everywhere by from about 300 to 500 percent—for some commodities, such as wheat, tenfold, and salt, twentyfold, in some places—with wholly unprecedented and devastating effects, social as well as economic; the capital accumulation, particularly by commercial and industrial sectors, by which the economic amalgam we know as capitalism was able to establish itself as dominant through most of Europe; the consequent elevation of the money economy as the norm for all transactions of society, and thus the elevation in society of bankers, merchants, traders, and manufacturers, those Marx was later to term "the rising bourgeoisie"; and the enormously profitable trade with the Far East, whose merchants would deal only in precious metals, largely silver.

And add this: American bullion was certainly responsible for the financing of the powerful militaristic government of Spain, whose foreign policies spread destruction and death across Europe, from Turkey to the Channel, in every decade of the sixteenth century from the 1520s on; in particular it was the sustenance of Spain's standing army, which grew from 30,000 men in the early years to at least 200,000 and maybe twice that by the century's end—the largest military force Europe had ever seen. Here, if anywhere, are sown the seeds of modern European militarism.

But gold and silver were by no means the only exploitable commodities of the Americas and, especially in countries other than Spain, more mundane resources were more important. Chief among them, prosaically enough, was fish—codfish mostly, but other kinds as well, and whale oil, too, from Newfoundland, the St. Lawrence, and the New England coast—which I calculate may have brought Atlantic

Europe income greater at times even than gold. These figures of
annual income, based on rough estimates, are indicative:

	GOLD	FISH
1520s	$611,000	$55,000–90,000
1550s	$5,328,000	$520,000
1610s	$1,107,000	$2,730,000
1630s	$155,000	$1,253,000

Fish, to be sure, were not likely to have the same economic effect as
ingots—there is not much of a multiplier effect in a cod—but their
impact was clearly important for western Europe as a whole and, for
a number of Atlantic ports of England, Holland, France, Portugal,
and Spain, indispensable. By 1519, contemporary observers said,
there were at least 100 European ships a year making the summertime
round trip to Newfoundland; by 1578 it was calculated that there
were more than 300 (150 French, 100 Spanish, 50 English, 50 Portuguese, and 20 to 30 Basque) enjoying such a "great abundance of
cod so that the hooke was no sooner overboard but presently a fish
was taken"; and in the early years of the seventeenth century, when
the fisheries were at their height, fleets must have reached as many
as 1,000 ships a year, loading upwards of 200 million cod each season,
if we can rely on the several estimates of the time. For England alone,
at this high point, the income was said to be around £120,000 to
£130,000 a year on a catch of 30 million cod or so, with maybe 10,000
sailors and a like number of dockside workers dependent on the trade;
Newfoundland, said a contemporary, was "Great Britaines Indies."

Of equal importance with fish, and for the French of paramount
significance, were furs, primarily the skins of beavers. This trade
probably began with the first land-daring fishermen in the 1490s, but
it did not play a major role in the European economy until the last
quarter of the sixteenth century, when fashion, and new methods of
processing, created a sudden great demand for American beaver. In-
sufficient research has been done to provide adequate figures on the
beaver trade—ships, pelts, profits—but we do know that by the 1620s
the Dutch and French alone were importing something like 30,000
beaver skins a year (and lesser amounts of marten, otter, rabbit, deer,
fox, and "other beasts' skins"); by the 1650s this had reached around
100,000 skins a year, with concomitant profits in Europe of perhaps

40 percent of investments; and by the 1690s as many as 286,000 furs (some suggest 300,000) were being imported each year, and that seems to have been the peak. All told, I would hazard a guess that between 10 and 15 million beavers, but perhaps as many as 20 million, were killed for fur in the seventeenth century, and maybe 1 to 2 million other animals as well.

The last principal element in this catalogue of European exploitation, especially important to the English, is what can loosely be called, as it was at the time, "commodities"—that is, produce both cultivated and wild, everything from sugar to timber, tobacco to sassafras, the products of the bountiful soils of the New World. The trade here began of course with Colón's first trip and increased as the sixteenth century went on—spices, fruits, dye-woods, medicines—but the all-out exploitation Europe viewed as commercially valuable generally had to await European settlement and on-the-spot horticulture and processing, usually by environmentally calamitous plantation farming. Fortunes were made on both sides of the Atlantic in various minor commodities such as cochineal, indigo, ship timber, cotton, and salt, but it was sugar and tobacco that proved most durable. Both were extremely easy to grow in the New World and extremely popular in the Old, established as essential staples by the middle of the seventeenth century, when some 30,000 tons of sugar and perhaps 5,000 tons of tobacco were imported from the Americas; both exacted terrible prices on both sides of the Atlantic, human as well as environmental.

One more element, the one literally underlying all the others, was the land itself. It was neither an export, of course, nor a medium of exchange, but it was, for the European, a commodity: to be acquired, bought, sold, deeded, and handed down, to be owned, used, developed, mined, and plowed, deforested and drained, depleted, abandoned. It was always an important factor in European economic and social life, and the Americas had an immense amount of it, and the European mind did not doubt that it was there to be taken.

This Century of Exploitation was unlike anything the world had seen before. Whether we think of it in terms of the New World's being the essential fuel of modern Europe—"America contributed fundamentally to the world's rapid growth during the sixteenth century," is how the French historian Pierre Chaunu has put it, and "weighed decisively in creating an imbalance oriented towards growth"—or see it as the Old World putting its characteristic stamp on America—"I would say that America was Europe's 'doing,' " as Fernand Braudel says somewhat poetically, "the achievement by which Europe most truly revealed her own nature"—there is no mistaking its overriding importance on both sides of the Atlantic. Neither participant would ever be the same again.

Not long before 1592, a fitting enough anniversary, Christopher Marlowe wrote The Tragical History of Doctor Faustus, *which became an immediate and lasting hit on the London stage. It was a poetic and durable version of that story, but it was only one among many, for the legend of the magical doctor, which seemed to express in some thrillingly forbidden way the elemental truths of the European soul, was extremely popular throughout the subcontinent.*

The legend was based on the true story of a German magician and traveling doctor of medicine in the first decades of the sixteenth century, Johann Faust, who practiced, a contemporary said, "up and down Germany, with unspeakable deceit, many lies and great effect." He was naturally a target of the witch-hunts of his time, although he seems somehow to have escaped official condemnation for more than three decades of conjuring and curing, and his success inspired wild tales about him even while he was alive. After his death—whether at the hands of the Devil or not—he almost immediately became a subject of plays and poems and parables, many of them following the line of Johann Spies of Frankfurt, whose book held that Faust had made a bargain with Lucifer so that he could practice the dark arts of Satan, including the power to know and control all the objects of the earth, in return for relinquishing his eternal soul. This version, published in 1587 and immediately sold out, then pirated in no fewer than four editions in later years, was the one that became known to Marlowe.

At about the same time that Faust met his end, in the 1540s, another learned European died, in the town of Frauenburg, Poland. His name was Nicholas Copernicus, and ironically it was on the day of his death, May 24, 1543, that a copy of his De revolutionibus orbium coelestium, *fresh off the presses, finally reached his bedside. He died before he ever saw it.*

Copernicus's book, setting forth the doctrine that the sun was at the center of the solar system and the earth revolved around it in a circular orbit, was important not so much for the novelty of its thesis or even the discomfort it caused in religious circles, leading Luther to snort that "the ass is trying to pervert the whole science of astronomy" and the Catholic Church to place it on its Index in 1616. Its importance lay in that, along with a half a dozen other such books of the mid-century, it sanctified the new approaches of the new Science, demonstrating that the Truths of the Universe could be understood by the dispassionate processes of research and reason alone and not by the exercise of faith or belief. Far from reducing humans and their earth to an insignificant role in a sun-dominated solar system, it rather convinced the sixteenth-century European of the quite wonderful brilliance of the human mind and the beauty of its rationalism. "The new astronomy that seemed to reduce man to nothingness," as Egon Friedell points out, "made him in reality the unveiler, the seer, and even the legislator of the cosmos."

This is precisely what the Faust story is all about: it celebrates, despite its hortatory ending, the victory of humans, freed from the impediments of religion and custom, over nature. Faust renounces God, as Marlowe shows us, and the pious promises of heaven, so that he may have the knowledge of the universe—all the planets in the firmament and all the plants and beings of the earth—and the power to make them do his bidding:

> *O what a world of profit and delight,*
> *Of power, of honor, of omnipotence. . . .*
> *All things that move between the quiet poles*
> *Shall be at my command.*

Thus Europe, crowned by Science, may rule the world.

The other reason, then, that it was England which picked up the Columbian mantle in the late sixteenth and early seventeenth centuries was that, in an era of exploitation, it had attributes for this unsurpassed by any other Atlantic nation.

To some extent, these were surprisingly like those enjoyed by Spain when it opened up the New World a century earlier. England was consolidating itself into a modern state, first with the firm-handed rule of a popular queen and then with the formal unification of its separate kingdoms. It was experiencing a new sense of nationalism, accompanied by a jingoistic hatred of a foreign enemy and a recent military vic-

tory over it. It had gotten rid of its Jewish population long before—
the official expulsion of Jews from England was in 1290—but it had a
despised religious minority in the unconverted Catholics at home and
the brutalized peasantry in Ireland. And it had a long tradition of
maritime trade, plus a body of experienced and able mariners on
whom it could count for Atlantic exploration and commerce.

In addition, England possessed some special features peculiar to
itself, and its time.

Geography—which as always is the essential determinant of human
constructs—had provided it with considerable insular protection, and
as a result the English monarchy, unique in Europe, had never developed a standing army or the resultant ability to levy independent
taxes, create its own legislation, or declare war at will. Thus England's
was a society with much more dispersed power than elsewhere in
Europe, in the hands both of the landed aristocracy and the rising
new sector of rich farmers, wealthy merchants, and successful manufacturers, whose fortunes expanded greatly in the inflationary cycles
of the sixteenth-century price revolution. It was these titans of the
new capitalism, for example, who from 1553 to 1603 were able to
invest in joint-stock companies with overseas interests, something
like £13 million, a prodigious sum, of which an estimated £584,000
went to New World ventures, and who had enough left over to sink
perhaps £4.4 million more in companies specializing in Atlantic piracy
(to return an estimated 60 percent on their investments).

Geographical isolation also played a part in the development of
England into a modern nation-state during this time. It had a single
national parliament, its only representative body, unlike the several
provincial parliaments of countries such as Holland and Switzerland;
it had a single set of laws for the whole country, unlike the jumble
of legal codes that prevailed in France; and it had a single national
language, from Cornwall to the Scottish lowlands, unlike the multiple
tongues of the Italian peninsula or eastern Spain. "Considered emo-
tionally or considered practically," says the English historian K. G.
Davies, "England was more of a 'nation' in 1600 than any other
European country. There was a special self-consciousness, heightened
by the Reformation and toughened by the war with Spain, a consciousness met time and time again in Elizabethan literature," including of course the deliberately imperial works of Richard Eden
and Richard Hakluyt.

England's isolation served also to keep the country, more than any other in Europe, out of war, and its comparatively painless embrace of Protestantism in 1534 spared it most of the effects of the internecine turmoil that engulfed the rest of the subcontinent. Thus it was able to concentrate the great part of its expenditures, both royal and private, on overseas expansion and the fleets with which to pursue it: from 1545 to 1625 the Royal Navy increased in both numbers and tonnage twofold, the merchant marine fivefold, and England was prepared to say, with Ralegh, "Whosoever commands the sea commands the trade, whosoever commands the trade of the world commands the riches of the world, and consequently the world itself."

Other attributes, too, all pointing in the same direction: a great "surplus" population, forced off the land by the sixteenth-century enclosure movement and massed in the crowded cities, unemployed, unproductive, and unwanted; the resulting rise in crime, leading to stiffer penalties (more crimes punishable by death than any other nation) and soon to the choice of transportation, which was seen as a reasonable alternative to decapitation by many convicted criminals; a large increase in Protestant immigrants who had been forced out of mainland Catholic countries, many of them artisans and skilled laborers, with no special ties to England and no barriers to overseas resettlement; and a religious ideology called Protestantism that not only removed impediments that hampered nascent capitalists elsewhere but positively honored credit, profit, interest, and even usury, and held virtuous thrift, industry, wealth, and—it is undeniable—exploitation.

And thus it was that, exactly a century after Colón's death, it was England, inheritor of the Columbian Legacy, that sent out the little fleet that would successfully challenge Iberian hegemony in the New World and set the foundation, though none could have possibly imagined it then, for the transformation of the land and people of North America.

> *And in regions far*
> *Such heroes bring ye forth*
>   *As those from whom we came,*
>   *And plant our name*
> *Under that star*
> *Not known unto our north.*

Chapter Eleven

1607–25

I

Jamestown

[May 1607.] When Captain Newport in his first Voyage, did not like to inhabit upon so open a roade, as Cape Henry, nor Point Comfort he plied it up to the River, still looking out for the most apt and securest place, as well for his Company to sit downe in, as which might give the least cause of offence, or distast in his judgement, to the Inhabitants. At length, after much and weary search ... they had sight of an extended plaine & spot of earth, which thrust out into the depth, & middest of the channell, making a kinde of Chersonesus or Peninsula, for it was fastened onely to the Land with a slender necke....

The Trumpets sounding, the Admirall strooke saile, and before the same, the rest of the fleete came to an ancor, and here ... to loose no further time, the Colony disimbarked, and every man brought his particular store and furniture, together with the generall provision ashoare: for the safety of which, as likewise for their owne security, ease, and better accommodating, a certain Canton and quantity of that little halfe Iland of ground, was measured, which they began to fortifie, and thereon in the name of God, to raise a Fortresse, with the ablest and speediest meanes they could.—William Strachey, 1610

On May 14, 1607, the second successful invasion of America formally began, 115 years after the first, as the hundred or so Englishmen from the Newport fleet disembarked on a low-lying peninsula on the north bank of what they were to call the James River. It was a moment of great significance for both the Old World and the New, for not only did it lead to the first effective implantation of the British nation overseas but, almost as if it had parted the waters, it began a period of colonial activity that in just three decades brought settlers from a half-dozen nations of Europe to the northern continent. Within the next four years, the French established a small *comptoir* in Quebec, the Dutch had explored the Hudson estuary, and the Spanish in Mexico had moved across the Rio Grande and encamped at Santa Fe; within the next thirty years there were no fewer than twenty-nine colonies established in North America, including the Caribbean, in addition to the dozen Spanish settlements in Mexico and the garrison in St. Augustine, with a total European population of close to 60,000 outside Mexico.[1]

There was no such thing as a typical European colony here: each one inevitably expressed the styles and strategies of the country (and the regions) whose peoples set it up, each adapted according to the conditions of its environment. The French settlements along the St. Lawrence were little more than trading posts, with a few families and an attachment of *religieux*; the Dutch colonies on the Hudson and the Delaware (as well as Swedish and Finnish posts on the latter) were similarly entrepôts, concerned chiefly with supplies of furs and skins for the European market and involved with agriculture only insofar as it was necessary to keep the little outposts going. The Spanish settlements in the Southwest were either mining camps or fortified mission villages, planned as little way-stations from which souls would be converted and gold and silver shipped. The English colonies, in New England and Maryland as well as Virginia, were generally more populous affairs, aimed to be places of permanent settlement and dependent on agricultural exploitation and the occupation of territory. All of the Caribbean settlements, with the exception of those on a few small islands used for trade or piracy, were designed for agricultural economies, dependent on poor-white and (increasingly) slave-black labor.

But if not exactly typical, Jamestown was at least in many ways representative—and, as the first successful outpost of the nation that was ultimately to win the battle of the continent, premonitory. Its story demonstrates with particular clarity how the next great colonizing power carried out the Columbian Legacy, with the same roughshod determination, the same mixture of bravery and cruelty, the same tragedy and triumph, as the first. Whatever the differences between English and Spanish forms of conquest, they were alike in their desire to emplace their own foreign populations, establish political and ideological hegemony, settle and control large stretches of land, effect military control over a subject people, exploit the resources of the soil—and achieve spiritual regeneration in the process.

They were alike, too, in the way they intended to build large permanent settlements, true extensions of the mother country. The peninsula on which the English decamped was, according to John Smith, "a verie fit place for the erecting of a great citie," and this he fully intended to accomplish—a great *European* city, let it be added, with English-style farms and English-style industries, houses and churches and storerooms right from the English countryside, and English men (and eventually women) imported to populate it.

And its first building, as at La Navidad and Isabela, was to be a fort.[2]

[May 1607.] Newport, with Smith, and 20 others, were sent to discover the head of the river: by divers smal habitations they passed, in 6 daies they arrived at a towne called Powhatan, consisting of some 12 houses pleasantly seated on a hill; before it 3 fertil Iles, about it many of their cornefields, the place is very pleasant, and strong by nature, of this place the Prince is called Powhatan, and his people Powhatans.—John Smith, 1612

About the Indians of the Chesapeake area in the seventeenth century we know essentially only what we are told by a handful of English invaders, not all unsympathetic but all rigidly Anglocentric, and only for the first few decades before the Indian population was decimated and scattered. Intermittent fieldwork was done in the late nineteenth and early twentieth centuries, but among tiny remnant groups by then so dislocated and so intermarried that they could hardly be called true descendants of the original culture at all, and little archeological work has been done at Indian (as opposed to colonial) sites in the Chesapeake, less even than in Española. Great caution is therefore appropriate.[3]

Yet it is probably safe to say that the peoples of the southwestern Chesapeake—it is difficult even to give them an apt name, though they have conventionally, if wrongly, been saddled with the name Smith gave them, probably pronounced "*po*-khah-tun"*—were then living in some form of loose association of villages and provinces that might be understood as a kind of chiefdom, with a titular elder in the position the English designated as "chief." It was clearly not either a "monarchy" or an "empire," as many of the early English naturally said, and certainly not an organized "confederacy," as Thomas Jefferson and a whole raft of modern commentators have described it; at best it was a linked alliance of what the English called "tribes" (more accurately villages, of between 200 and 1,000 people) connected by various sorts of family ties, clan affiliations, political allegiances, tributes and duties, and intermittent defense pacts.

One reason for its amorphous nature may be that it was probably a fairly new system of association, contrived perhaps in the 1580s or 1590s, joining at first a half-dozen and then later perhaps thirty villages or so. Whether this system was the result of social disruptions caused by epidemics from earlier European contacts, or in defensive response to what looked like a series of European invasions, there is no way to know, but it is thought that this was the only area east of Appalachia where such an interwoven society existed at this time, and its singularity may well rest on such outside causes as those.[4]

> *[June 1607.] Captaine Newport being gone for England, leaving us (one hundred and foure persons) verie bare and scantie of victualls, furthermore ... in danger of the Savages. ... The sixt of August there died John Asbie of the bloudie fluxe. The ninth day died George flowre of the swelling. The tenth day died William Bruster Gentleman, of a wound given by the Savages, and was buried the eleventh day. ...*
>
> *Our men were destroyed with cruell diseases as Swellings,*

---

*Other, more reliable English accounts suggest that this region of the tidewater was known to its native inhabitants as Tsenahkommaka (meaning "densely inhabited land," "long-inhabited land," or "land opposite"), and so the people might best be known collectively as the Tsenahkommakas. The village, or "tribe," of the principal chief was rendered variously as Powhatan, Poaton, or Poetan; the first form was the name the English gave not only to the chief but to the collectivity over which he presided, but there is no indication that the Indians themselves used any such designation.

*Fluxes, Burning Fevers, and by warres, and some departed
suddenly, but for the most part they died of meere
famine. There were never Englishmen left in a forreigne
Countrey in such miserie as wee were in this new
discovered Virginia.—George Percy, 1625*

The most compelling fact of life in the Virginia colony, from the
beginning and for many decades, was death.

It is hard to come by accurate figures, even with the help of the
sort of detailed account Percy provided, but there is no question that
the great majority of those sent out to Virginia between 1607 and
1625 lost their lives, most of them within a year. John Smith estimated
in 1631 that "neere eight thousand men's lives" had been "consumed"
in Virginia up to 1625, and such figures as we have seem to bear him
out: at least 7,289 people were listed for trips from London to Virginia
in those years (probably an undercount, since data for 1610–18
are sparse), and only about 1,210 people were alive when a rough
census was taken in 1625, of whom 85 percent had come out
since 1618. Thus we must assume that at least 6,000 people died in
or on their way to Jamestown, making the well-known assessment
of Governor William Berkeley later in the century—"Heretofore
not one of Five scaped the first yeare"—awful as it seems, a slight
underestimate.*

How to account for death on such a scale?

The simple, awful explanation is that, in the sad Columbian tradition, the Jamestown colonists, amid an abundance of nature so full
that a minimal amount of labor would bring forth easy sustenance,
did not know how to feed themselves and for the better part of two

---

*There is one other possible explanation, but it could not have been written about much,
and what was penned would have been censored by the Virginia Company, so we are left with
conjecture. But there are enough allusions to the attractiveness, or at least abundance, of the
Indian way of life—and repeated laws punishing those who ran away to the Indians—to suggest
that some number of potential colonists may simply have run into the woods and joined the
Powhatans. The Virginia Assembly itself, acknowledging that runaways who were captured
"were putt to sundry deaths as by hanginge, shootinge and breakinge upon the wheele,"
admitted that nonetheless starvation and cruelty "forced many to flee for reliefe to the Savage
Enemy." The figures for 1618–22, the most reliable, which indicate that 3,570 people were
shipped out (joining 700 already there) and only 1,240 remained in 1625, would suggest
incredibly high rates of mortality, on the order of 750 people a year, surely something that
would have attracted attention and have been mentioned in some records. But since no such
attention was paid, it may be assumed that an embarrassingly high number of good Englishmen
decided to become good Indians.

decades never learned. Time and again it is reported that the colonists were "not so provident . . . as to put corne in the g[r]ound for their winters bread" or "not compelled (since in themselves unwilling) to sowe Corne for their owne bellies, nor to put a Roote, Herbe, &c. for their owne particular good in their Gardens, or elsewhere." Time and again it is said that they succumbed to unaccountable "idlenesse and bestiall sloth," "laziness," and "unwillingnesse," and "had they not been forced . . . they would all have starved." Time and again, Percy said, "this starveinge Tyme."

This extraordinary functional disability has intrigued historians repeatedly over the years, as it intrigued contemporaries, and the reasons put forth have been numerous: the debilitating effects of disease, according to Percy and others since, although even the healthy men were apparently idle and unproductive, and upcountry settlements, less prone to disease, were similarly improvident; a lack of discipline, said John Smith, although even when he and successors ran the colony as a military camp there was never enough food and hundreds died at the "starving time"; too many gentlemen, others said, although as soon as a cash crop came along in later years these high-born dandies proved to be very hard-working and capable indeed; a communal store and lack of free enterprise, Ralph Hamor suggested, but even with a general switch to private plots and individual initiative after 1612 the starvation deaths went on and as late as 1619 the colony was still "in a great scarcity for want of corn."

This "extreme beastly idleness of our nation" is on the one hand so bizarre and yet on the other so recurrent—it is recorded over and over in colonies of the Spanish (e.g., Isabela), the French (e.g., France-Roy and Quebec), the Dutch (e.g., Fort Orange), and the English elsewhere (e.g., Plymouth)—that I think one can understand it only by trying to comprehend what it meant for the psyche of Europe to confront the wilderness of America. Not only did this powerful experience of trying to live amid nature in the raw—so very different from merely sailing by or journeying through—engender dark feelings of fear and hatred, as we might expect, but it also produced bewilderment, dislocation, and disorientation, a sense of being out of place, imprisoned in a hostile environment full of hostile strangers with none of the promised wealth or ease, where none of the familiar rules and assumptions obtain, where none of the attributes by which one has achieved self-definition—matters of one's birth, trade, learning, experience, or competence—seem to apply. In such circumstances the alienation from nature already ingrained in European culture—and the more so in settlers from distinctly urbanized societies such as southeastern England and southern Spain—might well create a psychological impotence, a withdrawal, a kind of mental fetal-positioning, that would read to the world as idleness and laziness. It might well produce a weighty and profound psychological barrier that for many became impossible to cross even in times of need.

Some support for this explanation is provided by studies made of others who have proven psychologically unable to cope with strange new conditions. The historian Karen Ordahl Kupperman has compared the reported symptoms of the early Jamestown colonists with those of prisoners of war, particularly Americans in Korea and Japan where the circumstances of their imprisonment were far beyond their cultural expectations, and found them remarkably similar. The apathy and lethargy so often noted in Jamestown, she suggests, might really be the same sort of "isolation and despair about the future," leading to a "fatal withdrawal from life," which was characteristic of the American POWs. This is all the more pronounced, she notes, when such men are deprived of both effective, nurturant leadership and acceptable, familiar work—conditions common to the American prisoners and the Jamestown settlers.

Withdrawal: apathy: famine: death. That, in pure form, was the pattern of the settlement of Jamestown for virtually all of its first two decades. Through its years of existence the Virginia Company was responsible for the loss of many more lives—English lives alone—than it ever saved.

[April 1608.] The worst mischiefe was, our gilded refiners with their golden promises, made all men their slaves in hope of recompence, there was no talke, no hope, no worke, but dig gold, wash gold, refine gold, load gold, such a brute [rumor] of gold, as one mad fellow desired to bee buried in the sandes, least they should by their art make gold of his bones. . . . Captaine Smith would not applaud all those golden inventions . . . he was not inamoured with their durtie skill, breathing out these and many other passions, never anything did more torment him, then to see all

*necessarie businesse neglected, to fraught such a drunken
ship with so much gilded durt.—John Smith, 1612*

When Christopher Newport first returned to London, in August 1607, he provided the officers of the Virginia Company with at least several barrels of stones he took to be gold-bearing along with promises of "a Kingdome full of the oare." The fact that the stones proved worthless apparently daunted no one: on his second voyage to Jamestown, in January 1608, Newport took two goldsmiths, two refiners, and a jeweler, as well as 115 more settlers, most of whose heads were apparently filled with what Smith dismissed as "golden inventions." The fruit of all their labors of digging and washing and loading is not recorded, but Newport did take additional samples with him when he completed his second round-trip sometime in the early fall. Thereafter the silence is deafening.

And anything but golden: company promoters from then on made no mention of ores of any kind, their praises having to do with the land being "large and great," the climate "most sweete and wholsome," the soil "strong and lustie," and the like. Of the prospects for "gilded durt," not a word.

The poor English. Not once in all their ventures were they to stumble upon "the mynes of gould and silver" that seemed simply to offer themselves everywhere to the Spanish. "It was the Spaniards good hap," John Smith wrote with some acerbity, "to happen in those parts, where . . . they had the use of gold and silver. . . . But we chanced in a lande, even as God made it. Where we found only an idle, improvident, scattered people; ignorant of the knowledge of gold, or silver, or any commodities." Not once in all those ventures, though, did they stop their dreaming, and when George Chapman wrote a masquerade for the celebrations of Princess Elizabeth's wedding in 1613 he centered the action upon a huge rock of gold, said to be the symbol of Virginia.

*[May 1610.] Cast up the reckoning together: want of
government, store of idlenesse, their expectations frustrated
by the Traytors, their market spoyled by the Mariners, our
Nets broken, the Deere chased, our Boats lost, our Hogs
killed, our trade with the Indians forbidden, some of our
men fled, some murthered, and most by drinking of the*

brackish water of James Fort weakened and indangered,
famine and sicknesse by all these meanes increased.
                                    —William Strachey, 1625

As an example of a colony in a shambles to match that of Española under Cristóbal Colón it would be hard to do better than Jamestown in its early years, only some of whose troubles were touched upon by Strachey. It was assuredly the victim of any number of "cruell diseases," caused in part because the site of the colony, in fine Columbian tradition, was markedly ill chosen: much of the Jamestown peninsula was a tidal marshland, a fecund breeding ground for mosquitoes and their malarial parasites (the latter, not native to the Americas, from London or via the Caribbean) and the source of the "brackish water" probably infected with typhoid bacteria. But its primary problems were manmade, including practically every sort of turmoil that human conflict could contrive: quarrels, feuds, lawsuits, schisms, brawls, plunder, robbery, fraud, desertion, mutiny, treason, piracy, murder, dismemberment, whipping, tortures, and execution, to say nothing of its cruelties to, and the revenges of, the Powhatans. "They neither feared God, nor man," Strachey said of the settlers, "which provoked the wrath of the Lord of Hosts, and pulled downe his judgements upon them."

That the colony survived at all in its first three years is remarkable, due in part to the tenacity of men such as John Smith and George Percy, the determination of the investors in London, and most of all—ironically—the supplies of corn provided regularly (given, bartered, or stolen) from the Powhatans' fields. Even so, among some 600 settlers in the fall of 1609, of the 1,900 or so who had been sent out, the population dwindled so rapidly that "within 6 monthes after there remained not many more than 60 most miserable and poore creatures." When Sir Thomas Gates and his 150 men arrived in Jamestown in May 1610 they found such a desperate and sickly company, full of "clamors and complaints, of accusing or excusing one another," that they decided within weeks to end the Virginia experiment and abandon the colony, and on June 7, 1610, the entire assemblage embarked for England.

[March 1610.] We thinke fitt your Lordship should reduce
them all into severall bandes and compaies of fifties or

more when you thinke good and to committ the charge of
them to severall officers and captaines to be exercised and
trained up in martiall manner and warlike discipline. . . .
A summary and arbitrary way of justice, mingled with
discreet formes of magistracy as shall in your discretion
seeme aptest for your Lordship to exercise in that place,
wilbe of most use both for expedicion and example and
for criminall causes, you are to deale therein according to
your commission and good discretion.
　　　　　—Virginia Company, to Lord De La Warr, 1610

The London investors, aware that things were literally falling apart
in Jamestown despite their considerable contributions of men and
money, determined in the spring of 1610 to refinance the company
and send out a well-born and seasoned soldier, Thomas West, Lord
De La Warr, to be the absolute ruler of Virginia, impose order on
the colonists, turn Jamestown into a military encampment, wage war
upon the troublesome natives—and make the colony profitable.

By one of those chances in which the English were content to see
the hand of providence, De La Warr sailed into the James River just
as Gates and the remnant colony were sailing out. They all returned
to the Jamestown site and on June 10, a Sunday, De La Warr disembarked and, "landing, fell upon his knees, and before us all, made a
long and silent Prayer to himselfe, and after, marched up into the
Towne" to read out his orders for military rule. Those orders, provided by the company and enlarged upon the following year, were
essentially to govern the colony for the next decade according to what
can only be called martial law, with a severity of punishments that
not only strike the modern temperament as harsh but were seen at
the time, by such as the Virginia secretary, Ralph Hamor, at least,
as "cruell, unusuall and barbarous."

The orders provide a lengthy list, in some sixty pages of small
print, of acts forbidden to the colonists, almost all of which end with
some variant of "shall bee punished with death." Death was prescribed, for example, for blasphemy, sedition, desertion, sodomy,
adultery, rape (including "maid or Indian"), robbery from church or
general store or neighbor (including apparel or tools), false oath, trade
with Indians, and a dozen other offenses; whipping was ordered for
washing clothes in public or throwing out wash water in the streets,

for daring "to doe the necessities of nature" within a quarter-mile of the fort, for "fornication, and evident proofe made thereof," and a variety of small infractions; and cursing was to be condemned by "severe punishment" the first time, having "a bodkin thrust through his tongue" the second, and death the third.

It cannot be denied that the Virginia colony managed to survive under such conditions, but whether because of them, as some historians maintain—following Captain Smith, who found them quite congenial—would be hard to establish. What can be said, though, is that it survived in such a way as to become the equivalent of a military invasion force in a foreign land.

> [*August 1610.*] *Then draweinge my sowldiers into Battalio placeinge a Capteyne or Leftenante att every fyle we marched towards the Towne. . . . And then we fell in upon them putt some fiftene or sixtene to the Sworde and Almoste all the reste to flyghte. . . .*
>
> *My Lieftenantt bringeinge w[i]th him the Quene and her Children and one Indyann prisoners for the W[hi]ch I taxed him becawse he had Spared them his Answer was thatt haveinge them now in my Custodie I might doe w[i]th them whatt I pleased. Upon the same I cawsed the Indians head to be cutt of. And then dispersed my fyles Apointeinge my Sowldiers to burne their howses and to cutt downe their Corne groweinge aboutt the Towne.*
>
> *And after we marched w[i]th the quene And her Children to our Boates ageine, where beinge noe sooner well shipped my sowldiers did begin to murmur becawse the quene and her Children weare spared. So upon the same A Cowncell beinge called it was Agreed upon to putt the Children to deathe the w[hi]ch was effected by Throweinge them overboard and shoteinge owtt their Braynes in the water.*—George Percy, 1612

It is horrible, and pitiable, to read from their own pens the descriptions of how the English—even the well-born George Percy, he of the gold-laced suits and beaver hats—had finally decided to come to terms with their native hosts, the more so in that the descriptions are so matter-of-fact, offered without anguish or remorse. This may be, as the historian Howard Mumford Jones has said, "very small beer" in comparison with the conquest of Mexico or Peru, but it is different only in scale, not in severity. There is but one excuse, or at least explanation: this was war, and Percy was a professional soldier.

Most historians write as if there were no such thing, but the evidence seems sufficient to show that there was indeed something that must be described as an Anglo-Powhatan War and that its first phase began with the landing of De La Warr in the summer of 1610. There is no mistaking his orders from the Virginia Company: the "enemy is the natives," they said, all of whose chiefs should be either taken prisoner or made into tributaries, "to acknowledge no other lord but Kinge James," and should be expected to provide regular tributes of corn and skins and regular supplies of workers as "a meanse of claringe much ground of wood and of reducing them to laboure." And if the natives should, understandably, resist such measures and "fly up into the countrey and foresake their habitacion," then the English forces should seize "half there corne and harvest" and kidnap the chiefs and their children to educate "in your manners and religion," whereupon "their people will easily obey you and become in time civill and Christian." This is nothing short of a declaration of war.

And so the English understood it. The opening skirmish took place in July, when Gates descended upon the village of Kecoughtan, a few miles downstream from the fort at the mouth of the James, "put five to the sword, wounded many others," and "the rest of the savages he put to flight," then burned the village and apparently destroyed its cornfields. Next Percy was sent to destroy the village of Paspahegh, just north of Jamestown, with the attendant bloodshed he described so coldly. Thereafter De La Warr unleashed what the modern historian J. Frederick Fausz, one of the few to understand the nature of these events, calls "a brutal and atrocity-ridden four-year war of revenge reminiscent of campaigns in Ireland" (where De La Warr had in fact served and been knighted), with raids on the towns of Waraskoyak, Nansamund, Chickahominy, Appomatuk, and Paspahegh more than once, in which numbers of warriors were slain, houses burned, canoes and weirs destroyed, and cornfields trampled and torched. De La Warr's successor from May 1611, Sir Thomas Dale, another soldier, carried on the conflict (with what Percy called "a greater supply" of men and "a greate store of Armour"), "makeinge more invasyons & excursions upon the salvages" all the way up the river to the farthest reaches of Powhatan territory at the fall line, fifty miles west of Jamestown.[5]

Ultimately the Powhatans sued for peace, or what was probably in their eyes something more like a truce. The cause of it was almost certainly the direct assault that Dale led on the village upstream that served as the headquarters of Wahunseneka, whom the English chose to call Powhatan, in the spring of 1614, or his crippling campaign against the previously invulnerable village of Pamunkey around the same time; but the occasion for it, face-saving to both sides, was the famous marriage of colonist John Rolfe to one of Wahunseneka's daughters, Matoakah, known to the English, and history, by her playful nickname, Pocahontas.* It is conceivable that there may have been, or developed, some affection between the two parties of this union—Ralph Hamor at the time asserted that "Rolfe had bin in love with Pocahuntas and she with him"—but it seems obvious that its primary motives were political, a means not only of ending the war but of establishing some sort of mitigative normalcy between two peoples now apparently living side by side. Rolfe declared to his military superiors at least that he sought the marriage not out of "the unbridled desire of carnall affection: but for the good of this plantation, for the honour of our Countrie . . . and for the converting to the true knowledge of God and Jesus Christ, an unbeleeving creature." Nothing, however, is recorded about Matoakah's feelings in the matter.

Thus ended, with a bizarre marriage and the effective victory of the armed and militant invaders, the First Anglo-Powhatan War. (There were to be two others, with the same military result, in 1622 and 1644.) It is an event that deserves to go down in history, for the pattern it set was tragic: never once after this defeat would the natives of America succeed in repelling and rejecting a single European colonial power.

If the spectrum of responses of the English to the people of America

---

*There is some reason for believing the name meant something like "little wanton," as the English rendered it, but I am persuaded it is a form of the Algonkian word *pocohaac*, which William Strachey tells us means "the privities or secret of a man," in other words, "penis," and has the suggestion of, as we would say, "cock-teasing." It seems probable that the Powhatans, like other Algonkian groups, put no sanctions against premarital sex—indeed, encouraged it as a method of courtship and mate selection—and that Matoakah, perhaps no more than twelve or thirteen when she first met the English in 1608 and already bearing that name, was rather more flirtatious than most. She was *not*, by the way, a princess, although the English always regarded her as such; she was the daughter of a chief, but since descent was in the female line, the next generation in power would be the sons and daughters of his eldest sister.

could range from slaughter to marriage—though, indeed, with the emphasis more on the former than the latter—what does that say about the way in which the second great colonial power responded to that part of the Columbian Legacy which in the Spanish was the tension between the Noble Savage and the Savage Beast?

It is not that the English were uniformly hostile to the Indians, either in Virginia or in New England and Maryland later; in fact there were those, even if a minority, who went to some pains to learn their languages, study their cultures, and record their beliefs and myths. But as the events of early Virginia suggest, there is very little of the Noble Savage tradition in English colonization, even less than in the Spanish, and one can go through the whole of England's record in this era without coming upon anyone remotely as sympathetic to the Indians as Las Casas. Some promotional types did push the Edenic image ("the people most gentle, loving, and faithful, void of all gile, and treason, and such as lived after the manner of the golden age"), but they were those who had never moved from England or had merely explored the coasts; the ones who came to settle and live among the actual peoples of the New World found little that was praiseworthy, and almost nothing noble, about them.[6]

Several factors explain the English response. First of all, the Indian populations were much smaller than those the Spanish encountered, their numbers drastically reduced after a century of lethal disease epidemics, and their tribal organizations, not as elaborate and statified in any case as those of Mesoamerica, were in disarray, their social and religious systems badly damaged, from the same decimating sicknesses. Second, after it turned out that there were no great mines of gold or silver into which the Indians could be enslaved and that the colonies would have to survive on plantation agriculture, the natives seemed merely to be in the way, careless occupiers of land that could be put to better use under an English plow. Last, in spite of occasional pieties to the contrary, neither Christianizing nor civilizing the Indians played any very large part in either the theory or practice of England's colonization, and nowhere were serious attempts made at a full-scale integration of native populations into European culture on the Spanish model. That is one of the reasons that there is no record in any part of the English colonies—in sharp contrast to the Spanish—of anyone following the Rolfe–Matoakah example and why sanctions and eventually laws grew up in the seventeenth century against Anglo-Indian intermarriage.

Hence the English were much readier to succumb to the image of
the Indian as the Savage Beast—in fact, to use those two words over
and over again in their writings to a degree unmatched by either the
French (who would more often use *peuple* or *barbars*), the north
Europeans (the Dutch used *wilden*, the Swedes *wildar*), or the Spanish
(who used *bestia* only occasionally, *Indios* most commonly).

"Savage" has occasionally been excused as a sort of neutral word,
with no weightier connotations than "person" or "native." But it is
nothing of the sort. Its deep richness of meaning was perfectly clear
to the seventeenth-century English—contemporary usages include
"not of a manne, but of a veraye brute and salvage beast," "not to
relent is beastly, savage," and "savage wild, degenerate men"—and
Shakespeare used it or its variants some forty-two times, never once
without connotations of wild, rude, fierce, cruel, and subhuman. It
is all the more resonant coupled with the images conveyed by "beast,"
which the English used for the Virginia natives from the start: "demeanour like to bruite beasts," "unbridled beastes," "these beests
which are of most wilde & savage nature," "cruell beasts," "more
brutish than the beasts they hunt," and on and on.

It all came down to this: the natives of the Americas were to be
understood as *less than human*, not in the literal sense, of course—
their handsome human physiques were often noted, their tribes
clearly measured against other human societies—but still in some real
and operative way that permitted the sort of psychological displacement we now know to be common in creating the image of the
Enemy, the Other: "consider what these Creatures are (I cannot call
them men)," "in order to make them Christians, they must first be
made Men," "the first task is to make them men." And thus they
could be used in exactly the manner that English circumstances and
American conditions set for the success of the colonial enterprise.
"To imagine the Indian as a savage beast," as the shrewd historian
Gary Nash has put it, "was a way of predicting the future and preparing for it and of justifying what one would do, even before one
caused it to happen." That meant, as with wild beasts anywhere:
controlled, fenced in, confined to parks or reservations; broken and
tamed, "domesticated," brought to the restraints of civilized society;
displaced and scattered, forced on to distant lands, with bounties on
any who strayed too close; or exterminated, hunted down and killed
outright on a regular basis and over a wide area.

Those are precisely the four elements of the policy toward the native population of North America that the English, and their United States successors, followed over the next four centuries.

> *[1616–21.] Your Majesty . . . prohibiting our importation of tobacco, the only commodity which we have had hitherto means to raise towards the appareling of our bodies and other needful supplements . . . we are plunged in so great extremities that now remaineth neither help nor hope, but that we must all here perish for want of clothing, and other necessaries. . . .*
>
> *May it therefore please your Majesty out of your princely compassion . . . either to revoke that Proclamation, and to restore us to our ancient liberty, or otherwise to send for us all home; and not to suffer the Heathen to triumph over us and to say "Where is now their God?"*
> *—Virginia colonists' petition to James I, January 1621*

James I was a well-known foe of tobacco, had in fact written a bitter pamphlet, *A Counterblaste to Tobacco*, in 1604 to try to discourage a habit even then growing among his citizens. To register his displeasure with the increasing importation of the weed from Virginia he issued a proclamation in 1620 to limit sharply the amount that could be sent to London from both Virginia and Bermuda. The Virginia planters, by then totally dependent on that single commodity for survival, as they make only too plain, wrote this anguished appeal in reply. It seems to have had an effect—that, along with the word passed to His Majesty that the colonists could find a ready market for their product in other European ports, thus depriving London, and the king, of lucrative import duties—for the trade was halted only temporarily and by 1623 Virginia and Bermuda were granted a virtual monopoly of the English market.

The first English experiments in growing tobacco were made around 1610, apparently by John Rolfe, and he was the one who eventually discarded the homegrown Virginia variety, said to be somewhat harsh, for a sweeter type he had brought in from the West Indies around 1611 or 1612. The first tobacco shipment was sent from Virginia to London in 1613 or 1614, a meager four barrels' worth but commanding such a good price—probably around 40 shillings a pound—that it encouraged the colonists to extend their fields. In

1616, 2,300 pounds was shipped, the next year 19,388, the next 49,528, and in 1620 some 60,000 pounds, by which time tobacco had become the all-consuming interest of the Virginia settlers: "The only commodity for Merchandizes in booth the Plantations is at this day no other than Tobacco: whereby there apparrell, tooles, impellments & all other necessarys (except victuall) are procured." But of course with all of this supply, prices in London quickly plummeted, going from 40 shillings a pound in 1614 to 3.5 shillings in 1619 and 1 to 3 shillings in 1625; thereafter they dropped steadily as production kept increasing, reaching as low as 2 to 3 pence a pound after 1640.

The response of the planters was inevitable: the only way to maintain income with falling prices was to move farther and farther out into Powhatan country and plant larger and larger fields, felling trees and clearing lands wherever they could, regardless of local populations or environments. Tobacco is a crop that needs a great deal of land in any case, but in Virginia it proved all the more voracious because the thin topsoils of the tidewater coast (not enriched by glacial mineral deposits, as northern soils are) were exhausted in a half-dozen years and plantations were abandoned and left to erosion. "Now the gre[e]dines[s] after great quantities of Tobacco," complained several prominent Virginians, "causeth them after 5 or 6 years continually to remove and therefore neither build good Houses, fence their grounds or plant any Orchards, etc." Modern ecologists have echoed the complaint: "Such farming," the ecohistorian Albert Cowdrey has said, "ensured that the minimum number of people would have the maximum impact on soil and forest," none of it beneficial. Even today the tidewater region shows the disastrous effect of plantation-tobacco culture.

Yet the lure of tobacco was irresistible. It provided a crop within a single year, it was relatively easy to grow (the hardest work, picking, could be done by indentured servants or slaves), it was lightweight and could be shipped in bulk, and if enough land was given over to it, it was enormously profitable. Compared to that, the fact that it was a product even then known to be odious ("harmefulle to the braine, dangerous to the Lungs," and "hurtful to the health of the whole body") was insignificant.

It is perhaps fitting that the first colony of what was to become the United States was saved by, and built entirely around, a product of human and environmental debilitation.

*[August 1619.] About the latter end of August, a Dutch
man of Warr of the burden of a 160 tunes arrived at
Point-Comfort. . . . [It] brought not any thing but 20. and
odd Negroes, w[hi]ch the Governor and Cape Marchant
bought for victualles.—John Rolfe, January 1620*

It was not the beginning of slavery in the English colonies, as is
usually alleged in the textbooks, but only in the technical sense that
these "20. and odd" captives were brought into Jamestown as indentured servants. Indentured servitude, which had for some years
provided most of the colony's labor force and would for a half-
century more, normally meant an obligation of two to eight years'
labor in return for the passage out and room and board, after which
the servant normally would be given a "freedom grant" of acreage
on which to establish a farm. Thousands of English men (and some
few women) were taken to Jamestown on these terms; surviving
records indicate that it was on such terms that these twenty-plus
Africans were traded, and at least some of them were later mentioned
as having completed their service and become free men.

Indenture, though, was only a short step from outright slavery,
even if freedom was its ultimate promise. Terms and conditions of
labor were much harsher than in England, wages were even lower
and not always paid, punishments for infractions were much more
severe—one couple even beat their two servants to death and got off
without penalties—and it was not uncommon for a man to be forced
into two and even more terms of servitude for supposed misbehavior
or to be sold to another master in the middle of his term, "like a
damnd slave," as one Thomas Best said when he was thus sold in
1623.

*[1618–25] We therefore the said treasurer and Company
upon a solemn treaty and resolution . . . require you the
said Governor and Council of Estate to put into Execution
with all convenient speed a former order of our Courts . . .
for the laying and setting out by bounds and metes of three
thousand Acres of land . . . to be called by the name
Governors Land . . . [and] three thousand Acres shall be
and so called the Companies Land. . . . Lastly we do hereby
require and Authorize you . . . to Survey or cause to be*

Survey'd all the Lands and territories in Virginia above mentioned.—Virginia Company letter to George Yeardley, November 1618

The Virginia Company, an unmistakable financial failure (indeed, at least £8,000 or £9,000 in debt) after twelve years and any number of promotional schemes and empty promises, decided in 1619 to reorganize, with Sir Edwin Sandys as its new treasurer. The new philosophy and the key to all investors' hopes was now summed up in a single word: land.

According to this letter, the so-called "greate Charter" of 1619, 100 acres were to be given to all the pre-1616 settlers still in the colony, plus an additional 100 acres for every share they might hold in the company; 50 acres were to be granted to any indentured servant after his period was up; London investors were given rights to land according to the number of their shares, plus 50 more acres for every tenant whose passage they would pay; and all officers of the company who would serve in Virginia would be given handsome estates— 3,000 acres for the governor, 1,500 for the treasurer, 100 for men of the cloth. In the next six years no fewer than 184 grants were made by the company, most of them of 200 acres but a number of 1,000, and for the rest of the century the average grant to English settlers in Virginia was 560 acres, just under a full square mile each.

Land, to be sure, had always been a measure of rank and stature, but it had been of no special importance in Virginia until a profitable cash crop—a land-devouring cash crop at that—had been found for it. That discovery set off a concerted land rush among the colonists that proved to be well-nigh insatiable and inspired the seizure of land wherever the local inhabitants proved to be too weak or sparsely settled to prevent it. Thus began a movement—it is not too much to call it an affliction—that would mark and decisively shape the whole tenor of American history. In the words of the historian Michael Rogin, "Land in America was not only a symbol of national identity, but also—in a more thoroughgoing fashion than anywhere else in the world—a commodity. . . . Land was the major economic resource, the major determinant of social status, and the major source of political power in early America."

The fact that the land so coveted was not exactly theirs to take was an inconvenience that did not trouble many of the English overmuch,

nor overlong. They believed (or at least regularly offered the justification) that land not actually built upon was unused and therefore
unowned, at best made use of only occasionally by the local Indians,
and so available: "We have done them no Injury by settling amongst
them," wrote one Englishman grandly in 1636, "we rather than they
being the prime occupants, and they only Sojourners in the land."
This was a total misperception of the careful and well-worked-out
patterns of Indian land use, but not even the most sympathetic English
colonist, not even Roger Williams, understood.

"Ask of me, and I shall give thee the heathen for thine inheritance,
and the uttermost parts of the earth for thy possession." So said the
work only recently translated by King James's scholars into English,
a book that continually provided comfort, sometimes in the most
practical ways, for the invaders of Virginia, as it would just a few
years later for those of Plymouth and Boston. It was not so far from
a view taken, ironically enough, by an Indian elder who in 1608
described the white strangers in the Powhatans' lands as "a people
come from under the world to take their world from them."

In its attitude to the land, and the creatures thereof, a culture reveals
the truest part of its soul. On the vast wild lands of North America,
Europe made manifest its character so clearly that two centuries after
it began its conquest the Frenchman Tocqueville could write:

> In Europe people talk a great deal of the wilds of America, but
> the Americans themselves never think about them; they are in-
> sensible to the wonders of inanimate nature and they may be
> said not to perceive the mighty forests that surround them till
> they fall beneath the hatchet. Their eyes are fixed upon another
> sight: the American people views its own march across these
> wilds, draining swamps, turning the course of rivers, peopling
> solitudes, and subduing nature. This magnificent image of them-
> selves does not meet the gaze of the Americans at intervals only;
> it may be said to haunt every one of them in his least as well as
> in his most important actions and to be always flitting before
> his mind.

He has caught it exactly: the blindness, the insensitivity, the discon-
nectedness, the exploitation, the destruction—and above all that mysterious obsessive need to try "subduing nature."

We may see all of these at work from the beginning. John Smith, for example, showed himself to be impervious to the wonders of the Virginia wilderness: in his "Proceedings of the English Colony," which takes 413 lines (in a modern edition) to describe the events of the first five years, only 83 have even the slightest reference to the elements of nature, fully a third of those devoted to the native foods on which the colonists' lives depended, and only once did he provide a description of the countryside through which he traveled so extensively; it reads, in its entirety, "the coast well watred, the mountaines very barren, the vallies very fertil, but the woods extreame thicke, full of Woolves, Beares, Deare, and other wild beasts." Since Smith's account was based on the diaries and letters of at least a dozen of his fellow settlers, it is clear that this deficiency of description was not Smith's alone, and indeed, the separate accounts by Percy, Archer, Strachey, and others were similarly barren. The world was all before them, but somehow they saw it not.

Part of this is no doubt explained by the lack of a tradition in European culture, particularly acute in England, to provide careful and close-hand description of the plant and animal worlds, much less the wilderness. The English had little experience in natural history —the great Hakluyt, for example, could compile enormous accounts of exploration and adventure around the world in which descriptions of topography, climate, animal habitat, and wild (unexploitable) vegetation were virtually nonexistent—and at best could point to a thin line of herbals and bestiaries, drawn almost entirely from laboratories rather than the field, and none too accurate at that.*

I suspect that this remarkable blindness, this *separateness*, is a part of that same mental blockading, the psychological distancing and numbing, that descended on the Jamestown settlers in their early decades. Not knowing how to assimilate the American wilderness, and in some sense knowing themselves inadequate to it, they withdrew, to find that mental refuge where they could imagine the wild did not really exist, or at least not sufficiently so to need evaluation and recounting. This is called denial, and it is a common mental

---

*John White, whose careful observations on his Roanoke voyage of 1585 produced a set of striking watercolors both beautiful and accurate, stands alone in the long history of English exploration almost until the late eighteenth century, and he is nowhere matched by a writer of similar stature, not even his companion Thomas Hariot, who was probably the best observer before Thomas Jefferson.

defense; but it has its psychological consequences, and they are not healthy.

When the English *did* see nature, it was with a vision, as we would expect, refracted by the marketplace—in the Tocquevillian sense, just as it was about to "fall beneath the hatchet." Nature was hardly more than a storehouse of commodities or potential commodities: John Smith, in one of the dense old-growth forests, observed that "many of their Oakes are so tall and straight, that they will beare two foot and a half square of good timber for 20 yards long"; Gabriel Archer, looking at a breathtaking waterfall where the James came down from the Piedmont, wrote that "the water falls downe from huge greate Rockes: making in the fall five or six severall Ilettes, very fitt for the buylding of water miles thereon"; Archer again, on the Virginia forest: "It is generally replenisht with wood of all kindes and that the fayrest yea and best that ever any of us (traveller or workman) ever sawe, being fitt for any use whatsoever, as shipps, howses, plankes, pales boordes mastes, waynscott, Clappboord, for pikes or elswhat."

The commodification of nature: prelude, and partner, to that long "march across these wilds."

But that march, as well as its goal of subjection, is impelled by something more than just exploitation, something darker: it begins, as we have seen, with fear, that "restless dread" of which Lucretius wrote, never more acutely felt than in the face of that aspect of nature seen as wilderness—which America had in abundance. It was to be found in almost every European who came to live in these aboriginal landscapes, but it was among the Protestants—who added to the long history of Christian antagonism to nature their own special animus against emotion and instinct and disorder—that it reached its height; and it was given to the English Puritans, a particularly pinched and dour Calvinist sect, to give this expression with all the biblical rhetoric at their command. William Bradford, the first governor of Plymouth and, to Cotton Mather, the Moses of England, set the dismal tone when describing the first Puritan landing in 1620:

> What could they see but a hidious & desolate wildernes, full of wild beasts & willd men? and what multituds ther might be of them they knew not. Nether could they, as it were, goe up to the tope of Pisgah, to vew from this willdernes a more goodly cuntrie to feed their hops; for which way soever they turnd their

eys (save upward to the heavens) they could have litle solace or content in respecte of any outward objects. For summer being done, all things stand upon them with a wetherbeaten face; and the whole countrie, full of woods & thickets, represented a wild & savage heiw.

It is a tone that sounded through the century: "a forlorne Wilderness . . . hideous, boundless and unknown" (Edward Johnson), "a vast and roaring wilderness" (Thomas Hooker), "a wilderness where are nothing but wild beasts and beastlike men" (John Winthrop), "a rude and unsubdued wilderness" (Richard Mather), "a wast howling wilderness" (Charles Chauncy). Whether or not the wilderness was howling, one certainly gets the impression of something at strident pitch.

To this terror of the wild the European mind opposed the serenity of the garden: nature tamed, nature subdued, nature, as it were, *denatured*. The mission to impose control—and its aesthetic analogue, order—on elements of the natural world was seen as the very duty, the very purpose, of civilization and above all its Christian form; Governor Winthrop, Good Book in hand, captured it exactly: "The whole earth is the Lords garden, and he hath given it to the sonnes of men, and with a general Commission: Gen: 1: 28: increase and multiplie, and replenish the earth and subdue it."*

But for all the talk of gardens, we must not forget that the task of control and subjugation was to be done violently, with all the technology of power at Europe's command—axe and saw and gun and knife and plow—and with exactly those men it had trained so long in warfare, who were everywhere its vanguard—the governors of Virginia, the conquistadors of New Spain, the chevaliers of New France—and who everywhere manned its outposts of empire, the fort. This was to be, in truth, nothing less than a war between man and nature, on a battlefield so vast and in a time so compressed as to be without precedent, and it could have but one outcome: human

---

*The historian Oscar Handlin pointed out some years ago why the passion for order might have been so strong in American settlers: "Many of those who made the crossing were people whose life was already in disorder. . . . Their migration was largely the product of their own helplessness, of social forces over which they had no control—persecution by the Established Church, changes in agriculture and the unavailability of land, the disruption of the wool trade and the growth in the number of men without employment." This, coupled with a sense of loss, of home, had to be taken out against something; it was.

violence "works" and nature can be subdued, if not defeated, in the short run, and it can be generations, even centuries, before the terrible and irreversible consequences of such a victory become evident. That was the sort of victory upon which the premise of America was based.

It began, from Virginia on, with the transformation of eastern North America in no more than a century into a homeland for what William Carlos Williams was later to call the "great voluptuary," the colonial American "full of a rich regenerative violence." It may well have been the swiftest and most dramatic environmental change ever wrought by human agency on the face of the earth up to that time —"the largest area in history to be so greatly changed so quickly," in the opinion of Richard Lilliard in his study of American woodlands.

No sure statistics exist, but the devastation of certain species important to the European economy was so glaring and widespread that it could not fail to have produced some impressionistic reports and estimates. Beavers, once numbering perhaps 60 million or more in North America, were effectively extinct in most parts of the northeast as early as 1640—a *Jesuit Relation* of 1635 reported that the "Hurons . . . have not a single beaver," Irokwa supplies were exhausted in the 1630s, and both the Massachusetts and Delaware coasts were depleted by 1640—and although the French fur network extended out into Manitoba and Saskatchewan to find supplies, even there the end of the next century saw the "exhaustion of the beaver fields" and everywhere the "disappearance of beaver." As with the beaver, so with almost all other fur-bearers (marten, wolf, otter, mink, muskrat), most of the large herbivores (deer, moose, antelope, elk, wood bison, caribou), and a great many of the game birds (turkey, duck, goose, heath cock, passenger pigeon)—vastly depleted in numbers, in some places exterminated, wherever the Europeans settled or their influence penetrated.

The great Eastern deciduous forest, too, was similarly exploited and depleted. The first areas to go were on the shores of the fisheries, where coastal encampments used great amounts of lumber for docks, buildings, and processing fuel; the coasts of Newfoundland, Labrador, northern New England, and the mouth of the St. Lawrence were denuded for miles inland ("a great pity to behold them") by about 1640, contemporaries report. Southern New England was similarly ravaged, but there a considerable lumber industry (fifty sawmills in Massachusetts Bay alone by 1675), including shipbuilding and mast-making, was added to such traditional uses as housing, fuel, fence-building, and clearing land for agriculture and pasture. (Between 1630 and 1800, it has been estimated, New Englanders cut down 260 million cords of wood.) In Virginia, as we have seen, where the forests were quickly cleared for tobacco plantations, some half a million acres were deforested by the end of the seventeenth century, and such species as the white oak, black walnut, and white cedar, which do not easily regenerate, were effectively exterminated there; gone forever were the old-growth woods and their majestic 250-foot denizens. A hundred years after the first landing, the English were well along in the process of eliminating the ancient Eastern woodlands from Maine to the Mississippi, in what would be the greatest deforestation in human history before the twentieth century.

The ripple effects of such an environmental disruption were, though more subtle, even more far-reaching. Extermination of the beaver, for example, meant the deterioration of beaver dams and ponds and the unchecked flow of stream waters, which destroyed riverine eco-systems, increased floods and topsoil runoff, promoted bank erosion and siltation, and reduced water tables. The destruction of old-growth forests meant the elimination of certain intricate econiches and their microbial and faunal patterns, the emigration of bird and animal populations, and the invasion of pioneer species that prevented the natural succession from ever producing again the great trees or the carpets of native wildflowers. Local and regional climatic changes followed, with new conditions of wind, temperature, humidity, and soil moisture, and even seasons that proved inhospitable to many kinds of plants and animals but to which the vast numbers of new European species—cattle, pigs, horses, rats, dandelions, and so on —adapted rapidly, without predators or pathogens to hinder them.

All in all, the presence of just a few hundred thousands of the European branch of the human species, within just a century after its landing, did more to alter the environment of North America, in some places and for many populations quite irretrievably, than the many millions of the American branch had done in fifteen centuries or more. It took a special kind of mind to see that impact as beneficial, as "progress," indeed as "civilization." But the European (and the American successor) possessed just such a mind: those English who clear-cut their way through ancient primordial forests actually spoke of "making land."

> *[March 1622.] Itt hath pleased God for our manyfo[ld] sinns to laye a most lamentable Afflictione uppon this Plantacon, by the trecherie of the Indyans, who one the 22th of march laste, attempted in most places, under the Coulor of unsuspected amytie, in some by Surprize, to have cutt us of all and to have Swept us away at once through owte the whole lande. . . . They p[re]vayled soe farr, that they have massacred in all partes above three hundred men women and Children, and have, since nott only spoyled and slaine Divers of our Cattell, and some more of our People, and burnte most of the Howses we have forsaken, but have alsoe enforced us to quitt many of our Plantacons.*
> —*Virginia Council, April 1622*

The Second Anglo-Powhatan War began in March 1622 with an attack, under the command of Wahunseneka's successor, Opechan-kano, on the colonists at Jamestown and several other settlements for at least a hundred miles on either side of the James. Figures on the number of dead vary—John Smith a few years later said, with some positiveness, 347, other contemporary estimates ranged to more than 400—but there is no doubt that this was a "lamentable Afflic-tione" on the colony, especially since the best estimates suggest that it had only some 1,240 settlers at the time. It might have been worse—it might indeed have succeeded in destroying the enterprise —except that one Powhatan servant apparently revealed the plot to his master (who "used him as a Sonne") and he was able to alert the main Jamestown settlement in time to allow it to resist the attack.

This second war, instigated by the increasing encroachment of English plantations (and livestock) onto Powhatan lands, and possibly also by two serious epidemics of 1617 and 1619, lasted roughly three years and ended much as the first had, with the defeat of the Indians at the hands of the English. Upon hearing of the massacre the Virginia Company sent out uncompromising orders, asking for what today we would recognize as genocide, for "a perpetuall warre without peace or truce" to "roote out from being any longer a people, so cursed a nation, ungratefull to all benefitte, and incapable of all good-nesse." The directions were followed assiduously. Four expeditionary forces under Governor George Yeardley and three other experienced soldiers were sent out at once, killing all Indians of any age or sex on sight, burning fields and villages, destroying canoes and weirs and any other artifacts in their way. Thereafter it was the colony's set policy to dispatch retaliatory raids by mobile and heavily armed fighting units—"harshe visits" in one euphemism—twice a year against nearby villages perceived to be hostile, forcing all but the most compliant Indians deeper into the western woods. Within a year the Virginia Council could boast that "by Computatione and Confessione of the Indians themselves we have slayne more of them this yeere, then hath been slayne before since the beginninge of ye colonie."

Details of these punitive raids are naturally scarce, but the surviving accounts indicate that once again the English were a match for their Spanish predecessors in ruthlessness and amorality. A raiding party in June 1623, for example, led by Captain William Tucker, sailed to a Powhatan village "under color to make peace" and arrange for the release of some English prisoners; when the captives had been delivered and a great crowd had gathered along the shore, the English ship opened fire indiscriminately and at least forty natives fell. Shortly thereafter Tucker led a force to negotiate a peace treaty with a village near the Potomac, carrying a butt of poisoned wine, and after they had concluded the treaty he persuaded their Indian hosts to drink a toast to it from their cask. An estimated two hundred Indians died instantly, after which the soldiers dispatched another fifty or so with more conventional weapons and "brought hom parte of ther heades."

With its declaration of open war the Virginia colony finally enacted the policy of all-out land confiscation and population removal it had been hoping to effect ever since tobacco proved profitable; in the words of one colonist:

> We, who hitherto have had possession of no more ground then their waste, and our purchase . . . may now by right of Warre, and law of Nations, invade the Country, and destroy them who sought to destroy us: whereby wee shall enjoy their cultivated places . . . and possessing the fruits of others labours. Now their cleared grounds in all their villages (which are situate in the fruitfullest places of the land) shall be inhabited by us.

With that came the practical end not only of Powhatan resistance to English colonization but of the Powhatan society as a cohesive political entity, destroyed by a generation and more of defeat, disease, displacement, dispersion, and devastation. Of the pre-Jamestown population of the Chesapeake tidelands, which may have been upwards of 40,000, there were probably no more than 5,000 left in 1625, most of them forced back to villages along the fall line: whether by microbe or musket, the English invasion had succeeded. In 1646, after a second failed uprising, the Powhatans were officially banished from their ancestral homelands, and by 1669, when a colonial census was taken, there were only 528 men (and perhaps about 2,000 people in all) still left, and these living largely as detribalized appendages to white settlements. By 1685 the Powhatans were said by the English to be extinct: in yet another way was the Columbian Legacy effected.

It was by no means compensatory, but the Second Anglo-Powhatan War also spelled the end of the Virginia Company. News of the massacre coincided with a vicious factional fight among the company's investors and the discovery of waste and mismanagement—"embezzlement" is probably not too strong a term—in the company's finances. Subsequent investigation by the King's Privy Council showed that after two decades and at least £100,000 in public subscriptions, not to mention thousands more brought in from a long-running public lottery, the company was bankrupt; that many of the three thousand souls it had sent out to Virginia from 1619 to 1624 had perished because of inadequate supplies to accompany them (and theft of what little there was by officials in Virginia); and that not one of the various schemes tried out to put the colony on an industrial footing had succeeded, despite the large amounts invested, because they were poorly planned and quite alien to what the environment of Virginia would permit. (The idea that the colony would be good for pineapples and citrus fruits, for example, was based on the company's unfounded notion that lands on the same latitude should produce the same products, and so what grew in Spain, say, should grow in Virginia.)

On August 26, 1624, the charter of the Virginia Company was officially revoked and the Virginia colony became the property, in English eyes at least, of the crown. Change of control meant a beneficial change of management but it was only partly because of this that the colony was subsequently able to put itself in order and in some measure prosper. The greater part was that, after the defeat of the Powhatans, the colonists (and especially the richest few) were able to spread their plantations out farther through the tidewater and for the next decade or so enjoy something of a boom. The population grew to some 2,600 by 1629 and then an estimated 8,000 a decade later.

Just after the 1622 massacre, Samuel Purchas, in his long compilation celebrating and promoting British colonization, wrote that the deaths of the slain English colonists, like the deaths of those who had been sent to Roanoke thirty-five years before, served only to establish the right of Europe to the lands of America. With that astonishing assurance by which all conquering nations somehow convince themselves of the justness of their conquest, he concluded that "their carkasses, the dispersed bones of their and their Countrey mens since murthered carkasses, have taken a mortall, immortal possession, and being dead, speake, proclaime and cry, This our earth is truly English, and therefore this Land is justly yours O English."

And so it was to be.

Chapter Twelve

1607–25

II

Powhatans and Others

IN THE fall of 1608, in accordance with instructions from the Virginia Company directors (and possibly, as has long been claimed, from King James I himself), Captain Christopher Newport undertook to enact the coronation of Wahunseneka, chief of the Powhatans, and thereby make him a vassal of the English king and an ally of the Virginia Colony. John Smith, then the colony's president, thought little of the idea, the military solution being always his preferred mode of diplomacy, but he agreed to accompany the captain on his journey upcountry to the fall line of the York River along with "50 of the best shot" and a boatload of presents for the vassal-to-be, including a "bason, ewer, bed & furniture," a scarlet suit and cloak, and a copper crown. However the idea was presented to Wahunseneka, it is certain that the notion neither of coronation nor of subinfeudation would have meant anything to him, but he was prepared to accept gifts from the the white strangers' chief. "If your king have sent me presents," he told Smith, "I also am a king, and this my land, 8 daies I will stay to receave them." On the chosen day, Newport and entourage ceremoniously presented their treasures to the chief, sitting among his council of elders, and he accepted them all with due dignity (even trying on the scarlet apparel after some hesitation), although when it came to the actual coronation itself he seemed reluctant to comply with the required English gavotte. John Smith reported the near-comic scene:

A fowle trouble there was to make him kneele to receave his crowne, he neither knowing the majestie, nor meaning of a Crowne, nor bending of the knee, indured so many perswasions, examples, and instructions, as tired them all. At last by leaning hard on his shoulders, he a little stooped, and Newport put the Crowne on his head.

It must have been quite a spectacle: one white-haired old man, minus an arm, trying to cajole another (described as "little less than eighty") to kneel before him, finally calling on his men (it seems) to force the Indian into a kind of slump, and placing a cheap copper crown on his head with appropriate medieval royal mumbo jumbo. And the second old man, who could not have known what the rigmarole was all about but who knew enough that he would not bend before this strange sea captain, at last deigning to wear the copper ornament the strangers were making such a fuss of—in return for which, "to congratulate their kindnesse, he gave his old shoes and his mantle to Captain Newport," to be conveyed to the English King. That mantle, a coat of skins decorated with beadwork and the insignia of two animals, perhaps rabbits, is today in the Ashmolean Museum, Oxford. Nothing is known of the whereabouts of the basin, bed, or crown.

This bizarre event, almost a parody of the kind of misunderstandings that were to beset the initial decades of contact among the two vastly different cultures as they vied for dominance in the New World, nonetheless reveals some important truths about the Chesapeake peoples who were the first representatives of the original—the receiving—culture. Through them we may begin to understand some of the essentials of that culture in the broad, the political and social instruments, the beliefs and values, and especially the behavior and attitude toward the natural world they lived within. Not all of those of the North American continent believed as they did, obviously—the differing environments ensured differing subcultures, and some were more statified than others—but it is generally accepted among historians and ethnologists that the societies of the continent north of the Tropic of Cancer shared enough in common, in both underlying principles and the practices they gave rise to, that these particular people of the Virginia tidelands may serve as well as any other as a window onto at least a substantial part of that world.[1]

The first thing to note is Wahunseneka's refusal to kneel, for this reveals much about the character of those assigned to leadership roles in Indian society and about the nature of that leadership.

In one sense, Wahunseneka did not have the humility to kneel, to take a subservient position before a European stranger in front of his assembled council. The quality that seems to have typified those chosen as leaders (and even where chieftaincies were hereditary, as with the Powhatans, tribal elders could exercise a degree of choice) was a quiet dignity, a self-evident strength of character combined with an aura of appropriate gravity that impressed even the Europeans; John Smith, for example, who professed no great admiration for the "subtile" Wahunseneka, nonetheless reported that he "carried himselfe so prowdly, yet discreetly (in his Salvage manner) as made us all admire his natural gifts considering his education." Similar comments are made again and again for other Indian chiefs, north and south: they seemed to be people unlikely to bend to foreign interlopers, literally or otherwise.

But in another sense, Wahunseneka did not have the power to kneel—that is, to be the embodiment of the tribe so as to bind all other members of it to whatever the English had in mind. As a rule, an Indian "chief"—even Wahunseneka, who may have gathered unusual power in the tribal upheavals following earlier European contacts—had only limited powers, was more a respected spokesperson than authoritarian monarch; he might be expected to ascertain and speak the will of a meeting of the council of elders, for instance, or represent the tribe in dealings with other peoples, but he would be unable to make laws or decisions unilaterally or to act in any way not sanctioned by the consensual agreements of the governing councils. That this figure was not some sort of powerful satrap of a familiar type was usually incomprehensible to Europeans, who consistently made the native "werowances" or "sachems" or "sagamores" into chiefs and those chiefs into kings and emperors, and almost never understood what their role and authority were or how to deal with them.

Of course it would have been hard for Europeans, steeped in systems of hierarchy and patriarchy, to have grasped the general egalitarianism of the typical nonstatified Indian society. Nowhere north of Mexico were there the elements of nation-states—apparatuses of government, powers of taxation, agencies of enforcement, fixed aristocracies, or the like—and even where chieftaincies were hereditary and in a predetermined lineage that conferred no significant trappings of power or elevated social role. Rules and codes there were, sometimes quite complex, and sanctions and taboos operated to give them effect, but to a great degree the individual was governed by the understood obligations of community (including the community of nature) rather than allegiance to a sovereign or recognition of laws or fear of civil retribution. Père Paul Le Jeune, a Jesuit missionary who spent a season with the Montagnais in 1634, conveyed some of this in his account in the *Jesuit Relations*:

> Nor do they endure in the least those who seem desirous of assuming superiority over the others, and [they] place all virtue in a certain gentleness or apathy. . . . All the authority of their chief is in his tongue's end, for he is powerful insofar as he is eloquent; and even if he kills himself talking and haranguing, he will not be obeyed unless he pleases the Savages.

Although it is true that the Montagnais were a less sedentary people than the Powhatans and other agricultural tribes, and therefore probably had looser systems of authority, this description seems to reflect with fair accuracy the practice of most Indian societies.[2]

One other significant aspect of this egalitarian polity is worth noting. At Wahunseneka's "coronation," if it was a ceremonial occasion similar to Newport's earlier meeting with the chief, "on each side [of] his house sate 20. of his concubines, their heads and shoulders painted red, with a great chaine of white beads about their necks, before those sate his chiefest men in like order in his arbor-like house." Smith could not have realized it, but what he was describing had nothing to do with concubinage: these men and women almost assuredly made up the central council of Wahunseneka's village, and the women, if they were not in fact equal vocal participants in the council deliberations (as, we are told, in some Eastern woodlands societies they were not), were there certainly to monitor the goings-on and presumably to participate in consensual decisions.

Women in general were accorded high status in Indian societies and were usually equal participants in both political and economic realms. I do not find much evidence that these were full-fledged gynecocracies, as some writers recently have suggested, but there is no doubt about certain salient features: women throughout the Algonkian and other cultures of the East Coast could and did become tribal chiefs (and in some societies, shamans) and through matrilineal descent—from an older brother or sister—rather than as an inheritance from a father or husband; matrilineality was the rule rather than the exception in North American tribes, and rights to certain houses or usufructure over certain fields and plots would be passed down the female line; women were full participants in economic life, usually responsible for field-tending and often harvesting, nut- and berry-gathering, clothes-making, food preparation, and household work, and they had control over the products of their labor, as their husbands were well aware;* women had considerable choice in the selection of a husband, done only after a man proved his competence not only as hunter and provider but as lover. Since this contrasted so sharply with the position of women in contemporary European society, where women's economic and social power, already constricted by a patriarchal culture, was further undercut by the new capitalist economies stressing production by men and outside the home, it is hardly surprising that the men who wrote about it were generally confounded about what they saw and even typically detected in it an inferior status of drudgery for women quite at odds with the truth.

But these men never really did understand the cultures they were intruding on, even though they often wrote about them at some length and occasionally with some care, and that is really what made the "coronation" such a fiasco. Out of a deep ethnocentric insensibility, the English then and after assumed that either the Powhatan culture was so superficial or the European one so irresistible that it should take no more than their very presence—their superior mode of dress, superior instruments of war, superior form of religion—to persuade the Indians to renounce their American past and become tawny English folk. Newport, and those behind in London who had cooked up this scheme, had the idea that this heathen chief would gladly swear allegiance to the great King James and that the conversion of the tribe to Christianity and civilization would inevitably follow.

---

*There is the story of the woman who, angry with her husband, hid the food, the cooking utensils, and his clothes, and then went out and took the bark off the family canoe before he interceded and came to terms with her.

When it became clear that the Powhatans had no desire to give up their culture, and indeed would resist that with some severity, the English response was simply dismissal and hostility and a reversion to warfare.

Yet a truly objective English observer (if there had been one) might well have concluded that the life of rural Chesapeake in 1607 was not inferior in any substantial way to that of rural England, save perhaps in such technologies as metallurgy and firearms, and in certain substantial ways, from abundance of vittles to individual freedom, could be reckoned superior.

It was certainly superior in its system of food supply, in terms both of efficiency and of nutrition. The Powhatan system, similar to that of probably most Indians north of Mexico, was a combination of hunting-gathering for perhaps two-thirds of the nutritional intake and shifting horticulture based on the corn-beans-squash triad for the other third; it was, as Albert Cowdrey says, "the most energy-efficient of all economic systems," based on "the most useful grain in the world"—corn, which the eastern Indians had in several varieties. This system had been developed over the centuries with a number of methods that assured its success: mound planting (similar to the Taino *conucos*) instead of row planting, for example, to prevent wind and water erosion; "three-sister" farming with corn stalks as a trellis on which beans would grow and squash as a moisture-retentive ground cover, all together providing both balanced soil nutrients and a balanced diet; limited areal planting, usually in nutrient-rich riverine fields, which were allowed to lie fallow after several years to restore fertility; selecting out and sometimes breeding of wild species to ensure the most beneficial and fertile nut and fruit trees, grapevines, and root plants; hunting within both territorial and seasonal limits that generally prevented overkilling or waste; fishing with complex woven wooden weirs, so intricate that the English couldn't even repair the ones they took from the Indians; and careful forest burns that were used both to drive big game in desired directions and to encourage pioneer plant species and smaller grass-loving animals. All in all, Cowdrey concludes, these methods, "fine-tuned by millennia of learning and transmission," created an Indian food system that "had long attained a high degree of subtlety and sophistication."

The New World was well endowed, of course, a land richer in

diversity and abundance of natural species than Europe, and it was kept that way by careful environmental practices; in the summary words of Carl Sauer, the historical geographer who was a pioneer in this area, "The eastern Indians lived well and at ease in a generous land which they used competently and without spoiling it." But there was more to it than that, for the Indians were also extremely competent cultivators who had worked out a horticulture that, even without domesticated animals, surpassed that of Europe. Sauer again:

> In general, it may be said the plant domesticates of the New World far exceeded in range and efficiency the crops that were available to Europeans at the time of the discovery of the New World. In grains Europe had nothing to match Indian maise as to productivity, food value, utility for hill lands, and varietal adaptions to many climates. . . . In plant proteins and fats, Europe again was poor and the New World richly supplied by cultivated plants. . . . The ancient Indian plant breeders had done their work well. In the genial climates, there was an excellent, high yielding plant for every need of food, drink, seasoning, or fiber. On the climatic extremes of cold and drought, there still were a remarkable number of plant inventions that stretched the limits of agriculture about as far as plant growth permitted.

To which should be added the Indians' use of plants in medicine. Only a small portion of native medical knowledge has survived to the present, but some 150 drugs from North American Indians and a third as many from South America have been taken into the modern U.S. pharmacopoeia. Early English settlers continually reported the efficacy of Indian medical practices and many benefited directly from their curatives ("Their charmes are of force to produce effects of wonderment"), although they were obviously baffled by much of it and were just as inclined to ascribe the remedies to "their curst magicke" and "diabolicall charmes" as to their "herbes, and rootes, and plants." There is evidence that native drugs were used as anesthetics, antiseptics, sedatives, laxatives, purgatives, anthelmintics, stimulants, antitoxins, and cauterizers, and that in general shamans would also have some knowledge of surgery, massage, and obstetrics (at which they have been said to be "probably more advanced" than contemporary Europeans), in addition to those forms of psychotherapy and self-healing dismissed as "witchcraft." Comparison is difficult, but it could be said that the Indian medical system was not less developed than the European, and in terms of its pharmacology was more extensive.

Other aspects of Indian life, as we may see it among the Powhatans, also do not suffer by comparison to Europe's. The villages were described as clean and neat, well laid out, often with palisades of tree trunks, and one of them so impressed John Smith ("no place so strong, so pleasant and delightful in Virginia") that he bought it outright and named it "Nonsuch." The houses were capacious and clean, made of wooden frames in a bread-loaf shape and covered with either woven mats or bark sheets that were protective in winter ("that notwithstanding either winde raine, or weather," said Smith, "they are as warme as stooves") and could be pulled back on either side to let in air and light the rest of the year. Artifacts were generally simple, although some were decorated with extreme intricacy, and they were plentiful, for purposes both utilitarian (clay pots and soapstone vessels, knives of reed and flint and beaver tooth, bows and bone-tipped arrows, dugout canoes up to fifty feet long, corncribs) and decorative or religious (animal sculptures, copper and pearl and bone ornaments, beaded belts and cloths, clay pipes). Clothing, usually fringed, was commonly of deer or raccoon skin; rabbit, wolf, and other pelts were also used, and thigh-high leggings and moccasins were worn for forest travel, and feathered headdresses of various elaborateness for ceremonial occasions. Nothing is known about the Powhatans' concepts or practices of sanitation, but the English were struck by their emphasis on washing themselves every morning and before meals, a custom that even the well-bred European (such as James I, who is reported never to have washed his hands) would have regarded as excessively ablutionary.

As with the Tainos, though, it was the warm behavior and general civility of the Chesapeake peoples—at least until open warfare broke out—that most impressed the English chroniclers, those who occasionally got beyond the "savage beast" stage at any rate. Whatever their inner doubts, the Indians behaved as "a most kind and loving people," "naturally most curteous," and "very cheerefully and friendly," and did not refuse hospitality even to strangers they had no reason to like: "we were entertained by them very kindly," "they entertained us with much welcome," "the meanest sort brought us such dainties as they had," and so on. And not to strangers alone: the gentle and intimate ways that parents related to their children were so striking that even such hard-bitten Englishmen as John Smith and Ralph Hamor remarked on it with approval, the latter noting that Wahunseneka declared he loved his daughter "as deere as his owne life . . . whom if he should not often beholde, he could not possibly live."

All this, carried out in a climate that was, except in the dead of winter, most benign and comfortable, must have added up to a quality of life that, even amid the disruptions brought by the Europeans, might reasonably have struck the Powhatans as hardly worth giving up for the hard, disputatious, violent, and unsettled life that the colony at Jamestown had to offer.

At this point it is important to enter a note of historiographical caution. It is not merely that the records we must work from are largely of English origin, assembled by the untutored and the condescending, or even that they cover such a limited span of years before communication between observer and observed was ruptured. It is rather that these accounts, and indeed all European accounts at the time of contact, can reflect but a pale glimmer of the original societies of the American natives. With the exception of the statified Mesoamerican cultures with surviving written glyphs and records, it is almost impossible to know anything with any great certainty about the precontact societies of the original people.

The reason is that all of those precontact societies were changed, and most quite radically so, by a century of lethal epidemics introduced from 1493 on that so devastatingly thinned their numbers— at least by two-thirds; the latest researches suggest *perhaps by as much as 95 percent*—that no aspect of life remained untouched. Among the diseases, new and ruinous to America, were smallpox, bubonic plague, measles, cholera, typhoid, pleurisy, scarlet fever, diphtheria, whooping cough, influenza, gonorrhea, viral pneumonia, malaria, yellow fever, dysentery, and alcoholism—perhaps, according to Russell Thornton, as many as ninety-three in all. The effect of such a high mortality, and in such a short period of time, could have been only to shatter or distort a great part of the Indians' belief systems, disrupt their political and social institutions, discredit their medical practices and the healers among them, produce psychological disorientation and demoralization, kill off most of the elders who were the repositories of tribal history and traditional knowledge, demand the simplification of the cultural inventory and its technologies, force migration and regrouping of remnant populations often in areas far from sacred lands, and increase the likelihood of warfare either in the clash of migrating groups or in the search for new populations. All of this must have so fundamentally altered the basic character of those societies that by the time they came into the historical record they were simply not the same as they had been through the earlier centuries; as the historian Henry Dobyns has put it, "Aboriginal times ended in North America in 1520–24 [the first widespread smallpox epidemic], and Native American behavior was thereafter never again totally as it had been."

The Powhatans may serve as an example of this population crash. We have impressionistic evidence that their numbers at one time were substantial—"What I have seen in this land," said a French missionary who came to the Chesapeake in 1570, "is that there are more people than in any part I have seen on the known coast"—and some modern reconstructions that suggest a sixteenth-century population somewhere around 40,000, though other estimates range as high as 60,000 and 100,000. In the years from 1520 to 1600 there were, according to Alfred Crosby, "perhaps as many as seventeen" serious epidemics in eastern North America, including the smallpox epidemic that made its way north from Mexico after 1519; the epidemic of 1528 begun by the Narváez expedition in Florida, probably typhus; the measles epidemic that spread from Mexico after 1531; the influenza epidemic spread by Cartier in 1535–36; the disease that the de Soto expedition called a "pest in the land" in 1538; and a disease begun by the Roanoke settlers in 1585, probably typhus, which Thomas Hariot described as "so strange a one that they did not know anything about it or how to cure it" but "the people began to die very fast." Any one of these contagions would have had effects we can scarcely imagine, running through these "virgin-soil" populations that had no immune defenses and probably felling whole villages, whole regions even: "I hav[e] seen the death of all my people thrice," Wahunseneka told Smith, "and not one living of those 3 generations, but my selfe." It is not clear whether the old chief is referring to his original village or something larger, but there is no doubt that the toll of these epidemics was great: Smith estimated in 1608 that there were only some 7,650 Powhatans left, which he later revised to 5,000, saying, "The men be few."

We have no record of how the remnant Powhatans coped with such a die-off, but some sort of realignment and resettlement of populations would have been almost inevitable. James Merrell, who has done a study of a Carolina Piedmont subculture going through such a process in the seventeenth century, indicates that generally the survivors were forced to go wandering in search of new disease-free villages, leaving sacred sites and familiar ecosystems behind, and would often have to merge with foreign tribes and learn new languages and customs: "In order to survive," he notes, "groups were compelled to construct new societies from the splintered remnants of the old." That some such process took place in the Chesapeake is indicated by the English sources suggesting that Wahunseneka "inherited" six "tribes" (probably merely villages) sometime between 1572 and 1597, and acquired another two dozen or so in the years before 1607, thus creating the "confederacy" of which he was said to be the "king." It would clearly have been a makeshift kind of association, understandably anxious about the new visitation of whites in 1607 but uncertain about how to respond to them—especially after that 1607 landing in fact introduced one more "great diseaze" that produced a "strange mortalitie"—and this helps to explain the puzzle of the vacillating nature of its reactions, all the way from marriage to massacre.

There is no record either of the psychological dislocations these survivors would have gone through, but we can imagine that the fact of deaths in this number, beyond the powers of comprehension much less cure, could be assimilable into the Indian consciousness only with considerable mental and moral upheaval, even the abandonment of parts of the ancient belief systems proven inadequate in the new circumstances. And where those new circumstances also included new settlements of the white invaders, new systems of trade, new market values, new means of survival, new technologies, and new intoxicants (woodlands Indians having nothing stronger than tobacco), the effects must have been particularly convulsive. Compounding which would have been the fact that those who might best have been able to work out an assimilation, the elders, were the most vulnerable to disease, and in such conditions a great many of the old customs and tenets must have been transformed. As a New England Indian said of his tribe under similar circumstances later in the century, "A long time ago, they had wise men, which in a grave manner taught the people knowledge; but they are dead, and their wisdom is buried with them, and now men live a giddy life, in ignorance, till they are white headed, and though ripe in years, yet then they go without wisdom to their graves."

Obviously not all ancient forms were jettisoned, but probably none was completely unaffected and no society could have remained as it had been. What the Europeans everywhere observed and recorded, then, although they assumed it to be a culture unchanged since the dawn of time, was one vastly altered and reordered and still in many places in a state of flux. That it could still present to them a face of such comparative stability and serenity, as it did almost everywhere, is a singular testament to what must have been the great strength and success of the original customs and beliefs.

What endured in the altered world the Europeans encountered, among the Powhatans as among Eastern woodlands societies generally, were those basic integuments subsequently recorded, such institutions as the hereditary chieftaincy, such systems as the matrilineal clan, such technologies as the dugout canoe and mixed-crop planting. But what endured most, it is clear, in these as in all Indian societies of which we know, was the intimate and abiding relationship with nature that informed all important acts in the passage of an Indian lifetime; it was no doubt touched and altered during the century of epidemics, but it lasted and it was there to be recorded again and again in the historical era because it was so obviously central to the worldview of Indian culture.

Europeans usually saw this relationship in terms of religion, but at its core was in fact a body of beliefs operating more widely and even more deeply than that. The standard way of labeling it is "animism" (from the Latin anima, "soul"), which sees life in all nature and all natural objects and processes—rain and wind and climate, mountains and rivers and rocks, as much as oaks and deer and turkeys—but that does not convey the complexities that such a relationship entails: of the resulting place of the human, for example, as another species of equal but not superior stature in that web of life; of the sacredness of this living world, whose special and delicate balance has to be maintained to conserve the human population; of the necessary reciprocal and mutually dependent relations among all parts of this world, the obligations of which must be especially appreciated (and met) by the human participants; and of the continual interaction among, and communication between, all these natural relatives, ordered in the way that ancestors have painstakingly come to understand and passed down in myth and story and legend, in dance and ritual and ceremony. All of this is not casual or peripheral, somewhere at the edge of daily life or confined to weekends, but rather primary and pivotal, at the very center of existence. Abuse it, and sickness or misfortune visits; disregard it, and calamity for the whole village follows.

There are any number of recorded expressions of this basic Indian attitude. Luther Standing Bear, for example, a chief of the Oglala Sioux:

> The Indian, as well as all other creatures that were given birth and grew, [was] sustained by the common mother—earth. He was therefore kin to all living things and he gave to all creatures equal rights with himself. . . . A great unifying life force . . . flowed in and through all things—the flowers of the plains, blowing winds, rocks, trees, birds, animals—and was the same force that had been breathed into the first man. Thus all things were kindred and brought together by the same Great Mystery.
>
> Kinship with all creatures of the earth, sky and water was a real and active principle. For the animal and bird world there existed a brotherly feeling that kept the Lakota [of which the Oglala were a branch] safe among them and so close did some of the Lakotas come to their feathered and furried friends that in true brotherhood they spoke a common tongue.

Or this recent statement of the Haudenosaunee (Irokwa):

> In our languages, the Earth is our Mother Earth, the sun our Eldest Brother, the moon our Grandmother, and so on. It is the belief of our people that all elements of the Natural World were created for the benefit of all living things and that we, as humans,

are one of the weakest of the whole Creation, since we are totally dependent on the whole Creation for our survival. This philosophy taught us to treat the Natural World with great care. Our institutions, practices and technologies were developed with a careful eye to their potential for disturbing the delicate balance we lived in.

Although the ceremonies of this earth-relationship were part of the entire life-cycle, it is important to appreciate the special role they played in that most crucial of all growing periods, adolescence. It was then that young men—and as near as we can now determine, in many societies young women as well—went through various rituals and trials that bound them intimately to nature with a closeness that was to last throughout their lives. The process differed from tribe to tribe, environment to environment, but it seems to have been practiced in one form or other by all Indian societies, most often through a version of the rite of passage we call the vision quest—"the single most distinctive spiritual characteristic of the Indians of the North American continent," in the words of the ecohistorian Thomas Berry.

In its classic form, the boy of thirteen to fifteen years preparing for a vision quest would consult with a shaman, or similar religious figure, and then go for three or four days into some remote area where he would be alone, directly confronting—and hoping to commune with—the forces of nature, without food, without weapon, without belongings. Some sort of self-testing would accompany this task: fasting, for example, from both food and water; isolation in the wilderness, away from clan and village; intense concentrated prayer; and especially among the Plains Indians, some self-afflicted pain, even cutting off of pieces of flesh to offer to Creation. From this, for most boys—though some would have to repeat the ritual several times— would come that transcendent vision in which the force of nature would be made manifest and through which the boy would enter into a direct spiritual relationship with nature, at its best an epiphanal experience:

And while I stood there [this is a vision of Black Elk, an Oglala Sioux, when he was only nine years old] I saw more than I can tell and I understood more than I saw; for I was seeing in a sacred manner the shapes of all things in the spirit, and the shape of all shapes as they must live together like one being. And I saw that the sacred hoop of my people was one of many hoops that made one circle, wide as daylight and as starlight, and in the center grew one mighty flowering tree to shelter all the children of one mother and one father. And I saw that it was holy.

Often this would be accompanied by the vision of a particular animal or bird which from then on would be his totem spirit, a part of, in some sense identical with, the boy-now-become-a-man:

And as I looked ahead, the people changed into elks and bison and all four-footed beings and even into fowls, all walking in a sacred manner on the good red road together. And I myself was a spotted eagle soaring over them. . . . I looked below and saw my people there. . . . Now the tepee, built and roofed with cloud, began to sway back and forth as in a wind, and the flaming rainbow door was growing dimmer. I could hear voices of all kinds crying from outside: "Eagle Wing Stretches is coming forth! Behold him!"

When I went through the door, the face of the day of earth was appearing with the day-break star upon its forehead; and the sun leaped up and looked upon me, and I was going forth alone.

This crucial rite of passage of course took many forms, and the English caught a glimpse of it among the Powhatans, although they had no idea what they were seeing and leapt to the conclusion, convenient for the conqueror—it was in fact their equivalent to Colón's "cannibalism"—that it was some sort of child sacrifice. One account described a ceremony in which a group of fourteen or fifteen boys were ritually beaten, forced to lie in a heap before a great fire while the women cried and moaned as if in mourning, and then sent out into the woods to die; another said the young men were given a drink "which makes them run mad" and then given bows and arrows before being sent to the woods, where they stayed for several weeks and afterward remembered "nothing of their former life," including their parents and their language. What they were describing is what the Powhatans called *huskanaw*, a ceremony of adolescent purgation in which the ritual mourning is for the "death" of childhood, the beating is to provide the suffering that is a kind of sacrifice to the spirit world, and the period of self-sufficiency in the woods is for the vision quest.

It is hard to convey the importance of this extraordinary ritual in the culture of North America, but it must be understood as something more than quaintness or quiddity. The American ecologist Paul Shepard, in his extraordinary *Nature and Madness*, argues that the process made the Indian (and other primary) societies *sane*, in contrast to those societies, especially of the West, which lack a means of instilling a oneness with nature in their youths. He argues that if adolescent children, at the stage when they are trying to come to terms with the meaning of life and their role in it, can be helped to achieve some kind of spiritual linkage with the natural world and an understanding of how humans must relate to it, that provides a connection, a *bonding* in psychological terms, which creates a healthy sense of identity and security, some comprehension of the purpose and cosmic order of the world around. "The framework of nature as metaphoric foundation for cosmic at-home-ness," Shepard says, "is as native to the human organism in its adolescent years as any nutritive element in the diet. Lacking it, he [*sic*] will always lack true reverence for the earth. The remaining choices for a logic of creation are an other-worldly orientation, materialist exploitation, or existentialist absurdity." Societies that lack this "true reverence for the earth," Shepard concludes, can aptly be said to be mad; societies that foster it live "the way of life to which our ontogeny was fitted by natural selection, fostering a calendar of mental growth, cooperation, leadership, and the study of a mysterious and beautiful world where the clues to the meaning of life were embodied in natural things." For the society as for the individual, rootedness is health.

Healthy Indian societies, in normal times at least, made their earth-relationship further manifest in how they lived on the land. Again, different environments fostered different approaches, but what is striking is the recurrent evidence that, as hunters or fishers or planters or pickers, Indians throughout North America were ritualistically conscious of and concerned about the effects of their actions on their surroundings and careful to see that limits and constraints were everywhere observed. Obviously the processes of getting food had to involve some interference with nonhuman nature—no society, no species survives without some such interference—and Indian societies of various times and places are known to have used fire circles to trap animals, for example, burned forest undergrowth to promote new species, planted corn in quite extensive acreage, and in places drew off streams into irrigation ditches. Still, in all of the nonstatified societies the fundamental respect for the land and its creatures formed such a crucial part of the belief systems that environmental damage was minimal, and nowhere so far as we know was the notion of humans versus nature, of conquest and control, ever practiced or even formulated.

Hunting, for instance, was an activity (before the advent of Europeans) surrounded with rituals that limited slaughter and discouraged overkilling. Hunts of particular animals would be confined to certain seasons or certain "preserves," with proscriptions against killing certain females and most pregnant animals, and even then would depend upon a general village-wide agreement that the time and targets were propitious, appropriately sanctioned by dreams in which the animals would be seen willingly giving themselves up, then appropriately prepared by rituals of forgiveness and atonement—often involving fasting, sexual abstinence, and purgation—before the hunting band ever took to the woods. If the hunt was successful, further rituals would offer apologies to the family and tribe from which the animal came, explaining the necessity of the kill and offering gifts to appease their understandable anger and loss: one Ojibwa woman is described as taking the head of a dead female bear in her hands, "stroking and kissing it several times" and "begging a thousand pardons for taking away her life"; subsequently her companion "blew tobacco smoke into the nostril of the bear" to appease its anger, and finally made a speech in which "he deplored the necessity under which men labored thus to destroy their *friends* [but] without doing so, they could by no means subsist."

Such regardful rituals of hunting were matched by equally careful and effective rituals of consumption. In virtually every society there operated some form or other of what has been called "potlatch" (from the Nootka *potshat'l*, "giving") among the Northwest Coast Indians—that is, a formal and obligatory distribution of food to the rest of the village from those individuals or bands who have been especially favored in hunt or harvest. This act—one that brings great honor and prestige to the donor but is entirely without embarrassment or debt for the donee—was so deeply ingrained in these societies that it applied even to visitors and strangers, even Europeans, thus accounting for the otherwise inexplicable generosity all explorers from Colón on encountered upon first meeting the American natives. Its particular beauty was that it served not only the social function of a kind of obligatory egalitarianism but an ecological one as well, discouraging overkills that might hinder future supplies, preventing excessive accumulation or hoarding, and providing for the regular and efficient recycling of foodstuffs.

Farming and foraging, too, were generally done with a careful sense of balance and respect, surrounded with rituals and ceremonies in which the beings of weather and the beings of plants were consulted and honored—corn, of course, received a special celebration, with songs, poems, dances, libations, sometimes sacrifices to it—and in which the successful harvest was unfailingly made an occasion of veneration and gratitude. With considerable knowledge of plant life —some tribes had forty words for different parts of a leaf—species were bred and nurtured (varieties of white grape, for example, which are not found in the wild), areas best for nut or fruit trees or tobacco were carefully delimited and maintained, and the harvesting of perennials was restricted to assure future sufficiency. And because farming was practiced with such concern for the health and protection of the soil, its long-range effect on the land was minimal indeed; we know from excavations that some tribes occupied the same limited number of acres for as long as ten centuries without despoliation.

"The land is sacred"—it is, really, as simple as that common phrase, known in one way or another in almost every tribe. Like the sun and wind and clouds and air, land was understood to be part of the numinous cosmic spirit, but it was so obviously precious and life-giving that it had to be accorded special reverence and respect; it had its special holy spots, besides—snow-capped mountains and fissured rocks and ancient mesas and thunderous waterfalls—which gave special evidence of the holiness of creation. Identification with territory was consequently very strong among tribes, and made more potent still by the knowledge that the history of the tribe was rooted there and the souls of its ancestors were mingled with the soils. "In a way that few Europeans could understand," a modern study has put it, "the land *was* Indian culture: it provided Native Americans with their sense of a fixed place in the order of the world, with their religious observances, and with their lasting faith in the importance of the struggling but united community as opposed to the ambitious, acquisitive individual." This is why the loss of land, forced upon them by European diseases and European expansionism, was so devastating: the appropriation of land meant nothing less than the extirpation of soul.

This identification with territory is not to be confused with *ownership*, and the distinction is important. Nowhere on record did Indians ever contrive concepts of land ownership, not by individual or family or village or tribe, and the idea would have been quite foreign. Owning the land, selling the land, seemed ideas as foreign as owning or selling the clouds or the wind. There were no doubt concepts we would identify as *usufruct*—that is, family or village claims to a planting field or hunting ground while it is being used, and only for so long as it is used regularly—but such ideas never had very high standing and did not in any case imply possession of the European it's-my-land-and-I-can-do-what-I-want-with-it type. When the Indians of Manahatta "sold" their island to the Dutch headman in the 1620s they no doubt understood themselves to be conferring some sort of usufructory privilege, though it is unlikely that they had in mind their own displacement from a treasured summer hunting and fishing spot—and it is certain that they had no idea they were supposed to relinquish claim to this land forever because it "belonged" to the white strangers.

The cosmology here is so fundamentally different from Europe's that it is difficult for an observer from that Western tradition, not excluding those with the blood of American ancestors, even to come to terms with it, much less find the European words and concepts to convey it. But if this too brief delineation of some of the basic ideas of the Indian earth-relationship is inadequate, at least it suggests how innocent what Calvin Martin calls "the Indian thought-world" is from a belief in the idea of progress, for example, or the utilitarian view of nature, or the transcendence of material possession, or any view of creation seen only through the eyes of a single large bipedal species. Trying to see from inside the hogan and tepee, we may at least understand how far from the mark the early European observers were in their assumptions that the Indians were "just like us," only darker, and would, occupying the only thought-world those Europeans could imagine, succumb to the same temptations and threats;

and how far from the mark have been most subsequent historians down to the present—most unfortunately the Marxist ones, mired in their materialist explanations—in their reluctance to shed preconceptions that prevent them from understanding a biocentric and ecological thought-world of considerable grandeur and pertinence.

One final aspect of the pervasive earth-relationship is perhaps most telling of all, but by no means without controversy. Although the Indians were settled across it in great numbers, particularly in the south and east, the land of North America was still by every account without exception a lush and fertile wilderness teeming with abundant wildlife in water, woods, and air. Indian societies had taken their livelihood from the land for eons, hunting, foraging, planting, fishing, building, trekking, burning, but there were still so many passenger pigeons that they darkened the sky in flight, so many sturgeons that, it was said, one could walk across the rivers, so many ancient trees that the forests often seemed impenetrable. Some reverence for nature, some elemental understanding of the human on the species level, must have been at work.

This becomes all the more impressive when we see how many people there may have been on the continent before European contact. This is a topic rife with dispute, even more so than the previous demographics of Española, for which there are at least Spanish censuses to rely on. In general there are two methods of estimation: one is to work back from what are hoped to be approximately reliable European surveys of the first half of the seventeenth century, figuring a depopulation of at least 70 percent and as much as 97 percent from the multiple epidemics of the previous century; the other is to try to calculate the number of people who might reasonably have been able to live in a given area with a given means of resource depletion, the settled horticulturists judged to be able to support larger numbers than hunter-gatherers. Such imperfect techniques inevitably have produced a wide range of population estimates, but there is now a rough academic consensus, quite sharply at odds with figures conventionally accepted earlier in this century, that the total number of Indians in the New World at the time of the Discovery was between 60 and 120 million people. (That compares to a population for Europe outside Russia of 60 to 70 million.) Estimates for North America alone similarly range from about 40 to 56 million, the bulk of which—perhaps 25 to 30 million—occupied the area of the Mesoamerican state sys-

tems south of the Tropic of Cancer and 8 million more the islands
of the West Indies. That leaves from 7 to 18 million people north of
Mexico, the majority of whom were probably in the mixed horti-
cultural-hunting belt in the Mississippi basin and along the Atlantic
coast to Maine. Henry Dobyns, who has been attacked for over-
optimistic assumptions and high-side estimates in his lengthy 1983
work, *Their Numbers Become Thinned*, has nonetheless argued (and
gained some support for) the case that the higher figure of 18 million
is most likely and may even be an underestimate, since it works out
to just 1.4 people per square kilometer and estimates for nonstate
horticultural people range as high as 2.4 per square kilometer; the
Indians could have reached such levels, he maintains, "because they
inhabited a relatively disease-free paradise and domesticated high-
yield cereals and tubers."

Whatever the exact figure—I myself incline to a tentative number
of 15 million north of Mexico—demographic and other scholars are
agreed on one point: pre-Columbian North America was fairly
densely populated, as such cultures go, and certainly was not the
empty wasteland and untouched wilderness that Europeans took it
to be. Yet it certainly gave off the aspect of an untouched world, a
prelapsarian Eden of astonishing plenitude, even in just those coastal
areas where population was the highest, and after centuries of occupation and use. In other words, we must imagine a sizable population, such as the European invaders did not achieve until the 1840s,
in some areas quite densely settled, that would have been trapping
and shooting small game and game birds day after day for centuries,
fishing any available stream and clamming any available coast, gathering fruits and nuts and roots of several hundred species over thousands of acres a year, hunting big game over hundreds of square miles
with many thousands of pounds of meat every year (more than 15,000
for a village of 400 in southern New England alone, one estimate
suggests), ringing and burning trees and planting crops on a scale of
perhaps an acre a person, clearing underbrush and driving animals
by fires any one of which might be as much as twenty miles around,
and, let us assume, occasionally blundering with a fire out of control
or a hillside denuded for firewood or a well dried up from overuse
—all that, and *still* occupying an environment that in important
ways was ebullient and wild, abundant in both kinds and numbers
of flora and fauna, functioning to all intents and purposes in its

original primal state. If that does not argue for the Indian cultures a very special, an *intrinsic*, regardfulness for nature, it is hard to know what would.

The fashion of looking to American natives as ecological models, begun in the 1960s and undiminished since, has come under heavy fire in recent years from those who resist what they see as the impossibly romantic notion of idealistic tribes living in natural benignity—as, in fact, a modern version of the myth of the Noble Savage. This, they say, is a distortion of history; those people are the tribe that must be known as the Nevawas.

"The Indian revered nature because he had no other choice," as the frontier historian W. H. Hutchinson put it in leading this countercharge. "He perceived nature as being controlled by supernatural forces he was obliged to propitiate if he hoped for success in life," and that was all there was to it, no overriding spirituality, no fancy earth-relationship. "We ought to dry our eyes and recognize that the Indian was above all a self-centered pragmatist when it came to land use."

The argument tends to run this way. Indian societies were violent ones, characterized by hunting and war, in which the additional destruction of nature came easily. Whatever spiritual relationship they had with nature, the Indians obviously feared the forces around them more than they revered them and thus had no special difficulty, when the opportunities arose, in destroying both flora and fauna to their own advantage. There is good reason to think that the mass extinctions of the Pleistocene were caused by the overkills of Paleolithic hunters, and for the postcontact period the evidence is plentiful that the Indians hunted the beaver to near extinction and were wasteful and careless in the slaughter of other desired animals. The only thing that prevented Indian societies from greater destruction before the Europeans was that their technologies were too primitive and their numbers too small, not that their values were too pure. The only Indians who lived any other way were the Nevawas.

It is a plausible tale, and it has won its converts. This is a murky area where sureties are not easy to come by, and hypotheses of this sort can be strung out at length with some persuasiveness. The difficulty with it, however, is that at too many points the argument rests on mere conjecture (and mean-spirited at that), and where there is evidence to test it against it does not stand up.

• There is no very good proof that precontact societies engaged in warfare that was either common or particularly fierce, and the weight of evidence suggests that they were for the most part pacific. The Indian scholar Darcy McNickle has estimated that fully 70 percent of North American tribes were pacifist, a figure hard to be sure of, although it does correlate with the estimated percentage of traditionally gynocentric tribes, characterized by high status for women and central female deities, which are said to have played down conflict and male heroics; at least two of them were recorded by Europeans as placing "all virtue in a certain gentleness or apathy" (Le Jeune) and being full of "women-like men [who] seeke rather to grow right by industrie, than famous by deeds of Chevalry" (William Wood). Additional support for such an estimate comes in the numerous oral histories of Indian societies, where it is clear that warfare played so little a part that many of them, perhaps two-thirds, simply did not have war stories or battle legends of any kind; both the Algonkians of the Eastern woodlands and the traditionally peaceful tribes of the Southwest had no war myths that can be traced back before European times. The famous and popular war stories generally come from the Plains Indians, whose warrior codes and cults indeed played an important role in the later centuries, but it is interesting that virtually every one of them involves horses—and these did not appear until the seventeenth century.

Warfare was certainly known in historic times after the European invasion, sometimes quite awful and destructive, as the Irokwa annihilation of the Hurons in 1640 in the contest to determine who would control the Laurentian fur trade. And it is probable that the devastation of epidemics triggered wars both in retaliation against those enemies presumed to have caused it and in search of additional population to make up for those lost; John Smith, for example, reported of the Virginia Indians that they fought "but for women and children, and principally revenge." But as to pre-Columbian warfare we know almost nothing, and what little we do know suggests that where wars took place they were infrequent, short, and mild; in fact "war" seems a misnomer for the kinds of engagements we imagine might have taken place, in which some act of bravery or retribution rather than death, say, or territory, would be the object, and two "war parties" might skirmish without much effect on either one and none at all on the home villages. Early European settlers often made a mockery of Indian warfare—John Underhill wrote of the Pequots that their wars were "more for pastime, then to conquer and subdue enemies," and Henry Spelman, who lived among the Powhatans, said that "they might fight seven yeares and not kill seven men"—and were disdainful of the Indians' "strategems, treacheries, or surprisals" that avoided out-in-the-open battles. Even among warrior societies that emerged in the Great Plains, "counting coup"—some witnessed act of bravery, such as stealing an enemy's horses or touching him with a "coupstick"—was considered more important, and honorable, than killing him.

Organized violence, in short, was not an attribute of traditional Indian societies, certainly not as compared with their European contemporaries, and on the basis of the imperfect record what is most remarkable about them is their apparent lack of conflict and discord.

• The idea of interpreting any Indian society as fearful of nature, living in constant dread of its impersonal forces, is quite unfounded. As we have seen, the scholarly consensus is that, in the words of the ecohistorian J. Donald Hughes, Indians lived with "reverence for the earth, kinship with all forms of life, and harmony with nature." Which is not to say that they did not have a considerable deep respect for the power, even the capriciousness, of nature, and an understanding of their intimate dependence on its successful continuance; it is not even to say that they could not have had moments of fear in the midst of thunderstorm or volcanic eruption, periods of dejection or bitterness during drought or famine or disease. But nowhere in what we know of the Indian earth-relationship, whatever its other ambiguities, is there anything remotely like the fearful and vengeful sky gods of the desert cultures of the Middle East, of which Europe became the eventual inheritor.

• Indian cultures in much of the continent used fire as a technology to change the environment for their own ends, and that inevitably entailed the destruction of certain plants and trees and the disruption of some animal habitats. But this technology was used, and used carefully, with a largely positive effect. Regular and controlled ground-burnings such as the Indians practiced, whether in the prairie grasslands or the hardwood forests, *increased* the number and diversity of species, the levels of their populations, the amount of nutrients in the soils, the quantity of forbs and grasses, and the quality of available forage for all herbivores. In the forests regular annual fires averted the danger of hot-burning and damaging wildfires in the accumulated underbrush and stimulated the growth of such desired and fire-resistant hardwoods as chestnuts and oaks; in the prairies they held back the growth of forest cover altogether to promote the populations of bison and small-game animals and birds.*

• The extinctions of the Pleistocene era may have been in some measure abetted by humans, but it is now generally agreed that they were by no means caused by it. The so-called Clovis hunters (Indians in several areas with better spear- and point-making techniques) seem to have come upon the scene about 11,000 years ago, just as a number of large mammals (woolly mammoths, mastodons, camels, etc.) died off in large numbers, some to extinction. But severe and abrupt climatic alterations are known to have taken place at the same time, producing great changes in the habitat of these large, mostly herbivorous animals, never very numerous in the first place and dependent on perhaps four to five hundred pounds of green fodder a day, which was unavailable in the new conditions. It is hard to see in any case how the peoples of that time suddenly could have come up with either the technologies or the motives to kill in such vast numbers; and the famous "cliff drives" and "bison jumps" that were responsible for large numbers of animal casualties two or three hundred years later were not extensive enough to have exterminated whole species (mammoths, for example, are not found at such sites). Moreover, the prime target of the Pleistocene hunters was the American bison, which in all respects was similar to the large mammalian species that eventually died out, and though it was hunted repeatedly and avidly it survived so successfully that even in the nineteenth century Europeans still could marvel at its astonishing numbers.

• About overhunting in historical times, however, there is no real question: the record is stained with verified accounts of slaughter, destruction, areal depletions, waste, profligacy, cruelty, everything that would characterize a culture that did not know the earth was alive and all beavers brothers. It was by no means universal and it

---

*A study reported by Henry Dobyns in *From Fire to Flood* found that the population of quail increased by 250 percent in one area, and that of jackrabbits by 350 percent, because of increased ovulation resulting from improved diets high in grasses produced in such burnt-over environments.

was mostly spasmodic, but any number of tribes scuttled their taboos and customs at certain times and for reasons still not clear, and participated in animal-killings on an extraordinary scale. The extirpation of the beaver in the eastern half of the century, incidents of wanton and needless slaughter of herds of caribou and bison, nineteenth-century accounts of Indians who were "so accustomed to kill every thing that came within their reach"—the evidence is undeniable. What then of the ecological Indian?

The short answer is that the postcontact Indian was a far different creature from the precontact Indian and the aberrations of those later societies can be laid to the effects of decimating diseases and the disruptive pressures of war, trade, technology, and alcohol. Calvin Martin's path-breaking *Keepers of the Game* is an elaborate attempt to show just how this European intervention in eastern Canada, for example, preceded by exotic epidemics that killed great numbers and left the surviving societies in spiritual disarray, effectively destroyed the "long-standing compact between the animal kingdom and man" and "the mutual obligation–mutual courtesy relationship" that previously existed. If these hunting tribes were not "conservationist-minded during the heyday of the fur trade," he concludes, and "indeed they were baldly exploitative," it was "because their traditional incentives to conserve wildlife were rendered inoperative."

But the ecological Indian did not wholly disappear with the arrival of the Europeans. What we know about precontact attitudes to hunting and overkilling, in fact, comes from the traditions that were strong enough to survive into the historical era and were there to be recorded by anthropologists and ethnologists of the past two centuries: Black Elk was not an invention of the Wilderness Society, nor was Luther Standing Bear—they and hundreds like them were authentic representatives of an ancient tradition that did not die away. Whatever anomalies were produced by the European invasion, they *were* anomalous, bizarre deviations from a norm not only durable but widespread. Nor did they affect all tribes in the same way or disrupt primal animal-bond beliefs everywhere; it seems from Martin's evidence that only nonhorticultural tribes heavily dependent on hunting game, and in which there might be a plausible reason actually to think that diseases were transmitted by animals, succumbed to the temptation to slaughter for the fur trade, or at least to the degree the eastern Canadian tribes did. Even where animal relationships changed and taboos about overkilling were discarded, the complex of other beliefs binding Indians to the other elements of nature, including animals, were not substantially altered and other parts of the environment were not subject to attack and destruction.

In short, despite the evidence of abnormal anti-ecological behavior in certain Indian tribes in the historical era, one can still conclude with Wilcomb Washburn, the principal Indian historian at the Smithsonian, that "there exist sufficient examples of Indian concern for killing only as much as was needed and only in the proper manner to support the assertion that the Indian was the first ecologist."

• To believe that such a phenomenon could exist only because this Indian did not have either the technologies or the numbers is the last refuge of one who cannot imagine that there might be a society that would not destroy nature if it could.

Indian societies had a variety of technologies, some quite sophisticated and many well beyond anything comparable in Europe at the time (Powhatan fishing weirs, for example, or bows and arrows far easier, faster, and safer than the musket), and certainly could have developed others if they felt any need to do so, particularly in regard to food supply. If they did not, there was likely to be a good reason: if they did not anywhere use the plow, for instance, that may have been because their methods of breaking the soil with a planting stick worked just as well with a tenth of the effort, or because they had learned that opening up and turning over whole fields would only decrease nutrients and increase erosion, or because their thought-world would not have allowed such disregardful violence. Technologies in a nature-relating society are selected with a mind to their ecological value and impact, not from some technological or accumulative or human-centered imperative: "Viewing the world through mythic eyes," as Calvin Martin has said, the American Indian had "no powerful incentive to dream up new technologies and associated strategies to assist human survival. The biological outlook on life does not spawn that sort of mentality or behavior."

The principal environment-altering technology Indians did have—fire—was certainly powerful and destructive enough to cause immense damage if they had let it. But it was a technology surrounded with age-old constraints and used with the utmost care, to enhance rather than despoil local environments. If such a technique had not been embedded in an earth-conscious ethos, the whole continent might well have been black and denuded by the time the Europeans arrived, instead of the lush and wooded forestland they found it to be.

The matter of population size here is even more revealing. Small size does not necessarily ensure against environmental damage, as any number of European examples from barren Greek islands to deforested English shires would testify. But it is true that large size is associated often with widespread depredation—at least when it takes the form of powerful state-based agglomerations, which everywhere in the world (not excluding Mesoamerica and environs) generally seem to be erected on principles of an ever more complex manipulation of nature to human whim—dams, irrigation systems, large-scale agriculture, extensive roadways, monumental buildings, cities—that ultimately succeed in bringing down on them the predictable revenge of ecosystems gone awry.

By and large the societies of North America above New Mexico did not go in this statified direction—the exceptions may have been the Mississippi mound cultures, but their degree of political stratification is still debated—and did not produce either large populations or environmental destruction. In fact, they seem to have been quite mindful of the necessity to minimize the human impact on the ecosystem, conscious in some way of what we would now call the "carrying capacity" of their tribal lands, and to have taken special efforts to hold the population down. Among the various techniques used, not all with equal success, were ritual sexual abstinence (before a hunt or major communal ceremonies, for example), sanctions against and punishments for infidelity, the spacing of children to allow each the undivided attention of the parents through childhood, voluntary emigration or suicide by the old or ill, and the use of plant abortifacients. On a different scale, there were practices to prevent villages from overstressing any one environment: summer and winter migrations to different camping sites, periodic (once-a-generation) relocation of villages and their farmlands and hunting grounds, and division and separation of villages grown beyond a certain size.

Thus in effect it *is* accurate to say that Indian societies did not have sufficient numbers to destroy their environments—only this seems to have been consciously and deliberately so, a practice of great ecological wisdom.

So much, in sum, for the argument against the Nevawas. Everything suggests that the first Americans were indeed the first ecologists, because they evolved belief systems that by and large ensured they would be, and did so in turn (like a great many other primal peoples the world over) because they understood that their survival, and happiness—and as they would see it, the survival and happiness of all other species—depended upon it. It is quite as simple as that.

That did not make America into a paradise precisely, but close enough that it was understandable why so many Europeans upon seeing it for the first time would speak of the Golden Age and the Garden of Eden, why the very first European actually was convinced he had been washed by a river from Earthly Paradise. It is not as understandable why, following the precedent of that first conqueror, passed from the Catholic kingdom of Spain after a century of heroic elaboration on to the Protestant kingdom of England, they would choose to occupy, dominate, and destroy that land and the people who were its offspring—to assure, in the words of the historian Francis Parkman as late as the mid-nineteenth century, that since the Indian would not "learn the arts of civilization, he and his forest must perish together."

But thus, the Columbian Legacy.

Chapter Thirteen

1625–1992
Columbus/Columbia

WHEN the Reverend Samuel Purchas announced in 1625 the rightful conquest of North America by his countrymen, alive and dead—"therefore this Land is justly yours O English"—he also provided a series of volumes on English navigation and discovery intended to justify this claim, in the second of which he included a lengthy description of "that Worthy of Men" whose Discovery originated that conquest. Depending chiefly on the accounts of Peter Martyr, Francisco López de Gómara, and Antonio de Herrera (whose expert history had recently been published), he told the story of how "Colombo" importuned the Castilian throne for years, finally succeeded in launching his voyage, and thus opened up "the Columbian (so fitlier named, then American) World" for Europe. Details about the actual voyages are sparse, and it is clear that the good churchman (who had been appointed chaplain to another Columbian champion, George Abbot, the archbishop of Canterbury, a decade before) had primarily a moral interest in his history: he offered Colombo as a model of patience and perseverance duly requited, so that others "may by this example learn to digest greater Stormes at home," and the reader is made to understand that his "diligence and wisdome" was rewarded principally because he was "carrying Christ in his heart" throughout. But Purchas was enough of a historian to know that the Discovery was important in a more practical sense: Cortés, even with his Mexican gold, and Pizarro, with his Peruvian silver, "were not comparable to their Masters Master-Peece, who found the New World, to find them work."

Like many others of his time, Purchas regarded his actors, like the

new lands on which they strode—none of which he had ever seen—
as more symbolic than real. The sort of three-dimensionality we now
take to be essential to historical analysis is missing: Colón remains a
stick figure, connotative, manipulable. Despite the fact that Fernando's biography of his father was certainly available in England at the
time—a third Italian edition had been produced in Milan in 1614,
though it would be another ninety years before an English translation
was published—the kinds of intimate details that book provided were
generally ignored up to that time, by routine chroniclers as by serious
historians of the Purchas stripe.

The story of Colón's standing and reputation over these next centuries is one of Symbol and Flesh, Myth and Reality, and the complex
mixture of those elements depending on whose hands are doing the
shaping and for what purpose. At first, as we have seen, he was
largely Symbol—Explorer, Discoverer, Hero—and was brought
forth as the occasion demanded to represent Italian genius and courage, or Spanish adventure and conquest, or Christian perseverance
and purpose; the details of his personal life, of his voyages, of his
government of Española, even of his subsequent difficulties with the
Spanish sovereigns, were generally ignored. Then, gradually, for the
immigrants of the northern continent who came to think of themselves, and be identified, as "Americans," he was distended into
Personification, a figure standing for the new lands and new peoples
seeking to become a new nation, the actual Genoese ship's captain
lost in the mists of patriotic purpose. Next, with the publication of
a raft of material from Spanish archives, he became Character, a
larger-than-life figure who, though flesh and blood and heir to human
failing, overcame all that with the force of genius, an almost fictional
personage out of romantic lore who nonetheless was enhanced in his
historical stature (and lost nothing of his symbolic usefulness). Finally, it was left largely for the present century to try to understand
him as Human, using the tools of scholarship to separate out the
elements of myth and make-believe, attractive as they were, and leave
behind a figure of much more complexity—and on both sides of the
Atlantic, of controversy—than previous eras had known. Thus the
progress of the Columbian Legacy.

The historian J. H. Elliott observed two decades ago that "the
historical reputation of Columbus is a subject which has not yet
received all the attention it deserves," a comment that still holds true

today, in fact may be said to be an understatement. And though it is not possible in a short compass to remedy the omission completely, a quick survey may at least illumine part of that historical trajectory over the centuries and serve to set the Discoverer, both Symbol and Flesh, in some historiographical perspective appropriate for the anniversary of his achievement.

1625–1740 "*L'Amérique ne commande pas seule,*" Fernand Braudel cautions darkly, but in fact in the seventeenth century the American continents did become of utmost importance for the states and economies of Europe, indeed were decisive in the process by which Europe became a world power. It was the conquest of America, in Elliott's analysis, that gave the subcontinent its "new confidence in its own capacities, new territories and sources of wealth, and a new and deeper awareness of the complex inter-relationship between treasure, population and trade, as the basis of national power." The Century of Exploitation, though it began to peter out after the 1650s, was followed by a century and more of immigration and settlement, trade and commerce, a vast crisscrossing of the Atlantic that anchored Europe's global empires in the West and established the New World not only in the economy but even more in the consciousness and culture of the Old.

Cristóbal Colón—whether as Colón, Colombo, Colom, Colomb, or Columbus—was the emblem of much of that, as he had been the century before. By then each nation might have picked a figure of its own, and various alternative sons were put forth from time to time, but it was Colón who continued to stand for the discovery and opening of the new hemisphere; whereas Cortés, for example, an imposing and striking figure who led Spain to far more wealth than ever the Admiral did, was mentioned in some two dozen books from 1600 to 1650, Colón appeared in more than 120 of them. He continued to have a place in the "famous men" collections—including the first in Spain, Fernando Pizarro y Orellana's *Varones ilustres* in 1639—and in almost every account of either Spanish or Ligurian history, as well as in general histories of European discovery and expansion. It is noteworthy that as the century wore on Fernando's biography seemed to gain greater currency as a historical source, until in 1704 it received its first (and quite capable) English translation—in fact the first translation out of the Italian anywhere in Europe—in a handsome series of volumes, Awnsham and John Churchill's *Collection of Voyages and Travels* (reprinted in 1733, 1744–47, and 1752).*

England continued to have a special affinity to the Discoverer, or at least an image of him, and he was given Purchas-like treatment in several historical works in the course of this period. For Francis Bacon, England's leading natural scientist in the early seventeenth century, he was a personage of particular fascination, appearing one way or another in at least six of his works; his popular *History of the reign of King Henrie the Seventh* (1622) argued that it was not Colón but the Welsh prince Madoc in the twelfth century who actually was first to discover western lands, but Bacon nonetheless bemoaned the fact that Henry did not take up the offer supposedly presented by Bartolomé on behalf of his brother, and his quasi-utopian *New Atlantis* (written c. 1626) provided for a statue of Columbus to stand in the hall of the "principall inventors" of all time. Perhaps the best, if most bizarre, indication of Colón's reputation among the English was the claim put out in *De jure maritimo et navali* in London in 1682 that he was one of their own—"a discontented Native of this Isle, the Famous Columbus . . . born in England, but resident at Genoa." Then, as if life were striving to imitate art, in 1716 the grandson of England's James II, given the name James Francis Fitz-James Stuart, married Catarina-Ventura de Portugal y Ayala, the direct-line great-great-great-great-great-granddaughter of Cristóbal Colón, and himself became Admiral of the Indies (and Duke of Veragua, the other hereditary title) in 1733; but for the "Glorious Revolution" that deposed James II in 1688, England might have had an Admiral of the Indies on its throne.†

Again it is in literature that we can perhaps best catch a sense of the stature accorded Colón at the time. The Italians in the seventeenth century celebrated him with no fewer than eight poems—one of which, Tommaso Stigliani's *Del mondo nuovo* (Piacenza, 1617; Rome, 1628) was a *"poema eroico"* in thirty-four cantos—plus two

---

*The introduction to this series was a discourse on the history of navigation "supposed to be written by the celebrated Mr. Locke," presumably John, who died that year, which was based largely on Herrera's accounts and included a long entry on Columbus that made no mention of his doings on land.

†It could not have detracted much from the Admiral's English fame that he was described by Thomas Fuller in 1642 as "the worthy Peter Columbus," in what was perhaps an echo of Lucio Marineo Siculo, who had written of "Pedro Colon" a century earlier (1539).

full-length plays (1621, 1691) and now, the first in a long line, an opera, *Il Colombo,* text and music by Cardinal Pietro Ottoboni, in 1690. (The Italians also came through with the first nonportrait paintings of Colón that we know of: a depiction of the Discovery done for the Ducal Palace in Genoa sometime in the mid–seventeenth century, by Giovanni Battista Carlone; another, also for the palace, by Domenico Fiasella which was later burned; and a third by Lazzaro Tavarone for the Saluzzo Palace in Genoa.) English literary attention was still mostly fleeting, as in a 1607 verse by Michael Drayton, but there are mentions of Colón in at least four more poems before mid-century (1629, 1630, 1633, 1638) and in one of 1667—

> . . . *such of late*
> *Columbus found th' American, so girt*
> *With feathered cincture, naked else and wilde—*

that is indisputably a towering poem of the language, Milton's *Paradise Lost.** French interest also was scattered, but two substantial poems concerned Columbus, one of which, although it gives out in the middle of the second canto, still managed to be more than five hundred pages long. The notable new entrant in the literary lists now was Spain, with the chaotic but very popular play by Lope de Vega, *El Nuevo Mundo descubierto por Cristóbal Colón,* in which the Discoverer is a quasi-chivalric hero, a dreamer mocked by a cruel and plodding world who persists and triumphs and thus comes to stand forever as the symbol of what is presumed to be the eternal human (though it is peculiarly European and modern) spirit of enterprise and discovery; this was followed at the end of the century (1701) by

---

*Since both Justin Winsor and Henry Harrisse claim that Baptist Goodall's 1630 poem *Tryall of Travell* was the first English poem to mention Columbus, it may be useful to note that this was preceded by Robert Seall's broadside of 1563, George Gascoigne's commendatory poem of 1576, Stephen Parmenius's *De navigatione* in 1582, Edward Fairfax's translation of Tasso in 1600, Drayton's dedicatory verse to D'Olivier de Serres's *The Perfect Use of Silkwormes* in 1607, and briefly in the *Epigrammaton opusculum duobus distinctum* by one Huntingdon Plumptre in 1629. The poem by Goodall, who bills himself as "merchant," is a wretched piece of junk written apparently to celebrate world trade and "worldes of wealth and raines of ore repleate," on the level of

> Collumbus and Magellan Prowdly venetrd
> Then Drake, Vespucius and our forbish enterd

which goes on for seventy-eight pages, and oughn't.

Francisco Botelo de Moraes e Vasconcelos's enormous *El Nuevo Mundo*, the first complete *"poema heroyco"* about Colón in Spanish, 968 pages of undistinguished but plainly heartfelt verse.

By the end of the seventeenth century, now two centuries after the Discovery, Colón seems fixed in the European mind rather as Lope de Vega saw him, although he could be made tragic in the hands of some, romantic for the purposes of others, and simply heroic according to the needs of still others. Oddly enough, though, we have no idea how he was regarded by the people who actually followed in his wake and made their way to live in the New World. It was not much of a bookish population, true, though the Spanish had established three universities and a printing press in their domains before the sixteenth century was over and the English two universities by 1700; nor was it a population with much leisure, even if it had had the inclination, for contemplation and historical rumination; and it was preoccupied in any case with self-enrichment, particularly the form of it that John Adams called "that avarice for land that has made upon this continent so many votaries of Mammon." Still, it is somewhat surprising to see how few books were written in any part of the New World about the history of the lands now so abundantly being settled, and to find, as near as I can tell, no published references at all during the seventeenth century and the first three decades of the eighteenth to the man who made it all possible.

That seems a shame, for the various colonies, especially on the northern continent, were very busy living out the Columbian Legacy: the dream of Paradise and a life of ease (Sir Robert Montgomery, for example, spoke of Georgia in 1717 as "our future Eden"); the use of violence and military force (the Pequot War, 1637; King Philip's War, 1675; Bacon's Rebellion, 1676–77; Anglo-French Wars, 1689–97, 1702–13; etc.); the search for riches beyond reckoning (Benjamin Franklin's forthright "Hints for Those That Would Be Rich" came out in 1736); the destruction of the forest lands and the Indians who had lived there (white control, and forest depletion, extended by 1740 from Quebec to Tobago and Plymouth to Appalachia and through the Mississippi valley); and the enslavement first of red and then of black (with the importation of some 2 to 3 million Africans delivered alive in the Americas before 1740). What might it have been like if there had been just one among all those settlers, among the 600,000 or so in North America, the half a million in South America, who would have stopped to reflect on all that and where its genesis lay?

The year 1692 passed by without a single word or recorded deed of commemoration of that genesis.

1692 Witch trials in Salem, Massachusetts, condemned twenty women to death, who were then executed to the full view, and approbation, of local crowds.

Cotton Mather published Fair Weather, A Midnight Cry, *and Political Fables, each full of high-minded Puritan religiosity for the heathen of all races.*

William and Mary College, the fifth institution of higher learning in North America, was chartered in Williamsburg, Virginia.

Governor Diego de Vargas led a force of Spanish soldiers out of El Paso to begin, brutally, the reconquest of New Mexico after a decade of Pueblo revolts, ending with the recapture of Santa Fe in October and the execution of seventy of its Indian leaders.

Baron Louis Armand de Lahonton returned to France after a sojourn in Canada to begin Dialogues . . . entre l'auteur et un sauvage, *a sympathetic treatment of North American Indians that, with Montaigne, began the Noble Savage tradition in French letters.*

The population of the natives of North America was probably no more than 4 million.

1740–1825 The pace quickened. The new peoples of the Americas came to see themselves—and to be seen in Europe—as a different breed, no matter what their European stock, those who were part of an accelerating wave of newcomers drawn to the New World no less than those of the several generations born there. They began to chafe at the bonds that tied them to the mother countries—sometimes, as in the English colonies, uncharitably and unreasonably so—just when they came to be considered paramount in the maintenance of empire, not only as providers of commodities but as trading partners and strategic allies, even as safety valves and dumping grounds for restless metropole populations. Their stirrings of self-reliance and self-determination, beginning as the eighteenth century moved to its midpoint, gathered force with each decade until that peculiarly American convulsion that created an independent United States in 1783 and reverberated outward through the hemisphere; by the end of this period a majority of the former colonies had declared their independence and become nations (in the European pattern, be it noted) on their own.

In Europe, England (or properly, with the Act of Union in 1707, Great Britain) continued to consolidate power as the economic center of gravity shifted northward, and by the beginning of this period its empire had effectively become the most important in the world, with North America its most important cornerstone. That was part of the reason for an awakened interest in history there at about this time, especially the history of the Western hemisphere, producing a spate of books—in 1704, 1708, 1727, 1739, 1743, 1759, and a half-dozen in the 1770s—in which Admiral Columbus played a significant part. Perhaps the most scholarly of them was William Robertson's *History of America* (1777), but clearly the most popular—the one that American children, including Washington Irving, were said to grow up reading—was *The World Displayed* (1759), a multivolume set (as were many at the time) whose first book was devoted entirely to Columbus and his immediate successors. The chief sources here, standard fare by now, were Fernando's biography and Herrera's history (and that in turn influenced by Las Casas's *Historia* manuscript), so the image of the Admiral was largely the one his son and his great admirer put forth, none too accurate as we now know but detailed and intimate nonetheless. What was *not* included, and what seems generally to have faded from British attention as they, too, produced a darkish colonial record, was the Black Legend of Spanish misdeeds, beginning with Colón's government of Española; missing as well, here as in every other account, was a good sense of Colón on land, Colón as governor, Colón the increasingly demented malcontent in his last years in Spain. Like the Italians and the Spanish before them, the British now preferred a less complicated hero.

In the rest of Europe the attention paid Colón continued to swell. Four path-breaking works of scholarship appeared, betokening a new kind of interest: a Spanish collection of Columbian documents, with 108 chapters on Colón, by Andrés González Barcia, in 1749; a large and sweeping life story by Chevalier de Langeac, complete with fifteen pages of poetry, in France in 1782; a *Historia del Nuevo-Mundo* by Juan Bautista Muñoz, who had access to many Spanish archival sources, in Spain in 1793; and a full-scale *Vita di Cristofero Colombo* by Luigi Bossi, said to be the first "modern" biography, in Italy in 1818; to which might be added the first printing of Colón's *Book of*

Privileges, in both Italy and England in 1823. Still, it was rather in plays and poems, even operas and ballets, that Europeans seemed to want to treat the Discoverer, being absorbed now more with the compelling drama of the story than with the flat historical details, even the embellished details allowed the creative historian of the time. Thus there were two more long epic poems in French (1756, 1773), plus five other shorter verses, and at least three plays, one by Rousseau (originally written in 1742, printed in 1782, and said to have had music for it, no longer extant), and another by Nepomucène Lemercier in 1809, so bad that it caused a riot when first performed; three operas, some said to be with ballets, were produced in Italy in 1770, 1778, and 1788, and two plays in 1775; in Germany, Schiller's famous *Kolumbus* was printed in 1795 and a play produced in 1812; and even England supplied a number of long poems, including the first on Columbus as far as we know by a woman (*Reflections on a Tomb*, by "a Lady," in 1791), and a play, the first on the Discoverer in English (*Columbus, or A World Discovered*, by Thomas Morton, performed and printed in 1792, subsequently performed in the United States in 1797).

But as we might imagine, it was in the Americas, specifically that part where the restless and ambitious peoples of Britain spread themselves, that Christopher Columbus came to have a special significance and the Columbian Legacy finally to take on new life. These were people who now thought of themselves as *Americans*, not Britons, some now three and four generations in the land, people who increasingly worked out who they were, as a distinct culture, in relation to that land: their mission (as they came to understand and proclaim it) was *progress*, the literal progress across the land, across the mountains and rivers, as far as one could go, as well as the material progress that turned the howling wilderness into productive cropland and range, prosperous hamlet and city, and the moral progress that brought the laws and customs of civilization to the shores and then to the hinterlands, to white and (should they submit) red alike—all leading to the political progress that pointed toward resistance, revolution, and independence, around which the image of Columbus was purposefully entwined.

The first full treatment of Columbus in an American volume seems to be in the first issue of *New American Magazine* in January 1758, a competent if slightly florid life of the Admiral to lead off a "History

of the Continent of America" series that went on thereafter to concentrate almost entirely on the feats of English explorers. (The British
at the time were trying to play up the image of John Cabot, who
after all did sail in the service of England and did most likely land
on mainland North America, unlike Columbus, but he always proved
too shadowy and indistinct a character for veneration.) Then perhaps
nothing more—nothing that has lasted—until 1772, the first act in
the drama that would make of Columbus the personification of America and the new nation to which it gave birth. That process was the
work of a most unlikely trio—a New York publicist and editor, a
well-to-do businessman and amateur poet, and a Boston clergyman
with a passion for history—who within the space of no more than
two decades provided the fledgling nation with just the symbol it
needed: someone decidedly un-English, who could stand as no other
historical figure could for America, and who embodied the necessary virtues of perseverance, courage, vision, sagacity, and heroism
besides.

Philip Freneau (1752–1832) has been called "the father of American
poetry," a paternity that his children may wish to deny, but it does
seem that he was the first American-born poet to have his works
collected in a commercial volume, in 1786. His graduation address
at Princeton, in 1771, was an unrhymed pentameter paean to Columbus (published as "The Rising Glory of America" in 1772 in *The
American Village* and collected in 1809), and he would go on to treat
the subject at least five more times, including a book-length verse in
eighteen stanzas, *The Pictures of Columbus, the Genoese*, in 1788.
Much of it is conventional mythology, enlivened with the sort of
self-pitying postures provided in Fernando's account—

> *through various toils,*
> *Famine, and death, the hero forced his way,*
> *Through oceans pregnant with perpetual storms,*
> *And climates hostile to adventurous man—*

but the underlying point is to establish the uniqueness of the American
continent, where, "secure from tyranny and base controul,"

> *Nations shall grow, and states not less in fame*
> *Than Greece and Rome of old!*

Even, perhaps, where

> *Paradise anew*
> *Shall flourish, by no second Adam lost. . . .*
> *A Canaan here,*
> *Another Canaan shall excel the old.*

Freneau is credited also with the first personification of the new nation as the spirit of the Discoverer, in a poem published around July 1775, soon after the battles of Lexington and Bunker Hill:

> *Ah see with grief fair Massachusetts' plains,*
> *The seat of war, and death's terrific scenes. . . .*
> *What madness, heaven, has made Britannia frown?*
> *Who plans our [or?] schemes to pull Columbia* down.*

The asterisk is Freneau's, and he adds, "Columbia, America sometimes so called from Columbus, the first discoverer," obviously on the model already established by "Virginia," "Georgia"—and "America."

By the time of the next act, a decade later, the nation had won its independence and Joel Barlow (1754–1812) could take a fairly expansive view of how Columbus's intentions had worked themselves out. His *Vision of Columbus* appeared in 1787, nine books in somewhat tedious rhymed couplets, addressed to Louis XVI (with thanks for "reaching the hand of beneficence to another hemisphere"). The poem is preceded by a rather nice biographical essay on Columbus that Barlow thought necessary because there was only one book available with "a sufficient account" of the Discoverer's life (Robertson's *History*) and "it is presumed, from the present state of literature in this country, that many persons . . . are but slightly acquainted with the life and character of that great man, whose extraordinary genius led him to the discovery of the continent, and whose singular sufferings ought to excite the indignation of the world."*

---

*After the fashion of the time, the printing for this volume was paid in part by a number of subscribers, and the prominence of the men on this list indicates Barlow's considerable standing in the new nation. Among them: Louis XVI himself, put down for twenty-five copies,

In the poem itself, an aged Columbus lies in a Spanish prison, typically whining about his fate, until an Angel comes and takes him to the New World again to show him its future, when

> *Ages unborn shall bless the happy day*
> *When thy bold streamers steer'd the trackless way. . . .*
> *Behold you isles, where first the flag, unfurl'd,*
> *Waved peaceful triumph o'er the newfound world,*
> *Where, aw'd to silence, savage bands gave place,*
> *And hail'd with joy the sun-descended race.*

On the northern continent Columbus is shown how

> *Freedom's unconquer'd sons, with healthy toil,*
> *Shall lop the grove and warm the furrowed soil,*
> *From iron ridges break the rugged ore,*
> *Smooth the pale marble, spire the bending shore.*

And he is pleased:

> *Columbus hailed them with a father's smile,*
> *Fruits of his cares and children of his toil;*
> *With tears of joy, while still his eyes descried*
> *Their course adventurous o'er the distant tide. . . .*
> *He saw the squadrons reach the rising stand,*
> *Leap from the wave and share the joyous land.*
> *Receding forests yield the heroes room,*
> *And opening wilds with fields and gardens bloom.*

The Admiral is forced to go through an interminable section witnessing the Revolutionary War and the American victory, after which he is finally treated to a vision of the American future rampant with progress and science and the bounty produced by the two of them, until

---

G. Washington (twenty copies), New York governor DeWitt Clinton, Alexander Hamilton, Robert Livingston, "Col. Aaron Burr," Benjamin Franklin (six copies), Thomas Paine, and Charles W. Peale, plus an assortment of soldiers, judges, and politicians from Boston to Baltimore.

Each orient realm, the former pride of earth,
Where men and science drew their ancient birth,
Shall soon behold, on this enlighten'd coast,
Their fame transcended and their glory lost.

And so, the angel finally consoles the Admiral:

Let thy delighted soul no more complain
Of dangers braved and griefs endured in vain,
Of courts insidious, envy's poison'd stings,
The loss of empire and the frown of kings;
While these bright scenes thy glowing thoughts compose,
To spurn the vengeance of insulting foes,
And all the joys, descending ages gain,
Repay thy labours and remove thy pain.

A bit cloying, no doubt, but understandably optimistic given the times, and it immediately won Barlow fame; sufficiently so that twenty years later he reworked the whole thing into *ten* books and 3,675 couplets, retitled it *The Columbiad*, dedicated it to Robert Fulton (whose steamboat was launched that same year), and embellished it with a series of engravings of New World scenes. In its review of this volume the *Edinburgh Review* was moved to declare about its author, "We have no hesitation in saying, that we consider him a giant."

The last act of the drama was the work of the Reverend Doctor Jeremy Belknap (1744–1798), who offered his contribution in the form of "A Discourse intended to Commemorate the Discovery of America by Christopher Columbus," read to the Historical Society of Massachusetts on October 23, 1792, and printed as a pamphlet later that year before being used as the first half of his Columbus sketch in his *Biographies of the Early Discoverers* in 1794. Belknap confines himself for the most part to prose, but of the effusive kind:

About the middle of the fifteenth century . . . a genius arose, whose memory has been preserved with veneration in the pages of history, as the instrument of enlarging the region of science and commerce beyond any of his predecessors. . . . He had a genius of that kind, which makes use of speculation and reason-

ing only as excitements to action. He was not a closet projector,
but an enterprising adventurer [and his voyage was one which]
opened to the Europeans a new world; which gave a new form
to their thoughts, to their spirit of enterprise and of commerce;
which enlarged the empire of Spain, and stamped with immortality the name of Christopher Columbus. . . . In the pages of
impartial history, he will always be celebrated as a man of genius
and science; as a prudent, skillful, intrepid navigator.

And so on, leading up to a long encomium on the virtues of science,
commerce ("the soul of navigation"!), and freedom, a combination
that the new United States happens to have fashioned together as
never before in history; and ending with an inevitable ode to Columbus and "his daring sail":

> The Western World appear'd to view,
>   Her friendly arms extended wide;
> Then FREEDOM o'er th' Atlantic flew,
>   With poor RELIGION by her side.

And God declares:

> "Sweet peace and heav'nly truth shall shine
>   On fair COLUMBIA's happy ground;
> There FREEDOM and RELIGION join
>   And spread their influence all around."

One may well understand why no one thought to cite the good doctor
to challenge Freneau's paternity to American poetry, but in fact he
was hailed in the nineteenth century, largely for his work on the
discoverers, as "the father of American history."

Leaving aside a literary judgment on this trio of early American
patriots, it is clear that their considerable efforts—along with those
of perhaps a half-dozen poetasters and journalists and songsmiths
whose names we know and probably dozens of others lost to
history—succeeded in establishing the importance of the Discovery
and the image of the Discoverer in the minds of most of the citizens
of the new-made country. As early as 1784, a college in New York
with the inappropriate name King's decided to call itself Columbia;

in 1785 (and again in 1786) copper, gold, and silver coins were struck by order of the Confederation treasurer Gouverneur Morris with an allegorical female figure labeled (in erroneous Latin) "Immune Columbia"; in 1786 the new capital of South Carolina was christened Columbia and the same year a *Columbian Magazine* was begun in Philadelphia (the longest-lasting and most distinguished of its era, with contributions by Barlow, Belknap, Noah Webster, and John Quincy Adams); in 1787 appeared the first printed version of the song "Columbia," by Yale tutor Timothy Dwight, so popular with Revolutionary troops that it was regarded as America's unofficial national anthem for decades; in 1789 some leading patriots established the St. Tammany Society, or Columbian Order, as a social and political club in New York City; in 1791 the framers of the new government decided that it should have a federal capital on the banks of the Potomac River, to be called "the Territory of Columbia"; and in 1792 a ship named *Columbia*, under a Captain Robert Grant, discovered a massive river feeding into the Pacific at about 46 degrees north and, claiming it on behalf of the United States, named it "Columbia's River."

At the end of its first decade as a new nation, then, it is not surprising that the United States should have commemorated the tercentennial of the Columbian landfall with something more than the stony silence of the century before. In Boston the Historical Society, honored by the governor and lieutenant governor and other dignitaries, sat through Belknap's speech and then retired to a dinner "where the memory of Columbus was toasted in convivial enjoyment" and Belknap's ode was sung by "a select choir." In New York, the Tammany Society unveiled a fourteen-foot-high (apparently temporary) obelisk dedicated to Columbus and provided an "evening's entertainment," according to a local paper, that featured an "elegant oration" and a series of toasts that included "To the memory of Christopher Columbus," "May the New World never experience the vices and miseries of the Old," "May the deliverers of America never experience that ingratitude from their country which Columbus experienced from his king," and "May peace and liberty ever pervade the United Columbian States." And in Baltimore the first public monument in the world to the memory of the Discoverer was unveiled, a forty-four-foot column of brick, covered with cement and decorated with a marble slab, the gift of General Charles d'Amanor, the French consul in Baltimore, to commemorate the friendship of the two nations. A historian a century later alleged that there were celebrations that month also in Providence, Richmond, and "numerous other towns."

In the decades that followed, and well into the nineteenth century, Columbia was firmly fixed as the allegorical symbol of the United States. The first uses were largely private—no fewer than sixteen periodicals and eighteen patriotic books (e.g., *The Columbian Arithmetician, a new system of math*, by "an American," 1811) used "Columbian" or a variant between 1792 and 1825—but public use gradually increased and a half-dozen scholarly societies chose the name, including the Columbian Institute for the Promotion of Arts and Sciences, in Washington, D.C., which eventually became the Smithsonian Institution. The first settlement to use the name in this period was apparently Columbus, Ohio, founded as the state capital in 1812, to be followed by other towns in Massachusetts, Georgia, and Indiana in the 1820s, and at about that time there was even some national debate about changing the last part of the country's name officially from "of America" to "of Columbia," even simply calling the whole country Columbia. This was speedily brought to an end in 1819 when the colony of Nueva Granada, one of the first in South America to assert its independence of Spain, declared itself to be Colombia Grande (with a certain justification, since it then included all the places on the continent to which Colón had sailed), later simply Colombia.

1792   *Mary Wollstonecraft published* A Vindication of the Rights of Woman, *one of the earliest works to assert female equality; it was ridiculed in a parody entitled* A Vindication of the Rights of Brutes.

Kentucky was admitted to the United States as the fifteenth state, and permitted to be slave-holding.

Louis XVI, friend to America but not the Jacobins, was tried and condemned, to be executed the following year.

Construction of the White House was begun in Washington, under the direction of James Hoban, though the District of Columbia would not become the official seat of the union until 1800.

The Kingdom of Denmark became the first nation of Europe officially to abolish the slave trade; although William Wilberforce's bill for Britain's abolition of the trade was carried in Parliament, it was another fifteen years before it became a law.

The world's first academic society devoted to the study and promotion of chemistry was established in Philadelphia.

The population of the natives of North America was perhaps 3 million, two-thirds in Mesoamerica.

1825–1892 Then the dam burst. Part of the outpouring resulted from the energy released by the ebullient and prosperous new nation, confident and robust, clearly destined to be a major actor on the world stage and even then enjoying, at least among its white families, what is thought to have been the highest material standard of living in the world. Part of it was the new romantic spirit which chose to see in America the ideal combination of a free, natural, unspoiled society, untainted by the decadence of Europe, and yet a modern and civilized one capable of enjoying all the benefits of science and commerce. And part of it was simply that more came to be known about Cristóbal Colón and his life than at any time before.

This last factor was due to the long and largely thankless labors of one Martín Fernández de Navarrete, who retired from the Spanish navy in 1789 to undertake a royal commission to collect and sort documents related to Spanish naval history. A year or so later, while going through the library of the Duque del Infantado, he came upon a manuscript of seventy-six large-sized paper folios, forty or fifty lines to the page, which turned out to be Las Casas's copy of the long-lost *Journal* of the historic First Voyage—and for the next thirty-five years, working mostly out of a small office in the Hydrographic Office in Madrid, Navarrete devoted himself to a dogged search of all available Spanish archives for material relating to Colón and his voyages. That search brought to light not only the *Journal* but a series of letters between the Admiral and the Sovereigns, letters from Colón to his son Diego in the last years of his life, some of the depositions from the *Pleitos* lawsuit between the crown and Diego, a Spanish manuscript of the *Lettera Rarissima*, and a host of other papers, some known only in incomplete texts, some hard to find, some never printed. These were finally published as *Viajes de Colón*, the first part of a three-volume *Colección de los viajes y descubrimientos* in 1826 (dated 1825, but in fact not off the presses until

January 1826). Columbian scholarship would never be the same again.*

As it happened, news of the impending publication of the *Journal* had become known in Madrid, and the American ambassador to Spain, Alexander Everett, thought it would be appropriate if some American would translate it immediately into English and have it ready for an American audience shortly after it appeared in Spain. His travels had recently taken him to France, where he had met an American writer named Washington Irving, who proved to be fluent in Spanish, and so he thought to send him a note asking if he would be interested in a quick translation job, probably lucrative, in Madrid. Irving, then forty-two and down on his luck, with very little money and repeatedly frustrated in his efforts to find a subject for a new book that would establish him as a serious writer, was immediately taken with the idea; it would be, he thought, the job of a couple of months, his languages were certainly up to the task, and it would prove a very neat answer to those American critics who had lately accused him of failing to write about authentic American heroes and turning his back on the young nation, so in need of its able artists, to live in decadent Europe. He immediately wrote a letter of agreement and sent feelers to a few publishers, and a few months later headed off to Spain.

But once he was in Madrid something happened. Irving saw the new book, Navarrete's own copy, in February 1826; he talked at length with the then aged compiler; he accepted a room at the home of the American bibliophile Obadiah Rich, full of volumes on Spanish discoveries and early American history; and in the next four months he sat down and tore off seven hundred pages of the first draft of a full biography of Columbus. Clearing this project with his publisher

---

*Actually, the first use of the *Journal* is said to have been made by Juan Bautista Muñoz, an earlier crown historian who began locating and transcribing documents on the Indies in 1779, and whose *Historia del Nuevo-Mundo* of 1793, Samuel Eliot Morison wrote, had the benefit of the copy of the *Journal* shown Muñoz by Navarrete shortly after its discovery. In addition, Muñoz is said, by the nineteenth-century American bibliophile Obadiah Rich, to have made a copy of the *Journal*, which Rich obtained in 1830 (today in the Rich Collection of the New York Public Library, where it is miscatalogued as a printed book). However, I can find no evidence that Muñoz made any use of this document in his history, and in any case his work was denounced by Spanish historians at the time (and his archival work suppressed by the Spanish Academy of History) because they objected to his repeated complaints—rightful, but put without much diplomacy—about the disgraceful condition of Spanish archives and their misuse by Spanish scholars.

took somewhat longer, and the revision at which he worked with great energy somewhat longer still, but by July 1827 he had a very large completed manuscript of some 340,000 words. "I had no idea of the Nature of the task when I undertook it," he wrote to a friend that month, and now that he was through he was "full of doubts and anxieties" about its fate, on which "my future comfort and I may say my future subsistence depends."

He need not have worried. The four-volume edition of *The Life and Voyages of Columbus*, published in London in 1828, and the subsequent three-volume edition, published in New York, were immediately popular and acclaimed; translations were very quickly produced in several languages and a dozen countries; Irving was elected to the Spanish Academy of History, given an honorary doctorate from Oxford, and honored by the British Royal Society of Literature. In the next three decades there were thirty-nine printings and editions of the biography in the United States and Britain and fifty-one more in Latin America and Europe. (It is today available throughout the world in nearly two hundred editions and imprints.)

It is in fact a curious book. Irving listed no fewer than 150 sources, his diaries and the text itself show him to have been a diligent researcher, and we know him to have been concerned with authenticity, as he declared that he "labored hard to make the work complete and accurate as to all information extant." He had the Navarrete documents in front of him, more than nine hundred pages' worth, and the full resources of Rich's library. And yet the work is full of errors and suppositions of fact that are quite unwarranted; details are invented for virtually every scene, sometimes the slimmest facts are elaborated into the most prodigious events, and made-up conversations and long interior monologues of no historical validity occur throughout. He made scant use of all the new primary material (his account of the First Voyage, for one notable example, is not even as detailed and *Journal*-based as that of Fernando, and he almost never used the Admiral's exact words when Las Casas provided them), and he tended to rely quite uncritically on untrustworthy secondary sources, especially Fernando and Las Casas, whom he used with sublime gullibility and whose biases he accepted whole.

It is all very dramatic and readable, and Columbus becomes an extremely compelling and fascinating character, an outsized protagonist for an outsized story, and that fact surely played a large part in the great popularity of the book. But it is still a glaring abdication of the responsibility of the historian in favor of the license of the novelist, creating an essentially fictional hero for whose actions it was not necessary to provide documentation; or worse, in favor of the venality of the nationalist hoping for popular approval and literary reputation at home. Instead of dispelling the myriad myths that had become attached to the Columbus story, Irving chose to toss them all in, in full fictional regalia—piratical voyages of Colón's youth, a brief university career, service for King René d'Anjou, the shipwreck off the coast of Lisbon, maltreatment by the Portuguese court, worse treatment by the Spanish court, a brave appearance before the learned council at Salamanca University which insisted that the world was flat, Isabella's offer to pawn her jewels, the mutiny at sea, the exultant return to a jubilant Barcelona, the egg that proved his genius, the instant approbation of the civilized world—and much, much more. Not one of them true, or at least none with substantial and independent verification, not one that should be accepted as anything but fanciful invention by anyone pretending to serious history—as was pointed out, in fact, by a few academic carpers of the time, who took Irving to task for writing "an enchanted falsehood" full of "gaudy and meretricious" tales. But it all made for a rich and dramatic narrative and, substantiated now by a presumably reputable author, became the essential inspiration for the vast array of popular histories and paintings and poems and plays that seemed to fill the skies of the rest of the nineteenth century in such profusion.

Irving's Columbus was fuller and more detailed than all those before, but still a man of epic proportions, flawed in minor ways yet heroic in all the elements that counted: a nineteenth-century romantic character who might have come from the pages of Walter Scott:

> Columbus was a man of great and inventive genius. . . . His ambition was lofty and noble, inspiring him with high thoughts, and an anxiety to distinguish himself by great achievements. He aimed at dignity and wealth in the same elevated spirit with which he sought renown. . . . His conduct was characterized by the grandeur of his views and the magnanimity of his spirit. Instead of ravaging the newly found countries . . . he sought to colonize and cultivate them, to civilize the natives. . . . A valiant and indignant spirit . . . ardent and enthusiastic imagination . . . a visionary of an uncommon kind.

What of his seeming madness?—"a poetical temperament" that "betrayed him into visionary speculations." And what of kidnapping and enslaving and killing innocent natives?—yes, "a blot on his illustrious name," but all "countenanced by the crown" and anyway "errors of the times" that should not be considered "his individual faults." All in all, like Romulus, the sort of progenitor of which any nation should be proud.

Washington Irving left Spain in 1829, having collected material for three more substantial books (*The Conquest of Granada*, 1829; *The Companions of Columbus*, 1831; and *The Alhambra*, 1832) that would go on to provide for the American imagination the dark, heroic, romantic past to which it could not otherwise lay any claim. More than that the son of a young nation could not do, and when Irving wrote of Herrera, "To illustrate the glory of his nation is one of the noblest offices of the historian," he might well and justly have been thinking of himself. His reward was fitting: the next time he returned to Spain, in 1842, was as the United States ambassador to Madrid.

Others in the meantime made use of the Navarrete material, and a few scholars were inspired to some original researches of their own. At least ten serious and substantial biographies followed Irving's in the course of the rest of the century (and at least twice that many books in English alone retelling the story for popular audiences); of particular note, especially because they move beyond the Irvingesque to the scholarly, are the biographies by the German Alexander von Humboldt in 1836–39, the French-American Henry Harrisse in 1884 and again in 1892, the Spaniard José Asensio y Toledo in 1888, and the American Justin Winsor in 1891, all important contributions to the now extensive world of Columbiana. (One might also note a singular book by Aaron Goodrich, in 1874, *A History of the Character and Achievements of the So-called Christopher Columbus*, substantially wrong in many of its presumptions but refreshing in being the first, I believe, to attempt to debunk—"What has hitherto been termed the history of a great man is but a gilded lie"—the Columbus mythologizing.) At the same time a great amount of new Columbiana came to light and was printed, most for the first time: Andrés Bernáldez's *Historia de los reyes católicos*, written about the Columbus years by a friend of the Admiral's, was first printed in 1856; Las Casas's *Historia de las Indias* was finally published and available to scholars worldwide in 1875, after more than three hundred years; the Cuneo manuscript describing the Second Voyage was first published in 1885; and in 1889 agents of the Librairie Maisonneuve of Paris found the single extant copy, lost for four hundred years, of the original Castilian printing of the Santangel Letter of 1493, the first translation of which into English was published in 1891. Two monumental achievements of scholarship crowned this period, the publication in Spain of forty-two volumes of additional documents from the Archives of the Indies in Seville, between 1864 and 1884 (followed by another series of twenty-five volumes between 1885 and 1932, providing a total of 3,807 documents); and the justly renowned *Raccolta di documenti*, thirteen volumes put out in Rome between 1892 and 1896 by Italian scholars supported by the Italian government, the first three volumes devoted to the complete writings of Columbus, in expert translations into Italian with first-rate scholarly apparatus by Cesare de Lollis.

Somehow, though, it wasn't the text of Colón's daily sailing records or the official documents from the archives that caught the public fancy; it was rather the scenes, whether fanciful or real, that made of Columbus that larger-than-life character, maltreated and triumphant, persevering and brave, glorious and unrecognized, who had in fact endured through the centuries from the sixteenth onward, only now given new life and historical stature by the pen of a gifted American storyteller. This was the figure who featured in more than several hundred poems written in English about Columbus in the remainder of the century (at least twenty of which appeared in book form, along with some twenty-eight in other languages), by such authors as James Russell Lowell, Walt Whitman, Ralph Waldo Emerson, Edward Everett Hale, Sidney Lanier, Joaquin Miller, Alfred Tennyson, and Arthur Hugh Clough;* in fourteen plays and seven operas, including one by Felicien David in 1847 and one by S. G. Pratt performed at the Metropolitan Opera in New York City in 1892; in the nine novels (one by James Fenimore Cooper, *Mercedes of Castile*) and three short stories that have survived; and, so one may imagine, in three rather important musical works of the time, Richard Wagner's *Columbus* overture of 1835, Antonin Dvořák's *Te Deum* chorale written for the New York City Quatercentennial ceremonies in 1892, and his Symphony No. 5 (later renumbered

---

*Algernon Charles Swinburne turned his hand to the subject, for a collection sponsored by the Italian Asiatic Society and a Milan publisher to commemorate the Quatercentennial; he wrote six truly pathetic lines and wisely gave up. More than six hundred poems were completed for that volume, however, and published in 1892.

9), *From the New World*, written for the Chicago Columbian Exposition of 1893 (and in a lesser but lasting piece of music, "Columbia, the Gem of the Ocean," written by David T. Shaw in 1843, published around 1855). And that is certainly the figure as well who stands in flamboyant gesture and heroic mien at the center of the innumerable paintings of this era that chose the Discoverer for their appropriately romantic themes—at least sixty-four such scenes (apart from the seventy-eight portraits then said to be in existence), according to the enumeration of Nestor Ponce de León in 1893, including perhaps the most famous, John Vanderlyn's 1846 *Landing of Columbus*, which was done (in Paris) for the rotunda of the U.S. Capitol, where it still hangs. About the artistic merit of these mostly grand canvases the less said the kinder, but it is appropriate to note that none of them is much concerned with historical accuracy—the Vanderlyn, for example, shows a Franciscan monk at the Guanahani landfall, although none such accompanied the voyage—and most, with some uncanny Irvingesque affinity, seem to choose just those events (the Barcelona entry, the Salamanca council) with the least historical foundation. (The Vanderlyn painting has done double duty: a reproduction of it is on the back of the first paper currency with Columbus on it, the $5 National Bank note of 1863, issued until 1875, which on the front has a scene of Columbus sighting land; Columbus appeared also on the front of the $1,000 U.S. note of 1869–80 and on the back of the $5 Federal Reserve note of 1914–22.)

It is said that after his visit to Peru and Chile as part of a papal delegation in 1823–25, a young Italian priest, Giovanni Maria Mastai Ferretti (later Pope Pius IX), complained that he knew of not one single stone or monument in either North or South America dedicated to the memory of the man who first discovered them for Europe. Obviously he had not heard of the column in Baltimore, but as far as we know there was at the time no other statue or plaque in Colón's honor on those continents, and in Europe but a single memorial, a bust on a large pedestal at the Municipal Building of Genoa, erected in 1821. That was a deficiency that was not long in being remedied.

It was remedied first, if we can trust the spotty historical records, in the lands Colón actually found, with a modest bust in Havana in 1828 and a statue in front of Government House, Nassau, in 1832. Next, in lands far from where he ever set foot, he was twice memorialized on the new Capitol in Washington: first, in 1846, with a marble group showing Columbus holding aloft a globe marked "America," on the east portico, said to be the first piece of statuary ever purchased by the U.S. government (it is, typically, inaccurate in dress and detail); then eighteen years later with a large bronze door at the main east entrance featuring scenes from the Discoverer's life, not all of them fanciful, and small portrait busts of the historians (including Irving) by whom his story was made known. Boston caused a small statue of Colón as a boy to be erected in Louisburg Square in 1849, and followed that with another in 1871, and Philadelphia put up a sizable monument for its commemorative world's fair of 1876. In Europe, Genoa naturally took the lead, dedicating a large monument and statue in 1862, and this was followed, surprisingly, by Liverpool, whose shipping interests erected a statue in 1866. By the time of the quatercentennial, at least according to those at the time compiling such data, there were twenty-eight major public monuments to Columbus in the United States (three each in New York City and Washington, D.C., two each in Baltimore and Boston, and one in Philadelphia, Chicago, St. Louis, Scranton, and Sacramento, plus thirteen unspecified), ten in the Caribbean* (including Santo Domingo, finally), two in Mexico, five in South America, and nineteen in Europe (three in France, seven in Italy, and nine in Spain, including six large monuments, four with statues of the Discoverer in various heroic poses atop, one of which, in Barcelona, is at 187½ feet the tallest in the world).

All in all, it seems like an extraordinary number of memorials and representations of a single individual, even for an age that apparently relished its statuary and its canvases. In fact, William E. Curtis, the director of the Bureau of the American Republics, a division of the 1893 Columbian Exposition, wrote then that it was "a fact that the effigy of 'the Admiral of the Indies' has been painted and carved more often, perhaps, than [that] of any other except the Saviour of Mankind, and that the world is reminded of its obligations to him by more monuments than have been reared to the honor of any other hero of history."

It was perhaps inevitable, certainly typical of the time, that such

---

*The statue of Colón facing the harbor at Port-au-Prince, Haiti, at the westernmost part of his Ysla Española, was toppled and thrown into the sea by demonstrators celebrating the overthrow of President Jean-Claude Duvalier in February 1986; on the empty pedestal someone attached a piece of paper reading, in Creole, *"Pa de blans en Hayti!"*—"No whites in Haiti!"

conspicuous attention should culminate in an attempt actually to have Colón recognized as an official saint by the Catholic Church. This move was largely initiated by a French writer, Antoine F. F. Roselly de Lorgues, with his *Christophe Colombe* in 1856, made more explicit in his *L'ambassadeur de Dieu et le Pape Pie IX* in 1874, and fastened upon as a worthy cause by various groups particularly in Italy and the United States, including an alliance of civic-minded American Catholics who established themselves as the Knights of Columbus in New Haven in 1882. In spite of such pressures (which continued until as late as 1918), the effort faced a number of serious difficulties—not least of which was Colón's unseemly alliance with Beatriz de Arana, which had produced an offspring without sanction of marriage, and the lack of proof of his having performed a genuine miracle, required for canonization—and in the end the Vatican apparently did not even begin the beatification process.*

1892   *Grover Cleveland was elected president of the United States for the second time, an act that he, and the nation, regretted just one year later, after the crash and panic of 1893.*

Alfred, Lord Tennyson, and Walt Whitman died; Pearl Buck was born.

Antonin Dvořák was installed as director of the Conservatory of Music in New York City, where he was to spend much of his time the first year composing his symphony From the New World *for the Columbian Exposition in Chicago.*

Rudolf Diesel, a German engineer, obtained a patent for his design of an internal-combustion engine that used crude oil instead of refined gasoline and proved efficient for large-scale means of transportation such as locomotives and ships; at the same time Henry Ford was at work perfecting his first automobile.

The first mass-produced picture postcard, developed for the Chicago exposition, was printed.

The population of the natives of North America was an estimated 4.5 million, no more than 500,000 of whom lived north of Mexico.

---

*In 1969 two saints were *removed* from the official Vatican calendar of canonization for lack of historical documentation as to their lives or miracles: St. George, patron of the church in which Colón and crew attended their last mass before sailing from Palos in August 1492, and St. Christopher, the Christ-bearer who inspired the Admiral's signature.

1892–93   To understand why the quatercentennial of the Discovery created such a stir, after two anniversaries had passed with apparent neglect and the third with only modest celebration, is to understand what America had become, what the Columbian Legacy had wrought, by the end of the nineteenth century. Columbus still served as the embodiment of the nation and the excuse for the kind of nationalistic fervor that inspired *The Youth's Companion* magazine that year to publish a "Pledge of Allegiance" specifically to mark the 400th anniversary; but the simple facts that nearly four times as much money was spent on the Columbian Exposition of 1893 as on the Centennial Exposition in Philadelphia seventeen years earlier and that it drew more than twice as many people suggest that out of the figure of Columbus the nation now made something more than just a patriotic symbol, something in fact that represented the official national deity, Progress, and such attendant seraphim as Science, Wealth, Power, and Civilization.

New York City led off the events of October 1892 with what the *Magazine of American History* the next month called a "monster celebration," five days of parades and floats and fireworks and speeches and military marches and naval pageants (and one unveiling and one opera) that attracted at least a million visitors (the city's population was then only twice that) and exceeded in scope anything the city had known before, "a spectacle of surpassing significance." New York put itself on display, the magazine said, as a "great commercial capital" that "stands in its glory to-day [as] a living, bustling, instructive monument to the honor of the pioneer of modern civilization." And then it used a picture of a Manhattan bank vault containing $72 million in gold to illustrate the speech of New York governor Roswell Pettibone Flower in which he said of the men of the First Voyage, "They dreamed of wealth, and here it is beyond imagination's farthest limit."

On Wednesday of that week, October 12, a memorial to Columbus was unveiled at the southwest corner of Central Park, in what was then rechristened Columbus Circle. This handsome column of Carrara marble, from Italy, with a statue by Gaetano Russo, an Italian (only Italian artists were invited to compete), was erected with money raised by the publisher of the New York *Progresso Italo-Americano*, from, as it says at the base, "the Italians resident in America." Its obvious provenance illustrates a social phenomenon that became more widespread and more exaggerated as time went on: the transformation, despite the obvious difficulties, of Cristóbal Colón into Cristoforo Colombo, a specifically Italian hero embraced both by native Italians hungry for progenitors of *their* new nation (united in 1861) and by the growing numbers of Italian immigrants in the United States eager to claim an authentic "American" figure as their own.

It was given to Chauncey Depew, president of the New York Central Railroad and principal agent for the Cornelius Vanderbilt fortunes, to put the imprimatur on the New York ceremonies. In a speech to operagoers at Carnegie Hall he exhibited considerable touchiness at a few less than idolizing articles that had recently been in the newspapers by historians such as Justin Winsor, then the leading Columbus scholar in America, and remarked, "If there is anything which I detest more than another, it is that spirit of critical historical inquiry which doubts everything; that modern spirit which destroys all the illusions and all the heroes which have been the inspiration of patriotism through all the centuries." The Quatercentennial, he argued, was not the proper occasion for such petty academicism. It was, rather, a time that "marks the wealth and the civilization of a great people," but even more than that, "it marks the things that belong to their comfort and their ease, their pleasure and their luxuries . . . and their power." Nothing could be clearer.

For the first time the federal government involved itself in the anniversary celebrations, with a joint resolution of Congress* and a declaration from President Benjamin Harrison calling upon citizens to observe the day at home, at work, and in school; Vice-President Levi Morton declared grandly to the nation that "we have added a new holiday to the American calendar . . . to be repeated at the expiration of each one hundred years to the furthermost limit of time." The government also issued a half-dollar memorial coin that month, the first commemorative U.S. coin ever struck, put on sale at a dollar to raise money for the Columbian Exposition; it had a portrait of Columbus in profile on one side (according to a U.S. Mint source, after a portrait in the Madrid Naval Museum) and the *Santa*

---

*In an attempt at historical accuracy, the congressional resolution called for national celebrations on the day of Discovery as it would be according to the modern calendar, that is, October 23 (though in this case the solons made it October 21, since the twenty-third was a Sunday that year and they felt the day should be marked particularly by schoolchildren). Such attempts, however, have never won popularity or recognition.

María on the reverse. The government also prepared its first commemorative stamp issue, an unprecedented printing of fifteen stamps
in a single series showing scenes of Columbus's life, from the sighting
of land on the one-cent to his profile portrait on the five-dollar
(though the latter was not of much practical use since the maximum
U.S. postage rate at the time was $1.28); this series was planned also
for the Columbian Exposition and since that had to be postponed it
was not released until the following year.

That great exposition proved to be so great that the city of Chicago
could not raise the money and complete the buildings in time for an
1892 opening, so the event had to be rescheduled for the following
spring. No one seemed to mind the wait, however, and when the
fair at last presented itself—officially known as The World's Columbian Exposition—it proved to be the most elaborate and extensive
yet undertaken in the world. On the opening day, May 1, 1893,
President Cleveland addressed a crowd estimated to be of more than
300,000 people, then concluded his remarks, exactly at noon, by
pressing a gold telegraph key with an inlaid ivory button that sent a
current starting the thousands of engines and gears and belts and
wheels that provided the electricity and drove the innumerable pieces
of machinery throughout the grounds. A contemporary account
reports:

> At one and the same instant the audience burst into a thundering
> shout; the orchestra pealed for the strains of the Hallelujah Cho
> rus; the wheels of the great Ellis engine in Machinery Hall com
> menced to revolve; the electric fountains in the lagoon threw
> their torrents towards the sky; a flood of water gushed from the
> McMonnies Fountain and rolled back again into the basin; the
> thunder of artillery came from the vessels in the lake; the chimes
> in Manufacturer's Hall and on the German Building rang out a
> merry peal, and, overhead, the flags at the tops of the poles in
> front of the platform fell apart and revealed two gilded models
> of the ships in which Columbus first sailed to American shores.

As that suggests, the whole event was an undertaking of superlatives. The site was a 664-acre stretch of parkland along Lake Michigan
(almost thirty times larger than the site for the Paris Exposition of
1855), on which were erected forty buildings for the main exhibitions,
some of immense size and all of elaborate ornamentation in high

Victorian style, and forty-two more for the displays of individual states, with another four score buildings and walkways for the exhibits of eighty foreign nations, colonies, districts, and corporations, all connected by canals and lagoons plied by gondolas and small steamboats. The cost of it all was an astonishing $30 million (as against $8 million each for the 1867 Paris and 1876 Philadelphia fairs)—just about the cost to build the Panama Canal more than a decade later —and it attracted nearly 24 million visitors, in a nation of 63 million people, the largest crowd for any single event in the history of the world to that point.*

It could not be said that Columbus the individual was entirely ignored amid all this. There was a large statue, *Columbus Taking Possession*, by Louis Saint-Gaudens at the main entrance of the chief administration building, a statue by Frederic-Auguste Bartholdi cast in silver (later melted down), and two smaller statues and a fountain frieze; a full-scale replica of the monastery of La Rábida outside Palos was provided by the Spanish government for a mere $50,000, with a copy of the original Capitulations, twenty-nine autograph letters of Columbus, one of his wills, and a copy of the *Profecías*; and in the lake were full-sized facsimiles of the three ships of the First Voyage (with a few added modern details, including hammocks and staysails, to ease the ocean passage from Seville, though in the event the *Niña* and *Pinta* were towed across). But the real point of the fair was the presumed end and glory for which Columbus had sailed—that is, those American exhibits devoted (in order of size) to Manufactures and Liberal Arts, Machinery, Agriculture, Transportation, Mines and Mining, Electricity, Horticulture, Forestry, and Fisheries. It was, in sum, an assemblage of modernity designed to convince the visitor, as one promotional pamphlet had it, "that all the marvels of the world, and the products of all the master geniuses in art and invention, are gathered there to delight and instruct—a very panorama of the possibilities of human ingenuity and persistent effort." How neatly a tribute to the Discoverer.

1893–1992 The past hundred years have not done much to change the position of Christopher Columbus as an American symbol—he is still the hero of scores of plays and operas and novels and poems,

---

*Almost a century later Chicago dropped out of competition for the 1992 World's Fair because it could not raise what it estimated was the $2.2 billion necessary for a repeat performance.

just as mythic as ever—but they have for the first time seen serious efforts to reassess his reputation in the light of the vast collection of new or previously unexamined documents. That reassessment, attempting finally to separate fact from fancy, has produced an unprecedented outpouring of scholarship on both sides of the Atlantic, an apparently endless flood of studies and monographs, some quite controversial, about every detail of the Discoverer's life and achievements, reaching its crest for the quincentennial. According to the count of Simonetta Conti in her 1986 bibliography, there were 3,271 articles and books published about Columbus and his times between 1880 and 1985, and some 800 of those were of sufficient scholarly importance to be included in the authoritative *Annotated Guide* put out by Foster Provost of Duquesne University in 1990.

Quite apart from the quantity, however, the quality of Columbian scholarship (leaving aside meretricious popularizations) has been of a reasonably high level, despite some nationalistic myopia and a tendency to succumb to the dreary debates over Colón's birthplace and the Landfall Question. Most of the basic documents have by now been published several times over, usually with proper scholarly apparatus, in one or another of the West European languages, and some have received several translations; the *Journal*, for example, which after its original English translation in 1827 did not have another treatment until the Hakluyt Society version by Clements Markham in 1893, has had eight English versions in this century, two in the past three years, and at least twenty-two translations into Italian, German, French, Portuguese, and modern Spanish, plus three transcriptions of the full manuscript and one complete reproduction in facsimile. The *Pleitos*, first published in 1892–94, has had a critical scholarly edition in Spanish in 1967, and the *Book of Privileges* a transcription and similar treatment in Spanish in 1951 and 1982, although neither has received scholarly treatment in English, and the *Pleitos* has never been translated; similarly, the *Book of Prophecies*, which both the Italians (1892) and the Spanish (1982) have reproduced and annotated, has yet to have an English version. (These and similar gaps presumably will be filled by the *Repertorium columbianum*, a project at UCLA under Fredi Chiappelli that is supposed to produce in the next decade a twelve-volume compilation and English translation of all of Columbus's writings.) At least six international symposiums devoted to Columbus have been held since 1950, and though the results have been predictably uneven it is safe to say that they have left no corner of Columbiana untouched. And at least three dozen books of first-rank scholarly importance have appeared, with more planned for the quincentennial and after; in English alone there have been substantial biographies by John Boyd Thacher (1903–04), Filson Young (1906, 1912), Salvador de Madariaga (1939), Daniel Sargent (1941), Samuel Eliot Morison (1942), G. R. Crone (1969), and Paolo Emilio Taviani (1985), with major ancillary volumes on various aspects of the Columbus corpus (again only in English) by G. E. Nunn (1924), Cecil Jane (1930–33), Otto Schoenrich (1949–50), Benjamin Keen (1959), Carl Sauer (1966), Alfred Crosby (1972), Troy Floyd (1973), and Fredi Chiappelli (1976).[1]

It has been said often in this period that original Columbian scholarship is over and there is no more to discover about the Discoverer, but the century has added a number of new details, including several letters written by Columbus and documents from Spanish archival sources. A notarial document showing that Columbus was a sugar merchant in Madeira and describing him unmistakably as "a citizen of Genoa" was uncovered in 1904; a 1513 map by the Turkish cartographer Piri Re'is, copied from a chart owned by "the Genoese infidel Colon-bo," was found in Istanbul in 1929, and it shows Española, Puerto Rico, and perhaps Cuba-an-island just off the coast of what is unquestionably a southern continent; the diligent searches in Spanish archives by Alice Gould in the 1920s and 1930s, amid papers that had been used as stable-bedding by Napoleonic troops in the Peninsular Wars and understandably left untouched thereafter, turned up a royal confirmation of Colón's presumed will of 1498 and several lists of crewmen on the First Voyage; and the historian Eugene Lyon in the 1980s found details about a 1498 voyage of the *Niña* that provided new information on her sails, rigging, and capacity. The condition of the various Spanish archives, with some records still uncatalogued and many still unread, and the renewed interest in the Discovery as its anniversary nears, make it seem probable that those finds will not be the last.

The most important effect of the new material and the new scholarship of this century has been to demythify Columbus the Discoverer and resuscitate Colón the Man, providing for the first time a much more complex, and more interesting, three-dimensional figure, including foibles, figments, and failures. Henry Vignaud, the American amateur historian who was a notable leader in the process of reassessment in the early part of this period, described it thus:

> The history of Columbus, as it came to us from Columbian sources, gathered such weight and credit that the only Columbus who was known was the one he himself and his intimates had depicted, whose career they had traced, and whose work they had explained.
>
> But criticism, which is no respecter of persons or things, turned at last her searching glance on the Columbian legend and closely scrutinized the sources whence it came. In addition to the documents of Columbian origin hitherto relied on, she discovered others of an independent character which were at singular variance with the former. . . . By studying these new sources of information it was found, little by little, that many of the facts set forth by Columbian traditions were controverted, and that it was necessary to submit the tradition itself to a close and severe inspection.

That inspection led to the realization that much of what Colón had said about himself, and what he presumably told his son Fernando and his admirer Las Casas, was simply not true, and much else was highly dubious or quite unprovable. Thus scholars of this century have inevitably come to be concerned with a reexamination not only of the Colón version of events—this is where the Vignaud school has held forth—but of the character and personality of the man himself, with a frankness and a skepticism that were not deemed suitable before.

The new areas of inquiry have been many, some frivolous even, but among the most important have been: Colón's religiosity, whether genuine or contrived to please the Sovereigns, and the importance in his enterprise of messianic zeal and mysticism rather than the lure of gold or love of adventure; the extent to which Colón is to be seen as a "medieval" as opposed to a "Renaissance" man and whether his ideas of geography and colonial governance, among others, are to be regarded as modern inventions or archaic survivals; the amount and kind of Colón's pre-Discovery reading and learning, the scholarly influences that made up the Grand Scheme, and the languages he may have known and been literate in; the character and skill of his navigation and the degree to which his successes were due to fixation and good fortune and his failures (to go west, for example, when he could have) to myopia and ill fortune; and his physical health, the cause and nature of his illnesses, and particularly the extent to which this might have affected his perceptions and judgments, his very sanity, on later voyages. I do not mean to suggest that such questions have received due attention from all serious writers of this era, for it must be said that most biographies still dwell upon the complexities of Colón's character lightly if at all—it is still common to avoid talking of Colón on land when at all possible and to fore-shorten his later years to a single deathbed scene—but they have informed the best of modern scholarship, most notably among the Spanish themselves, and certainly have served to provide a fuller and more realistic, if sometimes darker, portrait of the Discoverer.

Thanks also to the new "searching glance" of criticism, a number of old Columbian disputes have been largely laid to rest during this period. The argument over Colón's birthplace, for example, has died down considerably since the Spanish Academy of History in 1928 found that the documents produced earlier to support a Castilian background were forgeries, and the City of Genoa put out a 288-page volume in 1931 full of documents that established its case as Colón's native city; the odd Portuguese or Greek claimant does still surface, however, and there are still those who seriously advance theories of there being *two* Colóns, both Spanish-born but one of noble ancestry. And the question of the authenticity of some major documents—Fernando's biography, Las Casas's *Journal* transcription, the 1498 will, the *Profecías*—has been largely settled in favor of accepting the existing texts until further facts appear, although real questions still linger about the presumed correspondence between Colón and the Florentine humanist Paolo Toscanelli.

That still leaves plenty of room for contention, of course, and many issues remain in lively dispute: Colón's early years at sea, and whether he made the voyages (e.g., to Iceland and Africa) he claimed; the sequence of events during his first years in Spain and how "obdurate" (or merely preoccupied) the Spanish court was; the importance of the Pinzóns before and during the First Voyage and the motives for Martín Alonso Pinzón's "desertions"; the site of the 1492 landfall; the legitimacy or injustice of Bobadilla's treatment of the Colóns; the whereabouts of the Admiral's mortal remains. Perhaps the two most vexatious questions of the century, which can be phrased with de-ceptive simplicity, are still: what did Colón think beforehand he was going to discover? and what did he think afterward that he had discovered? The destination issue, as we know, has produced considerable scholarly heat, with the work of Vignaud (1905, 1911, 1921), Jane (1930), and Romulo Carbia (1936) to uphold the heading-for-new-lands view, and the work of Thacher (1903–04), Emiliano Jos (1935), Morison (1942), and Taviani (1974) on the sailing-for-Asia side, among many others; Morison's view, primarily because of the overall standing of his biography, is probably the more generally accepted today. The New-World-or-not question has received much less attention, and it is likely that the conventional idea of Colón going to his deathbed thinking he had found Asia is still the predominant (if, as seems clear, erroneous) one, but I suspect that the weight of scholarly opinion will shift on this point, perhaps in the light of Quincentennial reconsiderations.

One historiographical molehill threatens to become truly mountainous: the question of whether Colón was a Jew. There is, as I have indicated, no substance for such a notion, and yet it is raised repeatedly in both popular and serious writings and has exercised at least a half a dozen historians in the past century. The subject seems to have begun percolating late in the last century, and was directly taken up by Vignaud in 1913, Francisco Martínez Martínez in 1916, and Jacob Wasserman in 1929, until it finally became the pretext for a long biography by Madariaga in 1939. The argument has so little foundation that it properly belongs in the same corner of Columbiana where Colón is held to be Polish, resting as it does on the entirely unprovable supposition that Colón was a *converso* to Christianity, and I am sure it would not survive but for the concurrence of the expulsion of the Jews and the start of the First Voyage. Yet it surfaced once again in a book by the noted Nazi-hunter Simon Wiesenthal in 1972 (translated as *Sails of Hope* in 1973) and since then has enjoyed a strangely resilient currency. Specific undermining of the theory is to be found in the works of Antonio Ballesteros y Beretta (1945) and Armando Alvarez Pedroso (1942).

As with the explosion of scholarship, so has there been an explosion of creative works about Columbus, though I hasten to add that the two have almost nothing to do with one another. By my count there have been at least 143 such works so far in the twentieth century, including 11 book-length poems, 2 short stories, 39 novels, and no fewer than 51 plays and operas, a rather extraordinary tide to which the United States has contributed well over a third. It cannot, for all its bulk, be called a very distinguished lot, in fact it is astonishingly mediocre, but it does contain a competent opera by Darius Milhaud and Paul Claudel in 1927, a Louis MacNeice radio play in 1944, a show (words and music) by Meredith Willson in 1969, novels by C. S. Forester in 1940 and Cedric Belfrage in 1964, and a skillful poem by the bibliographer Foster Provost in 1989. And one would be seriously amiss not to mention a 1919 poem, "The History of the United States," written by Winifred Sackville Stoner, Jr., which contained the, alas, immortal lines

> *In fourteen-hundred and ninety-two*
> *Columbus sailed the ocean blue.*

During this same period the national celebration known as Columbus Day finally evolved into the annual shopping spree and Italo-American and Hispanic parade-day it has become. The idea of such a holiday had its supporters, largely in the Knights of Columbus, ever since the Quatercentennial, but it took the determined work of a first-generation Italian in Denver, a printer and part-time politician named Angelo Noce, to lobby through the first official noncentennial Columbus Day, decreed by Colorado governor Jesse F. McDonald in 1905 and made a state law two years later. Through the efforts of Noce, who traveled widely around the country, and Italo-American societies in many cities and states that took it over as a special ethnic cause, Columbus Day became an official holiday in fifteen states by 1910, thirty-four by 1938, and an official national holiday, latterly one of the movable ones, with a federal proclamation by Franklin Roosevelt in April 1934. Inasmuch as schools are thus closed in celebration every year and have been for more than half a century, one might presume that the historical reasons would be conveyed to the children who are thus excused; a 1986 survey by the National Endowment for the Humanities, however, found that *one-third* of the nation's seventeen-year-olds did not have the faintest idea of even what century it was that the Discovery was made and 4 percent imagined that it occurred after 1850.*

---

*By 1938, Columbus Day was celebrated also by twenty-two countries in South and Central America and the Caribbean; today it is a holiday throughout the area, usually designated in Spanish-speaking areas as El Día de la Raza, The Day of the Race. Canada, however, does not celebrate it, and Newfoundland's Discovery Day, June 20, is a commemoration of John Cabot's presumed landfall.

No matter; Columbus has at least a firm place on the map, if not in the classroom. A 1988 survey determined that there were as many as 65 geopolitical entities in the United States using "Columbus," "Columbia," or some variation thereof in 37 states (plus, of course, the District of Columbia), including 50 cities, 9 counties, 5 townships, and 1 Air Force base, but *not* including the rivers, capes, mountains, falls, lakes, glacier, peak, and plateau, nor the infinitude of streets, avenues, highways, circles, bridges, parks, plazas, squares, and buildings (nor, of course, the broadcast network, symphony orchestra, jazz band, string quartet, encyclopedia, movie company, colleges, railroads, banks, museums, journals, or space shuttle). Outside the United States, "Columbus" or "Colón" or derivations are used for one nation (Colombia), one national capital (Colombo, Sri Lanka, so named by the Portuguese in 1517), one major province (British Columbia), a series of small islands (in the Mediterranean, off Spain), an archipelago (in the Galápagos, where there are also places named after other figures associated with Colón, including Bartolomé and the Pinzóns), and towns and cities in every country of South America; pride of place, so to say, goes to Cristóbal, a suburb of Colón, Panama. In the English-speaking world, Christopher Columbus has given his name to more geographic places than any other actual figure in the history of the world, with the exception only of Queen Victoria; in the United States he surpasses all other eponyms except Washington.

That the Quincentennial that ends this latest century will be celebrated with more commotion and ceremony than ever before there is no question, though whether it will have much to do with the man it is supposed to commemorate there is real reason to doubt.

The official events, carefully planned, expensively mounted, and much ballyhooed, will involve every nation on both sides of the Atlantic and some few on the Pacific as well. As of 1989, thirty-two nations and twenty U.S. states and colonies had established official Quincentennial commissions, and they had authorized a bewildering array of celebrations, parades, pageants, fireworks displays, conferences, symposiums, exhibitions, projects, monuments, museum shows, contests, scholarships, grants, books, newsletters, magazines, scholarly compendiums, television programs, commemorative coins and stamps, memorabilia, sailing races, cruises, guided tours, and myriad other forms of observance, a great many hewing to the same spirit of gain that characterized the original voyage, though some of them guided by its sense of discovery and learning as well. Seville is to be host to the Columbian world's fair, with exhibits from a hundred nations at a cost of something like $4 or $5 billion; Genoa is planning its fifth international conference of Columbianists, an exposition of Columbiana collected worldwide (including a greenhouse with all the plants of the New World), and a new *Santa María*; Barcelona is to be the site of the Summer Olympic Games, dedicated to the Admiral; the Dominican Republic is hoping, after a delay of fifty years, to erect a 390-foot lighthouse in Santo Domingo, at a cost of some $10 million, that will be the largest Columbian monument in the world; the city of Columbus, Ohio, will hold something it calls "AmeriFlora '92," the nation's first international floral and garden exhibition, with $50 million worth of plants; the Spanish government will launch a communications satellite named, perhaps with no irony, after the sailor who first saw land and was deprived of his reward by his captain; an opera entitled *The Voyage*, written by the minimalist composer Philip Glass and Broadway playwright David Henry Hwang has been commissioned by New York's Metropolitan Opera for a premiere in October 1992; twelve full-scale replicas of the original ships have been planned, one commissioned by Japan, and Spain's official trio is expected to cost $4 million, about sixty times the amount paid for the entire first expedition;* and a private group in New York City has begun ceremonies to honor, so help me, the "marriage" of the Columbus monument in Barcelona to the Statue of Liberty in New York Harbor in 1990, to be followed by a honeymoon trip and what is called a "twin-monument birth" (one monument in each hemisphere) in 1992.

Obviously this foofaraw will exceed, in length, money, fervor, technology, publicity, self-congratulation, and bathos, any previous commemoration; Father Charles Polzer of the U.S. Quincentenary

---

*The project to build replicas of the First Voyage ships was originally overseen by Admiral Cristóbal Colón, seventeenth-generation descendant of the original admiral and the first direct descendant to serve as an officer in the Spanish navy. He was gunned down in Madrid in 1986 by unknown assailants, but his son, a navy lieutenant with the same distinguished name—and the hereditary titles of Admiral of the Ocean Sea, Governor of the Indies, and Duke of Veragua—stepped into the project and was slated to command the *Santa María* on her transatlantic voyage in 1992.

Jubilee Commission has described the attention drawn to it as "widespread and monumental," an understatement.

It is not, however, without its dissenters. Many of those who know well the cultures that once existed in the New World have reason to be less than enthusiastic about celebrating the event that led to the destruction of much of that heritage and the greater part of the people who produced it; some have insisted on labeling the events of 1492 an "encounter" rather than a "discovery" and having it so billed for 1992, some others have chosen to make it an occasion to direct attention to native American arts and achievements, and others still are planning to protest the entire goings-on as a wrongful commemoration of an act steeped in bloodshed, slavery, and genocide. The United Nations General Assembly, given several opportunities to endorse the Quincentennial, has been diplomatically stymied—by disputes about whether Colón was the first discoverer (Iceland and Ireland have both insisted on precedence), whether a commemoration that glorifies a colonialism from which many nations still suffer is apt, and whether West European world hegemony is a fit phenomenon for other continents to honor—and has taken no official action at all. And some of those who have sought to draw attention to the environmental destruction wrought in the aftermath of the Discovery, particularly members of various Green movements in the industrialized world, have decided to use the occasion to draw into question the nature of a civilization that could take the earth so close to ecocide.

In all of this, it seems certain, Cristóbal Colón will be quite lost, even Christopher Columbus quite hard to find, as his accomplishments are made the malleable and serviceable clay into which the breath of one cause or other, one patriotic mission or other, one testimonial to modernism or other, is blown. But that is in keeping, of course, for it is as the source of just such symbols that Colón has functioned through the five centuries of his life-after-death: from the time that he was made into a super-Hercules by Oviedo and Martyr to the time he became the early modern hero for the English who needed instigation and the Italians who needed inspiration; in the epics by which he became the personification of America as in the biographies that made him stand for wealth and progress; by the pageants that turned him into the image of this nation's skill or that one's genius and the celebrations that made him the agent of capitalist ingenuity and persistence . . . and beyond. It may be fitting, or only richly ironic, that, having seen the world as utilitarian, so has the world seen him.

Walt Whitman imagines Columbus on his deathbed, in Valladolid, in that May 1506, knowing the end is near, staring into the future:

> *What do I know of life? what of myself?*
> *I know not even my own work, past or present;*
> *Dim, ever-shifting guesses of it spread before me,*
> *Of newer, better worlds, their mighty parturition*
> *Mocking, perplexing me.*

Ah, but no, Colón, they do not mock and should not perplex: indeed, they live out your legacy, your destiny, more successfully and more grandly, if more terribly, than you ever could have dreamed.

1992 *Worldwide population is estimated at more than 5.6 billion.*

Rainforest area in the Western Hemisphere, originally 3.4 billion acres, is down to 1.6 billion, and going fast, at the rate of 25 million acres a year, or 166 square miles a day; U.S. forestland, originally more than a billion acres, is down to 500 million commercially designated acres, some 260 million having gone for beef production alone.

Topsoil depletion and runoff in the United States reaches a rate of 80 million feet per day, nearly 30 billion tons a year.

Twenty-five years after the U.S. Endangered Species Act went into effect, listing 500 of the several thousand threatened species in the country, twelve of the protected species have become extinct and 150 more are losing population at a rate that will lead to extinction within a decade. Two hundred threatened plants native to the United States have become extinct in the last five years. At least 140 major animal and bird species have become extinct since 1492, including four species of whales, seventeen varieties of grizzly bears, seven forms of bats, Eastern and Oregon buffalo, great auks, sea otters, sea minks, Eastern elks, long-eared kit foxes, Newfoundland and Florida wolves, Eastern cougars, Arizona and Eastern wapiti, Badlands bighorn sheep, heath hens, passenger pigeons, Jamaica wood rails, spectacled cormorants, Puerto Rico blue pigeons, Eskimo curlews, Puerto Rican conures, Carolina parakeets, Antigua and Guadeloupe bur-

rowing owls, Guadeloupe red-shafted flickers, ivory-billed wood-peckers, Berwicks wrens, Tecopa pupfish, harelip suckers, longjaw ciscos, and blue pike.

Wilderness areas, officially designated at 90 million protected and 50 million unprotected acres, have been reduced from about 2.2 billion acres in pre-Columbian times—a decrease of roughly 96 percent.

The population of the native people of North America is about 20 million, only 1.5 million outside of Mesoamerica.

Epilogue

BY THE 1780s, the question of the importance of the Discovery and its impact on the world had become a topic of some debate in the intellectual circles of France and in the writings of the reigning *philosophes*, an extension of the old *sauvage noble–bête sauvage* debates earlier in the century. It was so provocative a subject, in fact, that Abbé Guillaume Reynal, the author of a highly popular four-volume study, *A Philosophical and Political History of the Settlements and Trade of Europeans in the Two Indies*, decided to see if the matter could be set to rest, in appropriate *philosophe* tradition, by asking the learned men of the Academy of Lyons to hold an essay contest, invite entrants on all sides, and award a prize, which he would himself contribute, to the one they judged had made the best case. The topic of debate: "Was the discovery of America a blessing or a curse to humankind?"

Unfortunately the precise workings-out of that contest have not survived the ebb and flow of history, which was turbulent indeed in France, we may remember, at that time. It is known, however, that entries were submitted in 1787 and 1788, that the Lyons savants were unable to declare an outright winner, and that only eight essays, with a fair mixture of opinion on the several sides of the issue, survive. Of those survivors the one that is easily the most learned and lucid, as well as the most persuasive, is the one by the *abbé* himself.

Reynal was willing to concede some positive effects of the Discovery. "This great event hath improved the construction of ships, navigation, geography, astronomy, medicine, natural history, and some other branches of knowledge; and these advantages have not been attended with any known inconvenience." Moreover, the domains of the Indies "have given splendor, power, and wealth, to the states which have founded them," although it was true that great expenses had been lavished "to clear, to govern, [and] to defend them," and that eventually they would all inevitably assert their independence and be lost to the "country which has founded its splendor upon their prosperity." As well, "Europe is indebted to the New World for a few conveniences, and a few luxuries," but those were "so cruelly obtained, so unequally distributed, and so obstinately disputed" that they could not really be said to be worth the price in human lives and disruption—and "before these enjoyments were obtained, were we less healthy, less robust, less intelligent, or less happy?" And finally, although "the New World has multiplied specie amongst us," the cost was high for the peoples of the Americas, who still "languish in ignorance, superstition, and pride" and have lost "their agriculture and their manufactures" to boot, and even for Europe, where the benefits were largely overwhelmed by a concomitant inflation.

On the negative side, the effects loomed larger. For one, "the bold attempts of Columbus and of Gama" created "a spirit of fanaticism" for "making discoveries" in search of "some continents to invade, some islands to ravage, and some people to spoil, to subdue, and to massacre." Those who succumbed to such adventures became "a new species of anomalous savages" who "traverse so many countries and who in the end belong to none . . . who quit their country without regret [and] never return to it without being impatient of going out again," all so that they might "acquire riches in exchange for their virtue and their health." "This insatiable thirst of gold," moreover, had "given birth to the most infamous and the most atrocious of all traffics, that of slaves," the "most execrable" of crimes against nature. And with all that "the machine of government," overextended in resources both at home and in the Americas, had "fallen into confusion," with the poorest states being forced to languish "under the yoke of oppression, and endless wars," while those who were "incessantly renewed" by Indies treasure "harassed the globe and stained it with blood."

Such was the indictment from the learned philosopher. And here, in full, was his conclusion:

Let us stop here, and consider ourselves as existing at the time when America and India were unknown. Let me suppose that I

address myself to the most cruel of the Europeans in the following terms. There exist regions which will furnish you with rich
metals, agreeable clothing, and delicious food. But read this history, and behold at what price the discovery is promised to you.
Do you wish or not that it should be made? Is it to be imagined
that there exists a being infernal enough to answer this question
in the affirmative! Let it be remembered that there will not be a
single instant in futurity when my question will not have the
same force.

Let it be remembered.

Reynal was not alone in his condemnation. The thought had
haunted some few right from the start—Montaigne, for example, in
the expansionary sixteenth century, who said he was afraid "that we
shall have greatly hastened the decline and ruin of this new world by
our contagion"—and was not absent even from some, such as Henry
Harrisse, in the ebullient nineteenth century: "As to the sum of
happiness which has accrued to humanity from Columbus' discovery,
philosophers may deem it light and dearly purchased" . . . It is even
a mortal question whether the two worlds would not have been far
happier had they remained forever unknown to each other." The
vantage point of five hundred years allows us to appreciate the wisdom
of such few far more acutely than their contemporaries ever could.

It may be that all such judgments, including Abbé Reynal's, are
in the end fruitless: history is what happened, not what should have
happened. Certainly there are those who argue, with some merit,
that it is foolish to think that Europe could have been anything but
what it was, done anything but what it did. Why should one suppose
that a culture like Europe's, steeped as it was in the ardor of wealth,
the habit of violence, and the pride of intolerance, dispirited and
adrift after a century and more of disease and famine and death beyond
experience, would be able to come upon new societies in a fertile
world, innocent and defenseless, and not displace and subdue, if
necessary destroy, them? Why should one suppose such a culture
would pause there to observe, to learn, to borrow the wisdom and
the ways of a foreign, heathen people, half naked and befeathered,
ignorant of cities and kings and metal and laws, and unschooled in
all that the Ancients held virtuous? That, according to J. H. Elliott,
who had wrestled with just this question, would be asking "a great

deal of any society," but certainly more than the society represented by Europe in the fifteenth or even the sixteenth century.

Of course one may still wonder, and wonder long, about what that says about this society, the one now dominant in America, and the West, and the world. And one may even legitimately wonder, if it is not too painful, about what might have been. Was not Europe in its groping era of discovery in the fifteenth century in fact in search of salvation, as its morbid sonnets said, or of that regeneration which new lands and new peoples—and of course new riches—would be presumed to provide? Was that not essentially the arrangement Colón sold to the Sovereigns, confirmed in the Capitulations?

And there *was* salvation there, in the New World, though it was not of a kind the Europeans then understood. They thought first that exploitation was salvation, and they went at that with a vengeance, and found new foods and medicines and treasures, but that proved not to be; that colonization and settlement was salvation, and they peopled both continents with conquerors, and it was not that either; that progress and power and technics wrested from the new lands was salvation, and they made mighty nations and towering cities in its service, but it was not even that.

The salvation there, had the Europeans known where and how to look for it, was obviously in the integrative tribal ways, the nurturant communitarian values, the rich interplay with nature that made up the Indian cultures—as it made up, for that matter, the cultures of ancient peoples everywhere, not excluding Europe. It was there especially in the Indian consciousness, in what Calvin Martin has termed *"the biological outlook on life,"* in which patterns and concepts and the large teleological constructs of culture are not human-centered but come from the sense of being at one with nature, biocentric, ecocentric, and where there was myth but not history, circular rather than linear time, renewal and restoration but not progress, imaginative apperception far more subtle than science, understanding without words or even ideation, sacred rather than material interpretation of things, and an interpenetration into earth and its life-forms that superceded an identification with self or species.

It was there then, when Colón first encountered what he intuited, correctly, to be "in all the world . . . no better people nor better country," and it is there even now, despite the centuries of batterment, for those who stop and bend and open to hear it. It was

salvation then, it might possibly be salvation now. Certainly there is
no other.

An Irokwa woman in New York City, Doris Melliadis, said fifteen
years ago:

> Now they come to gather for the coming disaster and destruction
> of the white man *by his own hands*, with his own progressive,
> advanced, technological devices, that only the American Indian
> can avert. Now the time is near. And it is only the Indian who
> knows the cure. It is only the Indian who can stop this plague.
> And this time the invisible will be visible. And the unheard will
> be heard. And we will be seen and we will be remembered.

So we may hope. There is only one way to live in America, and there
can be only one way, and that is as Americans—the original
Americans—for that is what the earth of America demands. We have
tried for five centuries to resist that simple truth. We resist it further
only at risk of the imperilment—worse, the likely destruction—of
the earth.

There exists a nineteenth-century "bible" with the title *Oahspe*,
said to have been influential among the Irokwa of the last century,
which purports to be the words of "Jehovih" transmitted through a
Dr. John Ballou Newbrough in 1881, in which Christopher "Columbo" is mentioned as playing a special part in the Design of God.
In "one of the plans of God for redeeming the world"—a world
which He acknowledged had fallen upon sinful times—Columbo was
visited by the heavenly hosts and inspired by them "to go with ships
to the westward, across the ocean," there to find for Europe "a new
mortal anchorage," "a new country, where only the Great Spirit,
Jehovih, is worshipped." He makes the momentous voyage, but the
news of it is discovered by the agents of Satan, "the false Kriste,"
and his angels "did set the rulers of Spain against Columbo, and had
him cast in prison, thus breaking the chain of inspiration betwixt
Columbo and the throne of God"—and it is these evil spirits that
instead lead the people of Europe across the ocean "to the countries
Columbo had discovered" and there, to the consternation of Heaven,
did "evil take its course."

So it may have been. However one may cast it, an opportunity
there certainly was once, a chance for the people of Europe to find

a new anchorage in a new country, in what they dimly realized was the land of Paradise, and thus find finally the way to redeem the world. But all they ever found was half a world of nature's treasures and nature's peoples that could be taken, and they took them, never knowing, never learning the true regenerative power there, and that opportunity was lost. Theirs was indeed a conquest of Paradise, but as is inevitable with any war against the world of nature, those who win will have lost—once again lost, and this time perhaps forever.

Acknowledgments

IN THE SEVEN YEARS I have spent working on this book I have been helped by countless people, wittingly and otherwise, but I would particularly like to express my gratitude to these special few: Ben Apfelbaum, David Belsky, Jerry H. Bentley, David Buisseret, Gabriella Canfield, Richard Cornuelle, J. H. Elliott, W. H. Ferry, Lydia Freeman, David Gurin, David Henige, Janis B. Holm, Anna Jardine, Karen Kennerly, John E. Kicza, Joseph Laufer, Virginia Leonard, Pat and Dick Mackey, Mark Mirsky, Victor Navasky, the Newberry Library (Richard Brown, David Buisseret, Frederick Hoxie, Tina Reithmaier), Anne Paolucci, John Paulits, William Pomerantz, Foster Provost, Nan Rothschild, Norman Rush, Kalista Sale, Rebekah Sale, Roger Sale, William M. Sale III, Trudie Schafer, Elisabeth Scharlatt, Barbara Schneider, Joseph Spieler, Harrison Starr, Paolo Emilio Taviani, Gerald Theisen, Lionel Tiger, Frederick Turner, William Whitefeather, Bill Whitehead.

I owe special gratitude, for believing in this effort when not all agreed, to my agent, Joy Harris, and my editor, Elisabeth Sifton.

Notes

All short titles in the following notes refer to books listed on pages 393–94.

Chapter One 1492 (I)

1. The exact dimensions of the three ships are, and probably will forever be, unknown: there are no contemporary plans or drawings or documented descriptions or recorded measurements. The 1979 discovery, in Seville's Archives of the Indies, of a sheaf of documents called the *Libro de Armada* has provided some details about the *Niña*'s cargo, leading the marine historian Eugene Lyon to estimate her as 67 feet long, with a beam of 21 feet, a drift of just under 7 feet, and a cargo capacity of between 58 and 60 tons; he also reports that she may have been fitted out with a fourth mast, at least for the later 1498 journey detailed in the *Libro*, the additional spar being for a smaller countermizzen sail (*National Geographic*, vol. 170, November 1986). A recent work in this area, by Carla Rahn Phillips of the University of Minnesota, revises the size estimates down from this and most previous guesses; after a study of more than a hundred ships of the period, she estimates the *Pinta* to have been 55 to 65 feet in deck length, 16 to 18 feet abeam, and roughly of 75-ton capacity; the *Niña* at 49 to 59 feet, 14 to 16 feet, and 55 tons; and the *Santa María* at 58 feet, 19 feet, and 108 tons (in Gerace, *Columbus*, pp. 69ff). However, it is appropriate to note that as of 1985 there were no fewer than forty-four books in all languages specifically devoted to the kinds and sizes of ships Colón sailed in on his four voyages, and each book could put forth its own dimensions.

None of the many reproductions of these ships that have been made in the past —three ships for the Chicago Columbian Exposition of 1893, a *Santa María III* in 1927, a *Santa María IV* moored in the Barcelona harbor since 1951, and a copy of that shown in the United States—and none of those built for the Quincentennial, three *Santa Marías* in Spain alone—can possibly be but faint and erroneous replicas of the originals, however careful their research and construction.

2. The motivation for the expulsion of Jews from Spain, thus depriving it of many of its most important intellectuals, businessmen, bankers, and artisans, has long been a mystery. I suggest that the reasons lie in the problems of the prominent *conversos*, important in the courts of both Castile and Aragon though somewhat more prominent in the latter, faced with the growing pressures from the Spanish Inquisition.

The Inquisition was begun in 1478 as a means of ensuring religious unity in the fledgling state of Spain, and its explicit targets were the *conversos*, ostensibly Christians but suspected of containing large numbers of backsliders, pretenders, crypto-Jews, and Judaizers who practiced their Hebraic rites in secret. No *conversos*, not even the highest placed, were free from this pressure: Juan de Santangel, the *escribano de ración* for the court of King Ferdinand and one of his most important financial backers, was hauled before an Inquisition court in July 1491 and sentenced to wear a yellow robe through the streets as a sign of guilt and contrition, and all those in his family who escaped harsher terms were forced to undergo such public humiliation. It does not take much imagination to suppose that these powerful men eventually decided that a strategy of getting rid of the Jews was essential for them to remain in and secure their positions of power: without Jews around, *conversos* would have neither models nor lures for reversion and the Inquisitional courts would have less reason for suspecting them of being likely to do so. As J. H. Elliott has put it, *conversos* "afraid that their own position would be jeopardized by the back-sliding of their bretheren" decided on expulsion since it "would remove temptation from all those New Christians who still looked back uneasily to their abandoned faith"; he calls it nothing less than "the last, and greatest, triumph of the zealous *conversos*" (*Imperial Spain*, St. Martin's, 1963, pp. 96–98).

3. There is some reason to doubt that Colón ever made a journey to Iceland, despite assurances of those such as Morison (*AOS*, vol. 1, p. 32) that this was merely "one more adventurous voyage" of his. The only sources we have for it are Fernando and Las Casas, and Fernando quotes a note he says his father wrote thus: "I sailed in the year 1477, in the month of February, a hundred leagues beyond the island of Tile [Thule, or Iceland], whose northern part is in latitude 73 degrees north and not 63 degrees as some would have it be. . . . And at the season when I was there the sea was not frozen, but the tides were so great that in some places they rose 26 *braccia*, and fell as much."

The difficulties: First, the latitude, for all Colón's certainty, is wrong; Iceland *is* at 63 to 66½ degrees north. Second, there are no 26-*braccia* (50-foot) tides in Iceland, in fact nothing greater than 15 feet; there *are* occasionally tides that high at the Avenmouth, near Bristol, where Colón might have gone, as he says once in his *Journal* (December 21) and again in a postil in Pope Pius II's *Historia rerum*, but this reference seems clearly to be Iceland. Third, the seas of Iceland in February were not likely to be unfrozen, even though we do know that it was an especially mild winter that year; but at any rate it would have been the most extraordinary voyage to go to Iceland in midwinter at all, and no such sailings are recorded between England, or Ireland, and Iceland. Fourth, Colón almost assuredly could not have gone a hundred leagues "beyond"—i.e., west of—Iceland, for that would have taken him to Greenland, a fact he could scarcely have avoided mentioning; some have tried to make this passage read that Iceland is a hundred leagues (in circumference), but that figure is so far off as to be meaningless. And last, when Colón in his *Journal* boasts of having "seen all the East and West" in his travels (December 21), he says nothing about Iceland, which is peculiar if he had actually been there.

(Further discussions of the matter are in Vilhjalmur Stefansson's *Ultima Thule: Further Mysteries of the Arctic*, Macmillan, 1940, and in Taviani, *Columbus*.)

4. There is no way to be certain about the date of Colón's birth using existing documents, despite the assurances of those such as Morison who insist on August–October 1451. That date is based on two notarial depositions (see Morison, *JAOD*, pp. 7–9), one of 1470 and one of 1479, but the former says only "over 19" and the latter "twenty-seven years old, or thereabouts" ("*viginti septem annorum, vel circa*"), much too vague to provide a certain year, nor is there any reason to

suppose that Colón himself was necessarily sure, or that he was reckoning in the modern style instead of the Latin (in which both first and last year are included). Of them, the Italian Columbianist Taviani says authoritatively: "All we can say with certainty is that it [Colón's birth] happened between 1450 and 1452" (*Columbus*, p. 233).

There are additional sources of confusion. The contemporary historian Andrés Bernáldez, who knew Colón, says he was "about 70" when he died in 1506 (i.e., born in 1436). Colón himself in 1501 said he had "navigated for 40 years" and elsewhere that he went to sea at fourteen, according to Fernando (i.e., a birthdate of 1446–47); but his other figure (in 1492) of "at sea for twenty-three years" provides a still later date (1455) if we add the same fourteen years. The obvious and safest conclusion is that we do not know and likely never will.

5. There is real reason to doubt that this "prologue," which Las Casas places at the front of the *Journal*, was written first, and some reason to suppose it was written at the end of the journey. Its arch and formal tone has a different rhetorical character from the *Journal* entries, and it has the pontification of a document written after the accomplishment of discovery rather than before. It also mentions the terms by which the sovereigns "ennobled [past tense] me so that henceforth I might call myself Don and be Grand Admiral of the Ocean Sea," a title he would have had a right to only *after* his discoveries.

Many Columbus scholars believe it properly to be an epilogue or at least a writing from late in the journey (see *Studi colombiani*, vol. 2, pp. 89ff); some (including Cesare de Lollis and Cecil Jane) even doubt its authenticity altogether, suggesting that it may have been added on by Las Casas—or by someone clumsier still, since it refers to the expulsion of the Jews in January instead of August and calls the Sovereigns "King and Queen of the Spains [*dlas españas*]," a locution virtually unheard of at the time (although Peter Martyr did once use "Queen of the Spains" in 1488, he was an Italian, that was his first year in Spain, and he did not use this form again). Morison, however, maintains that the internal evidence "strongly suggests that he [Colón] wrote this prologue shortly after his departure" (*JAOD*, p. 48n), and cites in particular the fact that he praises his "three vessels well suited for such an enterprise," even though he had troubles with the *Pinta* and often complained about the *Santa María*. Morison also says that Colón's promise in the prologue to "record everything in a picture, by latitude . . . and longitude" must have been made in a moment of rashness before the journey, since he "notoriously failed to do" this in the *Journal* itself; but a straightforward reading of that passage shows rather that Colón is promising in some *other* document, not the *Journal* at hand, to "make a new chart of navigation . . . and, further, to compose a book, and record everything," etc.

6. On a number of points Morison's defense of India-all-along (see chiefly *AOS*, vol. 1, chap. 6) is shaky. He argues, for example, that Colón would have had no motive for contriving his deceit after the fact, although it seems obvious that only by asserting the claim that he had reached the Indies could he persuade the Sovereigns to sponsor a second voyage, the returns from the first being so meager; this subterfuge, indeed, he had been planning all along, according to Fernando's biography.

Morison says also that Colón would have had to go back and falsify the *Journal* after the discovery and there are no indications that this was done; the trouble here is that we don't know how much is Colón and how much Las Casas in the *Journal*, and the first time we get the word "Indians" in a direct transcription in Colón's words is not until October 17, five days after landfall, by which time the "Indies" deception could have been long decided upon. And to counter the argument that Spain could not have sent such a scanty and underarmed flotilla to confront the Grand Khan, Morison argues that Isabella and Ferdinand were "simple" and *did* suppose that Colón needed only present himself, and his credentials, to have the Khan and fellow potentates fall at his feet; such "simplicity" is not found elsewhere in the reign of these monarchs, nor does Morison ever claim to perceive it elsewhere.

Chapter Three   1492 (II)

1. The idea that Colón was deceiving his fellow sailors makes sense and is consistent with his later behavior, but it does not answer all of the puzzling questions that surround the alternative figures of the "false log." (For a lengthy if ultimately unsatisfactory analysis of the problems, plus a critique of other proffered explanations, see David Henige and Margarita Zamora, *The Americas*, vol. 46, no. 1, July 1989.) To pose a few: why did Colón begin this deception on September 10, just three days into the voyage and long before he would have needed to fool, or calm, the crew? Why are there no figures given for ten of the thirty-four days at sea, and on two days insignificant changes from 14 leagues to 13 and 14 to 11? Why were the variations so disparate, ranging from 54 to 94 percent of the "actual" leagues, and the longest not always diminished the most? Why, in the Las Casas text, are only a quarter of the distances in words, and the others written in either Roman or Arabic numerals, and why are a third of the verbs used in connection with them in the conditional? And why is there no mention of the Admiral's duplicity in the *Pleitos*, although the crown lawyers would surely have had access to Colón's original log and would surely have wanted to make out their antagonist as an untrustworthy liar? Questions abound; answers do not exist.

2. The Landfall Question, once it began to be raised after Navarrete's publication of the *Journal* in 1826, has occupied literally hundreds of researchers in dozens of countries, and in the past decade with increasing heat. *National Geographic* (November 1986) has provided the most recent full-scale claimant, Samana Cay, after a five-year, million-dollar research effort, but it has persuaded only a few of those who have studied the question, and criticisms have been sharp and cogent.

It is probably accurate to say that most Columbian scholars have accepted the island formerly known as Watlings as the most likely landfall site, and upon the evidence gathered for this theory the island's name was officially changed to San Salvador (Colón's name for his landfall) in 1926. The choice was given further weight by the imprimatur of Admiral Morison in his classic 1942 biography, an opinion he reinforced and made absolute in his subsequent edition of the *Journals* (Morison, *JAOD*).

Yet Morison's scholarship on this point is shoddy—there is no other word for it—and in some places dishonest. One may find some fairly elaborate criticisms in a recent landfall book (De Vorsey and Parker, *In the Wake of Columbus*), but the following may suggest their gravamen: (1) Morison mistranslates the *Journal* in at least half a dozen cases, some through inadvertence but some clearly to fit his preconceptions of what the landfall and the following route were—e.g., he mistranslates *isleta* (islet) as "island" in the reference to Guanahani, since his choice for that landfall is Watlings and that plainly is not an islet. (2) Morison claims that Colón couldn't fix a latitude by using the North Star, which is an impossibility for a navigator of that age; Colón's figures in the *Journal* (which *are* confusing) probably can be explained by the inference that he used a kind of quadrant that Morison never knew about, and perhaps misread a tangent scale for the degree scale, not by his ignorance of celestial reckoning. And Morison's conjecture that Colón made the mistake of shooting from the star Alfirk instead of Polaris is laughable: Alfirk is almost invisible to the naked eye and impossible to mistake for the bright Polaris. (3) Morison tries so hard to make Watlings fit in with Colón's landfall description of a "very level" island (it is in fact hilly) that he omits Kerr Mountain as well as its elevation (*AOS*, vol. 1, p. 299) from his map in the *Journal* edition (*JOAD*, p. 66); thereafter he makes Long Island large and flat and verdant when it is extremely thin, hilly, and relatively sparse. (4) Morison is reduced to speculating that Colón used a "land league" from time to time, so as to explain *Journal* entries violently at odds with his own reconstructions; there is no evidence in any European language at any time for such a league, nor does Colón ever suggest that he is using such a measurement.

Chapter Four
Europe (II)   *"The Earth Shall Quake Before Them"*

1. It has become fashionable in recent years to argue that this phrase is not meant quite so harshly as it sounds. The Hebrew *yirdu*, it is said, connotes "descent" as well as "control" and "dominion" and thus suggests some affinity of human and animal; other phrases—Adam is supposed "to till and to keep" the Garden, to "dress it and . . . keep it"—soften the heavenly suggestion of domination; and anyway, the ancient rabbis never interpreted "dominion" as permitting the Hebrews to act in an environmentally destructive way. Perhaps; but the Old Testament is so replete with images of violence and power and fear connected with nature not by accident, surely, but because it shows a religion established precisely to distance itself from others more animistic and "pagan" and intertwined with nature. (See especially Paul Shepard, *Nature and Madness*, Sierra Club, 1982; Lynne White, *Science*, March 10, 1967; John Passmore, *Man's Responsibility for Nature*, Scribner's, 1974; Merlin Stone, *When God Was a Woman*, Harcourt, 1976.)

It has become fashionable also to suggest that what the Bible really had in mind is expressed not in Genesis but, for example, in Psalm 24 ("The earth is the Lord's and the fullness thereof") and that it conveys the idea not of dominion but of *stewardship*, as in the heavenly covenant "which I make between me and you and every living creature that is with you." Perhaps; but this seems to me to require some creative reading; in any case, the concept of steward, either in its root English sense ("sty warden") or its Greek sense of *oikonomos* ("house manager"), suggests a warden-manager role very like a dominator-lord one. Ultimately, the important point is that whatever the Bible or the Ancients may have said or meant or done, medieval Christians interpreted the Bible to permit and encourage a dominant role for humans over nature.

Chapter Five 1492–93

1. While we bury the label "Arawak" for these Caribbean people, it might also be opportune to jettison "Lucayan," a contrivance apparently fashioned by Las Casas to describe the people of the Bahamian chain as distinct from those of Cuba and Española. There is no justification for creating such a separate tribal group for people who were clearly Tainan in language and custom, and who seem to have been in regular contact with their colleagues on the larger islands; at most we could follow Irving Rouse's idea of calling them sub-Taino, or western sub-Taino (see Gerace, *Columbus*), but that seems unnecessarily and artificially precious, too.

2. There is considerable historical controversy over how acute an observer of New World nature Colón was. One school is represented by the nineteenth-century German naturalist and historian Alexander von Humboldt, who regarded Colón as a shrewd and accurate observer and describer who "retained a profound feeling for the majesty of nature" even if he was more perceptive of people than their surroundings. Another is characterized by Filson Young, a Columbus scholar at the turn of this century who scorned Colón as being "childlike" in his descriptions and noted that his sense of comparisons was limited to whether something was like Spain's or not.

In a much cited but peculiar article in the *Proceedings of the American Philosophical Society* (July, 1941), Leonardo Olschki manages to come down firmly on both sides. On the one hand, he notes, "Columbus's own laconic and summary descriptions of landscapes, localities and events" are "devoid of exactness or color" and "lacking in color and detail," and he decides that "the insufficiency of details, as well as his exaggeration of dimensions and proportions, reveal that the natural aspects of the newly discovered islands did not especially attract the attention of the Admiral." The reason, Olschki says, is largely that Columbus was still part of a medieval, prescientific tradition in which "nature constitutes an accessory element of the narrative, being merely a frame for human activity, life and events," and so it was normal that he "followed the anthropocentric tendencies of his epoch." But then Olschki goes on to argue that Colón somehow develops an "increasing insight into the peculiarities of life and nature in the islands" and even looks "at reality with a spiritual eye and with a breadth of interest and a multifariousness of impressions that has no parallel in the history of voyages and discoveries." Colón's view of "natural aspects" became, he says, "personal and original . . . determined by an uncommon power of realistic observation," and his descriptions of Indians are "very detailed," "depicting their life and habits with a keen and expressive realism." One wonders how Olschki supposed he reconciled those quite different points of view.

Chapter Six 1493–94

1. All that we have any reason for believing about this reception at the Barcelona court is the account of Peter Martyr, the Italian humanist then serving as a tutor for the royal family; he says merely that Colón "was honorably received of the king and queen, who caused him to sit in their presence, which is a token of great love and honor among the Spaniards." The numerous other stories—of the "triumphal entry" into the city, "all the populace turned out to greet him" (as depicted, for example, on the bronze doors of the U.S. Capitol in Washington), and Ferdinand and Isabella praying and weeping with the Admiral—are fabrications, created decades later. Fernando Colón, for example, who was *not* there (and was four years old at the time), has a florid account about how "all the Court and the city came out to meet" the Admiral and how at his audience the Sovereigns "rose from their thrones as if he were a great lord, and would not let him kiss their hands." Las Casas, who also was not there, has his own fanciful embellishment (see p. 239).

2. The gullible like to adduce the death of Giovanni da Verrazzano on a Caribbean island in 1528 as proof of cannibalism, and some, such as Morison, accept it unquestioningly (complete with "a crowd of natives . . . licking their chops," in *Southern Voyages*, p. 315). But the voyage was entirely undocumented—we don't even know where his death took place, aside from some unidentified island—and the "cannibal" part is based solely on an account put forth in 1551, twenty-three years later, by an Italian poet who says he learned of it from Girolamo da Verrazzano, who accompanied his brother and claimed to have been an eyewitness; even that does not assert that Girolamo actually saw any flesh-eating, or indeed anything more than his brother's killing by unnamed Indians on an unnamed beach while he himself was in a longboat in a tossing surf several hundred yards away. Alberto Magnaghi has a persuasive article in the *Enciclopedia italiana* of 1937 effectively disputing the cannibal story; see also Marcel Trudel, *The Beginnings of New France*, McClelland & Stewart (Toronto), 1973.

3. The whole question of syphilis has vexed and fascinated the medical and historical professions for centuries. The most careful and developed analysis I know is in Alfred Crosby Jr.'s *The Columbian Exchange* (Greenwood [Westport, CN], 1972), where an entire chapter is devoted to the matter; Crosby rather tentatively sides with those who believe the devastating strain of this disease originated in the New World and may fairly be regarded as the Indians' revenge for the devastation and disease visited upon them.

4. Vespucci, a perplexing figure in the history of exploration, has had great champions and fierce detractors. The entire truth of his career is still unknown, but several conclusions seem reasonable.

First, he probably did make three voyages to the Western Hemisphere, one with Alonso de Hojeda in 1499 and two with Gonçalo Coelho along the South American coast in 1501–02 and 1503–04, but he almost certainly did not sail to, and "discover," South America in 1497, when records show him safe in Spain. Second, he was an able navigator (in spite of some wild theories to which his name is appended) and a man of sufficient skill and learning to have served as the first *piloto mayor* for the

Spanish Crown in 1508–12. Third, he was almost certainly the author of the four manuscript letters in his name (Vaglienti, 1500; Cabral, 1501; Bartolozzi, 1502; and Conti, 1502), which, although they contain exaggerations and some variant mythologizing, also contain some accurate New World descriptions. And finally, he was almost certainly not the principal author of the two works that made him famous (*Mundus novus*, 1502, and *Quattro viaggi*, 1505), both of which are full of wild tales and lies and specious science and are now held to be the work of some unknown pirate in Italy (possibly a Giovanni Giocondo) whose fanciful elaborations were chiefly responsible for the books' popularity.

Of course Vespucci is not to be blamed for the fact that Martin Waldseemüller came upon a copy of the *Quattro viaggi* around 1507 as he was putting together a new edition of Ptolemy, and determined that Vespucci was the first to discover the new continent in the Ocean Sea, which should therefore be called "*Amerige* or *Land of Americus*, or *America*" (Morison, *Southern Voyages*, p. 289). Waldseemüller may have given Vespucci this credit on the basis of the false claim that he had been to South America in 1497, or because Vespucci was the first explorer there to realize that this was indeed "a fourth part of the world." There was almost no way for him to have known that one Cristóbal Colón had found the southern continent on his Third Voyage in 1498, before any of Vespucci's genuine voyages there, or to know that Colón had declared it to be an "*otro mundo*"; Colón's journal and summary letter of that expedition were not printed until the nineteenth century and the voyage is only cursorily mentioned in the pirated version of Peter Martyr's "First Decade" of 1504, where, in the original, Martyr says, "Whether [his discovery] be continent or not, the Admiral does not much contend" (Arber, *First Three Books*, p. 90).

Waldseemüller, incidentally, eventually learned the truth, and in his 1513 edition of Ptolemy Colón is credited with the discovery of the mainland.

Chapter Eight   1500–06

1. Of those four copies, one in vellum was sent to be stored in Las Cuevas; one perhaps in vellum was given to his son Diego, then a page of the court, presumably to pass on to the Sovereigns; and two copies were sent to Nicolò Oderigo (or Odorico), a Genoese friend, presumably to show to the Bank of San Giorgio in Genoa—with whom Colón had obviously been dealing, no doubt about shipments back and forth from Española—so that its officers could collect from the crown money they had lent to Colón if the need ever came (although why *two* copies were necessary for this has never been explained). A discussion of the document and a facsimile of the title page may be found in Thacher, vol. 3. The first printing of the book was in the nineteenth century, from one of the San Giorgio copies, translated into Italian and then into English, in 1823, as *Memorials of Columbus* (Giovanni Batista Spotorno, Ponthenier [Genoa] and Treuttel and Winter [London]).

2. There was considerable communication among cosmographers in Spain and Italy around this time, and enough interest in Italy about the Western discoveries to inspire Bartolomé to go to that country after his brother's death in 1506; but it is not necessary to establish any direct links between the Colóns and the cosmog-

rapher Giovanni Contarini or the engraver Francesco Roselli to believe that the Contarini map is a fair expression of the Admiral's ideas. On that map—introduced with a verse, incidentally, that also confirms the newness of the hemisphere ("Stay, traveler, and behold new nations and a new-found world")—Colón's Tierra Firme is shown clearly as a large southern continent, beginning a few degrees above the Equator, labeled "Terra Crucis" on its eastern coast. To the north are both the Greater and Lesser Antilles, including Cuba clearly as an island, and about 20 degrees to their west is Cipango (Japan). Above them all, in a huge landmass beginning with a faintly Florida-like projection and then running off in a long southwesterly coastline, is Asia, with various Chinese cities labeled ("Cianaba," "Magna," "Kathay," etc.). All that is as the Admiral would have had it, but there are also two entries very much at odds with his vision: the discovery of South America is credited to "the most noble lord Pedro Alvares [Cabral] . . . in 1499 [actually 1500]" and a label off the far west of Asia says "Christopherus Columbus . . . sailing westwards . . . betook himself to this place ["Cianaba," Marco Polo's Chamba] which as Christopher himself . . . asserts, holds a great store of gold." Neither of those ideas could have come directly from Colón, since he would certainly have claimed credit for the discovery of South America himself and would not have imagined he was ever 100 degrees *west* of Tierra Firme where the map places "Cianaba." Nonetheless, the rest of the map so accords with what the Admiral suggests as his cosmographical image at about this time that I think we may at least take it as a fair representation of his thoughts, if not anything directly influenced by his own pen or hand.

It is pertinent here to confront the question of maplets attributed to Bartolomé Colón, collected and printed by Alessandro Zorzi in 1525 or so. Zorzi says that these little sketches were drawn from a map given to a Brother Jerome in Rome in 1506 by Bartolomé (though he does not say they or the original map was *drawn* by him), and on the basis of that some historians have claimed that they are Bartolomé's work and show the geographic conceptions of the Colón brothers at the time of the Admiral's death. The maplets are certainly not by Bartolomé, who we have reason to believe was for a time a mapmaker: they are terribly crude; the location of the Equator is inconsistent and misleading; the Caribbean islands are misplaced, and there isn't even any Cuba or Cipango. Whoever turned out these maplets, they can't represent Bartolomé's idea of the world, much less Cristóbal's. (The best treatment of this issue is John Bigelow, "The So-Called Bartholemew Columbus Map," *Geographical Review*, vol. 25, 1935.)

3. I do not know of a single complete critical study of the seafaring talents of the Admiral of the Ocean Sea, though E. G. R. Taylor's introduction to vol. 2 of Jane has some excellent scathing analysis. But consider a few obvious elements of such a study. Start with the fact that the Admiral lost five of the seven ships he took with him on the two most important and most extended voyages (one on the First, all four on the Fourth). He was continually in error on reading the heavens to find out where he was, sometimes making errors so egregious that his proponents have to assume he was confused about what stars to shoot from or what kind of degree to use; on the First, Third, and Fourth Voyages he gave latitude readings that are remarkably wrong, and at one point on the last he even declared that Veragua, some

9 degrees from the Equator, was "the same distance from the pole as the Equator."
And he repeatedly went to the wrong latitudes at the wrong times, as on the return
trip of the First Voyage, when he sailed the North Atlantic at its worst period, or
the outward passage of the Third Voyage, when he got himself stuck in the Doldrums
for two weeks, or the return passage of the Second, which took an agonizing three
months.

4. Colón's financial holdings are difficult to sort out, but there is no question
that his estate was worth a great deal and that his wealth at the time of his last will
was sizable, considering that it might have been in the neighborhood of $200,000
in pre-Depression dollars, roughly equivalent to $4 million in 1990 dollars, and that
an experienced ship's captain of Colón's time would be earning (in pre-Depression
dollars) perhaps $350 a year. We know, furthermore, that when Diego drew up *his*
will, in 1509, there was no doubt that he was a wealthy man, and he did not inherit
the whole estate.

When Colón's father, Doménico, died, sometime between 1494 and 1500, he died
poor and in debt, and in 1500 his estate was sued for money owed; whatever wealth
the Admiral had assembled before that date—and this was before the gold strike—
he did not feel it sufficient to use to relieve his father.

The figure of $15,000 for Colón's one-tenth of the gold profits due the crown is
estimated from Las Casas's estimate of 450,000 *pesos de oro* a year in 1502–09, or
9,000 ($27,000) as Colón's share; and from records for 1502 of exports of 200,000
pesos and for 1504 of 14,000 pesos, which would mean Colón's share was 4,000
($12,000) in the former year and 1,400 ($4,200) in the latter. (The figures for gold
exports from the islands are given, as complete as can be contrived, in Troy Floyd's
valuable book, *The Columbus Dynasty in the Caribbean, 1492–1526*, New Mexico,
1973.)

5. In this codicil, whose authenticity is not in dispute, Colón mentions that "when
I went from Spain in the year 1502, I made an order and *majorat* of my property
[the one presumably authorized by the crown]," but no copy of such a document
has ever been found. Instead, we have a copy of a will of February 22, 1498, printed
by Navarrete in 1825 from an original he says he saw but which was subsequently
destroyed, plus a royal confirmation of that will from September 1501, the original
of which has been found and authenticated. One scholar who has investigated this,
Enrique de Gandia, had decided that this 1498 will may not be entirely genuine and
that the form as Navarrete has printed it is not to be trusted (*Historia de Cristóbal
Colón*, Buenos Aires, 1942); other authorities, however, including Antonio Ballesteros y Beretta (*Cristóbal Colón y el descubrimiento de America*, Salvat [Barcelona/
Buenos Aires], 1945, vol. 1, p. 121) pronounce it authentic. Salvador de Madariaga
(*Christopher Columbus*, Oxford, 1939) offers the theory that it is a later forgery
based on the 1502 will, but does not explain the 1501 confirmation. This 1498 will
is printed in full, with the codicil, in Young, *Columbus*. Morison discusses it in
JAOD, and Taviani in *Columbus*.

The references to Beatriz, incidentally, which include the remark that she is "a
person to whom I am under very great obligation" and the assertion that "this matter
weighs heavily upon my soul" but the reason "is not fitting to write here," have

never been explained. Nor, in spite of his great attention to the details of other bequests, why he grants her only an unspecified "provision."

6. It is barely possible that the figure of St. Christopher at the western end of the Juan de la Cosa map of 1500 bears the likeness of the Admiral, with whom de la Cosa sailed, as was claimed in the nineteenth century, on uncertain authority, by R. H. Major in his *Select Letters of Christopher Columbus* (Hakluyt, 1847); and a Genoese numismatist, Gaetano Avignone, declared in 1892 that a bronze medal with a seaman on it done around 1505 was actually a portrait of Colón, possibly by the Modenese artist Guido Mazzoni, though there is no available evidence to give this story any credence, either. Aside from those two slim suppositions, there is no known contemporary portrait of the Admiral, none that we have any reason to think was even done in the Admiral's lifetime, not to mention in his presence. At least eleven portraits of the sixteenth century have been put forward as representations of Colón—most of them quite different from each other, of course—and the earliest that we can presumptively date is the "Giovian" portrait owned by Count Alessandro de Orchi, which would have been done sometime in 1551–56, since it was not included in Giovio's *Elogia* in 1551 but was reported to have been sent to the Uffizi Gallery by 1556.

7. The fate of Colón's remains is unknown and probably unknowable, though new attempts have been made for the quincentennial year to determine the truth.

The Santo Domingo casket has been opened and examined several times, and the fact that it contains a small lead bullet has led some to argue that it surely bears the authentic bones—since Las Casas says Colón was wounded in the battle off Portugal from which he swam ashore in 1476, and Colón himself in the *Lettera Rarissima* says "my old wound opened up" (though with no better evidence than that). An orthopedic surgeon from Yale who examined the coffin in 1960 reported that he found therein the bones of a man five feet, eight inches tall, with a large head, but he could make no positive identification and in fact suggested that the remains were of *two* bodies, identities unknown; hardly helpful.

Chapter Nine 1506–1606 (I) *The Columbian Legacy*

1. Aside from the works in his lifetime that mention Cristóbal Colón (nineteen versions of the Santangel Letter; Nicolo Scillacio on the Second Voyage; the *Lettera Rarissima*; and works by M. A. Sabellico, 1498, 1504, and later; J. F. Foresti, 1503 and later; Peter Martyr, 1504 and later; and Raffaele Maffei, 1506), the following is as complete a list as is possible to compile on the 142 printed volumes (and 385 editions and imprints) that appeared in Europe between 1506 and 1606, by author. The compilation is based on the John Carter Brown Library's *European Americana* (1980–82), vols. 2 and 3, supplemented principally by Joseph Sabin's classic *Dictionary of Books Relating to America*, Henry Harrisse's *Biblioteca Americana Vetustissima* and his *Notes on Columbus*, Justin Winsor's *Narrative and Critical History of America*, John Parker's *Books to Build an Empire*, and E. G. R. Taylor's *Late Tudor . . . Geography*. (See note to p. 221 below.) Repeated dates mean different imprints; "(x2)" means normally two editions of the same imprint.

Abbot, George, London, 1599, 1600, 1605
Alvarez, F., Antwerp, 1558
Baptista Mantuanus, Paris, 1509, 1512
Barros, João de, Lisbon, 1552; Venice, 1561
Barrough, Phillip, London, 1601
Benzoni, Girolamo, Venice, 1565(x2), 1572; Geneva, 1578, 1579, 1581, 1586;
 Basel, 1579, 1583; Frankfurt, 1594(x2), 1595(x2), 1597(x2); Wittenberg, 1606
Beuther, M., Basel, 1582
Bielski, M., Cracow, 1551
Bizzarri, P., Antwerp, 1579(x2)
Boemus, Johann, Venice, 1560, 1564, 1566, 1573, 1585; Geneva, 1586, 1604
Boissard, Jean Jacques, Frankfurt, 1597
Bonsi, Lelio, Florence, 1560
Bruno, Giordano, London, 1584
Buonfiglio Constanzo, Giuseppe, Venice, 1604
Capilupi, I., Antwerp, 1574
Caprioli, Aliprando (ill.), Rome, 1596
Carion, Johann, Swabia, 1537; Antwerp, 1537
Castellanos, Juan de, Madrid, 1589
Cataneo (Catanaei), Mariae, Rome, 1514
Cecchi, G. M., Florence, 1583
Cesalpino, Andrea, Rome, 1602–03, 1605, 1606
Chiabrera, Gabriel, Venice, 1591, Venice, 1605, 1606
Colón, Fernando, Venice, 1569, 1571
Conestaggio, Girolamo, Genoa, 1585; Munich, 1589; Besançon, 1596, 1601; London, 1600; Frankfurt, 1602
Coppo, Pietro, Venice, 1528
Croce, Giovanni, Venice, 1573, 1574, 1605
Cunningham, William, London, 1559
Doglioni, Giovanni, Venice, 1601
Dolce, L., Venice, 1561
Dordoni, G., Pavia, 1568
Eden, Richard (comp. and tr.), London, 1553, 1555, 1572, 1576, 1577
Emili, P., Paris, 1548, 1549, 1581; Basel, 1569, 1572, 1601
Falloppius, Gabriel, Padua, 1563–64
Foglietta, U., Rome, 1572, 1579; Genoa, 1579, 1585, 1597
Fontaine, Charles, Paris, 1554, 1559
Foresti, J. F., Nuremberg, 1506; Venice, 1506, 1513, 1524; Paris, 1535
Fossetier, J., Antwerp(?), 1525(?)
Fracastoro, Girolamo, Florence, 1530
Fregoso, B., Milan, 1509; Antwerp, 1565; Basel, 1567
Galvão, Antonio, Lisbon, 1555, 1563, 1601
Gambara, Lorenzo, Rome, 1581, 1583, 1585
García Matamoros, A., Alcalá, 1553
Garibay y Zamolloa, E., Antwerp, 1571

Garimberto, G., Venice, 1549; Lyons, 1559

Giglio, G., Venice, 1565

Gilbert, Humphrey, London, 1576

Giorgini, Giovanni, Iesi, 1591, 1596

Giovio, Paolo, Venice, 1548; Florence, 1551, 1554(x4); Granada, 1568; Basel, 1575, 1577, 1577, 1580, 1596

Giustiniani, Agostino, Genoa, 1516, 1537

Glen, Jean Baptiste de, Liège, 1601

Goes, D. de, Louvain, 1540, 1544

Gohory, Jacques, Paris, 1581

Gómara, Francisco López de, Saragossa, 1552, 1553(x2), 1554; Antwerp, 1554; Rome, 1556; Venice, 1557(x2), 1560(x2), 1564, 1565, 1576, 1599; Paris, 1568, 1569(x2), 1577, 1578, 1580, 1584, 1587, 1605

Grynaeus, Simon (comp.), Basel and Paris, 1532; Basel, 1534, 1537, 1555

Guicciardini, Francesco, Florence, 1561(x2); Venice, 1564; Basel, 1566, 1574, 1599; Paris, 1568, 1577; Bern, 1574; Baeza, 1581; London, 1579(x2), 1599; Dordrecht, 1599; Treviso, 1604

Hakluyt, Richard (comp.), London, 1582, 1589, 1598, 1599, 1600

Hall, Joseph, Frankfurt, 1605

Herrera, Antonio de, Madrid, 1601, 1601, 1601, 1612; Valladolid, 1606(x2)

Interiano, P., Lucca, 1551, 1551

La Popelinière, L. V. de, Paris, 1584

Laudonnière, René de, Paris, 1586; London, 1587; Frankfurt, 1591, 1603

Le Ferron, A., Paris, 1549(x2)

León, Andrés de, Valladolid, 1605

Le Pois, A., Paris, 1579

Lindschoten, John Huighen van, London, 1598

Lloyd, Humphrey, London, 1584

Madrignani, Angelo, Milan, 1508

Maffei, Giovanni Petri, Florence, 1588, 1589; Venice 1588, 1588, 1589; Cologne, 1589, 1590, 1593, 1595; Lyons, 1589, 1604; Ingolstadt, 1589; Bergamo, 1590; Antwerp, 1605

Magno, M. A., Naples, 1516

Malvenda, Tommaso, Rome, 1604

Manuzio, P., Venice, 1557; Paris, 1558

Martyr, Peter (Anghiera), Seville, 1511; Alcala, 1516, 1530, 1530; Basel, 1521, 1533, 1582, 1587; Nuremberg, 1524; Paris, 1532, 1587; Venice, 1534; Antwerp, 1536; London, 1555, 1572, 1576, 1577

Maurolico, F., Venice, 1543

Montalboddo, Fracanzano da, Vicenza, 1507; Geneva, 1508; Nuremberg, 1508(x2); Milan, 1508, 1508, 1512, 1519; Paris, 1515(x2), 1516, 1521, 1535; Venice, 1517, 1521

Münster, Sebastian, Basel, 1550–98 (18 eds. in German), 1552–65 (5 eds. in French), 1550–72 (5 eds. in Latin); London, 1553, 1572, 1574, 1576; Prague, 1554; Venice, 1558, 1575; Paris, 1575(x2); Cologne, 1575

Nauclerus, J., Cologne, 1564

Nicolay, N., London, 1585

Oviedo, Gonzalo Fernández de, Toledo, 1526; Seville, 1535; Salamanca, 1547, 1549; Paris, 1555, 1556; Valladolid, 1557

Padilla, J. de, Seville, 1521

Panciroli, G., Amberg, 1599

Pantaleon, H., Basel, 1550, 1572

Parmenius, Stephen, London, 1582

Passe, C. van de, Cologne, 1598

Paulus Middelburgensis, Fossombrone, 1513

Peckham, George, London, 1583

Petrarca, Venice, 1507

Peucer, K., Wittenberg, 1560; Antwerp, 1584; Lyons, 1584

Porchacchi, Tommaso, Venice, 1572, 1575, 1576, 1590

Ralegh, Walter, London, 1596

Ramusio, Giovanni Battista (vol. 3), Venice, 1556, 1565, 1606; Rouen, 1598

Resende, G. de, Lisbon, 1545, 1596

Rosaccio, G., Brescia, 1593; Venice, 1602

Ruscelli, G., Venice, 1566

Sabellico, M. A. (Coccio), Paris, 1509; Basel 1538; Coimbra, 1550

Sacro Bosco, Juan de, Paris, 1515; Alcala, 1526; Florence, 1572

Saint-Gelais, M. de, Lyons, 1574

Schöner, Johann, Nuremberg, 1533, 1551

Schottus, Andreas (ed.), Frankfurt, 1603–08

Seall, Robert, London, 1563

Servetus, Michael (ed.), Lyons, 1535

Stamler, Joannes, Augsburg, 1508; Venice, 1540(?)

Stella, Julius Ceasar, London, 1585; Lyons, 1585; Rome, 1585, 1590; Seville(?), 1586; Basel, 1590

Surius, L., Cologne, 1566, 1568; Paris, 1571

Szekely, I., Cracow, 1559

Tarcagnota, Giovanni, Venice, 1562

Tasso, Torquato, Parma, 1581(x5); Paris, 1581, 1595(x3); Madrid, 1587; Venice, 1593, 1595, 1600(x2); London, 1600; Rome, 1601

Testamento do Don Cristobal Colon, Memorial, Madrid(?), 1600(?)

Thilo, V., Basel, 1589

Thou, Jacques Auguste de, Paris, 1604(x3), 1606–09

Valori, Filippo, Florence, 1604

Veer, G. de, Amsterdam, 1598, 1598, 1598; Nuremberg, 1598; Paris, 1599; Venice, 1599

Venegas de Busto, A., Toledo, 1540

"Vespucci" (pirated), Florence, 1505–06; St. Die, 1507(x2), Strasbourg, 1509, Lyons, 1517–18

Villifranchi, Giovanni, Florence, 1602

Voerthusius, Johannes, Frankfurt, 1573

Waldseemüller, Martin (ed.), Strasbourg, 1513, 1522

Wytfliet, Corneille, Louvain, 1597; Douai, 1603
Zapata, Luis, Seville, 1566

Chapter Ten   1506–1606 (II)   England

1. This story is also used by Fernando and Las Casas, with very similar language, both saying that in fact Henry VII *accepted* the offer, but that by the time Bartolomé returned to Spain with that news the Discovery had already been announced. The story has no independent verification, although there is nothing to disprove it, and it seems far more likely that Henry would have rejected the offer than accepted it.

2. Sebastian Cabot's career is further illustration of the English-Spanish links of that period. He returned to Spain in 1512 or so, where he worked for the Spanish sailing office and was named its *piloto mayor* in 1518, but he kept up his ties with England, particularly with mariner friends he knew from his days in Bristol, some of whom sailed with him on a 1526–30 voyage to South America. Around 1548, sensing a change of mood in England—or perhaps having come under fire for inadequacies in his official duties, for which he faced a board of inquiry in Seville in 1545—he went back to London and began rounding up support for new English voyages to China, along "secret" passages to the north he assured everyone he knew well. Eventually he succeeded in getting what were called "merchant adventurers" of London to back a Cathay Company of 1553–56, of which he himself was governor and which undertook a voyage along the northeastern route to China but ended up, somewhat prosaically, in Russia instead. That venture, while it did not prompt any further explorations for another generation, did serve to open up a modest trade with Russia and to reward its instigator with a royal pension of £134 a year. Cabot died in 1557, a figure of triumph and tragedy, of bravery and bitterness, of great vanity and secretiveness, whom not a few have likened to Cristóbal Colón.

3. The books in English known to have made reference to Colón between 1553 and 1606 (information based in large part on John Parker's *Books to Build an Empire*) include:

Abbot, George, *A Briefe Description of the Whole Worlde*, 1599, 1600, 1605
Barrough, Philip, *The method of phisick*, 1601
Conestaggio, Girolamo, *History of Portugal and Spain*, 1600
Cunningham, William, *Cosmographical Glasse*, 1559
Eden, Richard, *A treatyse of the newe India . . :*, 1553; *The Decades of the newe
    worlde . . .*, 1555, 1572, 1576, rev. with Richard Willes as *History of travayle*,
    1577
Galvão, Antonio, *Discoveries of the world*, 1601
Gascoigne, George, in Humphrey Gilbert
Gilbert, Humphrey, *A Discourse . . . Catai*, 1576
Gómara, Francisco López de, *The pleasant historie . . .*, 1578, 1596
Guicciardini, Francesco, *The historie of Guicciardin*, 1579
Hakluyt, Richard, *Divers Voyages*, 1582; *Principall navigations . . .*, 1589, 1598,
    1600 (refs. by Fernando Colón, George Peckham, and René de Laudonnière)
Laudonnière, René de, *A notable historie . . .*, 1587

Lindschoten, John Huighen van, *his Discours of Voyages into y Easte & West Indies*, 1598

Lloyd, Humphrey, *History of Cambria*, 1584

Martyr, Peter, *Decades*. See Eden.

Münster, Sebastian, *Treatyse*. See Eden.

(?)Münster, Sebastian, *A briefe collection . . . Cosmographie*, 1572 (only copy incomplete)

Nicolay, N., *The navigations . . . into Turkie*, 1585

Parmenius, Stephen, *De navigatione . . . Humfredi Gilberti . . . carmen*, 1582

Peckham, George, *A true report*, 1583

Ralegh, Walter, *The discoverie of Guiana*, 1596

Seall, Robert, "A Comendation . . . of the wurthy Captain M. Thomas Stutely," 1563

Tasso, Torquato, *Jerusalem Delivered*, tr. Edward Fairfax, 1600

All of the above were published in London.

Chapter Eleven 1607–25 (1) *Jamestown*

1. By 1638, the English had thriving North American colonies in Virginia, Plymouth, Salem–Boston, Cape Ann, Connecticut, Rhode Island, Maryland, Guiana, St. Kitts, Barbados, Nevis, Antigua, Santa Catalina, and Tortuga; the French had outposts at Quebec–Cap de Tourmente, Trois-Rivières, Acadia, St. Christophe, and Martinique; the Dutch were at Albany, New Amsterdam, Delaware, St. Eustatius, and Curaçao; the Spanish, in addition to the sizable Mexican settlements and St. Augustine, had an outpost at Santa Fe and colonies on Española, Cuba, Jamaica, and Puerto Rico; the Swedes and Finns had established a few forts on the Delaware. In all, the population may have reached 200,000, but estimates here are notoriously chancy: the Spanish had something like 125,000 in Mesoamerica (though it may have been half again as many) and perhaps 20,000 in the Caribbean, the English had about 30,000 on the mainland and 25,000 in the Caribbean, the French had only a few hundred in Canada but maybe 5,000 in the Caribbean, and the Dutch had no more than 2,000 or so.

2. The sources with which to tell the Jamestown story in the opening decades are not as numerous as those for the Massachusetts settlements, and are a good deal less literary, and many of the official records of the Virginia Company in London and the early government in Virginia have been lost. But we do have the firsthand account of John Smith, who was in the colony until 1609, and his renderings of a variety of other colonists' diaries as he worked them for his 1612 *Map of Virginia*; the descriptions of William Strachey, secretary to the colony in 1610–11, in a long letter, published by Samuel Purchas in 1625, and in a manuscript of 1612, not published until the nineteenth century; two detailed diaries of the first year's events, by George Percy and Gabriel Archer, and a later account ("Trewe Relacyon") by Percy, not published until 1922; a collection of English records compiled by S. M. Kingsbury as *The Records of the Virginia Company of London*, in several

volumes; and an assortment of scattered letters, some of them in vol. 5 of Quinn, *NAW*. All in all, they tell us a good deal more about the settlers than the settled upon.

3. Such caution, I regret to say, has not generally been applied. Latter-day historians, anthropologists, ethnologists, and the like have been so willing to trust the early English eyewitness accounts that they construct virtually their entire picture of the Powhatan society out of them, right down to telling us its settlement patterns, political forms, burial and marriage practices, tribute systems, sumptuary rules, puberty rites, and the like, on the basis of little more than the perceptions of thoroughly Anglocentric and prejudiced men, not one of them trained for the task. The authoritative *Handbook of North American Indians* (ed. Bruce Trigger, No. 15, Smithsonian, 1978), for example, has a full chapter on the Powhatans with a complete description of their social and cultural habits as if some modern anthropologist had done fieldwork among them for years; in fact, the essay relies for almost all of its information on early English sources (and some English sources that date to a century later or more!), swallowing the prejudices and the misperceptions without a blink, and to back it up uses as reference only four archeological works (which tend to be much more reliable), two of which are not even about specifically Powhatan sites.

The result of such scholarship is not without interest, and not without some insights into parts of what the Powhatan society might really have been like, but it is mostly colonial concoction and it all rests on the assumption that, as we might put it, the bacterium is a reliable source of information about the behavior of its host.

4. The Powhatans and other peoples of the tidewater had a long history of contact with Europeans, for the most part hostile, and might well have concluded that the whites had every intention of taking over their land, necessitating alliances in response.

The record is imperfect, but there are reported European landings in this area in 1560, 1570, 1572, 1585, 1587, 1603, and 1607. In 1570 a Spanish mission was established in the Chesapeake area, presumed to be on the York River (the next river north of the James), and it caused enough friction (and probably disease) that it was, apparently, wiped out the next year, with the death of eight Jesuit priests; in 1572 a Spanish force under Pedro Menendez de Aviles landed and took revenge, killing at least twenty Indians in battle and hanging another fourteen. In the winter of 1485–86 a small party of Englishmen from the Roanoke settlement camped on the southern shore of the Chesapeake, and though no specific hostilities were reported Thomas Hariot acknowledged that in general the men of that voyage "were too harsh with [the Indians] and killed a few of their number," and the next spring commander Ralph Lane led a raiding party up the nearby Chowan River, where he attacked the Indians and later killed and beheaded a Roanoke chief. The fact that a handful of Indians ambushed a small party of Newport's men when they landed on this south shore in 1607 (no casualties, the Indians frightened away by musket-fire) suggests that they must have had prior provocation. And in 1603 the English captain Samuel Mace captured two "Virginia" Indians and took them to London, where they died, the best evidence indicating that the kidnapping must have taken place somewhere on the Chesapeake shores.

All this suggests that the peoples of the Chesapeake might well have had good reason to resist further European incursions and that a defensive alliance might have been one means to that end.

5. As I reconstruct events from the sparse and presumably self-censored accounts, the English effectively began the war just after Lord De La Warr landed in Jamestown in June 1610, armed with the sanctions from the Virginia Company elders. It might be said, however—and this is the position of J. Frederick Fausz (*Virginia Magazine of History*, vol. 95, no. 2, April 1987)—that it was the Powhatans who started things the previous winter, with attacks on small English encampments at Nonesuch and Nansemond, and with an apparent boycott of trade with Jamestown aimed at starving the colonists into submission. Thus the English attacks of 1610 could be seen as retaliations, a joining of the war, once they had sufficient arms and men for the task. The only trouble with this argument, it seems to me, is that one might then extend the tangled skein of provocations and affronts, first this side responsible and then the other, all the way back to the 1607 landing, or even back to the Powhatans' sixteenth-century contacts with hostile Europeans.

6. Karen Ordahl Kupperman has an entire book (*Settling with the Indians*, Rowman and Littlefield, 1980), and presumably a Ph.D. thesis besides, that seeks to show that Englishmen in the period 1580–1640 did *not* regard the Indians as subhuman and could at times in fact find elements to praise. The book is an interesting and useful reminder that some Englishmen did indeed sometimes describe Indian societies with something close to sympathy. But even the weight of her own evidence is clearly on the side of those who found the Indians alien and repellent (especially in the particular, no matter what homilies they would use for the general) rather than those who saw anything of value, anything worth emulating. One of her points seems especially revealing to me: not once in the entire record of early English settlement is there a single description of the *face* of any Indian (nothing of eye color, cheekbones, teeth, noses, lips, etc.), suggesting that they were seen as people who, however benignly regarded, were faceless, in some subtle way less than human.

Chapter Twelve   1607–25 (II)   *Powhatans and Others*

1. It is necessary to confront the problem of nomenclature. "Tribe" has become the accepted way to designate the larger Indian social/political unit and I have sometimes used that term, but this European derivative pasted onto American societies is both inadequate and misleading. "Tribe" at best might be serviceable to describe a language subgroup, as with the Powhatans, most of whom apparently spoke a common dialect of Algonkian, differing in some ways from that of the peoples of the Potomac or the Delaware or the Delmarva peninsula, although they were all identifiable as part of the Algonkian family of languages. This did not imply any necessary political or even social cohesion, however, and the basic political unit of most North American societies in pre-Columbian times seems to have been the village, or several villages in a conscribed area linked by kinship ties, although in times of need there might be additional outward alliances among the dialect group —usually temporary but in the case of the Irokwa and the Powhatans apparently

designed to be something more permanent. Because "tribe" has come to have certain derogatory connotations in certain quarters, "nation" has often been adopted as a more neutral term, but it has many specific European connotations of state systems that do not fit American conditions at all—and its own panoply of imprecisions. It is probably best when possible to use the term "people"—somewhat akin to the frequent Indian designations of themselves as "the people" or "the real people," although those were not intended to have political connotations—and to stumble along with the specific commonly used appellations, as inaccurate as those may be. ("Delaware," for example, is derived from the name of the English Lord De La Warr, and was stuck on an amalgam of remnant societies of the mid-Atlantic coast, of which the Leni Lenapies were but one part, who had in common only a general language affinity.) For a further discussion, see Robert Berkhoffer, in Howard Lamar and Leonard Thompson, eds., *The Frontier in History*, Yale, 1981.

2. Some dispute surrounds the extent to which Wahunseneka was an exception to the rule of general egalitarianism in Indian societies, since he is described as having sovereignty over some thirty Chesapeake "tribes" and is mentioned as having a complex "tribute" system below him, with the power to mete out punishment to recalcitrant subordinates. Even if we accept the accuracy of these kinds of English observations (and there is no special reason to, if we consider their generally misleading nature), it is clear that Wahunseneka was nothing like a "king" in the European sense of the word, set apart from his "subjects"; as John Smith noted, "For the King himselfe will make his owne robes, shooes, boews, arrowes, pots; plant, hunt, or doe anything so well as the rest" (Kupperman, *Settling with the Indians*, p. 145). I suspect that the English mistook for a tribute system what was a regular voluntary contribution to a common store of goods, to be apportioned in potlatch fashion or stored for another season; and what they thought was arbitrary punishment at the whim of Wahunseneka was more likely discipline sanctioned by the council of elders or tribal custom.

Chapter Thirteen   1625–1992   Columbus/Columbia

1. Among these biographies the Morison work—originally in two volumes, with useful notes, then cut and emaciated for the one-volume edition —has stood as the preeminent biography of the century, and thus deserves some comment. The original volumes certainly contain worthy scholarship, they are readable to the point of breeziness, and they offer the sensible navigational comments of one who traced the assumed routes of Colón's voyages in a small sailing boat. But they are seriously flawed, in ways that have escaped most of those who have relied heavily upon them in the past half-century. For one thing, they are erroneously *certain*, stating as facts (sometimes with disdainful dismissal of contrary views) some matters about which there are now (and were then) serious doubts, or at least fair controversy. (To mention just a few examples: about Colón's being necessarily the first transatlantic voyage of the fifteenth century; about the death and progeny of his first wife; about the Toscanelli letter; about the sequence of his years in Spain; about the lack of gold in Española; about Colón's ignorance of the magnitude of his discovery; even about

matters of reckoning and navigation, for which see De Vorsey and Parker.) For another, Morison refused to recognize a darker side of his hero—the side that Carl Sauer, for example, pointed to in *Early Spanish Main*—and in general refused to pay much attention to his deeds on land at all, where that side repeatedly showed itself. Finally, his assumptions about the manifest destiny of European imperialism, the inferiority of Indian cultures, and the inevitable justice of civilization's march —all of which may have been common coin in 1942—should strike a later age (as David Quinn has acknowledged in an introduction to the 1983 edition of Morison's book) as evidence of unacceptable bias, evident in almost every chapter.

Source Notes

All works cited here, except those directly below, are given a full citation when used first, a full title when used subsequently in a new chapter, and a short title in all other references; those listed below, the most frequently cited, are given by author (and short title where needed) throughout.

Arber, Edward, *The first Three English books on America*, Birmingham, 1885, Kraus (New York) reprint, 1971.

Braudel, Fernand, *The Structures of Everyday Life*, vol. 1 of *Civilization and Capitalism, 15th–18th Century*, Harper & Row, 1981, 1985.

Chiappelli, Fredi, ed., *First Images of America*, 2 vols., California, 1976.

Colón, Fernando, *The Life of the Admiral Christopher Columbus by His Son Ferdinand*, tr. Benjamin Keen, Rutgers, 1959. [Cited as "Fernando."]

Davies, K. G., *The North Atlantic World in the Seventeenth Century*, Minnesota, 1974.

De Vorsey, Louis, Jr., and John Parker, *In the Wake of Columbus: Islands and Controversy*, Wayne State, 1985.

Elliott, J. H., *The Old World and the New 1492–1650*, Cambridge, 1970.

Fitzhugh, William W., ed., *Cultures in Contact*, Smithsonian (Washington, DC), 1985.

Gerace, Donald T., ed., *Columbus and His World: Proceedings of the First San Salvador Conference*, Bahamian Field Station (Fort Lauderdale, FL), 1987.

Harrisse, Henry, *Notes on Columbus*, privately printed (New York), 1866.

Jane, Cecil, ed., *The Four Voyages of Columbus*, Hakluyt Society (London), series II, vols. 65, 70, 1930, 1933; Dover reprint, 1 vol., 1988.

Morison, Samuel Eliot, *Admiral of the Ocean Sea*, 2 vols., Little, Brown, 1942 (*not* the one-volume edition, 1942, or the Northeastern University reprint, 1983). [Cited as "*AOS.*"]

———, *The European Discovery of America*, Oxford, *Northern Voyages*, 1971; *Southern Voyages*, 1974.

———, ed. and tr., *Journals and Other Documents on the Life and Voyages of Christopher Columbus*, Heritage (New York), 1963. [Cited as "*JAOD.*"]

Provost, Foster, *Columbus: An Annotated Guide to the Study of His Life and Writings, 1750–1988*, Omnigraphics (Detroit)/John Carter Brown Library (Providence, RI), 1990.

Quinn, David Beers, *England and the Discovery of America 1481–1620*, Knopf, 1973. [Cited as "*EADA.*"]

———, ed., *New American World*, 5 vols., Arno Press/Hector Bye (New York), 1979. [Cited as "*NAW.*"]

Sauer, Carl O., *Early Spanish Main*, California, 1966.

———, *Sixteenth Century North America*, California, 1971.

Taviani, Paolo Emilio, *Christopher Columbus: The Grand Design*, Orbis (London), 1985.

Thacher, J. B., *Christopher Columbus*, 3 vols., Putnam's, 1903–04.

Winsor, Justin, *Narrative and Critical History of America*, vols. 1, 2, 8, Houghton
   Mifflin, 1889, AMS (New York) reprint, 1967.
Young, Filson, *Christopher Columbus and the New World of His Discovery*, Lip-
   pincott, 1912 (orig. 1906).

Prologue

p. 3 Gómara, *Historia general de las Indias*, Saragossa, 1552, dedication; and
Biblioteca de Autores Españoles (Madrid), 1852, vol. 23, p. 156.
   Le Roy, *De la vicissitude . . . en l'univers*, Paris, 1579, cited by Elliott, p. 10.
   Smith, *The Wealth of Nations*, London, 1776, bk. 4, chap. 7, pt. 3, in
R. H. Campbell and A. S. Skinner, eds., Clarendon (Oxford), 1976, p. 626.
   p. 5 Monuments and place names, see notes to pp. 347, 360, chap. 13 below.
   p. 6 Colón, *Lettera Rarissima*, 1503, Italian facsimile and English translation in
Thacher, vol. 2, pp. 669ff. The Navarrete Spanish version of a seventeenth-century
manuscript copy is transcribed and translated in Jane, vol. 2, pp. 72ff. Like all
translations here of Colón's writings, this is my own, informed by Thacher, Jane,
Morison, and others.

Chapter One   1492 (1)

p. 7 "at half an hour"—Colón, *Journal*, prologue, in Morison, *JAOD*, p. 49.
My translations are based largely on Oliver Dunn and James E. Kelley, Jr., *The
Diario of Christopher Columbus's First Voyage to America 1492–1493*, Oklahoma,
1989, with transcription of the Spanish original and facing English translation, supplemented by Morison, *JAOD* (which I generally have used for page citations, since
it is most accessible); Cecil Jane, *The Journal of Christopher Columbus*, rev.
L. A. Vigneras, Potter (NY), 1960; Robert Fuson, *The Log of Christopher Columbus*,
International Marine (Camden, ME), 1987; and Thacher, vol. 1, pp. 512ff, particularly valuable because he adds much of Las Casas's commentary and *Historia*
material. Additional sources on the First Voyage are in Provost, IV.E.2.
   Colón's ships: see José Maria Martínez-Hidalgo, *Columbus's Ships*, Barre (Barre,
ME), 1966; Morison, *AOS*, vol. 1, chap. 9; Eugene Lyon, *National Geographic*,
vol. 170, November 1986; C. R. Phillips, in Gerace, pp. 69ff; J. H. Parry, *The Age
of Reconnaissance*, World, 1963, pp. 53ff; Provost, V.O.
   p. 8 Colón, *Journal*, December 26, 1492, Morison, *JAOD*, p. 138.
   La Rábida: our knowledge of Colón in Spain before 1492 is quite sketchy. Fernando, the principal source, is quite unreliable; best is Juan Manzano Manzano,
Cristóbal Colón: Siete años decisivos de su vida, 1485–1492, Ediciones Cultura His-
pana (Madrid), 1964; also Foster Provost, in Gerace, pp. 57ff; Thacher, vol. 1, chap.
49; and Taviani, notes to chaps. 33, 34, 38.
   p. 10 *Pleitos*: Cesareo Fernández Duro, ed., *De los pleitos de Colón*, 2 vols.,
Madrid, 1892–94; Antonio Muro Orejón, *Pleitos colombinos*, Escuela de Estudios
Hispanoamericanos (Seville), 1967; see also Otto Schoenrich, *The Legacy of Columbus*, Clark (Glendale, CA), 1949–50; and Morison, *AOS*, vol. 1, p. 179.
   p. 11 Crew: Alice Bache Gould, *Nueva lista documentada de los tripulantes de
Colón en 1492*, Academia de la Historia (Madrid), 1984.

Colón, *Journal*, prologue, Morison, *JAOD*, p. 48.

Letter of Credence, ibid., pp. 30–31.

p. 12 Royal order, *Título*, ibid., p. 79.

Colón, *Journal*, ibid., p. 79.

Oviedo, *Historia general y natural de las Indias*, Seville, 1535; Salamanca, 1547, 1549; Valladolid, 1557; 4-vol. reprint, Academia de Historia (Madrid), 1851–55.

Crown agreement, Morison, *JOAD*; p. 28.

p. 13 "silversmith"—according to Gould, *Nueva lista*, and see Morison, *AOS*, vol. 1, pp. 190–91.

Expulsion: Cecil Roth, *A History of the Marranos*, Meridian, 1959; J. H. Elliott, *Imperial Spain 1469–1716*, St. Martin's, 1963, pp. 98–99; Angus MacKay, "Pogroms in Fifteenth-Century Castile," *Past and Present*, no. 55, 1972; Fernand Braudel, *The Mediterranean and the Mediterranean World*, Harper, 1966, pp. 823ff. Meyer Kayserling, *Christopher Columbus and the Participation of the Jews in the Spanish and Portuguese Discoveries*, Longmans, Green, 1893, Hermon (NY) reprint, 1968.

Old Spaniard: *Pleito* of Juan de Aragon, 1552; Morison, *AOS*, vol. 1, p. 194.

Colón, *Journal*, Morison, *JAOD*, p. 48.

p. 14 Colón, ibid., p. 49.

Decree, ibid., p. 33.

Sphericity of the earth: John Block Friedman in *The Monstrous Races*, Harvard, 1981, establishes that the medieval world knew the earth was round, as the Ancients had said; moreover, John Mandeville's spurious *Travels*, one of the most widely read books of the age, spoke of circumnavigation of the earth quite matter-of-factly. See also Taviani, pp. 456–57, 464–65.

p. 15 Colón: 1492—*Journal*, Morison, *JAOD*, p. 128; 1501—*Book of Prophecies*, see p. 188 below, and Fernando, p. 10; chart, *Journal*, Morison, *JAOD*, p. 57.

p. 16 Sailing career: Taviani, chaps. 7, 9, 15, 22, 24; Provost, IV.B, C; Jane, vol. 1, p. xxxvii, points out that Colón never claimed to be a sailor and even behaved most unseamanlike at times.

p. 17 Fernando, p. 9.

Oviedo, *Historia*, bk. 1, p. 12.

Beard, Las Casas, *Historia de las Indias*, 3 vols., ed. Augustin Millares Carlo and Lewis Hanke, Fondo de Cultura Económica (Mexico City), 1951, vol. 1, chap. 2; a truncated and unsatisfactory translation in English by Andrée Collard was printed by Harper & Row, 1971.

Braudel, p. 90.

p. 18 Colón's millenarianism: Pauline Moffitt Watts, "Prophecy and Discovery: On the Spiritual Origins . . . ," *American Historical Review*, vol. 90, February 1985; Leonard I. Sweet, "Christopher Columbus and the Millennial Vision of the New World," *Catholic Historical Review*, vol. 72, July 1986; Delno West, in Gerace, pp. 45ff; Alain Milhou, "Colón y su mentalidad mesiánica . . . ," *Cuadernos colombinos*, vol. 9 (Valladolid), 1983; see also Thacher, vol. 2, pp. 566–67, and vol. 3, pp. 660–64; Ann Williams, ed., *Prophecy and Millenarianism*, Essex, 1980; John Phelan, *The Millennial Kingdom of the Franciscans in the New World*, California, 1970; and Provost, V.G.

"Gold is most excellent"—*Lettera Rarissima*, Thacher, vol. 2, and Morison, *JAOD*, p. 383; see also Sauer, *Main*, passim; Jane, pp. cxviff.

Nebrija: Elliot, *Spain*, p. 117.

Colón, *Journal*, Morison, *JAOD*, p. 49.

p. 20 Mac Kie, *With the Admiral of the Ocean Sea*, McClurg (Chicago), 1891, p. 90.

Morison, *AOS*, vol. 1, pp. 158–59.

p. 22 Colón, *Journal*, Morison, *JAOD*, p. 49.

Footnote: De Vorsey and Parker, pp. 21, 64ff; Gerace, pp. 115ff, 122, 189; Morison, *AOS*, vol. 1, pp. 247–48, 260–61; *National Geographic*, vol. 170, November 1986.

p. 23 DESTINATION/"ENTERPRISE": The best discussions of this thorny question are Morison, *AOS*, vol. 1, chap. 6, and Taviani, notes to chaps. 29–31, for the India-all-along school; and Jane, introduction, and Henry Vignaud, *The Letter and Chart of Toscanelli*, Sands (London), 1902, Books for Libraries (Freeport, NY) reprint, 1971, for the Doubters' school. See also notes to p. 357 below.

"laughter and mockery"—1501 letter, Fernando, p. 10.

Prologue: Morison, *JAOD*, pp. 47–49; Jane, vol. 1, pp. xcii–xcix.

Passport and letter, Morison, *JAOD*, pp. 30–31; Taviani, pp. 394–95.

Simancas document in Taviani, pp. 393–94.

p. 24 Vignaud, "Letter to Whitelaw Reid," in Young, p. 379.

Fernando, p. 23.

Footnote: Quinn, *NAW*, vol. 1, pp. 78ff.

p. 25 Capitulations, in Morison, *JAOD*, pp. 27–30.

Da Gama: J. H. Parry, ed., *The European Reconnaissance*, Macmillan, 1968, chap. 4; Parry, *Reconnaissance*, pp. 141–42.

p. 26 Nicolet: see Marcel Trudel, *The Beginnings of New France*, tr. Patricia Claxton, McClelland & Stewart (Toronto), 1973, p. 183.

Vignaud, *Histoire critique de la grande entreprise de Christophe Colomb*, Welter (Paris), 1911; *Le vrai Christophe Colomb et la légende*, Picard (Paris), 1921; see also his "Letter," in Young.

Ferdinand: Townsend Miller, *The Castles and the Crown*, Coward-McCann, 1963, p. 149.

p. 27 Colón, *Journal*, Morison, *JAOD*, pp. 51–52.

Chapter Two   Europe (1)   *"The End of the World Is Near"*

p. 28 Nuremberg *Book of Chronicles*: see Paul Herrmann, *The Great Age of Discovery*, Harper, 1958, pp. 3–8.

p. 29 Huizinga, *The Waning of the Middle Ages*, Doubleday Anchor, 1954, p. 138.

Herrmann, *Great Age*, pp. 6–7.

Friedell, *A Cultural History of the Modern Age*, Knopf, 1964 (orig. 1930), vol. 1, chap. 3.

Grünpeck, in Paul Herrmann, *Conquest by Man*, Harper, 1954, pp. 426–27.

p. 30 Cohn, *The Pursuit of the Millennium*, Oxford, 1970.

Colón, *Book of Prophecies*, in Cesare de Lollis, *Raccolta di documenti . . .*, 13 vols., Ministro della Pubblica Istruzione, pt. 1, vol. 2, 1894, pp. 75ff; see also Thacher, vol. 2, pp. 660ff. Colón's marginalia are found in the *Imago mundi* edition put out by the Massachusetts Historical Society, Boston, 1927.

Huizinga, *Waning*, p. 31.

p. 31 Deschamps, ibid., p. 33 (my translation).

Huizinga, ibid., p. 37.

Violence: e.g., Howard Mumford Jones, *O Strange New World*, Viking, 1964, pp. 127ff; Peter Burke, ed., *Economy and Society in Early Modern Europe*, Routledge (London), 1972.

Marineo Siculo, in Miller, *The Castles and the Crown*, p. 30.

p. 32 Huizinga, *Waning*, p. 24.

Inquisition: e.g., Elliott, *Imperial Spain 1469–1716*, chap. 6.

p. 33 Mariana, *Historia general . . .*, Barcelona, 1839, vol. 4, p. 390.

Severity of war: Quincy Wright, *A Study of War*, Chicago, 1965; Pitirim Sorokin, *Social and Cultural Dynamics*, vol. 2, American Book, 1937.

Disease: e.g., Margaret Aston, *The Fifteenth Century*, Norton, 1968, pp. 15ff; Braudel, pp. 78–92; Leonard Sagan, *The Health of Nations*, Basic, 1987.

p. 34 Epidemics: Fielding Hudson Garrison, *An Introduction to the History of Medicine*, W. B. Saunders (Philadelphia), 1929 (orig. 1913), p. 186.

Savonarola, in Aston, *Fifteenth*, p. 15.

p. 35 Kempis, ibid., p. 18.

Famine: e.g., Braudel, pp. 71ff; see also his *The Mediterranean and the Mediterranean World*. Interesting material on Spain is in MacKay, "Pogroms," *Past and Present*.

Andalusia: MacKay, "Pogroms."

Burgundy: Braudel, p. 78.

p. 36 Sánchez, in MacKay, "Pogroms."

French poet, in Huizinga, *Waning*, pp. 33–34 (my translation).

Friedell, *Cultural History*, chap. 3.

p. 37 Leonardo, in Astor, *Fifteenth*, p. 46.

Cattons (Bruce and William B.), *The Bold and Magnificent Dream: America's Founding Years*, Doubleday, 1978, p. 12.

Trithemius, in Astor, *Fifteenth*, p. 154.

Machiavelli, *The Prince*, Chap. 18.

Nicholas of Cusa, in Astor, *Fifteenth*, p. 83.

p. 38 Humanism: e.g., David Ehrenfeld, *The Arrogance of Humanism*, Oxford, 1978; Morris Berman, *The Reenchantment of the World*, Cornell, 1981.

Ficino, in Lauro Martines, *Power and Imagination: City-States in Renaissance Italy*, Knopf, 1979, p. 216.

Alberti, in Kenneth Clark, *Civilisation*, Harper & Row, 1969, p. 89.

p. 39 Pico, *Oration on the Dignity of Man*, c. 1486.

Martines, *Power*, p. 205.

p. 40 "What they had"—Alexandre Koyre, "Galileo to Plato," *Journal of the History of Ideas*, vol. 18, 1957.

p. 41 20 million books: Peter Burke, *Popular Culture in Early Modern Europe*, New York University, 1978, p. 250.

"By the end"—S. B. Clough and C. W. Cole, *Economic History of Europe*, Heath (Boston), 1952, p. 91.

p. 42 Mathias, *Science and Society 1600–1900*, Cambridge, 1972, p. 78.

Materialism: e.g., Braudel, pp. 285ff.

Clark, *Civilisation*, pp. 101, 106.

p. 43 Alberti, in Clark, *Civilisation*, p. 106.

Palmieri, in Aston, *Fifteenth*, p. 150.

p. 44 "Jews are"—in Braudel, *The Perspective of the World*, Harper & Row, 1984, p. 563.

Mumford, *The Condition of Man*, Harcourt, 1973, p. 162.

p. 45 Toynbee, *Mankind and Mother Earth*, Oxford, 1976, p. 500.

p. 46 Friedell, *Cultural History*, ch. 5.

Turner, *Beyond Geography*, Viking, 1980, p. 255.

Pérez de Oliva, in Elliott, p. 15.

Chapter Three   1492 (II)

p. 47 Colón, *Journal*, Morison, *JAOD*, pp. 51–52.

Colón, ibid., p. 57.

p. 48 False log: see James E. Kelley, in De Vorsey and Parker, pp. 91–92 and app. C, for a somewhat tortured explanation; and David Henige and Margarita Zamora, "Text, Context, Intertext," *Americas*, vol. 46, 1989, for a deconstructionist analysis raising many important questions, answering none.

Fernando, pp. 48, 56.

p. 49 Morison, *AOS*, vol. 1, p. 266.

Colón, *Journal*, in Morison, *JAOD*, p. 167.

p. 50 Canaries: Alfred W. Crosby, Jr., *Ecological Imperialism*, Cambridge, 1986; and Felipe Fernández-Armesto, *Before Columbus: Exploration and Colonization from the Mediterranean to the Atlantic, 1229–1492*, Pennsylvania, 1987.

p. 51 Birthplace: documents in Morison, *JAOD*, pp. 5ff.; discussion in Taviani, pp. 223ff; complete documents in City of Genoa, *Christopher Columbus: Documents and Proofs of His Genoese Origin*, Istituto d'Arti Grafiche (Genoa), 1932, in English and German (Italian ed., 1931).

Will: Young, pp. 356ff.; Thacher, vol. 3, pp. 646ff. See Morison, *JAOD*, p. 6, and Enrique de Gandia, *Historia de Cristóbal Colón, añalisis crítico . . .* , Buenos Aires, 1942, for questions of authenticity.

Book count: Simonetta Conti, *Un secolo di bibliografia colombiana 1880–1985*, Cassa di Risparmio di Genova e Imperia (Genoa), 1986.

Footnote: Madariaga, *Christopher Columbus*, Oxford, 1939; Wiesenthal, *Sails of Hope*, Macmillan, 1973; and see notes to p. 358 below.

p. 52 Portuguese wreck: ibid., pp. 13–14; see Taviani, notes to chap. 10, for a discussion of alternative theories. I must say that I am persuaded by the analysis of Jacques Heers, *Christophe Columb*, Hachette (Paris), 1981, that argues it all to be Colonic deception.

Pirate captain: this was effectively demolished by Henry Harrisse, *Christophe Colomb*, E. Leroux (Paris), 1884, vol. 1, pp. 254ff; see also Taviani, pp. 281–85, and Ernle Bradford, *Christopher Columbus*, Viking, 1973, pp. 24–25.

Mapmaking: Thacher, vol. 1, pp. 190–93; Provost, IV.C. Since we have a document showing Colón to have been in Madeira in 1478 as a business agent for a Genoese trader (Morison, *JAOD*, pp. 8–9), it is reasonable to assume that this, not mapmaking or bookselling, was his career. The freehand map of Española, incidentally, once said to have been the work of this mapmaking Colón, is now generally agreed to be by another, unknown hand—as should have been obvious all along since "La Navidad" is rendered as "Nativada." The Italian chroniclers are Agostino Giustiniani, Antonio Gallo, and Bartolomé Senarega.

Footnote: Fernando, p. 10.

p. 53 Footnote: V. I. Milani, "The Written Language of Christopher Columbus," *Forum italicum* (SUNY: Buffalo), 1973; Cecil Jane, "The Question of the Literacy of Christopher Columbus," *Hispanic American Historical Review*, vol. 10, 1930; and several articles in *Studi colombiani*, SAGA (Genoa), vol. 2, 1952.

p. 54 Wills: Young, pp. 356ff; Thacher, vol. 3, pp. 646ff.

Felipa Perestrello (also Filipa Perestrelo): Thacher, vol. 1, chap. 48; Taviani, notes to chap. 20; Henry Vignaud, *Études critiques . . .* , Welter (Paris), 1905, pp. 424ff.

Beatriz de Arana: José de la Torre, *Beatriz Enríquez de Harana*, Iberoamericana (Madrid), 1933; Manzano, *Cristóbal Colón*; Taviani, pp. 468ff.

Xp̄o FERENS: Thacher, vol. 3, p. 454, with facsimiles of the signature in chap. 12, passim; Morison, *JAOD*, p. 202. The tilde, peculiarly, is variously over the "p" (rho), the "o" (omicron), and both.

p. 55 Vincenzo Colombo: Taviani, pp. 290ff.

Footnote: Fernando, p. 4.

p. 56 Colón, *Journal*, Morison, *JAOD*, p. 54.

Compass: e.g., Parry, *The Age of Reconnaissance*, pp. 80–89.

p. 57 Braudel, pp. 402, 412.

p. 58 Colón, *Journal*, Morison, *JAOD*, p. 54.

Pico, in Martines, *Power and Imagination*, pp. 216-17.

Colón, *Journal*, Morison, *JAOD*, pp. 55, 53–56.

p. 59 Colón, *Journal*, ibid., p. 62.

Footnote: Morison, *JAOD*, p. 60.

p. 60 Mutiny: Morison translates the February 14 entry (*JAOD*, p. 165) as "mutiny against him," but *"alcar se contra"* (Las Casas fol. 62R, li. 13) is best rendered as "rise against him," as Markham, Fuson, and Dunn and Kelley have it, though even that is an exaggeration. Fernando, who had the original in front of him, has two long paragraphs on the October events that say nothing about either rising or mutinying, and later he writes only that the Admiral dissuaded them "from turning back as they often resolved to do" (p. 92). Martyr's mutiny story is in the first book of his *Decades*, in Arber, p. 66; Oviedo's is in his *Historia general y natural de las Indias*, bk. II, chap. 5

The reference to "the Indies" in the October 10 entry is typical of Las Casas's editing, and says nothing sure about Colón's intentions. It seems obviously in context to be an interpolation by Las Casas as he transcribes the log, substituting what he knew forty years later for what would have been the more cumbersome phrases of the original, done with no intention to deceive, I am sure, only to clarify.

Pleitos, Duro ed., *De los pleitos de Colón*, vol. 2, pp. 127, 217–19, 407–10. The idea that the crew gave Colón a three-day deadline is another myth nowhere found in the *Journal*, and apparently drawn from *Pleitos* testimony (vol. 2, p. 75; vol. 1, p. 421) of Juan Moreno and Francisco Morales, though neither was on the First Voyage.

p. 61 Diaz: Parry, *Reconnaissance*, p. 137.

p. 62 Colón, *Journal*, Morison, *JAOD*, pp. 62–63.

"two hours," ibid., p. 63; the lookout's name is given in the *Journal* as "Rodrigo de triana," meaning that he came from the town of Triana, near Seville, but Alice Gould, *Nueva lista*, has established the form given here as his real name.

p. 63 Legacy money: Morison, *JAOD*, p. 64, n. 5; Meyer Kayserling, *Christopher Columbus and the Participation of the Jews.*

p. 64 Colón, *Journal*, Morison, *JAOD*, p. 64.
Colón, ibid., p 67.
Colón, ibid., p. 78.
Fernando, pp. 23, 17.

p. 65 Landfall: the essential works for an examination of this tedious but tenacious issue—and they in turn cite others of use—are De Vorsey and Parker; Morison, *JAOD* and *AOS*, vol. 1, chap. 16 and n. 1; Gerace; Fuson, *The Log of Christopher Columbus*; Joseph Judge et al., *National Geographic*, vol. 170, November 1986; and Edwin A. and Marion C. Link, *A New Theory on Columbus's Voyage Through the Bahamas*, Smithsonian Miscellaneous Collections No. 135, 1959; Provost, IV.E.2. lists others.

p. 67 Colón, *Journal*, Morison, *JAOD*, pp. 61, 167.
Letters from the Sovereigns: September 15, 1493, August 16, 1494, in Thacher, vol. 2, pp. 554–56, 618; also Gerace, p. 109.

p. 68 Behaim globe, variously reproduced, e.g., Quinn, *NAW*, vol. 1; *National Geographic*, vol. 170.
Müntzer letter, Morison, *JAOD*, pp. 15–17.
Colón, *Journal*, Morison, *JAOD*, p. 64.

p. 69 Early American voyages: see especially the works of David Beers Quinn, e.g., *NAW*, vol. 1, pt. 1; *EADA*; *North American Discovery, Circa 1000–1612*, South Carolina, 1971; and "The Argument for the English Discovery of America Between 1480 and 1494," *Geographical Journal*, vol. 127, September 1961. See also Gwyn Jones, *The Norse Atlantic Saga*, Oxford, 1964; Robert McGhee, "Contact Between Native Americans and the Medieval Norse," *American Antiquity*, vol. 49, January 1984; Fitzhugh, pt. 1; Morison, *Northern*; and Taviani, with an extensive bibliography, pp. 347ff. Two recent additions to the fringe literature are Paul Chapman's *The Man Who Led Columbus to America*, Judson (Atlanta), 1973, which takes St. Brendan seriously, and Arthur Davies in *Geographical Journal*, vol. 150, November 1984, which takes Scolvus seriously.

p. 70 Discovery: the meaning of the event, and the word, is discussed in Edmundo O'Gorman's strange *The Invention of America*, Indiana, 1961; and in Wilcomb E. Washburn, "The Meaning of 'Discovery' in the Fifteenth and Sixteenth Centuries," *American Historical Review*, vol. 68, October 1962.
Harrisse, *Discovery of North America*, Henry Stevens (London), 1892, N. Israel (Amsterdam) reprint, 1969; see also Samuel Eliot Morison, *Portuguese Voyages to America in the Fifteenth Century*, Harvard, 1940.
Bristol: see Quinn, works cited in note to p. 69 above, and especially *Geographical Journal*.
Day letter, *NAW*, vol. 1, p. 98.

p. 73 Colón, *Journal*, Morison, *JAOD*, pp. 64–65.

Chapter Four
Europe (II)   *"The Earth Shall Quake Before Them"*

p. 75 EUROPE AND NATURE: of the immense literature here, I find most useful: Morris Berman, *The Reenchantment of the World*, Cornell, 1981; Thomas Berry, *Dance of the Earth*, Sierra Club, 1988; Richard Bernheimer, *Wild Men in the Middle Ages*, Harvard, 1952; Alfred Biese, *The Development of the Feeling for Nature in* the Middle Ages and Modern Times, Routledge, 1905; Olive Dickason, The Myth of the Savage, Alberta, 1984; Edward Dudley and Maximillian E. Novak, eds., The Wild Man Within, Pittsburgh, 1972; H. R. Fairclough, Love of Nature Among the Greeks and Romans, Longmans, 1930; John Block Friedman, The Monstrous Races in Medieval Art and Thought, Harvard, 1981; Clarence Glacken, Traces on the Rhodian Shore, California, 1967; William Leiss, The Domination of Nature, Braziller, 1972; David C. Lindburg, ed., Science in the Middle Ages, Chicago, 1978; Carolyn Merchant, The Death of Nature, Harper, 1981; Roderick Nash, Wilderness in the American Mind, Yale, 1979; Evelyn Page, American Genesis, Gambit, 1973; Lawrence D. Roberts, ed., Approaches to Nature in the Middle Ages, Center for Medieval and Early Renaissance Studies, SUNY Binghamton, 1982; John Rodman, "The Dolphin Papers," Antæus, no. 57, Fall 1986; Paul Shepard, Nature and Madness, Sierra Club, 1982; John M. Steadman, Nature into Myth: Medieval Renaissance Moral Symbols, Duquesne, 1979; J. V. Thirgood, Man and the Mediterranean Forest, Academic, 1981; Keith Thomas, Man and the Natural World, Pantheon, 1983; Lynn White, "The Historical Roots of Our Ecological Crisis," Science, March 10, 1967.

p. 76 Andrew, reprinted in Noel Hudson, An Early Version of Hortus Sanitatis, London, 1954.

Thomas, Man, p. 258.

p. 77 More, Cambden, North, Howell, in Thomas, ibid.

Footnote: see E. T. McLaughlin, Studies in Medieval Life and Literature, Putnam's, 1894.

Bloch, Feudal Society, Chicago, 1961.

p. 78 Wild Man: see especially Bernheimer, Wild Men, and Friedman, Monstrous Races.

Thomas, Man, pp. 77–78.

Separation: see especially Shepard, Nature.

p. 79 Mappemondes: Rodney W. Shirley, The Mapping of the World, Holland (London), 1984.

p. 80 Gardens: e.g., Ellen C. Eyler, Early English Gardens and Garden Books, Folger (Washington, DC), 1963.

Friedman, Monstrous Races, p. 200.

Purchas, Virginias Verger, in Hakluytus posthumus, or Purchas his pilgrimes, 1625, MacLehose (Glasgow) reprint, vol. 19, 1905–07.

p. 81 Thomas, Man, p. 18.

Bacon, in Berman, Reenchantment, p. 30; Ficino, in Glacken, Traces, chap. 10; Hall, The Scientific Revolution 1500–1800, Longmans (London), 1954, p. 29.

Ecological heritage: see especially J. Donald Hughes, Ecology in Ancient Civilizations, New Mexico, 1975; Thomas, Man; Braudel.

p. 82 20 percent wooded: Thomas, Man, p. 193.

p. 83 City calculation: Braudel, p. 486.

Braudel, p. 421.

Braudel, p. 124.

p. 84 Wood: ibid., p. 362ff.

p. 85 Guevara, Épistres dorées . . . , Biblioteca de autores españoles (Madrid), 1850, vol. 13, p. 93.

James I, in Thomas, Man, p. 198.

Churchman, ibid., pp. 18–19.

Footnote: Braudel, pp. 341ff.

p. 86 Thomas, *Man*, p. 145.

Henneberg/Saxony, Brandon, *New Worlds for Old*, p. 76.

p. 87 Braudel, p. 215.

Thomas, *Man*, p. 274.

p. 88 European exceptionalism: e.g., William Woodruff, *Impact of Western Man*, St. Martin's, 1967; Darcy Ribeiro, *The Americas and Civilization*, Dutton, 1971; Lewis Mumford, *The Pentagon of Power*, Harcourt, 1970; Turner, *Beyond Geography*; Nash, *Wilderness*; and Passmore, *Man's Responsibility*.

p. 89 Kue Hsi: Nash, *Wilderness*, p. 21.

Technophilia: e.g., Lewis Mumford, *The Myth of the Machine*, 2 vols., Harcourt, 1967, 1970; and *Technics and Civilization*, Harcourt, 1934, 1962; Jacques Ellul, *The Technological System*, tr. Joachim Neugroschel, Continuum (NY), 1980.

Mumford, *Technics*, p. 4.

p. 90 Braudel, *The Perspective of the World*, Harper & Row, 1984, p. 387.

p. 91 Woodruff, *Impact*, p. 16.

Chapter Five 1492–93

p. 92 Footnote: Fernando, p. 44; on financing of the First Voyage, see Thacher, vol. 1, chaps. 54, 55; Taviani, pp. 497ff; Manzano, *Cristóbal Colón*, p. 196; Consuelo Varela, in Gerace, pp. 33ff.; Kayserling, *Christopher Columbus and the Participation of the Jews in the Spanish and Portuguese Discoveries*; Charles McCarthy, "Columbus and the Santa Hermandad in 1492," *Catholic History Review*, vol. 1, 1915.

p. 93 Río de Gracia: Morison, *AOS*, vol. 1, p. 398.

p. 94 "the administering"—Capitulations, April 30, 1492, in Morison, *JAOD*, p. 30.

p. 95 Colón, *Journal*, ibid., p. 64.

Fernando, pp. 59–60.

Colón, *Journal*, Morison, *JAOD*, pp. 64–65.

Footnote: Morison, *AOS*, vol. 1, p. 308.

p. 97 Madariaga, *Christopher Columbus*, p. 217.

"Taino"—Colón uses this word, in the form "Nitayno" on December 23 (Morison, *JAOD*, p. 133) and says he doesn't know if it means "noble, or governor, or judge."

TAINOS: there is a paucity of material on the Tainos, extirpation proving a considerable hindrance to scholarly investigation. The classic work is Sven Loven, *Origins of Tainan Culture*, Elanders Bokfryckeri Akfiebolag (Göteborg), 1935, but it is dense, dated, and dull. More up-to-date work has been produced by Irving Rouse, in *Handbook of South American Indians*, Julian H. Steward, ed., Bureau of American Anthropology, 1948, Cooper Square (NY) reprint, 1963, vol. 4, pp. 495ff; *Migrations in Prehistory*, Yale, 1986 (adapted for Gerace, pp. 293ff); and "Whom Did Columbus Discover in the West Indies?" *American Archeology*, vol. 6, 1987; and by Antonio M. Stevens-Arroyo, *Cave of the Jaguar*, New Mexico, 1988. Two general works are especially interesting, Carl Sauer's *Early Spanish Main* and David Watts's *West Indies*, Cambridge, 1987. Kathleen Deagan has done some archeological work on the Tainos, and her contribution (and its bibliography) are in Fitzhugh; similar work is in Ricardo E. Alegria, *Ballcourts and Ceremonial Plazas in the West Indies*, Yale Department of Anthropology Pamphlet No. 29, 1983.

p. 99 Watts, *West Indies*, p. 60; Sauer, *Main*, p. 68.

p. 100 Santangel Letter, Morison, *JAOD*, p. 184.

p. 101 Sauer, *Main*, p. 69.

Colón, *Journal*, Morison, *JAOD*, p. 67.

Island vegetation: Watts, *West Indies*; John Winter, in Gerace, p. 313ff.

p. 103 Species mistakes: Morison, *JAOD*, is particularly useful here, since he enlisted the services of some Harvard colleagues and others to identify correctly the plant, fish, and animal species that Colón names incorrectly.

Ferro, in Gerace, pp. 99, 102.

p. 104 Elliot, pp. 19–20.

Oviedo, ibid., p. 21.

Colón, *Journal*, Morison, *JAOD*, p. 70.

p. 105 Gerbi, *Nature in the New World, from Christopher Columbus to Gonzalo Fernández de Oviedo*, tr. Jeremy Moyle, Pittsburgh, 1985, p. 18; Iglesia, *Columbus, Cortés, and Other Essays*, tr. Lesley B. Simpson, California, 1969, chap. 1.

COLUMBUS AND NATURE: in addition to Gerbi, *Nature*, see Ferro, in Gerace, pp. 99ff.; Jane, vol. 1 introduction, especially p. xxxviii; Jones, *O Strange New World*, chap. 1; Tzvetan Todorov, *The Conquest of America*, tr. Richard Howard, Harper & Row, 1984, pt. 1; Alexander von Humboldt, *Examen critique . . . du nouveau continent . . .*, Gide (Paris), 1856, vol. 1; Leonardo Olschki, "What Columbus Saw on Landing in the West Indies," *Proceedings of the American Philosophical Society*, vol. 84, July 1941, and "Columbian Nomenclature of the Lesser Antilles," *Geographical Review*, vol. 33, 1943 (although the first is as confused as piece of *academica* as I've ever read); G. V. Scammel, *Historical Journal*, vol. 23, September 1980; Margaret T. Hodgsen, *Early Anthropology in the Sixteenth and Seventeenth Centuries*, Pennsylvania, 1964 (though she uses "Carib" where Taino is meant).

p. 106 Footnote: The postils are reprinted in de Lollis, *Raccolta di documenti . . .*, vol. 1, and some are translated in Morison, *JAOD*, pp. 22–31; see also Jane, vol. 1, introduction, pp. xxvii, xc, xci.

p. 108 Colón, *Journal*, Morison, *JAOD*, p. 78.

p. 109 Summary letter: Santangel Letter, facsimile and tr. in Thacher, vol. 2, pp. 17ff; facsimile in Bjorn Landström, *Columbus*, Macmillan, 1966, endpapers; translations in Morison, *JAOD*, pp. 182ff; Jane, vol. 1, pp. 3ff, and his note, pp. cxxiiiff; R. H. Major, *Letters of Christopher Columbus*, Hakluyt (London), 1847, Corinth (NY) reprint, 1961, pp. 1ff; Edward Gaylord Bourne, in Julius E. Olson and E. G. Bourne, eds., *The Northmen, Columbus, and Cabot*, Scribner's, 1925, pp. 263ff.

p. 110 Colón, *Journal*, Morison, *JAOD*, p. 89.

p. 111 "And Your Highnesses"—ibid, p. 105.

p. 112 Morison, *AOS*, vol. 1, p. 319.

p. 113 Colón, *Journal*, Morison, *JAOD*, pp. 115–16.

p. 114 "Your Highnesses"—Colón, *Journal*, Morison, *JAOD*, pp. 133–34.

Footnote: Gerbi, *Nature*, p. 7.

p. 116 "Sent all . . ."—Colón, *Journal*, Morison, JAOD, p. 136.

Footnote: INA contact, Robert C. Smith, College Station, TX 77843.

p. 117 Footnote: see Deagan, in Gerace, pp. 341ff; *New York Times*, August 27, 1985, sect. C.

p. 118 Colón, *Journal*, Morison, *JAOD*, pp. 136–37.

p. 120 Colón, ibid., pp. 151–52.
p. 121 Colón, ibid, p. 155.

Chapter Six   1493–94

p. 123 Colón, *Journal*, Morison, *JAOD*, p. 179.

Santangel Letter: see note to p. 109 above. The single extant copy is the pride of
the Lenox Collection of the New York Public Library.

p. 125 Venetian chronicle: Morison, *AOS*, vol. 2, p. 34. Papal bull, ibid., p. 22,
text in *Book of Privileges* (in English as *Memorials of Columbus*, ed. Giovanni Battista
Spotorno, Treuttel and Winter [London], 1823).

"caused Europe"—John Carter Brown Library essay for IBM exhibit, February
1988.

Hirsch, in Chiappelli, vol. 2, pp. 537ff. See also *European Americana*, John Carter
Brown Library, Readex (New Canaan, CT), vol. 1, 1980.

p. 126 Sovereigns, in Fernando, pp. 105–06.

Colón memorial: Thacher, vol. 3, pp. 100ff (with facsimile); Morison, *JAOD*,
pp. 199ff; and Bourne, in Olson and Bourne, eds. *The Northmen, Columbus, and
Cabot*, pp. 273ff. There is no date recorded on this memorial, and some have argued
for a later date (e.g., Jane, vol. 1, p. cxlvi), but de Lollis is probably right in assigning
it to 1493 (*Raccolta di documenti* . . . , vol. I, pp. lxxvff), as does Thacher.

p. 127 Footnote: Colón's signature is reproduced and discussed in Thacher, vol.
3, chap. 123.

p. 128 For the Second Voyage, see especially Thacher, vol. 2, chap. 75; Morison,
JAOD, pt. 3; Jane, vol. 1, pp. 20ff.; Fernando, chaps. 46–50, 54–58, 62–03; Provost,
IV.E.3; and original sources in note to p. 129 below.

Footnote: Kayserling, *Christopher Columbus and the Participation of the Jews in
the Spanish and Portuguese Discoveries*, citing a record of May 20, 1493, and orders
of May 23, 1493 (reprinted on pp. 157–69).

p. 129 Original sources: Chanca, originally in Navarrete, *Colección de los viajes
y descubrimientos . . . del siglo xv*, Imprenta Real (Madrid), 1825, vol. 1, pp. 198ff
(see Jane, vol. 1, pp. cxliii–iv), translated by Jane with facing Spanish text, pp. 20ff,
and Thacher, vol. 2, chap. 77. Cuneo, first printed in 1885, and found in de Lollis,
Raccolta, pt. 3, vol. 2, pp. 95ff, translated by Morison, *JAOD*, pp. 210ff, and in
J. H. Parry and Robert G. Keith, eds., *New Iberian World*, Times, 1984. Coma,
in *De insulis meridiani . . . nuper inventis*, put together from his letters by Nicolo
Scillacio (also Syllacio), in Pavia, 1494–45; facsimile and translation in Thacher, vol.
2, pp. 223ff, and translation in Morison, *JAOD*, pp. 229ff.

Coma, Morison, *JAOD*, p. 233.

p. 130 CANNIBALISM: The chief sources here are Anthony Pagden, *The Fall of
Natural Man*, Cambridge, 1982 (and its sources); Eli Sagan, *Cannibalism*, Harper
& Row, 1974; W. Arens, *The Man-Eating Myth*, Oxford, 1979 (with an excellent
bibliography); Robert A. Myers, "Island Carib Cannibalism," *New West Indies
Guide* (Utrecht), vol. 58, 1984; and Michael Palencia-Roth, "Cannibalism and the
New Man of Latin America," *Comparative Civilizations Review*, no. 12, Spring
1985. Arens has been taken to task (Donald Forsyth, "Three Cheers for Hans
Staden," *Ethnohistory*, vol. 32, 1985) for his dismissal of Hans Staden's eyewitness
account (*True History of His Captivity*, McBride [NY], 1929), and Arens is probably
too ready to dismiss the many other descriptions of some forms of ritualistic flesh-
eating, but his basic point and proofs remain largely sound.

The question of sacrifice and cannibalism as a source of protein for human diets received a good deal of attention a few years ago thanks to Michael Harner, "The Ecological Basis for Aztec Sacrifice," *American Ethnologist*, February 1977, and Marvin Harris, *Cannibals and Kings*, Random House, 1977, but they didn't stand up even on their own terms, as Marshall Sahlins (*New York Review of Books*, November 23, 1978), among others, demonstrated. Stanley Garn and Walter Block also have made a good case (*American Anthropologist*, vol. 72, February 1970, and vol. 81, December 1979) that the nutritional value of cannibalism is slim indeed, particularly if calories expended are compared with calories acquired. Montaigne's famous essay on the subject (1580), widely available, is most notable for its rare, perhaps then unique, tone of cultural relativism.

Colón on Caribs, *Journal*, Morison, *JAOD*, pp. 151–52.

p. 131 Cuneo, Morison, *JAOD*, p. 212. Although Chanca claimed (Jane, vol. 1, p. 30) that the Europeans were able to distinguish between Caribs and others by the bands of cotton around their legs, Fernando later makes clear (pp. 170–71) that all the island people wore leg wrappings of various kinds.

Guadeloupe: see Rouse, in Gerace, for extent of Carib settlement.

Breton, in Myers, "Cannibalism."

p. 132 Chanca, Jane, vol. 1, p. 32 (references on pp. 26 and 30 to human bones do not indicate cannibalism, only ritual use); Fernando, p. 170.

Breton, in Myers, "Cannibalism."

Las Casas, in Arens, *Man-Eating*, p. 54.

Sheldon, ibid.

Footnote: Keen (Fernando), p. 170; Morison, *JAOD*, p. 248.

p. 133 Breton, in Myers, "Cannibalism."

Arens, *Man-Eating*, p. 21, p. 54.

Martyr, in Arber, p. 67. In this and all subsequent quotations from Eden's six-teenth-century Englishing of Martyr, I have modernized the spelling and punctuation.

p. 134 "slaves"—Santangel Letter, Morison, *JAOD*, p. 186.

Footnote: Pagden, *Fall*; Forsyth, "Three Cheers"; Braudel, *Structures*, p. 78.

"the said Canibales"—Torres Memorandum, Jane, vol. 1, pp. 90–91; Thacher, vol. 2, chap. 80.

p. 135 Gómara, *Historia general de las Indias*, vol. 1, p. 36.

Cuneo, Morison, *JAOD*, p. 212.

p. 136 Chanca, Jane, vol. 1, p. 36.

Coma, Morison, *JAOD*, p. 238.

p. 137 Cuneo, ibid., p. 222.

Fernando, pp. 170, 144.

p. 138 Memo: Torres Memorandum, Jane, vol. 1, pp. 92–93.

Cuneo, Morison, *JAOD*, p. 226.

p. 139 Coma, ibid., pp. 238, 239–40.

p. 140 SYPHILIS: the literature here is vast. Most pertinent are Alfred W. Crosby, Jr., *The Columbian Exchange: Biological and Cultural Consequences of 1492*, Green-wood (Westport, CT), 1972, chap. 4; Morison, *AOS*, vol. 2, pp. 193–218. See also Francisco Guerra, in Chiapelli, vol. 2 (inconclusive); Theodore Rosenberg, *Monthly Review*, vol. 25, April 1974 (non-Columbian); Richard Holcomb, *Who Gave the World Syphilis?* Frober (NY), 1937 (scattershot); Provost, V.E.3. Colón remarks on the health of his crew on November 27; and see *AOS*, vol. 2, pp. 208–09.

Cuneo, Morison, *JAOD*, p. 212.

Vespucci (properly "Vespucci," since this is from the *Mundus novus* probably concocted from copies of his genuine letters in Florence without Amerigo's even knowing about it), tr. George T. Northrup, in the Princeton Project ed., vol. 5, Princeton, 1916.

p. 141 Cuneo, Morison, *JAOD*, p. 213.

p. 142 Coma, ibid., pp. 243–44.

Las Casas, in Thacher, vol. 1, pp. 123–24.

p. 143 Cuneo, Morison, *JAOD*, pp. 214–15.

Footnote: Thacher, vol. 2, pp. 283–84.

p. 144 Cuneo, ibid.

Gold cargo: Morison, *AOS*, vol. 2, p. 105, citing no source; Troy Floyd, *The Columbus Dynasty in the Caribbean 1492–1526*, New Mexico, 1973, app. 2, gives a figure from royal sources of 25,000 *pesos de oro*, or about $76,125 in pre-Depression dollars.

p. 145 Fernando, p. 128.

Martyr, in Arber, p. 80.

Fernando, pp. 122–23.

Colón, Santangel Letter, Morison, *JAOD*, pp. 186, 183.

p. 146 Hojeda, in Fernando, p. 129.

Cuneo, Morison, *JAOD*, p. 215.

Cuneo, ibid., p. 221; the "98" is no doubt an exaggeration or an error, since probably not more than twenty-five sailors each would be assigned to these small ships—one of which, incidentally, was the *Niña* from the First Voyage.

p. 147 Cuba trip: Fernando, chaps. 54–58; Cuneo, Morison, *JAOD*, pp. 221–25; Andrés Bernáldez, *Historia de los reyes católicos*, printed first in Grenada, 1856, in de Lollis, *Raccolta*, vol. 1, and in Jane, vol. 1, p. 114; Cecil Jane, "The Opinion of Columbus Concerning Cuba and the Indies," *Geographical Journal*, vol. 73, 1929. One may safely ignore the attempts by William J. Wilson (e.g., *Hispanic American Historical Review*, vol. 22, February 1942) to claim that Colón discovered South America on this journey.

"Cuba-no-island" oath: text in Young, pp. 350ff, and Thacher, vol. 2, pp. 322ff.

p. 148 Cuneo, Morison, *JAOD*, p. 227.

Morison, *AOS*, vol 2, p. 160.

Martyr, in Arber, p. 90.

Fernando, p. 145.

Chanca, Jane, vol. 1, p. 66; Fernando, p. 128.

p. 149 Cuneo, Morison, *JAOD*, p. 217.

Fernando, pp. 135, 146, 145.

Colón's illness: the most persuasive analysis, among many over the centuries, is Gerald Weissman, *They All Laughed at Christopher Columbus*, Times, 1987, chap. 1, convincingly arguing for Reiter's syndrome. *The New York Times* (October 27, 1987) connects Reiter's with immune-system infections like AIDS, both of which can be spread by sexual contact. Dr. John Politz of New York has theorized (personal communication) that Colón's bones would show signs of Reiter's and that an examination of the various remains might prove whether he was so inflicted or not, but no such inquiry has been undertaken.

p. 151 Fernando, p. 119; italics mine.

Chapter Seven   1495–1500

p. 152 Española: the best sources for Colón's governorship, other than Fernando and Las Casas, *Historia general y natural de las Indias* (bk. I, chaps. 100–122; bk. 2, chaps. 3–4, 7–11), are Floyd, *The Columbus Dynasty in the Caribbean 1492–1526*; Sauer, *Main*; Deagan, in Gerace; Thacher, vol. 2, chap. 86; Parry and Keith, eds., *New Iberian World*, vol. 2, pt. 2; and Stuart B. Schwartz, *The Iberian Mediterranean and Atlantic Traditions in the Formation of Columbus as a Colonizer*, Minnesota, 1986.

p. 153 Elliott, p. 15.

Fernando, pp. 147–48, 149; *AOS*, vol. 2, p. 170, gives March 27, not 24.

p. 154 Las Casas, *Historia*, chap. 90.

Caonabó: Fernando, p. 152; Thacher, vol. 2, p. 349; Morison, *AOS*, vol. 2, p. 171.

Martyr, in Arber, p. 81.

Bartolomé: Fernando, pp. 167–68.

Gallows: John Stuart Collis, *Christopher Columbus*, Stein & Day, 1977, p. 136.

p. 155 Tribute: Fernando, pp. 149–50; and see "List of products received in tribute by the Admiral," Parry and Keith, eds., *New Iberian*, p. 212.

Las Casas, *Historia*, chap. 105.

Encomienda: see Elliott, *Imperial Spain 1469–1716*, pp. 59ff; and Lewis Hanke, *The Spanish Struggle for Justice in the Conquest of America*, Pennsylvania, 1949, especially the bibliography, pp. 182–83, 189.

Las Casas, in Pagden, *The Fall of Natural Man*, p. 35.

p. 156 Royal letters, in Navarrete, *Colección de los viajes y descubrimientos . . .* , vol. 1, pp. 280ff.

Las Casas, *Historia*, and, e.g., *The Spanish Colonie* (one among many English versions of his *Brevisima relación*, London, 1583, University Microfilms reprint, 1966); see also Thacher, vol. 2, pp. 348ff, and Frances A. MacNutt, *Bartholomé de las Casas*, Putnam's, 1909, pp. 316–21, for some of Las Casas's life and work.

p. 157 "A Spaniard"—Las Casas, *Historia*, vol. 3, chap. 29; Todorov, *The Conquest of America*, p. 141. This latter took place in Cuba, with troops under Pánfilo de Nárvaez, but could not have been different in kind from those in Española under Colón.

Oviedo, *Historia general y natural de las Indias*, chaps. 29, 30, 37.

p. 158 Las Casas, last words, Todorov, *Conquest*, p. 245.

p. 159 Las Casas, Thacher, vol. 2, pp. 348ff.

DISEASE: see especially Crosby, *The Columbian Exchange*, chap. 2, and *Ecological Imperialism*; Henry Dobyns, *Their Numbers Become Thinned*, Tennessee, 1983; P. M. Ashburn, *The Ranks of Death*, Coward, 1947; John Duffy, *Epidemics in Colonial America*, Louisiana State, 1953; Russell Thornton, *American Indian Holocaust and Survival*, Oklahoma, 1987; and specifically for Española, Francisco Guerra, "La epidemia americana de influenza en 1493," and "El efeto demografico . . ." in *Revista de Indias*, vol. 45, 1985, and vol. 46, 1986.

Crosby, *Imperialism*, p. 196.

p. 160 DEMOGRAPHY: essential is Sherburne F. Cook and Woodrow Borah, *Essays in Population History*, vol. 1, California, 1971, especially chap. 6; see also William Deneven, ed., *The Native Population of the Americas in 1492*, Wisconsin, 1976;

Henry Dobyns, *Native American Historical Demography* (a bibliographical study), Indiana, 1976, and *Numbers*; Thornton, *Holocaust*.

Footnote: Dobyns, *Numbers*, p. 35, though he has in this respect been accused of overoptimism, e.g., by David Henige, *Journal of Interdisciplinary History*, vol. 16, 1986.

p. 161 Spanish record: see especially Hanke, *Spanish Struggle*, and its extensive bibliography, pp. 200ff; and Salvador de Madariaga, *The Rise of the Spanish American Empire*, Hollis & Carter (London), 1947.

Footnote: Jose Barreiro, *Cultural Survival Quarterly*, vol. 13, no. 3, 1989.

p. 162 Crosby, *Exchange*, chap. 3; quote, p. 66.

Cuneo, Morison, *JAOD*, p. 217.

Footnote: Morison, *AOS*, vol. 1, p. 51, no citation.

p. 163 ECOLOGICAL IMPACT: see especially Crosby, *Exchange* and *Imperialism*; Watts, *West Indies*; Sauer, *Main*; and a defensive David R. Harris, *Plants, Animals and Man in the Outer Leeward Islands*, California Publications in Geography, vol. 18, 1965; Provost, V.E.3.

p. 164 Las Casas, and Crosby, *Exchange*, pp. 111, 75, 99.

Footnote: for *repartimiento*, see Fernando, pp. 211–14.

p. 165 Crosby, *Imperialism*, p. 165.

Colón, in Fernando, p. 143, and Morison, *JAOD*, p. 261.

Zuaso, in Parry and Keith, eds., *New Iberian*, vol. 2, pp. 273–74.

p. 166 Las Casas, in MacNutt, *Las Casas*, p. 318.

Colón, Letter to Juana de Torres, Morison, *JAOD*, pp. 290ff; Jane, vol. 2, pp. 48ff (with Spanish text; and see vol. 1, p. lxxxvi); Thacher, vol. 2, pp. 423ff (also with Spanish text); Bourne, in Olson and Bourne, eds., *The Northmen, Columbus, and Cabot*, pp. 369ff. Quote from Morison, p. 291.

Return trip: Fernando, p. 169, is the only source for this, and it is basically unbelievable for so many people to have been on two small ships; I suspect an error in the Italian transcription from the (lost) original Spanish manuscript.

Las Casas, in Morison, *AOS*, vol. 2, p. 126.

p. 167 "and made enough"—Fernando, p. 170.

"faces the color"—Morison, *AOS*, vol. 2, p. 191.

p. 168 Morison, *AOS*, vol. 2, p. 222.

Fernando, p. 174.

Third voyage: Fernando, chaps. 66–73; Las Casas, *Historia*, chaps. 127–46; Las Casas abstract of Colón journal in Morison, *JAOD*, pp. 259ff, Thacher, vol. 2, chap. 91, and Bourne, in *Northmen*, pp. 317ff; Las Casas copy of a (similar) Letter to the Sovereigns (October 1498), in Jane, vol. 2, p. 2 (with Spanish text), and R. H. Major, *Select Letters of Christopher Columbus*, pp. 104ff; see also Louis A. Vigneras, *The Discovery of South America and the Andalusian Voyages*, Chicago, 1976; Provost, IV.E.4.

p. 169 "go with"—order of June 15, 1497; see Morison, *AOS*, vol. 2, pp. 226, 231.

Cabot: see Quinn, *NAW*, vol. 1, chap. 10. Morison thinks Cabot landed on Newfoundland (*Northern Voyages*, pp. 170ff), but Sauer says flatly it was New England (*Sixteenth*, p. 6).

Da Gama: see Parry, *The European Reconnaissance*, chap. 7.

p. 170 Colón, Morison, *JAOD*, p. 266.

"were perishing"—ibid., p. 275.

"to tell them"—ibid., p. 280.

Colón, ibid., p. 279.

p. 171 Colón, ibid., pp. 259, 262.

Colón, ibid, pp. 279–80.

p. 172 Maps: see, e.g., Shirley, *The Mapping of the World*; Quinn, *NAW*, vol. 1; Seymour I. Schwartz et al., *The Mapping of North America*, Abrams, 1980.

p. 173 Colón, Morison, *JAOD*, p. 281.

p. 174 Pearls, ibid., p. 273; "robbed me," *Lettera Rarissima*, ibid., p. 385.

p. 175 *Journal* entries, ibid., pp. 261, 264, 279, 281, and Jane, vol. 2, p. 22.

"the Terrestrial Paradise"—Morison, *JAOD*, p. 282.

Letter to Sovereigns, ibid., p. 285ff, and Jane, vol. 2, pp. 2ff. Morison translates *"ingenio"* as "ability" and Jane as "intelligence," although Morison argues in *AOS*, vol. 1, p. 73, that the word really means "creative talent" such as "the creative artists of the Renaissance displayed."

Las Casas, in Morison, *AOS*, vol. 2, p. 285. Las Casas, *Historia*, vol. 1, pp. 142ff, has a discussion of the placement of Earthly Paradise, and Washington Irving devotes one of his appendix notes (no. 35) (in Twayne edition, op. cit, vol. 12, pp. 333ff) to the subject. Maps with Paradise were fairly common in the second half of the fifteenth century, as for example the Fra Mauro Map of 1458–59 and the Paris Map of 1490.

p. 177 Colón, Morison, *JAOD*, p. 283.

p. 178 Mumford, *The City in History*, Harcourt, 1961, pp. 192–93.

Fernando, p. 191; Martyr, in Arber, p. 90.

Footnote: Fernando, p. 191.

p. 179 Colón's wealth: "four millions," Morison, *JAOD*, p. 292; figures on gold extraction and other details of Colón's estate are in Floyd, *Dynasty*, p. 170.

Fernando, pp. 206ff.

Colón, "For six," Torres Letter, Morison, *JAOD*, pp. 292, 296; the letter is also in Jane, vol. 2 (with Spanish text), pp. 48ff; Bourne, in *Northmen*, pp. 371ff; and elsewhere.

p. 180 Colón, Morison, *JAOD*, p. 297.

Morison, *AOS*, p. 486, and *JAOD*, p. 298.

Torres Letter, Morison, *JAOD*, pp. 292, 294.

p. 181 Gold production: Floyd, *Dynasty*, p. 68, and app. 2; Earl J. Hamilton, *American Treasure and the Price Revolution in Spain 1501–1650*, Harvard, 1934; Braudel, pp. 466–67. The salaries on Colón's Fourth Voyage are in Morison, *JOAD*. pp. 315ff; Bobadilla as governor had an annual salary of 180,000 maravedis.

Torres Letter, Morison, *JAOD*, p. 297.

"Gold is most excellent"—*Lettera Rarissima*, Morison, *JAOD*, p. 383.

p. 182 Bobadilla: Fernando, pp. 221–23; Floyd, *Dynasty*, pp. 239–40; Morison, *JAOD*, pp. 299ff.

Fernando, pp. 221–23.

Trasierra, in Floyd, *Dynasty*, p. 46.

p. 183 Colón, *Lettera Rarissima*, Morison, *JAOD*, p. 385.

Fernando, p. 223.

Tennyson, "Columbus," 1880.

Chapter Eight   1500–06

p. 184 Torres Letter, Morison, *JAOD*, p. 290.

Sovereigns, December 12, in *Book of Privileges*, Spotorno, ed., *Memorials of*

Columbus; see Thacher, pp. 559–60. Fernando gives December 17 as the date for this, but by then Colón was being received at Court.

p. 185 Ruiz: Bobadilla memo to the archbishop of Toledo, October 12, 1500; see Floyd, *The Columbus Dynasty in the Caribbean 1492–1526*.

"*otro mundo*"—Morison, *JAOD*, pp. 276, 288, 296; Jane, vol. 2, pp. 44, 66.

Voyages to Paria: Harrisse, *Discovery of North America*, pp. 361ff; Morison, *Southern*, chap. 9.

Book of Privileges, Spotorno, ed., *Memorials*; see also Thacher, vol. 2, chap. 99; in addition to the Spotorno version, there is Benjamin Franklin Stevens, ed., *Christopher Columbus: His Own Book of Privileges, 1502*, London, 1893, with a long introduction by Henry Harrisse.

p. 186 Footnote: Martyr, in Arber, pp. 94, 96; *Libretto*, Venice, 1504; Fourth Voyage: Morison, *JAOD*, p. 315.

p. 187 Sovereigns, Decree of September 27, 1501, in Morison, *JAOD*, pp. 300ff. Footnote: Colón, Morison, *JOAD*, p. 165; see Jane, vol. 2, p. xxv.

p. 188 *Book of Prophecies*, in de Lollis, *Raccolta di documenti . . .* , pt. 1, vol. 2, pp. lviiff.; part of its prefatory letter is in Fernando, p. 10; see also Watts, "Prophecy and Discovery," *American Historical Review*.

p. 189 Winsor, in Gerace, p. 50; Young, p. 146; Morison, *AOS*, vol. 2, p. 312.

p. 190 Torres Letter, Morison, *JAOD*, p. 291.

Footnote: ibid., p. 384.

p. 191 Colón, *Journal*, ibid., p. 139.

p. 192 Royal assent: ibid., pp. 309ff.

Crew: for the roster, ibid., pp. 314ff; *AOS*, vol. 2, pp. 318–20, has wrong figures. The chief source for the voyage is Fernando; Morison's translation of the relevant chapter is in *JAOD*, pp. 322–70.

"*el alto viaje*"—*Pleitos*, Duro, ed., *De los pleitos de Colón*, vol. 2, p. 227.

Fernando, p. 245.

29 June: Fernando, pp. 228–29.

p. 193 Colón, *Lettera Rarissima*, Morison, *JAOD*, pp. 373: see also Thacher, vol. 2; Bourne, *Northmen*, pp. 389ff.

Footnote: Martyr, in Arber, p. 105.

p. 194 Colón, in Morison, *JAOD*, pp. 373, 374, 376, 377.

Fernando, pp. 247, 230; also Morison, *AOS*, vol. 2, p. 327.

p. 195 Colón, Morison, *JAOD*, p. 381.

Fernando, pp. 243, 234.

p. 196 "Gold"—Morison, *JAOD*, pp. 377, 374.

14 August: Fernando, p. 235.

p. 197 NOBLE SAVAGE/SAVAGE BEAST: several works dealing with this theme are cited in the note to p. 75 above, especially Bernheimer, Dickason, Dudley and Novak, and Friedman. See also Elliott; Pagden, *The Fall of Natural Man*; Hanke, *The Spanish Struggle for Justice in the Conquest of North America*; Todorov, *The Conquest of America*; William Brandon, *New Worlds for Old* especially rewarding; Laura Schrager Fishman, *How Noble the Savage?*, Ph.D. diss., CUNY, 1979 (University Microfilms, 1981); *Europe and Its Encounter with the Amerindians*, special issue, *History of European Ideas*, vol. 6, 1985; Robert Berkhoffer, *The White Man's Indian*, Vintage, 1979, and its notes to pt. 1; Francis Jennings, *The Invasion of America: Indians, Colonialism, and the Cant of Conquest*, Norton, 1976 (orig. 1975).

Santangel Letter, Morison, *JAOD*, pp. 182–86, and other versions in note to p. 109 above.

"Vespucci," *Mundus novus,* tr. Northrup, Princeton, 1916.

Footnote: Hirsch, in Chiapelli.

p. 198 Martyr, in Arber, pp. 71, 78.

p. 200 Researcher: William Brandon, *New Worlds.*

Arciniegas, *America in Europe: A History of the New World in Reverse,* Harcourt, 1975, p. 51.

p. 201 Colón, *Lettera Rarissima,* Morison, *JAOD,* pp. 378, 381, 382, 385, 296.

Ortiz, in Todorov, *Conquest,* pp. 150–51.

p. 202 Sepúlveda, in Hanke, *Struggle,* pp. 122–23.

"Vespucci," edition printed in Rostock, 1505; see Susi Colin, in Christian Feest, ed., *Indians and Europe,* Rader Verlag (Aachen), 1987.

Thevet, in Elliott, in Chiapelli; my italics.

p. 203 9 November: Fernando, pp. 244–45.

p. 204 Pedro Mateos, in Sauer, *Main,* p. 141.

p. 205 Bastidas, ibid., pp. 116–18, 122; Morison, *Southern,* p. 199.

Colón, *Lettera Rarissima,* Morison, *JAOD,* pp. 374–75, 385; see also Thacher, vol. 2, pp. 589–93.

p. 207 Maps: e.g., Shirley, *The Mapping of the World,* and Quinn, *NAW.* The British Museum copy of the Contarini map was published by Oxford (London, 1924) with a large foldout facsimile; the Piri Re'is is discussed by Paul E. Kahle, *Geographical Review,* vol. 23, 1933.

Colón, *Lettera Rarissima,* Morison, *JAOD,* p. 378.

p. 208 Landström, *Columbus,* p. 191; similarly, Fuson, *The Log of Christopher Columbus,* p. 23, and Quinn, foreword to *AOS,* 1983. For discussions of Colón's later geographical ideas see Thacher, vol. 2, pp. 568, 617–21, and vol. 3, pp. 560–62; Sauer, *Main;* Harrisse, *Discovery;* Cecil Jane, "The Opinion of Columbus Concerning Cuba and the Indies," *Geographical Journal,* vol. 73, 1929, and introduction to *Four Voyages,* vol. 1; Vignaud, *Études critiques* . . . ; John Bigelow, "The So-Called Bartholomew Columbus Map of 1506," *Geographical Review,* vol. 25, 1935; Provost, V.E.2.a and IV.E.5. G. E. Nunn has produced several noted works (e.g., *The Geographical Conceptions of Columbus,* American Geographic Society, 1924, pt. 3; *The Columbus and Magellan Concepts of South American Geography,* privately printed, Glenside (CA?), 1932; and *Imago Mundi,* vol. 2, 1937, but I find most of his conclusions erroneous and some downright silly (for example, his idea that the Bartolomé maplets are genuine).

p. 209 Eve of St. John's Day: Fernando, pp. 264–65; Morison, *JAOD,* p. 354, makes this "the night before" the eve (June 22) and the marooning at Santa Gloria June 25.

Colón as mariner: E. G. R. Taylor, introduction to Jane, vol. 2, and "Columbus the Navigator," *Journal of the Institute of Navigation,* vol. 14, 1961; also Morison, "Columbus as a Navigator," *Studi colombiani,* vol. 2, 1952; Provost, V.L.

p. 210 Colón, *Lettera,* Morison, *JAOD,* pp. 376, 379, 373, 377, 379–80.

p. 211 Colón, ibid., p. 385.

p. 212 Colón's wealth: see his will, in Young, pp. 356ff; Floyd, *Dynasty;* Schoenrich, *The Legacy of Columbus,* especially pp. 57ff; Morison, *AOS,* vol. 2, pp. 412–13. All figures here are in pre-Depression dollars.

p. 213 Colón, *Lettera Rarissima,* Morison, *JAOD,* pp. 374, 381; Fernando, p. 240.

Morison, *AOS,* vol. 2, p. 410.

Codicil, Young, pp. 367ff.

p. 214 Death: Fernando, p. 284; Cesare de Lollis, *Cristoforo Colombo nella leggenda e nella storia*, Rome, 1923, p. 313.

PORTRAITS: no adequate study exists, but approaches toward it may be found in William Eleroy Curtis, *Christopher Columbus: His Portraits and His Monuments*, Chicago, 1893; Nestor Ponce de León, *The Columbus Gallery*, self-published (New York), 1893; Thacher, vol. 3, pp. 8ff; A. A. Pedroso, in *Studi colombiani*, Genoa, vol. 3; Winsor, vol. 2, pp. 69ff; Hugh Honour, *The European Vision of America*, Cleveland Museum of Art, 1975; Morison, *AOS*, vol. 1, pp. 65–67, 73; Provost, V.M.

Martyr, see Thacher, vol. 1, chaps. 1–16; "Colonus being"—in Arber, p. 106.

Impact of the New World on the Old: much has been written but probably sufficient are Elliott, especially chap. 1; Antonello Gerbi, *The Dispute of the New World*, tr. Jeremy Moyle, Pittsburgh, 1973; Honour, *Vision*; and essays by Elliott, Gerbi, and Myron P. Gilmore in Chiappelli, vol. 1.

p. 215 "America"—see endnote 7 to chap. 8; Waldseemüller's *Cosmographiae*, 1507, with maps, and "Vespucci," *Four Voyages* (modern ed.), tr. C. G. Hebermann, Books for Libraries Press (Freeport, NY), 1969; John Noble Wilford, *The Mapmakers*, Knopf, 1981; Daniel Boorstin, *The Discoverers*, Random, 1983; Las Casas is quoted in S. F. Bemis, *Yale Review*, vol. 57, March 1968.

p. 216 Remains: Thacher, vol. 3, pt. 9, chaps. 124–43; Morison, *Southern*, pp. 269–71, too dogmatic, as usual; *Encuentro* (University of New Mexico), Spring 1988; Provost, V.N.

Chapter Nine   1506–1606 (1)   *The Columbian Legacy*

p. 217 Oviedo, in Arber, pp. 209, 236; spelling and punctuation are modernized from Eden's translation of Oviedo's 1526 *Sumário*.

p. 218 Spanish monuments: by 1892 there were monuments in six cities, though the ones in Salamanca and Huelva had no statues of Colón; there was also a smaller statue in Seville, and an indoor statue and bust in Madrid; see Curtis, *Christopher Columbus*, and Thacher, vol. 3.

Oviedo, in Elliott, p. 11.

p. 219 Corte Real: Quinn, *NAW*, pp. 150–51.

Gomes, in Morison, *Northern*, p. 331.

Beothuks: Peter Such, *Vanished Peoples*, NC Press (Toronto), 1978.

p. 220 Printing of Colón voyages: see note to p. 109 above.

p. 221 Colón bibliography: see endnote 1 to chap. 9; *European Americana* (Reader Books, New Canaan, CT, 1980–82) is quite incomplete, and must be supplemented by Joseph Sabin, *A Dictionary of Books Relating to America*, 12 vols., 1870, N. Israel (Amsterdam) reprint, 1961; Henry Harrisse, *Biblioteca Americana Vetustissima*, New York, 1866, Paris, 1872 (updated by Carlos Sanz, Suarez [Madrid], 1960), and *Notes on Columbus*; Winsor; John Parker, *Books to Build an Empire: Bibliographical History of English Overseas Interests to 1620*, N. Israel (Amsterdam), 1965; E. G. R. Taylor, *Late Tudor and Early Stuart Geography*, Methuen, 1934, Octagon (New York) reprint, 1968. See also Quinn, introduction to *NAW*, vol. 5, pp. lxivff; Provost, VI.

Polyglot Psalter, reproduced in Thacher, vol. 1, chap. 29.

p. 222 Martyr, in Arber, tr. Richard Eden; for the details of its printing history, as for the other works mentioned in the text, see endnote 1 to chap. 9; see also Elizabeth Baer, "Richard Eden's Copy of the 1533 Decades," in *Essays Honoring Lawrence C. Wroth*, Anthoesen (Portland, ME), 1951.

p. 223 Penrose, *Travel and Discovery in the Renaissance 1420–1620*, Harvard, 1952, p. 277.

Martyr, in Arber, pp. 90, 103.

"a huge"—Gerbi, *Nature in the New World*, p. 129.

p. 224 Oviedo, on Colón, in Arber, p. 209; and *Historia general y natural de las Indias*, vol. 1, p. 167; vol 2, 13:1; vol. 6, 8:1.

Oviedo's burial: Thacher, vol. 2, p. 548.

Gómara, *Historia general de las Indias*, and Arber, pp. 340ff.

p. 225 Münster, *A treatyse of the new India*, tr. Richard Eden, London, 1553, in Arber, pp. 3ff, especially pp. 29–36; it is the earliest Latin edition, Basel, 1550, that has "Columbus," on p. 1099.

Ramusio: Quinn, *NAW*, vol. 1, p. lxv.

p. 226 La Roque: Morison, *Northern*, pp. 434ff; Quinn, *NAW*, vol. 1, chap. 22, pp. 337–39; *"il y a infiny"*—Davies, p. 22.

p. 228 Giovio: Thacher, vol. 3, pp. 9ff.

p. 229 Epic poems: see Leicester Bradner, in *Essays . . . Wroth*.

p. 230 Tasso: Edward Fairfax translation, London, 1600; a modern version (which does not actually do much more justice to these stanzas) is Joseph Tusiani, tr., *Jerusalem Delivered*, Fairleigh Dickinson, 1970.

p. 231 Fernando: see especially Keen's introduction; Jane, vol. 1, especially pp. xxviff; Taviani, pp. 470–71 (and references, principally de Armas); the full title is fifty-two words long, beginning *Historie del S.D. Fernando Colombo. . . .*

p. 232 Irving, in Fernando, p. v.

Frobisher: Morison, *Northern*, chaps. 15, 16; Quinn, *NAW*, vol. 4, chap. 80; Vilhjalmur Stefansson, *The Three Voyages of Martin Frobisher*, London, 1938; "which as many"—in Quinn, p. 207.

p. 233 Cortés: a no doubt apocryphal remark given us by William Prescott, *History of the Conquest of Mexico*, Philadelphia, 1873, vol. 3, pp. 217–18.

Camden, in Morison, *Northern*, p. 545.

p. 235 Gilbert, in Richard Hakluyt, *Principall navigations, voiages & discoveries of the English nations*, London, 1598, MacLehose-Glasgow University reprint, 1903–05, vol. 7, p. 464.

p. 236 Eden, in Arber (Münster), p. 6

Abbot, London, 1599.

p. 237 Seall, "A Comendation of the adulterus viage of the wurthy Captain M. Thomas Stutely [sic] and others, towards the Land called *Terra Florida*," 1563; a replica is in the New York Public Library.

p. 238 Egg story: Benzoni, *Historia*, Venice, 1565, p. 12; translation here by Morison, *AOS*, vol. 2, p. 15; refutation by de Lollis, *Cristoforo Colombo nella leggenda e nella storia*, p. 139.

Footnote: Quinn, *EADA*, p. 266; *NAW*, vol. 3.

p. 239 Barcelona: Las Casas, tr. Thacher, vol. 1, pp. 668–69; see also Morison, *AOS*, vol. 2, pp. 10–11; Antonio Rumeu de Armas, *Colón en Barcelona*, Editorial Católica (Seville), 1944.

Chapter Ten 1506–1606 (II) England

p. 241 Jamestown voyage of 1606–07: see Quinn, *NAW*, vol. 5, pt. 23, with original sources of Percy, pp. 267ff, and Smith, pp. 310ff; John Smith, *Travels and Works* . . . , Edward Arber, ed., English Scholars Library (Birmingham), 1884; Philip L. Barbour, *The Three Worlds of Captain John Smith*, Houghton Mifflin, 1964, and *The Jamestown Voyages Under the First Charter*, Hakluyt Society/ Cambridge (London), 1969; Matthew Page Andrews, *The Soul of a Nation: The Founding of Virginia and the Projection of New England*, Scribner's (Sponsors' Edition), 1944.

"to digg"—Virginia Company charter, April 10, 1606, in Quinn, *NAW*, vol. 5, pt. 23, p. 194.

p. 242 Ralegh, quoted by A. L. Rowse, *American Heritage*, June 1959, p. 106. *Antony* is generally thought to be c. 1606–07, after *Lear*.

"gentlemen"—Barbour, *Three Worlds*, says 59; Andrews, *Soul*, says 58; Smith himself (*Travels*, pp. 93–94) lists only 29 gentlemen and 6 well-born members of the governing council.

Percy wardrobe: Rukeyser, *Traces*, p. 202; but records show he was also sent a beaver hat with band in 1611.

Four failures: Roanoke, 1585 and 1587; Gosnold in New England, 1602; Leigh in Guiana, 1605; Gilbert and Frobisher also had taken men to establish colonies, but did not do so. See Quinn, *EADA*.

Footnote: Muriel Rukeyser, *The Traces of Thomas Hariot*, Random, 1970, 1971, p. 204.

p. 243 Andrews, *Soul*, p. 50.

Royal patent: Quinn, *NAW*, pp. 193–96.

Hakluyt, in Louis B. Wright, ed., *The Elizabethans' America*, Harvard, 1965, pp. 156ff, and elsewhere.

Newport: see Quinn, *EADA*, p. 209; and especially K. R. Andrews, "Christopher Newport of Limehouse, Mariner," *William and Mary Quarterly*, vol. 9, January 1954.

p. 244 "a Mariner"—Smith, in Quinn, *NAW*, p. 310.

p. 245 Poem, Michael Drayton, "To Virginia," in, e.g., Wright, *Elizabethans'*.

Ralegh: Norman Lloyd Williams, *Sir Walter Raleigh*, Penguin (London), 1965, pt. 5; death sentence, p. 215 ("to be strucken" is from the version in Rukeyser, *Traces*, p. 177).

Footnote: Andrews, *Soul*, p. 7.

p. 246 Purchas, *Virginias Verger*, in *Haklytus posthumus, or Purchas his pilgrimes*; *True Relation* and *A Map of Virginia*, in Smith, *Travels*, and Philip L. Barbour, ed., *The Complete Works of John Smith*, 3 vols., North Carolina, 1986.

"where we suffered"—Percy, in Quinn, *NAW*, p. 267.

p. 247 "Canibals"—ibid.

Smith, ibid., p. 311.

Newport voyage: Quinn, *EADA*, pp. 452–53.

Percy, Quinn, *NAW*, p. 268.

St. Augustine: Carl O. Sauer, *Seventeenth Century North America*, Turtle Island (Berkeley), 1980, chap. 2.

p. 248 Witchcraft: e.g., Brian P. Levock, *The Witchhunt in Early Modern Europe*, Longmans, 1987; G. R. Quaife, *Godly Zeal and Furious Rage*, Croom Helm (London), 1987 (with a good bibliography, and fair estimate of deaths, p. 79); Norman Cohn, *Europe's Inner Demons*, Sussex University, 1975; Jeffrey B. Russell, *Witch-craft in the Middle Ages*, Cornell, 1972; Hans Peter Duerr, *Dreamtime*, tr. Felicitas Goodman, Blackwell, 1985. For the Supreme Tribunal see Robert Ergang, *Europe from the Renaissance to Waterloo*, Heath, 1939, p. 173.

p. 249 *Malleus*, in Friedell, *A Cultural History of the Modern Age*, p. 285.

p. 251 Bartolomé visit: Oviedo, in Quinn, *NAW*, vol. 1, pp. 135–36; Fernando, pp. 36–37; see also Quinn, *EADA*, p. 75ff; Taviani, pp. 474–75.

Day/Say Letter: Quinn, *NAW*, vol. 1, pp. 98–99; and *EADA*, pp. 5ff, 94ff.

p. 252 John Cabot: ibid., ch. 10.

Sebastian Cabot, in Arber, p. 288; "is believed"—Quinn, *EADA*, p. 102. For Sebastian's career see Quinn, *NAW*, vol. 1, chap. 12; Morison, *Northern*, chap. 6.

Brant, in Quinn, *NAW*, vol. 1, pp. 128–29.

p. 253 "Armenica"—Arber, pp. xxvff.

Hyckescorner, in Quinn, *NAW*, vol. 1, pp. 128–29, and *EADA*, pp. 169–70. *Four Elements*, in Quinn, *NAW*, vol. 1, p. 171; in Arber, pp. xx–xxi; and complete in Percy Society Manuscripts, London, 1848, vol. 22. For its date, see Parker, *Books to Build an Empire*; Quinn, *EADA*, p. 167; Hirsch, in Chiapelli, vol. 1.

Early English voyages: Quinn, *EADA*, chaps. 1, 6; and in *Geographical Journal*, vol. 127, 1961.

Münster, *A treatyse of the newe India*, tr. Richard Eden; a copy is in the New York Public Library.

Penrose, "First Book About America Printed in England," *Pennsylvania Magazine*, January 1949.

p. 254 ENGLISH BOOKS MENTIONING COLON: Parker, *Books*; Taylor, *Late Tudor and Early Stuart Geography*; Franklin T. McCann, *The English Discovery of America to 1585*, King's Crown (Columbia University), 1952; D. B. Quinn, *The New Found Land*, John Carter Brown Library (Providence, RI), 1965; P. Lee Phillips, "List of Books Relating to America in the Register of the London Company of Stationers, from 1562 to 1638," *American Historical Association Annual Report*, vol. 1, 1896.

Footnote: Baer, "Richard Eden's Copy of the 1533 Decades," in *Essays Honoring Lawrence C. Wroth*.

p. 255 Parmenius: D. B. Quinn and Neil M. Cheshire, ed. and tr., *The New Found Land of Stephen Parmenius*, Toronto, 1972; this first-rate edition has a useful general bibliography, pp. 227ff.

Gilbert, *A discourse for the discoverie for a new passage to Cataia*, London, 1576; and in Hakluyt, *Principall navigations voiages, & discoveries of the English nation*, vol. 7, pp. 188–89.

Seall, "A comendation . . ."; see note to p. 237 above.

Hakluyt, preface to the second edition of *Principall navigations*, vol. 1, p. xli.

Footnote: Bridenbaugh, *Vexed and Troubled Englishmen*, Oxford, 1968.

p. 256 Abbay, in Smith, *Travels*, p. 43; it is always difficult to know how much of Smith's *Map* is his own language, but I see no reason to think that this dedication is anyone's work but that of Abbay, who signed it.

St. Bartholomew's Day Massacre: e.g., Ergang, *Europe*, pp. 320–21, with mention of Philip on p. 321n; see also James Westfall Thompson, *The Wars of Religion in France 1559–1576*, Ungar (New York), 1909?.

p. 258 Donne and Virginia: Rukeyser, *Traces*, p. 215.

Donne: *Elegie: Going to Bed*.

America as maiden: see especially Annette Kolodny, *Lay of the Land*, North Carolina, 1975, chap. 2; Merchant, *The Death of Nature*. Thomas Morton's *New English Canaan*, London, 1637?, provides a typical later example of this attitude.

p. 259 Barlowe, in D. B. Quinn, ed., *The Roanoke Voyages 1584–1590*, Hakluyt Society/Cambridge, 1955, vol. 1, p. 91; Settle, *A true report* . . . , London, 1577, in Quinn, *NAW*, vol. 4, pp. 210, 214; Eden, in Arber, p. 269; Harcourt, *A Relation of a voyage to Guiana*, Hakluyt Society (London) reprint, 1928, p. 106; Axtell, *The European and the Indian*, Oxford, 1981, p. 41; Hamilton, in Chiapelli, vol. 2.

GOLD: Hamilton, *American Treasure and the Price Revolution in Spain 1501–1650*, and "The Role of Monopoly in the Colonial Trade and Expansion of Europe," *American Economic Review*, vol. 38, 1948, and in Chiappelli, vol. 2; Pierre Chaunu, *European Expansion in the Late Middle Ages*, North-Holland (Amsterdam/New York), 1979, and with Huguette Chaunu, *Seville et l'antique 1504–1650*, 11 vols., Colin (Paris), 1955; Braudel, pp. 459ff; Peter Burke, ed., *Economy and Society in Early Modern Europe*, Routledge (London), 1972, especially chaps. 3–5; Elliott, pp. 59ff, and *Imperial Spain 1469–1716*, chap. 5, pt. 3. Gold and silver figures, from Hamilton, *Treasure*, p. 34, at $2.32 per ducat, equal $1.245 billion; Clough and Cole, *Economic History of Europe*, p. 127, estimate $924 million, using $35 per ounce for gold.

p. 260 Spanish army: William H. McNeill, *The Pursuit of Power*, Chicago, 1982, pp. 110–11, and Paul Kennedy, *The Rise and Fall of Great Powers*, Random, 1987, pp. 45–46.

FISH: Harold A. Innes, *The Cod Fisheries*, Yale, 1940; Gillian T. Cell, *English Enterprise in Newfoundland 1577–1660*, Toronto, 1969; Charles Burnet Judah, Jr., *The North American Fisheries and British Policy to 1713 (University of Illinois Bulletin)*, vol. 31, 1933; Charles Bréard and Paul Bréard, *Documents relatifs à la marine normande*, Lestringaut (Rouen), 1889; D. B. Quinn, *North America from Earliest Discovery to First Settlements*, Harper & Row, 1977, pp. 511ff; Davies, pp. 12–16.

p. 261 Gold/fish table: gold figures from Clough and Cole, *Economic History*; fish figures are mine, from the sources listed in the preceding note, with the English pound equivalent to $5 to $7 in pre-Depression dollars (cf. Innes, *Fisheries*).

"great abundance"—John Davis, in Innes, *Fisheries*, chap. 3.

"Great Britaines"—in Cell, *Enterprise*, introduction.

FURS: Harold A. Innes, *The Fur Trade in Canada*, Yale, 1930 (rev. 1956, 1970, Toronto); O. C. Phillips, *The Fur Trade*, Oklahoma, 1961; H. P. Biggar, *The Early Trading Companies of New France*, Warwich (Toronto), 1901; W. J. Eccles, "The Fur Trade and 18th-Century Imperialism," *William and Mary Quarterly*, vol. 40, 1983, and *The Canadian Frontier 1534–1760*, Holt, 1969; Trudel, *The Beginnings of New France*; Calvin Martin, *Keepers of the Game*, California, 1978; Davies, pp. 16ff.

p. 262 COMMODITIES: in addition to sources above, George Louis Beer, *The Origins of the British Colonial System 1578–1660*, Macmillan, 1908; Charles F. Carroll, *The Timber Economy of Puritan New England*, Brown, 1973; G. D. Ramsay, *English Overseas Trade During the Centuries of Emergence*, Macmillan (London), 1957; Eric Williams, *From Columbus to Castro: The History of the Caribbean*, Vintage, 1970; Braudel; Davies, especially "Bibliographical Note."

Chaunu, *European Expansion*, p. 65.

p. 263 Braudel, *The Perspective of the World*, p. 387.

Faust: Joseph Campbell, *Creative Mythology*, Viking, 1968, pp. 596–99; "up and down"—p. 597.

p. 264 Friedell, *A Cultural History of the Modern Age*, pp. 224–28; quote, p. 212.

ENGLISH ASCENDANCY: e.g., ibid., pp. 322–26; Bridenbaugh, *Vexed*; Davies; Catton and Catton, *The Bold and Magnificent Dream:America's Founding Years*; Theodore K. Rabb, *Enterprise and Empire: Merchant and Gentry Investment in the Expansion of England, 1575–1630*, Harvard, 1967; C. B. Macpherson, *The Political Theory of Possessive Individualism*, Clarendon (Oxford) 1962, pp. 263ff; D. B. Quinn and A. N. Ryan, *England's Sea Empire 1550–1642*, Allen & Unwin, 1983; R. H. Tawney, "The Rise of the Gentry 1558–1640," *Economic History Review*, vol. 11, 1941; F. J. Fisher, "Commercial Trends and Policy in Sixteenth Century England," *Economic History Review*, vol. 10, 1940.

p. 265 Investments: Rabb, *Enterprise*, pp. 57–62; he figures a pound sterling of that era as worth $100 in mid-1960 currency, which seems too high.

Davies, p. 51.

p. 266 Ralegh, in Rabb, *Enterprise*, p. 15.

Chapter Eleven   1607–25 (I) *Jamestown*

p. 267 JAMESTOWN: in addition to works cited for p. 241, see: William Strachey, *Historie of Travell Into Virginia Britania*, 1610–12, Louis B. Wright and Virginia Freund, eds., Hakluyt Society/Cambridge (London), 1953; and *True Reportory*, in Purchas, *Hakluytus posthumus, or Purchas his pilgrimes*, vol. 19; George Percy, "Trewe Relacyon . . . ," *Tyler's Quarterly*, vol. 3, 1922, and Kraus reprint, 1969; Ralph Hamor, *A True Discourse of the Present Estate of Virginia*, London, 1615, and in Purchas, *Pilgrimes*, vol. 19; Quinn, *NAW*, vol. 5; Edmund S. Morgan, *American Slavery, American Freedom*, Norton, 1975; Wesley Frank Craven, *The Southern Colonies in the Seventeenth Century 1607–1689*, Louisiana State, 1949; Louis B. Wright, *The Dream of Prosperity in Colonial America*, New York University, 1965; Jack P. Greene, ed., *Great Britain and the American Colonies 1606–1763* (documents), South Carolina, 1970; and the full series published under E. G. Swem, Jamestown 350th Anniversary Historical Booklets, University Press of Virginia, 1957, especially *A Selected Bibliography of Virginia 1607–1699*.

Strachey, in Quinn, *NAW*, p. 294.

p. 268 North American European population: Davies, with particular attention to his notes for chap. 3; Sauer, *Seventeenth Century North America*; Charles M. Andrews, *The Colonial Period of American History*, vol. 1, Yale, 1934; Stella H. Sutherland, *Population Distribution in Colonial America*, Columbia, 1936 (to be used with caution, as, e.g., her total misreading of Berkeley, p. 184).

On original Jamestown sources, see especially Quinn, *NAW*, introduction to pt. 23, pp. 187–89 (though "E. D. Morgan" there is really Edward S. Morgan); and in Morgan, *Slavery*, pp. 433ff; see also Edward M. Riley and Charles E. Hatch, eds., *Jamestown in the Words of Contemporaries*, National Park Service source book series no. 5, Washington, D.C. 1944.

p. 269 "a verie fit"—Smith, *Travels and Works . . .* , p. 6.

Smith, in Quinn, *NAW*, p. 311.

p. 270 Powhatans: see notes to chap. 12 below for sources.

European invasions: sources for note 4 for chap. 11 include Quinn, *EADA*, chap. 15, pp. 426–29, and chap. 17; Clifford M. Lewis and Albert J. Loomie, eds, *The Spanish Jesuit Mission in Virginia 1570–1572*, North Carolina, 1953; Christian Feest, "Virginia Algonquians," in Bruce G. Trigger, ed., *Handbook of North American Indians*, no. 15, Smithsonian, 1978; and Fausz, in Fitzhugh, pp. 231ff.

Powhatan singularity, Fitzhugh, p. 188.

Percy, Quinn, *NAW*, pp. 272–73.

Footnote: see J. Frederick Fausz, in Fitzhugh, p. 236; Strachey, *Historie of Travell*.

p. 271 Deaths: Smith, *Advertisements for the unexperienced Planters of New-England*, in *Travels*, p. 929; John L. Cotter, *Archeological Excavations at Jamestown*, National Park Research Series #4, Washington, D.C., 1988; Morgan, *Slavery*, pp. 101–07; S. M. Kingsbury, ed., *Records of the Virginia Company of London*, 3 vols., U.S. Government Printing Office, 1906; P. M. Ashburn, *The Ranks of Death: A Medical History of the Conquest of America*, Coward, 1947. Berkeley, quoted in Davies, p. 72.

Footnote: see Kingsbury, ed., *Records*, vol. 3, p. 536, and vol. 1, p. 158; "were putt"—vol. 1, p. 363.

p. 272 "not so provident"—Hamor, *Discourse*, p. 26; "not compelled"—Quinn, *NAW*, p. 290; "idlenesse"—ibid., p. 299; "this starveinge"—Percy, "Trewe Relacyon."

Functional disability: Morgan, *Slavery*, chap. 4; Smith, in Quinn, *NAW*, p. 313; Hamor, *Discourse*, p. 17; "in a great"—Yeardley, in Morgan, *Slavery*, p. 83.

"extreme beastly"—John Chamberlain, July 9, 1612, in Barbour, *The Three Lives of Captain John Smith*, p. 304.

p. 273 Kupperman, "Apathy and Death in Early Jamestown," *Journal of American History*, vol. 66, 1979.

Smith, Quinn, *NAW*, p. 317.

p. 274 "a Kingdome"—Sir Walter Cope, conveying Newport's report to the Earl of Salisbury, in Andrews, *The Soul of a Nation*, p. 87.

Praises: Quinn, *NAW*, pp. 238–39.

Smith, ibid., p. 335.

Strachey, ibid., p. 300.

p. 275 Strachey, ibid.

"within 6 monthes"—Smith, ibid., p. 344; "clamors"—ibid., p. 345.

Virginia Company, ibid., pp. 219–20, and Kingsbury, ed., *Records*, pp. 24–29.

p. 276 "landing, fell"—Strachey, Quinn, *NAW*, p. 295; Hamor, *Discourse*, p. 27.

Orders, instructions to De La Warr, 1610, and "Lawes divine, morall, and martiall," for Thomas Dale, 1611, complete in Peter Force, *Tracts and Other Papers* . . . , 1836, Peter Smith (Gloucester, MA) reprint, 1963, vol. 3; abridged in Quinn, *NAW*, pp. 221ff.

p. 277 Percy, "Trewe Relacyon."

p. 278 Jones, *O Strange New World*, p. 142.

Virginia Company, in Quinn, *NAW*, p. 215.

"put five"—Percy, "Trewe Relacyon."

Fausz, in Fitzhugh, p. 241.

Percy, "Trewe Relacyon."

p. 279 Hamor, *Discourse*, p. 10.

Rolfe, in Andrews, *Soul*, pp. 191–92.

Footnote: Strachey vocabulary, in John P. Harrington, ed., *The Original Strachey Vocabulary of the Virginia Indian Language (1612)*, U.S. Bureau of American Ethnology, Anthropology Papers no. 46, vol. 157, U.S. Government Printing Office, 1955. Algonkian sexways: e.g., Regina Flannery, *Analysis of Coastal Algonkian Culture*, Catholic University (Washington, DC) Anthropology Series no. 7, 1939.

p. 280 SAVAGE BEAST: useful here, beyond the works cited for p. 197 above, and for the English in particular, are Jennings, *The Invasion of America*, chaps. 4, 5; Axtell, *The European and the Indian*, especially chap. 3; Jones, *O Strange*, chaps. 2, 4; Karen Ordahl Kupperman, *Settling with the Indians: The Meeting of English and Indian Cultures in America 1580–1640*, Rowman & Littlefield (Totowa, NJ), 1980; Roy Harvey Pearce, *The Savages of America*, Johns Hopkins, 1953 (rev. 1965), pt. 1.

"the people most"—Arthur Barlowe, in, e.g., Hakluyt, *Principall navigations, voiages & discoveries of the English nation*, vol. 8, p. 350.

Christianizing: Jennings, *Invasion*, is very good on English Christianizing failures; Pearce, *Savages*, is wrong, incidentally, in saying (p. 9) that fifty missionaries were sent out—see Kingsbury, ed., *Records*, vol. 1, p. 603, and vol. 3, pp. 165–66, which makes it clear that local planters, not missionaries, were to do proselytizing work if they wished.

Intermarriage: see David D. Smits, "Abominable Mixture," *Virginia Magazine of History*, vol. 95, 1987.

p. 281 "Savage"—a typical excuse is Kupperman, *Settling*, p. 112; contemporary usages are in the *Oxford English Dictionary* and any concordance to Shakespeare; "demeanour"—Pearce, *Savages*, p. 6; "unbridled"—Quinn, *NAW*, p. 239; "these beests"—Robert Gray, *A good speed to Virginia*, London, 1609; "cruell"—Smith, *Works*, p. 574; "more brutish"—Purchas, *Pilgrimes*, vol. 19, p. 231.

"Consider"—Christopher Brooke, "A Poem on the Late Massacre," in Berkhoffer, *The White Man's Indian*, p. 30; "in order"—Axtell, *European*, p. 44; "the first task," William Crashaw, *Sermon*, London, 1610; Nash, in Dudley and Novak, eds., *The Wild Man Within*, p. 61; see also Nash, in Nash and Richard Weiss, eds., *The Great Fear*, Holt, 1970, and his *Red, White, and Black*, Prentice-Hall, 1974, 1982.

p. 282 Virginia colonists, in Andrews, *Soul*, pp. 287–88.

Tobacco: e.g., Beer, *The Origins of the British Colonial System*; Wright, *Dream*; Melvin Herndon, *Tobacco in Colonial Virginia*, Jamestown 350th Anniversary Booklet, Virginia, 1957; Morgan, *American Slavery*, p. 90, and chaps. 6, 9; Davies, pp. 144ff.

p. 283 "The only commodity"—in Beer, *Origins*, p. 87.

"Now the gre[e]dines[s]," in Morgan, *American Slavery*, p. 183.

Cowdrey, *This Land, This South*, Kentucky, 1983, p. 30; and see Carl O. Sauer, *Selected Essays 1963–1975*, Turtle Island (Berkeley), 1981, pp. 67, 353.

"harmefulle to the braine"—James I, *A Counterblaste to Tobacco*, London, 1604; and in, e.g., Riley and Hatch, eds., *Jamestown*, p. 7.

p. 284 Rolfe, ibid., p. 11.

Indenture, and "like a damned"—Morgan, *American Slavery*, pp. 126–30; Abbot E. Smith, *Colonists in Bondage*, North Carolina, 1947.

Virginia Company, Kingsbury, ed., *Records*, pp. 98ff, 153ff. Land grants: Cowdrey, *This Land*, p. 202; also W. Stitt Robinson, *Mother Earth: Land Grants in Virginia 1607–1699*, Jamestown 350th Anniversary Booklet, Virginia, 1957.

p. 285 Rogin, *Fathers and Children: Andrew Jackson and the Subjugation of the American Indian*, Knopf, 1979, p. 79.

p. 286 "We have done"—in Berkhoffer, *White Man's*, p. 131.

"a people come"—in Smith, *Travels*, p. 427.

ATTITUDE TO NATURE: in addition to sources listed for p. 75 above, and Turner, *Beyond Geography*; Berkhoffer, *White Man's*; Rogin, *Fathers*; Pearce, *Savages*; and Jennings, *Invasion*, these are useful: Wilson O. Clough, *The Necessary Earth: Nature and Solitude in American Literature*, Texas, 1964; William Cronon, *Changes in the Land*, Hill & Wang, 1983; Richard Drinnon, *Indian-Hating and Empire-Building*, Minnesota, 1980; Hans Huth, *Nature and the American*, California, 1957; Leo Marx, *The Machine in the Garden*, Oxford, 1964; Charles L. Sanford, *The Quest for Paradise*, Illinois, 1961; Bernard W. Sheehan, *Savagism and Civility*, Cambridge, 1980; Richard Slotkin, *Regeneration Through Violence: The Mythology of the American Frontier 1600–1860*, Wesleyan, 1973; William M. and Mabel S. C. Smallwood, *Natural History in the American Mind*, Columbia, 1941; Lionel Tiger, *The Manufacture of Evil*, Harper & Row, 1987.

Tocqueville, *Democracy in America*, tr. and ed., Phillips Bradley, Knopf, 1945, p. 74.

p. 287 Smith, Quinn, *NAW*, pp. 310–51; quote, p. 320.

English nature tradition: see E. G. R. Taylor, *Tudor Geography*, Methuen, London, 1930, chap. 1; and *Late Tudor and Early Stuart Geography*, chap. 7.

Footnote: White's watercolors are in Stefan Lorant, *The New World*, Deull, Slaoan, 1946, 1965.

p. 288 Smith, *Travels*, p. 56; Archer, Quinn, *NAW*, p. 274.

Bradford, *Of Plymouth Plantation*, chap. 9, in Harvey Wish, ed., Capricorn, 1962, p. 60.

p. 289 Johnson, Hooker, Winthrop, Mather, Chauncy, in Peter N. Carroll, *Puritanism in the Wilderness . . . 1629–1700*, Columbia, 1969.

Winthrop, *Conclusions for the Plantation in New England*, London, 1629; quoted in Nash, *Wilderness*, p. 31.

Footnote: Handlin, in James Morton Smith, ed., *Seventeenth Century America: Essays in Colonial History*, North Carolina, 1959, pp. 11ff.

p. 290 Williams, *In the American Grain*, Boni, 1925, p. 130.

Lilliard, *The Great Forest*, Knopf, 1947, p. 32.

Environmental impact: see Turner, *Beyond Geography*; Innes, *The Fur Trade in Canada*, including *Jesuit Relations*; Martin, *Keepers of the Game*; Carroll, *The Timber Economy of Puritan New England*; Cronon, *Changes*; Lilliard, *Great Forest*; James E. Defebaugh, *History of the Lumber Industry in America*, Chicago, 1907, vol. 1; Carl Bridenbaugh, "Yankee Use and Abuse of the Forest," *Massachusetts Historical Society Proceedings*, vol. 89, 1977; Michael Williams, *Americans and Their Forests: A Historical Geography*, Cambridge, 1989; Avery Craven, *Soil Exhaustion . . . Virginia and Maryland 1606–1860*, Illinois Studies in the Social Sciences, vol. 13, 1926.

p. 292 Virginia Council, in Riley and Hatch, eds., *Jamestown*, p. 12 (*u*'s modernized to *v*'s).

Smith, *Advertisements*, in *Travels*, p. 931; "used him"—Riley and Hatch, eds., *Jamestown*, p. 12.

Virginia Company, letter of August 1, 1622, Kingsbury, ed., *Records*, vol. 1, pp. 660–73.

p. 293 "harshe visits"—in Fausz, in Fitzhugh, p. 246.

"by Computatione"—ibid., p. 213.

Tucker raids, Kingsbury, ed., *Records*, pp. 221–22.

"We, who"—Edward Waterhouse, ibid., vol. 3, pp. 556–67.

p. 294 Population: see notes to p. 304 below.

Virginia Company: see especially Morgan, *American Slavery*, chap. 5; Craven, *Southern Colonies*, pp. 138ff; Andrews, *Soul*, pp. 317ff, 332; none, however, understands quite so readily as Jennings, *Invasion*, p. 79, that it was "looted by its organizers." Morison, by the way, figures a loss of £400,000 (*Northern*, p. 678), but the more careful Quinn and Ryan (*Sea Empire*, p. 176) and the scholarly Rabb (*Enterprise*) estimate only £200,000.

p. 295 Purchas, *Pilgrimes*, vol. 19, p. 228.

Chapter Twelve 1607–25 (II) *Powhatans and Others*

p. 296 Coronation: Smith, Quinn, *NAW*, vol. 5, pp. 323–25; Andrews, *The Soul of a Nation*, pp. 109ff.

Smith, Quinn, *NAW*, p. 325.

p. 297 POWHATAN SOCIETY: Fitzhugh, pt. 3; Flannery, *Analysis of Coastal Algonkian Culture*; Christian Feest, Wilcomb Washburn, and Douglas W. Boyd, in Trigger, ed., *Handbook of North American Indians*; Philip L. Barbour, *Pocahontas and Her World*, Houghton Mifflin, 1970 (although some caution is required); Charles Hudson, *The Southwestern Indians*, Tennessee, 1976; Ben C. McCary, *Indians in 17th Century Virginia*, Jamestown 350th Anniversary Booklet, Virginia, 1957; Frank G. Speck, *Chapters on the Ethnology of the Powhatan Tribes of Virginia*, Indian Notes and Monographs Series No. 5, Museum of the American Indian (New York), 1928; J. Leitch Wright, Jr., *The Only Land They Knew*, Free Press, 1981; J. Frederick Fausz, in Gary Nash and David Sweet, eds., *Struggle and Survival in Colonial America*, California, 1981; Hu Maxwell, "The Use and Abuse of Forests by the Virginia Indians," *William and Mary Quarterly*, vol. 19, 1910; James H. Merrell, "The Indians' New World," *William and Mary Quarterly*, vol. 41, 1984; Clyde A. Milner, in Howard Lamar and Leonard Thompson, eds., *The Frontier in History*, Yale, 1981; Maria Mook, "Virginia Indians," *William and Mary Quarterly*, vol. 23, nos. 1, 2, 4, 1943; Bernard Sheenan, "Indian-White Relations in Early America," *William and Mary Quarterly*, vol. 26, 1969; Charles C. Willoughby, "Virginia Indians in the Seventeenth Century," *American Anthropologist*, vol. 9, 1907.

p. 298 Smith, Quinn, *NAW*, p. 316.

p. 299 Le Jeune, in R. G. Thwaites, ed., *Jesuit Relations*, Burrows (Cleveland), 1906, vol. 6, p. 233.

"on each side," Smith, Quinn, *NAW*, p. 316.

p. 300 Gynecocracies: e.g., Paula Gunn Allen, *The Sacred Hoop*, Beacon, 1986; women's status: Allen, *Sacred Hoop*; Mona Etienne and Eleanor Leacock, eds., *Women and Colonization*, Praeger, 1980, especially Robert Steven Grumet on female chiefs; Eleanor Leacock and N. O. Lurie, eds., *North American Indians in Historical Perspective*, Random, 1971.

p. 301 Agriculture: see Cowdrey, *This Land, This South*, pp. 13ff, with quotes, pp. 16–17; Sauer, *Sixteenth*, pp. 286ff, *Seventeenth Century North America*, pp. 8off, 228–29, and *Selected Essays, 1963–1975*, chap. 3; McCary, *Indians*.

p. 302 Sauer, *Seventeenth*, p. 296; *Essays*, pp. 46–47.

Medicine: e.g., Marshall T. Newman, *American Journal of Physical Anthropology*, vol. 45, November 1976; Virgil J. Vogel, *American Indian Medicine*, Oklahoma, 1970.

"Their charmes," "diabolicall"—William Wood, *New Englands Prospect*, London, 1634, pp. 82–83; "their curst," "herbes"—William Morrell, *New-England*, London, 1625, p. 19; "probably more"—Newman, *Physical Anthropology*.

p. 303 Smith, "no place"—Quinn, *NAW*, p. 342; "that notwithstanding"—*Travels and Works. . .*, p. 67.

"a most kind"—Quinn, *NAW*, p. 276; "naturally"—Robert Cushman, *A Sermon Preached in Plimmoth*, London, 1622, p. A3; "very cheerfully"—Barlowe, in Hakluyt, *Principall navigations, voiages and discoveries of the English nation*, vol. 8, p. 383; "we were"—Quinn, *NAW*, p. 269; "they entertained"—ibid., p. 270; "the meanest"—ibid., p. 269; "as deere"—Hamor, *A True Discourse of the Present Estate of Virginia*, p. 38.

p. 304 Diseases: in addition to works cited for p. 159 above, see Merrell, "Indians' New World," D. H. Ubelaker, "Prehistoric New World Population Size," *American Journal of Physical Anthropology*, vol. 45, 1976, and *Reconstruction of Demographic Profiles from Ossuary Skeletal Samples*, Smithsonian Contributions to Anthropology No. 18 (Washington, DC), 1974; Henige, *Journal of Interdisciplinary History*, vol. 16, 1986; Thornton, *American Indian Holocaust and Survival*.

p. 305 Dobyns, *Their Numbers Become Thinned*, p. 25.

"What I have"—in Sauer, *Sixteenth*, pp. 224–25.

60,000: extrapolated from the figures in Ubelaker, *Reconstruction*; Wright, *Only Land*, says 100,000.

Crosby, *The Columbian Exchange*, p. 38; de Soto, in Merrell, "Indians' New World"; Hariot, in Lorant, *The New World*; Wahunsenekah, in Quinn, NAW, p. 276; Smith, *Travels*, p. 65.

p. 306 Merrell, "Indians' New World."

"great diseaze"—Archer, in Quinn, *NAW*, p. 276.

p. 307 "A long time"—Trigger, ed., *Handbook*, p. 88.

INDIANS AND NATURE: Martin, *Keepers of the Game*; Shepard, *Nature and Madness; Akwesasne Notes*, ed., *Basic Call to Consciousness* (Mohawk Nation), 1978, 1981, 1982; W. H. Capps, ed., *Seeing With a Native Eye: Essays on Native American Religion*, Harper & Row, 1976; Jamake Highwater, *Primal Mind*, Harper & Row, 1981; J. Donald Hughes, *American Indian Ecology*, Texas Western, 1983; Wilbur R. Jacobs, *Dispossessing the American Indian*, Scribner's, 1972; Calvin Martin, *The American Indian and the Problem of History*, Oxford, 1987; Peter Nabokov and Robert Easton, *Native American Architecture*, Oxford, 1989; Christian Vecsey and Robert C. Venables, ed., *American Indian Environments*, Syracuse, 1980: J. Baird Callicott, in Robert Elliott and Arran Gare, eds., *Environmental Philosophy*, Queensland/Pennsylvania State, 1983.

p. 308 Standing Bear, *Land of the Spotted Eagle*, Houghton Mifflin, 1933, p. 193.

Haudenosaunees, *Akwesasne*, ed., *Basic Call*, p. 2.

p. 309 Vision quest: Gary Witherspoon, *Language and Act in the Navajo Uni-*

verse, Michigan, 1977; Joseph Espes Brown, *Parabola 7*, Summer 1982; Robin Ridington, *Anthropologica*, vol. 13, nos. 1, 2, 1971; Thomas Berry, "Vision Quest," *Creation*, vol. 2, 1987.

Black Elk, *Black Elk Speaks*, as told by John G. Neihardt, Nebraska, 1961, pp. 43, 37, 45–46.

p. 310 English accounts: see Kupperman, *Settling with the Indians*; Wright, *Only Land*, pp. 6off; Flannery, *Analysis*.

p. 311 Shepard, *Nature and Madness*, chap. 3; quote, p. 71.

p. 312 Ojibwas: Martin, *Keepers*, p. 80.

p. 313 Farming/foraging: see works listed for p. 301 above, and Vecsey and Venables, *Environments*; Sauer, *Sixteenth*, pp. 288–89, mentions the grapes.

"In a way"—Charles M. Segal and David C. Stineback, *Puritans, Indians, and Manifest Destiny*, Putnam's, 1977, p. 28.

p. 314 Martin, *American Indian*, p. 27.

p. 315 Population: see the sources for pp. 159, 160 above, especially Dobyns, *Numbers*, and Thornton, *Holocaust*. Among the attacks on Dobyns, valid but not sufficient to do more than temper his conclusions, are William Sturtevant, *American History Review*, vol. 89, December 1984, and William Cronon, *Journal of American History*, vol. 71, September 1984.

p. 316 For specific Indian environmental effects, see Cronon, *Changes in the Land*, pp. 47ff; Hughes, *Indian Ecology;* Martin, *Keepers*, especially the epilogue. Maxwell's article "Use and Abuse" is a specious and self-serving U.S. Forestry Service version.

15,000 pounds: Cronon, *Changes*, p. 47.

p. 317 Nevawas argument: W. H. Hutchinson, "Dissenting Voice . . . Against the Myth of the Noble Savage," *Westways*, October 1972; Shepard Kretch III, ed., *Indians, Animals and the Fur Trade: A Critique of* Keepers of the Game, Georgia, 1981.

p. 318 McNickle, in Allen, *Sacred Hoop*, p. 266; Allen's book is intended to show the basic pacifism of North American Indian societies. See also Kupperman, *Settling*, pp. 55–56; Jennings, *The Invasion of America*, chap. 9.

Le Jeune, *Jesuit Relations*, vol. 6, p. 233; Wood, in Kupperman, *Settling*, pp. 55–56.

Smith, *Travels*, p. 71.

p. 319 Underhill, *Newes from America*, London, 1638, p. 40; Spelman, in Smith, *Travels*, p. cxiv; "strategems"—Smith, ibid., p. 72.

Hughes, *Indian Ecology*, p. 9.

Indian burning: ibid; and Henry Dobyns, *From Fire to Flood: Historic Human Destruction of Sonoran Desert Riverine Oases*, Ballena (Socorro, NM), 1981.

p. 320 Extinctions: e.g., Martin, *Keepers*, pp. 168ff; Paul S. Martin and H. E. Wright, eds., *Pleistocene Extinctions: The Search for a Cause*, Yale, 1967.

p. 321 "so accustomed"—Martin, *Keepers*, p. 165.

"longstanding," "mutual," "conservationist-minded"—ibid., pp. 184–85.

p. 322 Washburn, *The Indian in America*, Harper p. 56.

Martin, *American Indian*, p. 197.

p. 324 Parkman, *The Conspiracy of Pontiac*, 1851, Collier reprint, 1962, p. 63.

Chapter Thirteen   1625–1992   Columbus/Columbia

p. 325 Purchas, *Haklytus posthumus, or Purchase his pilgrimes*, vol. 2, pp. 19–32.

p. 326 Elliott, p. 10.

p. 327 Braudel, ibid., p. 78.

Elliott, ibid., p. 102.

Books: *European Americana*, vol. 2.

p. 328 Stuart marriage: Thacher, vol. 3, p. 637.

p. 329 Italian paintings: see Raffaele Soprani, *Vite de' pittori, scultori, architetti genovesi*, vols. 1, 2, Genoa, 1768.

p. 330 Adams, in Jones, *O Strange New World*, p. 159.

Early colonies: see especially Davies; Wright, *The Dream of Prosperity in Colonial America*; Craven, *The Southern Colonies in the Seventeenth Century 1607–1689*; Carl Becker, *Beginnings of the American People*, Cornell, 1915, 1960; Michael Kammen, *People of Paradox: An Inquiry Concerning the Origins of American Civilization*, Vintage, 1973.

p. 332 English histories: 1704, Churchill, *Collection of Voyages*; 1708, John Oldmixon, *British Empire in America*; 1727, Herman Moll, *Modern History . . .* ; 1739, *The British Sailor's Discovery*; 1743, *The American Traveller*; 1759, *The World Displayed*; 1770s, three anonymous histories, Robertson's *History*, and William Russel, *The History of America from the Discovery by Columbus*; and see E. G. Cox, *A Reference Guide to the Literature of Travel*, Washington University, 1938, vol. 2.

Scholarship: the Barcia book is mentioned in Muñoz; it is Winsor, vol. 2, chap. 1, who calls Bossi the first "modern" work.

Book of Privileges, Spotorno, *Memorials of Columbus*.

p. 333 Rousseau, *La découverie du Nouveau Monde*, in *Oeuvres*, Paris, 1826 (orig. Geneva, 1782), vol. 2, p. 435, an "opera with words and music," but the author apparently did not preserve the latter.

Morton, *Columbus*, London, 1792 (and 1799); first performed in America in 1797 in New York City, published in Philadelphia, 1794, and Washington, D.C., 1823; a new scene and a patriotic song were added by North Carolina senator Alexander Martin, printed in Philadelphia, 1798.

p. 334 Freneau: F. L. Pattee, *The Poems of Philip Freneau*, 3 vols., Princeton, 1902, calls him "the father of American poetry"; Freneau's first composed Columbus poem was apparently "Columbus to Ferdinand," probably written in 1770, but it was not published (in *The United States Magazine*) until 1779. The "Columbia" poem is "American Liberty."

p. 335 Barlow, *The Vision of Columbus*, Hudson & Goodwin (Hartford), 1787, Baltimore, 1814; redone as *The Columbiad*, Philadelphia, 1807, 1809 (2 eds.), Paris, 1813.

p. 337 Belknap, *Biographies of the Early Discoverers*, 1794, reprint 1856 (where Belknap is called "the father of American history"); "A Discourse" published by Belknap and Hall (Boston), 1792.

p. 339 Coins: Walter Breen, *Complete Encyclopedia of U.S. and Colonial Coins*, ECI/Doubleday, 1988.

Columbian Magazine: see L. N. Richardson, *History of Early American Magazines*, Thomas Nelson, 1931; a copy of Dwight's song is in the New York Public

Library; "Columbia's River"—*Voyages of the 'Columbia,'* Massachusetts Historical Society, 1941.

1792 celebrations: Edward F. deLancey, *Magazine of American History*, November 1893; Charles T. Thompson, William Eleroy Curtis, *Chautauquan*, November 1892.

p. 340 Books and periodicals: in the New York Public Library catalogue.

p. 341 Standard of living: E. J. Perkins, *Economics of Colonial America*, Columbia, 1980, p. 145.

For Navarrete, see his *Colección de los viajes y descubrimientos . . .*, now available in ms. facsimile, Nendeln (Lichtenstein), 1971; and Carlos Seco Serrano, ed., *Obras de Navarrete . . .*, Madrid, 1954. See also Morison, "Texts and Translations of the Journal," *Hispanic American Historical Review*, vol. 19, August 1939; John Harmon McElroy, ed., introduction to *The Life and Voyages of Christopher Columbus*, vol. 9 of *The Complete Works of Washington Irving*, Twayne (Boston), 1981.

p. 342 Washington Irving: McElroy, introduction to Irving, *Columbus*, and *Letters of Washington Irving*, 2 vols., same series; "I had no idea"—July 27, 1827, *Letters*, vol. 2, p. 239; "labored hard"—ibid., p. 243; John D. Hazlett, "Literary Nationalism and Ambivalence in Washington Irving's *The Life and Voyages of Christopher Columbus*," *American Literature*, vol. 55, December 1983 (although his nonsense about a "subtext" saying that "civilization is evil" should be discounted); Jones, *O Strange*, pp. 95ff.

Footnote: Rich Collection, New York Public Library, cat. ed. Edwin Blake Brownrigg, 1978.

p. 344 "Columbus was" etc.—Irving, *Columbus*, chap 46.

p. 345 "To illustrate"—McElroy, introduction to Irving, *Columbus*, p. lxxxvii.

Biographies: Humboldt, *Examen critique . . . du nouveau continent . . .*; Harrisse, *Christophe Colomb, Discovery of America*, and *Christophe Colomb devant l'histoire*, Paris, 1892; Asensio y Toledo, *Cristóbal Colón: su vida, sus viajes, sus descubrimientos*, 2 vols., Barcelona, 1888; Winsor, *Christopher Columbus and How he Received and Imparted the Spirit of Discovery*, Houghton-Mifflin; Goodrich, Appleton, 1874.

New Columbiana: Granada, 1856, and 2 vols., Seville, 1869; Las Casas, *Historia de las Indias*; Cuneo, Olindo Guerrini, ed., Bologna, 1885; Santangel Letter in English, Michael Kerney, *The Spanish Letter of Columbus to Luis de Sant' Angel*, Quaritch, London, 1891.

p. 346 Seville Archives: Joaquin F. Pacheco, et al., *Colección de documentos . . . del Real Archivo de Indias*, Madrid, 1864–84, 1885–1932; de Lollis, *Raccolta*, holdings in Provost, no. 9.

Works on Columbus: my figures here depend on the records provided for me by Foster Provost, supplemented by the sources cited for pp. 221 and 254 above, and the New York Public Library catalogue; and, e.g., Sara Agnes Ryan, *Christopher Columbus in Poetry, History and Art*, Mayer and Miller (Chicago), 1917; and Hilah Paulmier and R. H. Schauffer, *Columbus Day: Prose and Verse on Christopher Columbus*, Dodd, Mead, 1938.

Footnote: see *Columbus, An Unfinished Poem*, a small monograph by John S. Mayfield, Jacksonville, FL, 1944, with a 6-line fragment by Swinburne; the Italian volume is *Albo di onoranze internazionali a Cristoforo Colombo*, Vallardi (Rome and Milan), 1892.

p. 347 Paintings: chiefly Ponce de León, *The Columbus Gallery*.

Currency: Gene Hessler, *The Comprehensive Catalog of U.S. Paper Money*, Regnery, 1974.

MONUMENTS: see sources for p. 214 above; and Charles Weathers Bump, in Herbert B. Adams and Henry Wood, *Columbus and His Discovery of America*, Johns Hopkins, 1892, reprinted in Anne and Henry Paolucci, eds., *Columbus*, Council on National Literatures (Whitestone, NY), 1989; Frank Owen Payne, *Munsey's Magazine*, October 1920.

p. 348 Curtis, *Chautauguan*, p. 4.

p. 349 Canonization: Angelo Sanguineti, *La canonizzazione di Cristoforo Colombo*, Genoa, 1875; Giovanni Odoardi, in *Studi colombiani*, vol. 3, p. 261ff.

1892: for New York, *Magazine of American History*, vol. 28, November 1892; for Chicago, *Chautauquan*, December 1892, January–March, 1893; and H. S. Smith, *Columbus and Columbia*, National (Chicago), 1892, pt. 4.

Footnote: *New Yorker*, December 4, 1989, p. 68.

p. 351 Memorial coin: Breen, *Encyclopedia*.

p. 352 Commemorative stamps: e.g., Douglas and Mary Patrick, *The International Guide to Stamps and Stamp Collecting*, McClelland & Stewart, 1962, p. 43.

"At one and the same"—H. D. Northrup, *Popular History of America*, Hampden (Springfield, MA), 1898, p. 395.

p. 353 "that all the marvels"—Smith, *Columbus*, p. 814.

p. 354 Conti, *Un secolo di bibliografia*; Provost, *Annotated Guide*.

Journal in English: Samuel Kettell, 1827; Clements Markham, 1893; John Boyd Thacher, 1903; Edward Gaylord Bourne (using Markham), 1906; Van Wyck Brooks (using Kettell without saying so), 1924; Cecil Jane, 1930, and rev. L. A. Vigneras, 1960; Samuel Eliot Morison, 1963; Robert Fuson, 1987; Oliver Dunn and James E. Kelley, Jr., 1989.

p. 355 New discoveries: notarial document, in Morison, *JAOD*, pp. 8–9; Piri Re'is map, in Quinn, *NAW*, vol. 1, no. 25; Gould, see Morison, *JAOD*, p. 6; Lyon, *National Geographic*, November 1986.

Vignaud, "Letter to Whitelaw Reid," in Young, pp. 373ff; quote, pp. 374–75.

p. 356 For twentieth-century historiography up to 1966, see Charles E. Nowell, *American Historical Review*, vol. 44, 1939; Martin Todorash, *Hispanic American Historical Review*, vol. 46, 1966. Some additional attention is in Jacques Heers, *Le projet de Colomb*, Darflet (Genoa), 1983.

p. 357 City of Genoa, *Christopher Columbus: Documents and Proofs of His Genoese Origin*. To give a flavor of the alternative theories, I should mention some recent examples: Brother Nectario Maria, *Juan Colon . . . Was a Spanish Jew*, Chedney (New York), 1971; W. R. Anderson, *Viking Explorers and the Columbus Fraud*, Valhalla (Chicago), 1984?; and Manuel Luciano da Silva, *Columbus Was 100% Portuguese*, self-published (Bristol, RI), 1989.

Toscanelli: despite Morison's weight on the side of this correspondence as genuine (vol. 1, chap. 6), the arguments of Vignaud (*The Letter and Chart of Toscanelli* and other works) and others have by now moved enough scholars into—or beyond— the realm of doubt where Pauline Watts could say in 1985 ("Prophecy and Discovery," *American Historical Review*, vol. 90) that "on the basis of what is currently known, it seems extremely unlikely that Toscanelli and Columbus corresponded directly"; she probably overstates the case in adding that "Toscanelli wrote most of the first letter" (its information does seem meager and unimpressive for such a learned man) and that "Columbus no doubt read it" (for he never once mentions it in all of his geographic meanderings). It doesn't deserve all the attention it has received, if it even existed, because Colón didn't need it to prove that there was an Indies over there someplace, and didn't want it if he was in fact hoping for *new* lands.

p. 358 Destination: Vignaud, *Études critiques sur la vie de Colomb avant ses découvertes*, Welter (Paris), 1905, *Histoire critique de la grande entreprise de Christopher Colomb*, Welter (Paris), 1911; *Le vrai Christophe Colomb et la légende*, Picard (Paris), 1921; Rómulo Carbia, *La nueva historia del descubrimiento de América*, Coni (Buenos Aires), 1936; Emiliano Jos, in *Reseña . . . Congreso Internacional de americanistas*, Seville, 1935.

Colón/Jew: Provost, V. J; Vignaud, "Columbus a Spaniard and a Jew?" *American History Review*, vol. 18, 1913; Martínez Martínez, *El descubrimiento de América y las joyas de doña Isabel*, Seville, 1916; Wasserman, *Christoph Columbus*, S. Fischer (Berlin), 1929, *Columbus: Don Quixote of the Seas* (tr. Eric Sutton), Little, Brown, 1930; Madariaga, *Christopher Columbus*; Wiesenthal, *Sails of Hope* (tr. Richard and Clara Winston), Macmillan, 1973; Ballesteros, *Cristóbal Colón y el descubrimiento de América*, Salvat (Barcelona/Buenos Aires), 1945; Alvarez, "Cristóbal Colón no fue hebreo," *Revista de Historia de América* (Mexico City), 1942.

Creative works: again, I rely primarily on the records of Foster Provost and the New York Public Library catalogue; Conti, *Un secolo di bibliografia Columbiana 1880–1985*, counts eighty-six works, but her list is glaringly incomplete.

p. 359 Noce: Alfred K. Allan, "Forgotten Founder of Columbus Day," *Columbia*, October 1966.

Holiday: see U.S. House Judiciary Committee, *Hearings*, April 19, 1910; Paulmier and Schauffer, *Columbus Day*.

1986 survey: *New York Times*, August 31, 1987.

p. 360 1988 survey: *Discovery Five Hundred*, newsletter of the International Columbian Quincentenary Alliance (Columbus, NJ), October 1988.

Eponyms: George Stewart, *Names on the Land*, Houghton Mifflin, 1958; C. M. Matthews, *Place-Names of the English-Speaking World*, Weidenfeld & Nicolson (London), 1972.

p. 361 Polzer, *Five Hundred* (U.S. Quincentenary Jubilee Commission), May–June, 1989.

Footnote: *New York Times*, February 7, 1986.

p. 363 Whitman, "Prayer of Columbus," from *Two Rivulets*, 1876.

Epilogue

p. 365 Reynal and the America debate: Henry Steele Commager and Elmo Giordanetti, *Was America a Mistake?*, Harper & Row, 1967; Durand Echeverria, *Mirage in the West*, Princeton, 1968, especially pp. 172ff; Antonello Gerbi, *The Dispute of the New World*. This Reynal is from his *Histoire . . .*, tr. J. O. Justamond, London, 1776, pts. 7, 8, but is said to be similar to his later *Discours composé en 1788 . . . quelle a été l'influence de l'Amérique sur . . . l'Europe?*, Paris, 1792.

p. 367 Montaigne, in "Of Coaches"; Harrisse, *Notes on Columbus*, final page. Elliott in Chiappelli, vol. 1.

p. 368 Martin, *The American Indian and the Problem of History*, p. 197 (my italics). Turner, *Beyond Geography*, is especially eloquent about the lost opportunity—e.g., pp. 118ff, 171ff.

p. 369 Melliadis, in Sam Steiner, *The Vanishing White Man*, Harper & Row, 1976, p. 282.

Oahspe: The Words of Jehovih . . . , John Ballou Newbrough, Essenes of Kosmon (Montrose, CO), 1882, 1910, 1935, passages 735, 737, 790.

Index

A Note About the Author

KIRKPATRICK SALE is the author of five previous books, including *SDS*, *Power Shift*, and the prize-winning *Human Scale*, and is a contributor to many periodicals, among them *The New York Review of Books*, the San Francisco *Chronicle*, *The New York Times Magazine*, and *The Nation*. He is co-director of the E. F. Schumacher Society, a founder of the New York Green Party, and for the past fifteen years a member of the board of the PEN American Center. He has lectured on numerous college campuses and has twice been a recipient of the Columbus Quincentennial Scholarship of the Newberry Library, Chicago. Mr. Sale lives with his wife in New York City and Cold Springs, New York.

A Note on the Type

THIS BOOK was set in Garamond, a typeface originally designed by the famous Parisian type cutter Claude Garamond (1480–1561). This version of Garamond was modeled on a 1592 specimen sheet from the Egenolff-Berner foundry, which was produced from types thought to have been brought to Frankfurt to Jacques Sabon (d. 1580).
Claude Garamond is one of the most famous type designers in printing history. His distinguished romans and italics first appeared in *Opera Ciceronis* in 1543–44. While delightfully unconventional in design, the Garamond types are clear and open, yet maintain an elegance and precision of line that mark them as French.

Composed by Crane Typesetting Service, Inc., West Barnstable, Massachusetts. Printed and bound by The Haddon Craftsmen, Scranton, Pennsylvania. Designed by Virginia Tan.